Savitri Devi

The Lightning and the Sun

Third Edition
Complete and Unabridged

The Savitri Devi Archive

The Centennial Edition of Savitri Devi's Works
R.G. Fowler, General Editor
Each volume will be released in a limited cloth edition of 200 numbered copies.

Volume One:
AND TIME ROLLS ON
THE SAVITRI DEVI INTERVIEWS

Volume Two:
GOLD IN THE FURNACE
EXPERIENCES IN POST-WAR GERMANY

Volume Three:
FOREVER AND EVER
DEVOTIONAL POEMS

Volume Four:
DEFIANCE
THE PRISON MEMOIRS OF SAVITRI DEVI

Volume Five:
THE LIGHTNING AND THE SUN
(complete and unabridged)

Volume Six:
PILGRIMAGE

Future Volumes:
MEMORIES AND REFLECTIONS OF AN ARYAN WOMAN

THE LOTUS POND
IMPRESSIONS OF INDIA

HARD AS STEEL

LONG-WHISKERS AND THE TWO-LEGGED GODDESS
OR, THE TRUE STORY OF A "MOST OBJECTIONABLE NAZI" AND . . .
HALF-A-DOZEN CATS

IMPEACHMENT OF MAN

A SON OF GOD
THE LIFE AND PHILOSOPHY OF AKHNATON, KING OF EGYPT
(complete and unabridged)

AKHNATON'S ETERNAL MESSAGE
(and other writings on Akhnaton)

A WARNING TO THE HINDUS
(and THE NON-HINDU INDIANS AND INDIAN UNITY)

NOT "FOR NOTHING": LETTERS OF SAVITRI DEVI, VOLUME 1

SAINT SAVITRI: LETTERS OF SAVITRI DEVI, VOLUME 2

Savitri Devi

The Lightning and the Sun

Third Edition
Complete and Unabridged

Edited by R. G. Fowler

A Savitri Devi Archive Book
Counter-Currents Publishing, Ltd.
San Francisco
2015

Copyright © 2015 The Savitri Devi Archive

All rights reserved

Printed on acid free paper
No animal products were used in the creation of this book.
Dust-jacket and cover by Kevin I. Slaughter

ISBNs:
Limited Hardcover Edition: 978-1-935965-53-4
Library Hardcover Edition: 978-1-935965-72-5
Paperback Edition: 978-1-935965-54-1
Electronic Edition: 978-1-935965-55-8

Library of Congress Cataloging-in-Publication Data

Savitri Devi.
 The lightning and the sun / Savitri Devi ; edited by R.G. Fowler. -- Third edition, Complete and unabridged.
  p. cm. -- (The centennial edition of Savitri Devi's works ; volume 5)
 Includes bibliographical references and index.
 "A Savitri Devi archive book."
 "Each volume will be released in a limited cloth edition of 200 numbered copies"--T.p. verso.
 Originally published: Calcutta : Temple Press, 1958.
 ISBN 978-1-935965-53-4 (hardcover limited edition : acid-free paper) -- ISBN 978-1-935965-54-1 (pbk. : acid-free paper) -- ISBN 978-1-935965-55-8 (electronic edition)
 1. Hitler, Adolf, 1889-1945. 2. Genghis Khan, 1162-1227. 3. Akhenaton, King of Egypt. 4. Heads of state--Germany--Biography. 5. Mongols--Kings and rulers--Biography. 6. Egypt--Kings and rulers--Biography. I. Fowler, R. G. II. Title.
 DD247.H5S263 2012
 321.0092'2--dc23
                     2012047172

To the god-like Individual of our times;
the Man against Time;
the greatest European of all times;
both Sun and Lightning:

ADOLF HITLER,

as a tribute of unfailing love and loyalty, forever and ever.

1. Shiva

(in his "Tandava Nritya"—Dance of Destruction—at the end of every successive Time-cycle)

"The foolish disregard Me, when clad in human semblance..."

— The Bhagavad-Gita, IX, verse 11.

"Was der Tod der Elf einmal bedeuten wird, vermögen heute nur wenige zu ahnen — noch weniger kann ich darüber schreiben. Wir stehen mitten in einer grossen Zeitenwende. Was wir alle durchmachen sind ihre Geburtswehen. Alles scheint negativ — und einmal wird dann doch Neues and Grosses geboren werden..."[1]

— Rudolf Hess[2]

---

[1] "Today we are able to know little and write less about what the death of the eleven will mean. We are in the midst of a great historical turning point. We are going through its birth pangs. Everything seems negative — and yet something New and Great is being born." — Trans. R. G. Fowler.

[2] From a letter to his wife, written on the 28th October, 1946 — twelve days after the hanging of the Martyrs of Nuremberg

Contents

Illustrations ❖ ii

Editor's Foreword ❖ iii

Author's Preface ❖ ix

Part I: Timeless Perfection & Cyclic Evolution
1. The Cyclic View of History ❖ 3
2. Time & Violence ❖ 22
3. Men in Time, Above Time, & Against Time ❖ 37

Part II: The Lightning: Genghis Khan
4. The Child of Violence ❖ 59
5. The Will to Survive ❖ 63
6. The Will to Conquer ❖ 87
7. From the Danube to the Yellow Sea ❖ 108

Part III: The Sun: Akhnaton
8. "The Beautiful Child of the Living Aton" ❖ 129
9. The Heat-and-Light-within-the-Disk ❖ 135
10. The Seat of Truth ❖ 159
11. Too Late & too Early ❖ 195

Part IV: Both Sun & Lightning: Adolf Hitler
12. The Late-Born Child of Light ❖ 211
13. The Struggle for Truth ❖ 217
14. The World against Its Saviour ❖ 269
15. Gods on Earth ❖ 357

Part V: Epilogue: Kalki, the Avenger
16. Kalki, the Avenger ❖ 417

Index ❖ 437

About the Authoress ❖ 456

Illustrations

1. Frontispiece: Shiva as Dancer of Destruction

2. Savitri Devi photographed on 6 December 1948, the day before she completed Chapter 3 of *The Lightning and the Sun* ❖ 55

3. Genghis Khan ❖ 58

4. Akhnaton ❖ 128

5. Adolf Hitler: The Late-Born Child of Light ❖ 210

6. Adolf Hitler in the Early Days of the Struggle ❖ 216

7. Adolf Hitler: ". . . he spoke with the wild eloquence of emergency . . ." ❖ 268

8. Adolf Hitler during the Second World War ❖ 316

9. Adolf Hitler: The Man against Time ❖ 356

10. Hari Hara: A Twelfth-Century Indian Statue from Bihar ❖ 416

Editor's Foreword

The Lightning and the Sun is Savitri Devi's *magnum opus*. The book was written over an eight-year period, from 1948 to 1956, and was published in 1958. In terms of intellectual creativity, political commitment, high-stakes adventure, and all-round intensity, these years were the peak of Savitri Devi's life.

The Lightning and the Sun took so long to complete because Savitri set it aside, often for years at a time, to work on four other books: *Gold in the Furnace*, *Defiance*, *Forever and Ever*, and *Pilgrimage*.[1] Of course, Savitri may well have worked on these other books because the ideas of *The Lightning and the Sun* took longer to fructify. *The Lightning and the Sun* also required extensive research, whereas the other volumes primarily relate Savitri's personal experiences.

Chapter 1 of *The Lightning and the Sun* was written in Edinburgh, Scotland on 9 April 1948 while Savitri was working as a wardrobe assistant in the Ram Gopal dance company.[2] Chapters 3, 4, and 5 of *The Lightning and the Sun*, and possibly chapter 2 as well, were written while Savitri worked on *Gold in the Furnace*.

Gold in the Furnace relates Savitri's experiences in occupied Germany in 1948 and 1949. Savitri began writing *Gold in the Furnace* on 3 October 1948 (the date of the Introduction) in Alfeld an der Leine, Germany.[3] She finished the book on 16 July 1949, in the Werl Prison in Westphalia, where she had been

---

[1] Savitri Devi, *Gold in the Furnace: Experiences in Post-War Germany*, ed. R. G. Fowler (Atlanta: The Savitri Devi Archive, 2006); *Defiance: The Prison Memoirs of Savitri Devi*, ed. R. G. Fowler (Atlanta: The Savitri Devi Archive, 2008); *Forever and Ever: Devotional Poems*, ed. R. G. Fowler (San Francisco: Counter-Currents, 2012); and *Pilgrimage* (Calcutta: Savitri Devi Mukherji, 1958).

[2] Savitri Devi, *The Lightning and the Sun*, ed. R. G. Fowler (San Francisco: Counter-Currents, 2015), p. 21 below. On Savitri's time with the Ram Gopal dance troupe, see Savitri Devi, *And Time Rolls On: The Savitri Devi Interviews*, ed. R. G. Fowler, 2nd ed. (San Francisco: Counter-Currents, 2012), p. 54.

[3] *Gold in the Furnace*, p. xviii.

imprisoned for distributing National Socialist leaflets and posters in occupied Germany. *Gold in the Furnace* was published in Calcutta in 1952 by Savitri's husband, A. K. Mukherji, sometime after 21 August, the date of the Foreword.[4]

Chapter 3 of *The Lightning and the Sun* was completed in the railway station of Karlsruhe, Germany, on 6 December 1948,[5] while Savitri was on her second propaganda mission in Germany.[6] During her third propaganda mission, Savitri was arrested in Cologne on the night of 20–21 February 1949.[7] Savitri started writing chapter 4 of *The Lightning and the Sun* on 8 April 1949 in the Werl Prison,[8] and by 30 May 1949 she had finished it and completed part of chapter 5 as well. On that date, her cell was searched, and her manuscripts were confiscated.[9] She was told they would be destroyed, but on 17 June they were returned.[10] She completed *Gold in the Furnace* on 16 July, then resumed work on chapter 5 of *The Lightning and the Sun*,[11] completing it sometime in August 1949, before her release on the 18th. At this point, Savitri apparently set aside work on *The Lightning and the Sun* until 1951.

After her release from Werl, Savitri was expelled from occupied Germany and went back to her hometown of Lyons, France. She then began to write *Defiance*, the story of her arrest and imprisonment, which she completed in Lyons, on 29 August 1950 (the date of the Foreword).[12] *Defiance* was published in 1951 in Calcutta by A. K. Mukherji. (Since the frontispiece photo was taken in September 1951, the book must have been published after that.)

Chapters 6 and 7 of *The Lightning and the Sun* were written

---

[4] *Gold in the Furnace*, p. xiii.

[5] *The Lightning and the Sun*, p. 55.

[6] Savitri tells the story of her first propaganda mission in *Gold in the Furnace*, chapter 4, "The Unforgettable Night" and in *And Time Rolls On*, pp. 54–57; she tells the story of her subsequent missions in *Defiance* and in *And Time Rolls On*, pp. 57–60.

[7] *Defiance*, chapter 2, "The Arrest"; *And Time Rolls On*, pp. 60–69.

[8] *Defiance*, pp. 187–88.

[9] *Defiance*, chapter 10, "The Search."

[10] *Defiance*, pp. 355–56.

[11] *Defiance*, pp. 356, 370.

[12] *Defiance*, p. xv.

in Lyons in 1951 and 1952, completing Part II, "The Lightning: Genghis Khan."[13] At this point, Savitri again set aside *The Lightning and the Sun*, perhaps for as much as two years. There is no record of when she began Part III, "The Sun: Akhnaton," but she finished it on 23 May 1954 in Emsdetten, Germany,[14] i.e., after the completion of two other books: *Forever and Ever* and *Pilgrimage*.

Forever and Ever was probably begun in Lyons in 1952 and completed in Athens on 26 March 1953.[15] It was not published until after Savitri's death.

Pilgrimage tells the story of Savitri's visits to sacred sites related to National Socialism in Austria and Germany in April and May of 1953, as well as the Herrmann Monument and the Externsteine in October 1953. The book was begun on 3 June 1953 (the date of the Introduction[16]) in Emsdetten and finished there on 6 February 1954.[17]

On 16 December 1954, Savitri's room in Emsdetten was searched by German police, she was interrogated for ten hours, and the manuscript of *Pilgrimage* was seized. There was another search on 26 December. The manuscript of *Pilgrimage* was returned about a year later, sometime in 1955.[18] *Pilgrimage* was published by Savitri in Calcutta. The Preface is dated 12 December 1958, but the book likely appeared in print in early 1959.[19]

After finishing *Pilgrimage*, Savitri completed *The Lightning and the Sun* without turning to other projects. As noted above, she finished Part III on 24 May 1954. She wrote chapter 12,

---

[13] *The Lightning and the Sun*, p. 126.

[14] *The Lightning and the Sun*, p. 208.

[15] *And Time Rolls On*, p. 194.

[16] *Pilgrimage*, p. 8.

[17] *Pilgrimage*, p. 354.

[18] Savitri Devi, *Long-Whiskers and the Two-Legged Goddess, or the True Story of a "Most Objectionable Nazi" and . . . Half-A-Dozen Cats* (Calcutta: Savitri Devi Mukherji, n.d.; printed in England in 1965), pp. 80–83. Savitri recounts the seizure and return of the manuscript of *Pilgrimage* in a letter to Matt Koehl written in Prien, Germany, 3 September 1982.

[19] *Pilgrimage*, p. ix. Savitri's close friend Muriel Gantry was likely an early recipient of *Pilgrimage*. Savitri's inscription in her copy is dated 15 March 1959.

"The Late-Born Child of Light," which is the first chapter of Part IV, "Both Sun and Lightning: Adolf Hitler," in Emsdetten on 14 August 1954.[20] Chapter 13, "The Struggle for Truth," was completed on 4 May 1955 in Emsdetten.[21]

After that, Savitri was forced to leave Emsdetten. Eventually, she found a cottage in Oberricklingen near Hanover. Chapter 14, "The World Against Its Saviour," and chapter 15, "Gods on Earth," were completed on 15 February 1956, probably at Oberricklingen, although she does not give the location.[22] Part V, "Epilogue: Kalki, the Avenger" (chapter 16), was completed in Hanover on 21 March 1956, the Spring Equinox.[23]

More than two years passed before *The Lightning and the Sun* was published, because Savitri had to save up the money to publish it and several other works.

In May of 1957, Savitri left Europe for Calcutta, where she published *The Lightning and the Sun* in the latter half of 1958 (the Preface was written in Calcutta on 21 July 1958).[24] Around the same time, Savitri also published her pamphlet *Paul de Tarse, ou Christianisme et Juiverie* (Paul of Tarsus, or Christianity and Jewry), written on 18 June 1957 in El Maahdi, a suburb of Cairo, as well as *Pilgrimage* and *Impeachment of Man*, which had been written in India in 1945–1946.[25]

Savitri had 1,000 copies of the *Lightning and the Sun* printed, in both hardcover and paperback.[26] The original edition of *The Lightning and the Sun* was reprinted in 1979, with an introductory "Commentary" by Christof Friedrich (Ernst Zündel) and additional photographs.[27]

---

[20] *The Lightning and the Sun*, p. 215.
[21] *The Lightning and the Sun*, p. 267.
[22] *The Lightning and the Sun*, p. 414.
[23] *The Lightning and the Sun*, p. 436.
[24] *The Lightning and the Sun*, p. ix.
[25] Savitri Devi, *Paul de Tarse, ou Christianisme et Juiverie* (Calcutta: Savitri Devi Mukherji, 1958); *Impeachment of Man* (Calcutta: Savitri Devi Mukherji, 1959).
[26] I do not know how many hardcover copies of *The Lightning and the Sun* were printed. Savitri did, however, print 100 hardcover copies of her *Souvenirs et réflexions d'une Aryenne* [Memories and Reflections of an Aryan Woman] (Calcutta: Savitri Devi Mukherji, 1976).
[27] Savitri Devi, *The Lightning and the Sun* (Buffalo, N.Y.: Samisdat

William L. Pierce's abridged edition of *The Lightning and the Sun* omits two-thirds of the text and was published without Savitri Devi's editorial input, thus it cannot be regarded as one of her works.[28]

ON THE PRESENT EDITION

No manuscripts or typescripts of *The Lightning and the Sun* are known to have survived. Therefore, this edition is based entirely on the 1958 first edition. I have omitted everything added by Ernst Zündel to his 1979 Samisdat edition.[29]

Like Savitri Devi's other self-published books, the first edition of *The Lightning and the Sun* contains many errors and stylistic inconsistencies. My goal as editor was to make the minimum number of editorial interventions necessary to bring *The Lightning and the Sun* into accord with today's standards.

In keeping with Savitri's British English, I corrected errors of spelling and grammar and made the style consistent throughout. I also corrected a few "foreignisms": unidiomatic diction and syntax based on French and German, the languages Savitri regularly spoke while writing *The Lightning and the Sun*. I usually preserved Savitri's sometimes eccentric capitalization practices and worked to make them consistent.

Savitri Devi's use of punctuation was also eccentric. She did not use commas and semicolons merely to organize information on a page, but to indicate dramatic pauses in real or imaginary speech. I have tried to maintain these punctuation practices, with five exceptions. First, I updated the use of hyphens, e.g., in "to-day" and "to-morrow." Second, I regularized

---

Publishers, 1979).

[28] Savitri Devi, *The Lightning and the Sun*, ed. William L. Pierce, *National Socialist World*, no. 1 (Spring 1966): 13–90. The Pierce edition has been reprinted twice: *The Lightning and the Sun*, ed. William L. Pierce (Paraparaumu Beach, New Zealand: Renaissance Press, 1994) and *The Lightning and the Sun*, ed. William L. Pierce (Hillsboro, West Virginia: National Vanguard Books, 2000).

[29] Zündel added a two-page "Commentary" and a frontispiece photo of Savitri to the front of his edition and a number of photographs and a description of some of Savitri's other works to the back.

the use of commas before conjunctions, following American usage, because it eliminates certain ambiguities. Third, I removed a few commas that seemed to be obvious strays, conforming neither to accepted usage nor to Savitri Devi's style. Fourth, I eliminated commas and, in a couple of cases, colons and semicolons that were adjacent to dashes. Fifth, in a number of places I substituted commas for semicolons linking dependent clauses where they were not needed for clarity.

Where possible, I have supplied complete bibliographical information for books mentioned. I also checked Savitri's citations, sometimes against her own personal copies. Where useful, I have provided editor's notes, which are clearly marked as such.

Except for image no. 2, the photographs in this edition are scans from the first edition of *The Lightning and the Sun*. Unfortunately, their quality is generally poor, but I was unable to find better versions of the exact same images, so I have done everything possible to improve the scans.

Those who wish to check my editorial labours against the original should email me at archivist@savitridevi.org, and I will provide a photocopy of the first edition at cost or a PDF free of charge.

I wish to thank those friends of Savitri Devi and/or of the Savitri Devi Archive who helped make this new edition of *The Lighting and the Sun* possible. Special thanks are due Gabriella Anelauskaitė for the tedious and time-consuming task of scanning the first edition of *The Lightning and the Sun*, Matthew Peters and T. R. for carefully reading the page proofs and spotting numerous errors, James J. O'Meara for the index, Matt Koehl for providing the cover image, Kevin Slaughter for realizing the dust jacket/cover, J. M. for a generous donation at a crucial time, and Michael Polignano for creating the e-book and for technical help throughout the entire process.

I wish to dedicate this new edition of *The Lightning and the Sun* to the memory of Matt Koehl of the New Order, for his kindness to Savitri during her lifetime and his invaluable aid to my research on her life and work over the past 15 years.

R. G. Fowler
1 February 2015

Preface

This book—begun in Scotland in the spring of 1948, and written, at intervals, in Germany, between that date and 1956—is the result of life-long meditations upon history and religions, as well as the expression of life-long aspirations, and of a scale of moral values, which was already mine before the First World War.

It could be described as a personal answer to the events of 1945 and of the following years. And I know that very many people will *not* like it. But I have not written it for any other purpose than that of presenting a conception of history—ancient *and* modern—unassailable from the standpoint of *eternal* Truth. I have therefore endeavoured to study both men and facts in the light of that idea of the succession of Ages, from pristine Perfection to inevitable chaos, which pertains not merely to "Hinduism," but to *all* forms of the One, universal Tradition—the Hindus being (perhaps) but those who have retained somewhat more of that Tradition than less conservative people.

It may sound ironical that so intense a yearning after faithfulness to Tradition should have led me to an interpretation of historic personalities so different from that of most people who profess interest in things of the spirit. The endless future alone will tell who has understood divine Wisdom the best: those people or myself.

SAVITRI DEVI
Calcutta, 21st of July, 1958

Part I

Timeless Perfection
&
Cyclic Evolution

Chapter 1

THE CYCLIC VIEW OF HISTORY

The idea of progress—indefinite betterment—is anything but modern. It is probably as old as man's oldest successful attempt to improve his material surroundings and to increase, through technical skill, his capacity of attack and defence. Technical skill, for many centuries at least, has been too precious to be despised. Nay, when displayed to an extraordinary degree, it has, more than once, been hailed as something almost divine. Wondrous legends have always been woven, for instance, around such men as were said to have, by some means, been able to raise themselves, physically, above the earth, be it Etana of Erech who soared to heaven "borne upon eagle's wings," or the famous Icarus, unfortunate forerunner of our modern airmen, or Manco Cápac's brother, Auca, said to have been gifted with "natural" wings which finally fared hardly better than Icarus' artificial ones.[1]

But apart from such incredible feats of a handful of individuals, the Ancients as a whole distinguished themselves in many material achievements. They could boast of the irrigation system in Sumeria; of the construction of pyramids revealing, both in Egypt and, centuries later, in Central America, an amazing knowledge of astronomical data; of the bathrooms and drains in the palace of Knossos; of the invention of the war chariot after that of the bow and arrow, and of the sand clock after that of the sundial—enough to make them dizzy with conceit and over-confident in the destiny of their respective civilisations.

Yet, although they fully recognized the value of their own work in the practical field, and surely very soon conceived the possibility—and perhaps acquired the certitude—of indefinite *technical* progress, they never believed in progress as a whole,

---

[1] While Icarus fell into the sea, the Peruvian hero was turned into stone on reaching the top of the hill destined to become the site of the great Temple of the Sun, in Cuzco.

in progress on all lines, as most of our contemporaries seem to do. From all evidence, they faithfully clung to the traditional idea of cyclic evolution and had, in addition to that, the good sense to admit that they lived (in spite of all their achievements) in anything but the beginning of the long-drawn, downward process constituting their own particular "cycle" — and *ours*. Whether Hindus or Greeks, Egyptians or Japanese, Chinese, Sumerians, or ancient Americans — or even Romans, the most "modern" amongst people of Antiquity — they all placed the "Golden Age," the "Age of Truth,"[2] the rule of Kronos or of Ra, or of any other Gods on earth — the glorious Beginning of the slow, downward unfurling of history, whatever name it be given — far behind them in the past.

And they believed that the return of a similar Age, foretold in their respective sacred texts and oral traditions, depends, not upon man's conscious effort, but upon iron laws, inherent to the very nature of visible and tangible manifestation, and all-pervading; upon cosmic laws. They believed that man's conscious effort is but an expression of those laws at work, leading the world, willingly or unwillingly, wherever its destiny lies; in one word, that the history of man, as the history of the rest of the living, is but a detail in cosmic history without beginning or end; a periodical outcome of the inner Necessity that binds all phenomena in Time.

And just as the Ancients could accept that vision of the world's evolution while still taking full advantage of all technical progress within their reach, so can — and so do — to this day, thousands of men brought up within the pale of age-old cultures centred around the self-same traditional views, and also, in the very midst of the over-proud industrial cultures, a few stray individuals able to think for themselves. They contemplate the history of mankind in a similar perspective.

While living, apparently, as "modern" men and women — using electric fans and electric irons, telephones and trains, and aeroplanes, when they can afford it — they nourish in their hearts a deep contempt for the childish conceit and bloated hopes of our age, and for the various recipes for "saving mankind," which zealous philosophers and politicians thrust into

---

[2] *Satya Yuga*, in the Sanskrit Scriptures.

circulation. They know that nothing can "save mankind," for mankind is reaching the end of its present cycle. The wave that carried it, for so many millenniums, is about to break, with all the fury of acquired speed, and to merge once more into the depth of the unchanging Ocean of undifferentiated existence. It will rise, again, some day, with abrupt majesty, for such is the law of waves. But in the meantime *nothing can be done to stop it.* The unfortunate — the fools — are those men who, for some reason best known to themselves — probably on account of their exaggerated estimation of what is to be lost in the process — would like to stop it. The privileged ones — the wise — are those few who, being fully aware of the increasing worthlessness of present-day mankind and of its much-applauded "progress," know how little there is to be lost in the coming crash and look forward to it with joyous expectation as to the necessary condition of a new beginning — a new "Golden Age," sunlit crest of the *next* long drawn downward wave upon the surface of the endless Ocean of Life.

To those privileged ones — amongst whom we count ourselves — the whole succession of "current events" appears in an entirely different perspective from that either of the desperate believers in "progress" or of those people who, though accepting the cyclic view of history and therefore considering the coming crash as unavoidable, feel sorry to see the civilisation in which they live rush towards its doom.

To us, the high-resounding "isms" to which our contemporaries ask us to give our allegiance, *now*, in 1948, are all equally futile: bound to be betrayed, defeated, and finally rejected by men at large, if containing anything really noble; bound to enjoy, for the time being, some sort of noisy success, if sufficiently vulgar, pretentious, and soul-killing to appeal to the growing number of mechanically conditioned slaves that crawl about our planet, posing as free men; all destined to prove, ultimately, of no avail. The time-honoured religions, rapidly growing out of fashion as present-day "isms" become more and more popular, are no less futile — if not more: frameworks of organised superstition void of all true feeling of the Divine, or — among more sophisticated people — mere conventional aspects of social life, or systems of ethics (and of very elementary ethics at that) seasoned with a sprinkling of out-dated rites and symbols of which hardly anybody bothers to seek the original meaning; devices in the hands of clever men in power to lull the simpletons into permanent obedience; convenient names, around which it might be easy to rally converging national aspirations or political tendencies; or just the last resort of weaklings and cranks: that is, practically, all they are—all they have been reduced to in the course of a few centuries—the lot of them. They are dead, in fact—as dead as the old cults that flourished before them, with the difference that those cults have long ceased exhaling the stench of death, while they (the so-called "living" ones) are still at the stage at which death is inseparable from corruption. None—neither Christianity nor Islam nor even Buddhism—can be expected now to "save" anything of that world they once partly conquered; none have any normal place in "modern" life, which is essentially devoid of all awareness of the eternal.

There are no activities in "modern" life which are not futile, save perhaps those that aim at satisfying one's body's hunger: growing rice, growing wheat, gathering chestnuts from the woods or potatoes from one's garden. And the one and only sensible policy can but be to let things take their course and to await the coming Destroyer, destined to clear the ground for the building of a new "Age of Truth": the One Whom the Hindus name Kalki and hail as the tenth and last Incarnation of Vishnu; the Destroyer Whose advent is the condition of the preservation of Life, according to Life's everlasting laws.

We know all this will sound utter folly to those, more and more numerous, who, despite the untold horrors of our age, remain convinced that humanity is "progressing." It will appear as cynicism even to many of those who accept our belief in cyclic evolution, which is the universal, traditional belief expressed in poetic form in all the sacred texts of the world, including the Bible. We have nothing to reply to this latter possible criticism, for it is entirely based upon an emotional attitude which is not ours. But we can try to point out the vanity of the popular belief in "progress," be it only in order to stress the rationality and strength of the theory of cycles which forms the background of the triple study which is the subject of this book.

卐 卐 卐

The exponents of the belief in "progress" put forth many arguments to prove — to themselves and to others — that our times, with all their undeniable drawbacks, are on the whole, *better* than any epoch of the past, and even that they show definite signs of improvement. It is not possible to analyse all their arguments in detail. But one can easily detect the fallacies hidden in the most widespread and, apparently, the most "convincing" of them.

All the advocates of "progress" lay enormous stress upon such things as literacy, individual "freedom," equal opportunities for *all* men, religious toleration, and "humaneness," progress in this last line covering all such tendencies as find their expression in the modern preoccupation for child-welfare, prison-reforms, better conditions of labour, state aid to the sick and destitute, and, if not greater kindness, at least less cruelty to animals. The dazzling results obtained, in recent years, in the application of scientific discoveries to industrial and other practical pursuits, are, of course, the most popular of all instances expected to show how marvellous our times are. But that point we shall not discuss, as we have already made it clear that we by no means deny or minimise the importance of *technical* progress. What we do deny is the existence of any progress at all in the value of man as such, whether individually or collectively, and our reflections on universal literacy and other highly praised "signs" of improvement in which our contemporaries take pride, all spring from that one point of view.

We believe that man's value — as every creature's value, ultimately — lies not in the mere intellect but in the spirit: in the capacity to reflect that which, for lack of a more precise word, we choose to call "the divine," i.e., that which is true and beautiful beyond all manifestation, that which remains timeless (and therefore unchangeable) within all changes. We believe it with the difference that, in our eyes — contrarily to what the Christians maintain — that capacity to reflect the divine is closely linked with man's race and physical health; in other words, that the spirit is anything but independent from the body. And we fail to see that the different improvements that we witness today in education or in the social field, in government or even in technical matters, have either made individual men and women more valuable in *that* sense, or created any new lasting type of civilisation in which man's possibilities of all around perfection, thus conceived, are being promoted. The Hindus seem to be, today, the sole people who, by tradition, share our views; and they have, in the course of time, failed to maintain the divine order—the rule of the natural ruling castes. And we, the only people in the West who have tried to restore it in modern times, have been materially ruined by the agents of those forces of false equality that the modern world calls forces of "progress."

Progress?—It is true that, today, at least in all highly organised (typically "modern") countries, nearly everybody can read and write. But what of that? To be able to read and write is an advantage—and a considerable one. But it is not a virtue. It is a tool and a weapon; a means to an end; a very useful thing, no doubt; but not an end in itself. The ultimate value of literacy depends upon the end to which it is used. And to what end, is it generally used today? It is used for convenience or for entertainment, by those who read; for some advertisement, or some objectionable propaganda—for money-making or power-grabbing—by those who write; *sometimes*, of course, by both, for acquiring or spreading disinterested knowledge of the few things worth knowing; for finding expression of or giving expression to the few deep feelings that can lift a man to the awareness of things eternal, but not more often so than in the days in which one man out of 10,000 could understand the symbolism of the written word. Generally, today, the man or woman whom compulsory education has made "literate" uses writing to communicate personal matters to absent friends and relatives, to fill out forms—one of the international occupations of modern civilised humanity—or to commit to memory little useful, but otherwise trifling things such as someone's address or telephone number, or the date of some appointment with the hairdresser or the dentist, or the list of clean clothes due from the laundry. He or she reads "to pass time" because, outside the hours of dreary work, mere thinking is no longer intense and interesting enough to serve that purpose.

We know that there are also people whose whole lives have been directed to some beautiful destiny by a book, a poem—a mere sentence—read in distant childhood, like Schliemann, who lavishly spent on archaeological excavations the wealth patiently and purposely gathered in 40 years of dreary toil, all for the sake of the impression left upon him, as a boy, by the immortal story of Troy. But such people always lived, even before compulsory education came into fashion. And the stories *heard* and remembered were no less inspiring than stories now read. The real advantage of general literacy, if any, is to be sought elsewhere. It lies not in the better quality either of the exceptional men and women or of the literate millions, but rather in the fact that the latter are rapidly becoming intellectually more lazy and therefore more credulous than ever — and *not* less so; more easily deceived, more liable to be led like sheep without even the shadow of a protest, provided the nonsense one wishes them to swallow be presented to them, in printed form and made to appear "scientific." The higher the general level of literacy, the *easier* it is, for a government in control of the daily press, of the wireless, and of the publishing business — these almost irresistible modern means of action upon the mind — to keep the masses *and* the "intelligentsia" under its thumb, without them even suspecting it.

Among widely illiterate but more actively thinking people, openly governed in the old autocratic manner, a prophet, direct mouthpiece of the Gods, or of genuine collective aspirations, could always hope to rise between secular authority and the people. The priests themselves could never be quite sure of keeping the people in obedience forever. The people could choose to listen to the prophet, if they liked. And they did, sometimes. Today, wherever universal literacy is prevalent, inspired exponents of timeless truth — prophets — or even selfless advocates of timely practical changes, have less and less chance to appear. Sincere thought, real *free* thought, ready, in the name of superhuman authority or of humble common sense, to question the basis of what is officially taught and generally accepted, is less and less likely to thrive. It is, we repeat, by far easier to enslave a literate people than an illiterate one, strange as this may seem at first sight. And the enslavement is more likely to be lasting. The real advantage of universal literacy is to tighten the grip of the governing power upon the foolish and conceited millions. That is probably why it is dinned into our heads, from babyhood onwards, that "literacy" is such a boon. The capacity to think for one's self is, however, the real boon. And that always was and always will be the privilege of a minority, once recognised as a natural élite and respected. Today, compulsory mass education and an increasingly standardised literature for the consumption of "conditioned" brains — outstanding signs of "progress" — tend to reduce that minority to the smallest possible proportions; ultimately, to suppress it altogether. Is that what mankind wants? If so, mankind is losing its *raison d'être*, and the sooner the end of this so-called "civilisation" the better.

What we have said of literacy can roughly be repeated about those two other main glories of modern democracy: "individual freedom" and equality of opportunities for every person. The first is a lie — and a more and more sinister one as the shackles of compulsory education are being more and more hopelessly fastened around people's whole being. The second is an absurdity.

One of the funniest inconsistencies of the average citizen of the modern industrialised world is the way in which he criticises all institutions of older and better civilisations, such as the caste system of the Hindus or the all-absorbing family cult of the Far East, on the ground that these tend to check the "liberty of the individual." He does not realise how exacting — nay, how annihilating — is the command of the collective authority which *he* obeys (half the time, unknowingly) compared with that of traditional collective authority, in apparently less "free" societies. The caste-ridden or family-ridden people of India or of the Far East might not be allowed to do all that they like, in many relatively trifling and in a few really all-important matters of daily life. But they are left to *believe* what they like, or rather what they can; to feel according to their own nature and to express themselves freely about a great number of essential matters; they are allowed to conduct their higher life in the manner they judge the wisest for them, after their duties to family, caste, and king have been fulfilled. The individual living under the iron and steel rule of modern "progress" can eat whatever he fancies (to a great extent) and marry whom he pleases — unfortunately! — and go wherever he likes (in theory at least). But he is made to accept, in all extra-individual matters — matters which, to us, really count — the beliefs, the attitude to life, the scale of values and, to a great extent, the political views, that tend to strengthen the mighty socio-economic system of exploitation to which he belongs (to which he is forced to belong, in order to be able to live) and in which he is a mere cog. And, what is more, he is made to believe that it is a privilege of his to be a cog in such an organism; that the unimportant matters in which he feels he is his own master are, in fact, the most important ones — the only really important ones. He is taught not to value that freedom of judgement about ultimate truth, aesthetical, ethical, or metaphysical, of which he is subtly deprived. More still: he is told — in the democratic countries at any rate — that he is free in *all* respects; that he is "an *individual*, answerable to none but to his own conscience" . . . after years of clever conditioning have moulded his "conscience" and his whole being so thoroughly according to pattern, that he is no longer capable of reacting differently. Well can such a man speak of "pressure upon the individual" in any society, ancient or modern!

One can realise to what an extent men's minds have been curved, both by deliberate and by unconscious conditioning, in the world in which we live today, when one encounters people who have never come under the influence of industrial civilisation, or when one happens, oneself, to be lucky enough to have defied, from childhood onwards, the pernicious pressure of standardised education and to have remained free amidst the crowd of those who react as they were taught to, in all fundamental matters. The cleavage between the thinking and the unthinking, the free and the slaves, is appalling.

As for "equality of opportunities," there can be no such thing anyhow, strictly speaking. By producing men and women different both in degree and in quality of intelligence, sensitiveness, and will-power, different in character and temperament, Nature herself gives them the most unequal opportunities of fulfilling their aspirations, whatever these might be. An over-emotional and rather weak person can, for instance, neither conceive the same ideal of happiness nor have equal chances of reaching it in life, as one who is born with a more balanced nature and a stronger will. That is obvious. And add to that the characteristics that differentiate one race of men from another, and the absurdity of the very notion of "human equality" becomes even more striking.

What our contemporaries mean when they speak of "equality of opportunities" is the fact that, in modern society—so they say—any man or woman stands, more and more, as many chances as his or her neighbour of holding the position and doing the job for which he or she is naturally fitted. But that too is only partly true. For, more and more, the world of today—the world dominated by grand-scale industry and mass-production—can offer only jobs in which the best of the worker's self plays little or no part if he or she be anything more than a merely clever and materially efficient person. The hereditary craftsman, who could find the best expression for what is conveniently called his "soul" in his daily weaving, carpet-making, enamel work, etc., even the tiller of the soil, in personal contact with Mother Earth and the Sun and the seasons, is becoming more and more a figure of the past. There are fewer and fewer opportunities, also, for the sincere seeker of truth—speaker or writer—who refuses to become the expounder of broadly accepted ideas, products of mass-conditioning, for which he or she does not stand; for the seeker of beauty who refuses to bend his or her art to the demands of popular taste which he or she knows to be bad taste. Such people have to waste much of their time doing inefficiently—and grudgingly—some job for which they are *not* fitted, in order to live, before they can devote the rest of it to what the Hindus would call their *sadhana*—the work for which their deeper nature has appointed them: their life's dedication.

The idea of modern division of labour, condensed in the oft-quoted sentence "the right man in the right place," boils down, in practice, to the fact that *any* man—any one of the dull, indiscriminate millions—can be "conditioned" to occupy *any* place, while the best of human beings, the only ones who still justify the existence of the more and more degenerate species, are allowed no place at all. Progress . . .

There remain the "religious toleration" of our times and their "humaneness" compared with the "barbarity" of the past. Two jokes, to say the least!

Recalling some of the most spectacular horrors of history—

the burning of "heretics" and "witches" at the stake, the wholesale massacre of "heathens," and other no less repulsive manifestations of Christian civilisation in Europe, conquered America, Goa, and elsewhere — modern man is filled with pride in the "progress" accomplished, in one line at least, since the end of the Dark Ages of religious fanaticism. However bad they be, our contemporaries have, at any rate, grown out of the habit of torturing people for such "trifles" as their conception of the Holy Trinity or their ideas about predestination and purgatory. Such is modern man's feeling — because theological questions have lost all importance in his life. But in the days when Christian churches persecuted one another and encouraged the conversion of heathen nations by means of blood and fire, both the persecutors and the persecuted, both the Christians and those who wished to remain faithful to non-Christian creeds, looked upon such questions as vital in one way or another. And the real reason for which nobody is put to torture, today, for the sake of his or her religious beliefs, is *not* that torture as such has become distasteful to everybody, in "advanced" 20th-century civilisation, *not* that individuals and states have become "tolerant," but just that, among those who have the power of inflicting pain, hardly anybody takes any vivid, *vital* interest in religion, let alone in theology.

The so-called "religious toleration" practised by modern states and individuals springs from anything but an intelligent understanding and love of all religions as manifold, symbolical expressions of the same few essential, eternal truths — as Hindu toleration does, and always did. It is, rather, the outcome of a grossly ignorant contempt for all religions; of indifference to those very truths which their various founders endeavoured to reassert, again and again. It is no toleration at all.

To judge how far our contemporaries have or not the right to boast of their "spirit of toleration," the best is to watch their behaviour towards those whom they decidedly look upon as the enemies of their gods: the men who happen to be holding views contrary to theirs concerning not some theological quibble, in which they are not interested, but some political or socio-political Ideology which they regard as "a threat to civilisation" *or* as "the only creed through which civilisation can be saved." Nobody can deny that in all such circumstances, and especially in war time, they all perform—to the extent they have the power—or condone—to the extent they have not, themselves, the opportunity of performing—actions in every respect as ugly as those ordered, performed, or tolerated in the past, in the name of different religions (if indeed the latter ugly be). The only difference is, perhaps, that modern cold-blooded atrocities only become known when the hidden powers in control of the means of herd-conditioning—of the press, the wireless, and the cinema—decide, for ends anything but "humanitarian," that they should be, i.e., when they happen to be the enemy's atrocities, not one's own—nor those of one's "gallant allies"—and when their story is, therefore, considered to be "good propaganda," on account of the current of indignation it is expected to create and of the new incentive it is expected to give the war-effort. Moreover, after a war, fought or supposed to have been fought for an Ideology—the modern equivalent of the bitter religious conflicts of old—the horrors rightly or wrongly said to have been perpetrated by the vanquished are the only ones to be broadcasted all over the world, while the victors try as hard as they can to make believe that *their* High Command at least never shut its eyes to any similar horrors. But in 16th-century Europe and before, and among the warriors of Islam, conducting *"jihad"* against men of other faiths, each side was well aware of the atrocious means used, not only by its opponents for their "foul ends," but by its own people and its own leaders in order to "uproot heresy" or to "fight popery," or to "preach the name of Allah to infidels." Modern man is more of a moral coward. He wants the advantages of violent intolerance—which is only natural—but he shuns the responsibility of it. *Progress*, that also.

The so-called "humaneness" of our contemporaries (compared with their forefathers) is just lack of nerve or lack of strong feelings—increasing cowardice, or increasing apathy.

Modern man is squeamish about atrocities—even about ordinary, unimaginative brutality—*only* when it happens that the aims for which atrocious or merely brutal actions are performed are either hateful or indifferent to him. In all other circumstances, he shuts his eyes to any horrors—especially when he *knows* that the victims can never retaliate (as it is the case with all atrocities committed by man upon animals, for whatever purpose it be), and he demands, at the most, not to be reminded of them too often and too noisily. He reacts as though he classified atrocities under two headlines: the "unavoidable" and the avoidable. The "unavoidable" are those that serve or are supposed to serve modern man's purpose—generally: "the good of humanity" or the "triumph of democracy." *They* are tolerated, nay, justified. The "avoidable" are those which are occasionally committed, or said to be committed, by people whose purpose is alien to his. They alone are condemned, and their real or supposed authors—or inspirers—branded by public opinion as "criminals against humanity."

What are, anyhow, the alleged signs of that wonderful "humaneness" of modern man, according to those who believe in progress? We no longer have today—they say—the horrid executions of former times; traitors are no longer "hung, drawn, and quartered," as was the custom in glorious 16th-century England; anything approaching in ghastliness the torture and execution of François Damien, upon the central square of Paris, before thousands of people purposely come to see it, on the 28th of May, 1757, would be unthinkable in modern France. Modern man also no longer upholds slavery, nor does he (in theory, at least) justify the exploitation of the masses under any form. And his wars—even his wars, monstrous as they may seem, with their elaborate apparatus of costly demoniacal machinery!—are beginning to admit, within their code (so one says), some amount of humanity and justice. Modern man is horrified at the mere thought of the wartime habits of ancient peoples—at the sacrifice of twelve young Trojans to the shade of the Greek hero Patroclus, not to speak of the far less ancient but far more atrocious sacrifices of prisoners of war to the Aztec war god Huitzilopochtli. (But the Aztecs, though relatively modern, were not Christians, nor, as far as we know, believers in all-round progress.) Finally—one says—modern man is kinder, or less cruel, to animals than his forefathers were.

Only an enormous amount of prejudice in favour of our times can enable one to be taken in by such fallacies.

Surely modern man does not "uphold" slavery; he denounces

it vehemently. But he practises it nevertheless—and on a wider scale than ever, and far more thoroughly than the Ancients ever could—whether in the capitalistic West or in the Tropics, or (from what one hears outside its impenetrable walls) even in the one state supposed to be, today, the "workers' paradise." There are differences, of course. In Antiquity, even the slave had hours of leisure and merriment that were all his own; he had his games of dice in the shade of the columns of his master's portico, his coarse jokes, his free chatter, his free life outside his daily routine. The modern slave has not the privilege of loitering, completely carefree, for half an hour. His so-called leisure itself is either filled with almost compulsory entertainment, as exacting and often as dreary as his work, or—in "lands of freedom"— poisoned by economic worries. But he is not openly bought and sold. He is just *taken*. And taken, not by a man in some way at least superior to himself, but by a huge impersonal system without either a body to kick or a soul to damn or a head to answer for its mischief.

And similarly, old horrors have no doubt disappeared from the records of so-called civilised mankind, regarding both justice and war. But new and worse ones, unknown to "barbaric" ages, have crept up in their place. One single instance is ghastly enough to suffice. The long-drawn trial not of criminals, not of traitors, nor regicides, nor wizards, but of the finest leading characters of Europe; their iniquitous condemnation, after months and months of every kind of humiliation and systematic moral torture; their final hanging, in the slowest and cruellest possible manner—that whole sinister farce, staged at Nuremberg in 1945-1946 (and 1947) by a pack of victorious cowards and hypocrites, is immeasurably more disgusting than all the post-war human sacrifices of the past rolled in one, including those performed according to the well-known Mexican ritual. For there, at least, however painful might have been the traditional process of killing, the victims were frankly done to death for the delight of the tribal god of the victors and of the victors themselves, without any macabre mock-pretence of "justice." And they were, moreover, taken from all ranks of captured warriors, not malignantly selected from the élite of their people only. Nor did the élite of the vanquished people represent, in most cases—as it actually did in the shameful trial of *our* progressive times—the very élite of their continent.

As for such unthinkable atrocities as took place in France and in Spain, and many other countries, from the Middle Ages onwards, one would find quite a number of episodes of the recent Spanish Civil War—not to mention the no less impressive record of horrors performed, still more recently, by the "heroes" of the French *résistance*, during the Second World War—to match them and, more often than not, to outdo them.

And, curiously enough—although (they say) they "hate such things"—a considerable number of men and women of today, while lacking the guts to commit horrible actions personally, seem to be just as keen as ever on watching them being performed or, at least, on thinking of them and gloating over them, and enjoying them vicariously, if denied the morbid pleasure of watching. Such are the people who, in modern England, gather before the prison gates whenever a man is to be hanged, expecting goodness knows what unhealthy excitement from the mere fact of reading the announcement that "justice has been done"—people who, if only given an opportunity, would run to see a public execution, nay, a public burning of witches or heretics, no doubt as speedily as their forefathers once did. Such are also millions of folk, hitherto "civilised" and apparently kind, who reveal themselves in their proper light no sooner a war breaks out, i.e., no sooner they feel encouraged to display the most repulsive type of imagination in competitive descriptions of what tortures every one of them "would" inflict upon the enemy's leaders, if he—or more often *she*—had a free hand. Such are, at heart, all those who gloat over the sufferings of the fallen enemy *after* a victorious war. And they are also millions: millions of vicarious savages, mean at the same time as cruel—unmanly—whom the warriors of the so-called "barbaric" ages would have thoroughly despised.

But more cowardly and more hypocritical, perhaps, than anything else, is "progressive" modern man's behaviour towards living Nature, and in particular towards the animal kingdom. Of *that* I have spoken at length in another book,[3] and

---

[3] *Impeachment of Man*, written in 1945–46, and yet unpublished.

I shall, therefore, here, be contented with underlining a few facts.

Primitive man—and, often, also, man whose picturesque civilisation is anything but "modern"—is bad enough, it is true, as far as his treatment of animals is concerned. One only has to travel in the least industrialised countries of southern Europe, or in the Near and Middle East, to acquire a very definite certitude on that point. And not all modern leaders have been equally successful in putting an end to age-old cruelties to dumb beasts, whether in the East or in the West. Gandhi could not, in the name of that universal kindness which he repeatedly preached as the main tenet of his faith, prevent Hindu milkmen from deliberately starving their male calves to death, in order to sell a few extra pints of cow's milk. Mussolini could not detect and prosecute all those Italians who, even under his government, persisted in the detestable habit of plucking chickens alive on the ground that "the feathers come off more easily." There is no getting away from the fact that kindness to animals on a national scale does not ultimately depend upon the teachings of any superimposed religion or philosophy. It is one of the distinctive characteristics of the truly superior races. And no religious, philosophical, or political alchemy can turn base metal into gold.

This does not mean to say that a good teaching cannot *help* to bring the best out of every race, as well as out of every individual man or woman. But modern industrial civilisation, to the extent it is man-centred—not controlled by any inspiration of a super-human, cosmic order—and tends to stress quantity instead of quality, production and wealth instead of character and inherent worth, is anything but congenial to the development of consistent universal kindness, even among the better people. It hides cruelty. It does nothing to suppress it, or even to lessen it. It excuses, nay, it exalts any atrocity upon animals, which happens to be directly or indirectly connected with money-making, from the daily horrors of the slaughterhouses to the martyrdom of animals at the hands of the circus trainer, the trapper (and, also, very often, of the skinner, in the case of

---

[*Impeachment* was published in 1959: Savitri Devi, *Impeachment of Man* (Calcutta: Savitri Devi Mukherji, 1959).—Ed.]

furry creatures), and of the vivisector. Naturally, the "higher" interest of human beings is put forward as a justification—without people realising that a humanity which is prepared to buy amusement or luxury, "tasty food," or even scientific information or means of healing the sick at such a cost as that, is no longer worthy to live. The fact remains that there has never been more degeneracy and more disease of all descriptions among men, than in this world of compulsory or almost compulsory vaccination and inoculation; this world which exalts criminals against Life—torturers of innocent living creatures for man's ends, such as Louis Pasteur—to the rank of "great" men, while condemning the really great ones who struggled to stress the sacred hierarchy of human races before and above the over-emphasised and, anyhow, obvious, hierarchy of beings, and who, incidentally, built the only state in the West whose laws for the protection of dumb creatures reminded one, for the first time after centuries (and to the extent it was possible in a modern industrial country of cold climate), of the decrees of Emperor Asoka and Harshavardhana.[4]

Such a world may well boast of its tender care for prize dogs and cats and for pet animals in general, while trying to forget (and to make better civilisations forget) the hideous fact of a million creatures vivisected yearly, in Great Britain alone. It cannot make *us* overlook its hidden horrors and convince us of its "progress" in kindness to animals, any more than of its increasing kindness to people "irrespective of their creed." We refuse to see in it anything else but the darkest living evidence of that which the Hindus have characterised from time immemorial as the "Kali Yuga"—the "Dark Age"; the Era of Gloom; the last (and, fortunately, the shortest) subdivision of the present Cycle of history. There is no hope of "putting things right" in such an age. It is, essentially, the age so forcefully though laconically described in the Book of books—the Bhagavad-Gita—as that in which "out of the corruption of women proceeds the confusion of castes; out of the confusion of castes, the loss of memory; out of the loss of memory, the lack of understanding; and out of this, all evils"[5];

---

[4] I refer to the laws against cruelty to animals that were, in my eyes, one of the glories of the National Socialist régime in Germany.

[5] The Bhagavad-Gita, trans. Eugène Burnouf, I, 47 and following

the age in which falsehood is termed "truth" and truth persecuted as falsehood or mocked as insanity; in which the exponents of truth, the divinely inspired leaders, the real friends of their race and of all the living—the god-like men—are defeated, and their followers humbled and their memory slandered, while the masters of lies are hailed as "saviours"; the age in which every man and woman is in the wrong place, and the world dominated by inferior individuals, bastardised races, and vicious doctrines, all part and parcel of an order of inherent ugliness far worse than complete anarchy.

This is the age in which our triumphant democrats and our hopeful Communists boast of "slow but steady progress through science and education." Thanks very much for such "progress"! The very sight of it is enough to confirm *us* in our belief in the immemorial cyclic theory of history, illustrated in the myths of all ancient, natural religions (including that one from which the Jews—and, through them, their disciples, the Christians—borrowed the symbolical story of the Garden of Eden, Perfection at the *beginning* of Time). It impresses upon us the fact that human history, far from being a steady ascension towards the better, is an increasingly hopeless process of bastardisation, emasculation, and demoralisation of mankind; an inexorable "fall." It rouses in us the yearning to see the end— the final crash that will push into oblivion both those worthless "isms" that are the product of the decay of thought and of character, and the no less worthless religions of equality which have slowly prepared the ground for them; the coming of Kalki, the divine Destroyer of evil; the dawn of a new Cycle opening, as all time-cycles ever did, with "Golden Age."

Never mind how bloody the final crash may be! Never mind what old treasures may perish forever in the redeeming conflagration! The sooner it comes, the better. We are waiting for it— and for the following glory—confident in the divinely established cyclic Law that governs all manifestations of existence in Time: the law of Eternal Return. We are waiting for it, and for the subsequent triumph of the Truth persecuted today; for the triumph under whatever name of the only faith in harmony with

---

[*Le Bhâgavata Purâna ou histoire poétique de Krichna*, 3 vols. (Paris, 1840-1847). — Ed.].

the everlasting laws of being; of the only modern "ism" which is anything but "modern," being just the latest expression of principles as old as the Sun; the triumph of all those men who, throughout the centuries *and* today, have never lost the vision of the everlasting Order, decreed by the Sun, and who have fought in a selfless spirit to impress that vision upon others. We are waiting for the glorious restoration, this time on a world-wide scale, of the New Order, projection in time, in the next as in every recurring "Golden Age," of the everlasting Order of the Cosmos.

It is the only thing worth living for—and dying for, if given that privilege—now, in 1948.

Written in Edinburgh, on the 9th of April, 1948 – the 707th anniversary of the famous battle of Liegnitz

Chapter 2

TIME & VIOLENCE

From the few facts that I have recalled in the preceding chapter, it is pretty clear that there are no cruelties in ancient history—no Assyrian horrors, no Carthaginian horrors, no old Chinese horrors—which the inventiveness of our contemporaries of East and West, aided by a perfected technique, has not outdone. But cruelty—the violence of cowards—is merely one expression of violence among many, though admittedly the most repulsive one. Aided and encouraged by more and more staggering scientific achievements, which can be put to use for *any* purpose, man has, throughout history, become more and more violent—and not less and less so, as people fed on pacifist propaganda are often inclined to think! And, which is more, *it could not have been otherwise; and it cannot be otherwise* at any period of the future, until the violent and complete destruction of that which we call today "civilisation" opens for the world a new "Age of Truth," a new Golden Age. Until then, violence, under one form or another, is unavoidable. It is the very law of Life in a fallen world. The choice given us is not between violence and non-violence, but between open, unashamed violence, in broad daylight, and sneaking, subtle violence—blackmail; between open violence and inconspicuous, slow, yet implacable persecution, both economic and cultural: the systematic suppression of all possibilities for the vanquished, without it "showing"; the merciless "conditioning" of children, all the more horrible that it is more impersonal, more indirect, more outwardly "gentle"; the clever diffusion of soul-killing lies (and *half*-lies); violence under the cover of non-violence. The choice is also between selfless ruthlessness put to the service of the very Cause of truth; violence without cruelty, applied in view of bringing about upon this earth an order based on everlasting principles that transcend man; violence in view of creating, or maintaining, a human state in harmony with Life's highest purpose, and violence applied to selfish ends.

The two parallel alternatives are indeed one and the same. For it is a fact that, the more disinterested be its aims and the more selfless its application, the more frank and straightforward violence is; while, on the other hand, the more sordid be the motives for which it is in reality used, the more it is, itself, hidden, nay, denied; the more the men who resort to it boast of being admirers of non-violence, thus bluffing others and sometimes also themselves; acting as deceivers and being deceived — caught in the network of their own lies.

As time goes on and as decay sets in, the keynote of human history is *not* less and less violence; it is less and less honesty about violence.

Only an "Age of Truth" — in which all is as it should be, a world in which the social and political order on earth is a perfect replica of the eternal Order of Life — can be non-violent. And in the eloquent legends of all old nations, the ideal society at the dawn of Time is said to have been naturally so. There was, then, nothing to be changed; nothing for which to shed one's own or other people's blood; nothing to do but to enjoy in peace the beauty and riches of the sunlit earth, and to praise the wise Gods — the "*devas*," or "shining Ones," as the ancient Aryans called them — Kings of the earth in the truest sense of the word. Every man and woman, every race, every species was, then, *in its place*, and the whole divine hierarchy of Creation was a work of art to which and from which there was nothing either to add or to take away. Violence was unthinkable.

Violence became a necessity from the moment the sociopolitical order in this world ceased to be the undistorted reflection of the eternal cosmic Order; from the moment a man-centred spirit, exalting indiscriminately the whole of humanity at the expense of glorious living Nature, on one hand, and at that of the naturally superior individuals and naturally privileged races, on the other, arose, in opposition to the life-centred Tradition which had been sanctioning, for no one knows how many happy millenniums, the harmonious, divinely ordained hierarchy of peoples, animal species, and vegetable varieties; from the moment a vicious tendency to uniformity — ultimately leading to disintegration — set in, in opposition to primeval Unity within infinite, disciplined diversity. From that moment onwards, we repeat, violence became the law of the world, for good and for evil. The only way to avoid resorting to it was, henceforth, either to cut one's self off, entirely, from the world as it is, to turn one's back to life and to move about in an artificial, dream-like time — the illusion of an illusion — or else, to live outside Time altogether. Pretty few individuals were sufficiently foolish to take the first course, and fewer still sufficiently evolved and, at the same time, sufficiently indifferent, to take the second.

But violence is not a bad thing in itself. True, it set in as a necessity only after the world had become, to a great extent, "bad," i.e., unfaithful to its timeless archetype; no longer in keeping with the creative dream of the universal Mind, that it had once expressed. The very appearing of violence was a sign that the "Age of Truth" was irretrievably closed; that the downward process of history was gaining speed. Yet, violence cannot be judged apart from its purpose. And the purpose is good or bad; worth its while, or not. It is worth its while when those who pursue it do so, not merely unselfishly — with no primordial desire of personal glory or happiness — but also in keeping with an Ideology expressing timeless, impersonal, more-than-human truth; an Ideology rooted in the clear understanding of the unchanging Laws of life, and destined to appeal to all those who, in a fallen world, still retain within their hearts an invincible yearning for the perfect Order as it really *was* and will again be; as it cannot but be, at the dawn of every recurring Time-cycle. Any purpose which is intelligently, objectively consistent with the war-aims of the undying Forces of Light in their age-old struggle against the forces of Darkness, i.e., of disintegration — that Struggle illustrated in all the mythologies of the world — any such purpose, I say, justifies any amount of selfless violence. Moreover, as the "Era of Gloom" in which we are living proceeds, darker and darker and fiercer and fiercer year after year, it becomes more and more impossible to avoid using violence in the service of truth. No man — no demigod — can bring about, today, even a relative amount of real order and justice in any area of the globe, without the help of force, especially if he has but a few years at his disposal. And, unfortunately, the further this world advances into the present age of technical wonders and human abasement, the more the great men of inspiration are submitted to the factor of *time*, as soon as they attempt to apply their lofty intuitive knowledge of eternal truth to the solution of practical problems. They just *have to act*, not only thoroughly, but also *quickly*, if they do not want to see the forces of disintegration nip their priceless work in the bud. And whether they like it or not, thoroughly *and* quickly means, almost unavoidably, with unhesitating violence. One can say, with more and more certainty as the "Dark Age" goes on, that the god-like men of action are defeated, at least for the time being, *not* for having been too ruthless (and thus for having roused against themselves and their ideas and their collaborators the indignation of the "decent people"), *but for not having been ruthless enough* — for not having killed off their fleeing enemies, to the last man, in the brief hour of triumph; for not having silenced both the squeamish millions of hypocrites and their masters, the clever producers of atrocity-tales, by more substantial violence, more complete exterminations.

From all this it is quite clear that to condemn violence indiscriminately is to condemn the very struggle of the Forces of Life and Light against the Forces of disintegration — struggle, all the more heroic and all the more desperate, also, as the world rushes on towards its doom. It is to condemn that struggle which, at every one of its age-long, varying phases, and even through temporary disaster, has been securing for the world, beyond its deserved doom, the glorious new Beginning, which the few alone deserve. Within the bondage of Time, especially within this "Kali Yuga," one cannot be consistently non-violent without contributing, willingly or unwillingly, knowingly or unknowingly, to the success of the forces of disintegration; of what we call the Death-forces.

As for that violence which is used to forward the war-aims of the Death-forces, it is and has always been twofold: directed on one hand against Life itself — first, against the whole of innocent living Nature, then against the vital interests of higher mankind, in the name of "the common man" — and, on the other, against those particular men who, more and more conscious of the tragic realities of a darkening age, put up a stand in favour of the recognition of Life's eternal values and of the restoration of order upon its true, eternal basis.

In the attempt to bring about the triumph of the worthless

and the slow but steady disintegration of culture, in fact, less and less violence is needed. The world evolves naturally towards disintegration, with accelerated speed. It might have been, once, necessary to push it on along the slippery path. It has no longer been so, for centuries. It rolls on to its own doom, without help. In that direction, therefore, the champions of disintegration enjoy an easy task. They only have to follow and flatter the vicious tendencies of the increasingly despicable majority of men to become the world's darlings. But in their war against the few but more aware and practical exponents of the higher values — the upholders of the natural hierarchy of races; the worshippers of light, of strength, of youth — they are (and are bound to be) more and more violent, nay, more and more relentlessly cruel. Their hatred grows, as history unfolds, as though they knew — as though they felt, with the sharpness of physical perception — that every one of their victories, however spectacular it be, brings them nearer the final redeeming crash in which *they* are bound to perish, and out of which their now persecuted superiors are bound to emerge as the leaders of the New Age — the supermen at the beginning of the next Time-cycle — more like gods than ever. Their hatred grows, and their ferocity too, as the redeeming crash draws nigh, and, along with it, the dawn of the universal New Order, as unavoidable as the coming of spring. As the history of the last three years has shown[1] — as the history of darkest Europe (and of proud, unfortunate Japan) would show today, if only its hidden horrors were revealed — nothing surpasses in violence the persecution of the world's best men and women by the agents of the Death-forces, during the last period of the "Era of Gloom." Like the children of Light, these too — though for contrary reasons — act under the inexorable pressure of time. They have but a few years to try to stamp out the undying, divine Ideology; to crush as many of its votaries as they can, before they are, themselves, ground to dust in a fratricidal war of demons against demons.

They are in a hurry — not, as the heroic "élite," out of generous impatience; not out of any longing to see the "Age of Truth" re-established before its time, but out of feverish lust; out of the will to snatch from the world, for themselves, all the material

---

[1] This chapter was written in 1948.

advantages and all the satisfactions of vanity they possibly can, before it is too late. And as time goes on, their hurry amounts to frenzy. The one obstacle that stands in their way and still defies them — that will always defy them, till the end — is precisely that proud élite that disaster cannot discourage, that torture cannot break, that money cannot buy. Whether consciously or unconsciously, whether they be, themselves, thoroughly wicked, or just blind, through congenital stupidity, the workers of disintegration wage war upon the men of gold and steel, with unabated, hellish fury.

But theirs is not the frank, unashamed violence of the inspired idealists striving to bring forth, speedily, a lofty sociopolitical order too good for the unworthy world of their times. It is a sneaking, creeping, cowardly sort of violence, all the more effective that it is, outwardly, more emphatically denied, both by the scoundrels who apply it, or condone it, and by the well-meaning fools who actually believe that it does not exist. It is prompted by such feelings as one cannot possibly exhibit, even in a degenerate world, without running the risk of defeating one's own purpose: by bare hatred, rooted in envy — the hatred of worthless weaklings for the strong, for no other reason than they are strong; the hatred of ugly souls (incarnated, more often than not, in no less ugly bodies) for the naturally beautiful ones; for the noble, the magnanimous, the selfless, the real aristocracy of the world; the hatred of the unhappy, and, even more so, of the bored — of those who have only their pockets to live for, and nothing at all to die for — for those who live, and are ready to die, for eternal values. Such is, more and more, the widespread violence of our times, less and less recognised, in its subtle disguise, even by the people who actually suffer through it.

The Ancients knew better than our contemporaries who were their friends and who were their enemies. And this is natural. In a world rushing to its doom, there is bound to be increasing ignorance — ignorance precisely of those things one should know the best, in order to survive. The Ancients suffered, and knew whom to curse. Modern men and women, as a rule, do not know; do not really care to know; are too lazy, too exhausted, too near the end of *their* world to take the trouble to enquire seriously. And clever rascals, themselves the authors of all the mischief, incite them to throw the blame of it upon the only people whose unfailing wisdom and selfless love could have saved them, had they but wanted to be saved; upon that hated élite that stands against the current of Time, with the vision of the glorious new Beginning beyond the doom of the present-day world, clear and bright before its eyes. The whole amount of nonsense written and spoken since the end of the Second World War (and already before its end, in the newspapers and from the radio stations controlled by the democratic powers) about the sufferings of the European people, is the latest glaring instance of this broad-scale systematic lying, more and more common as the forces of disintegration become, with time, both more successful and more sneaking. Europe lies in ruins—the consequence of six years of inhuman bombing. The United Nations did the bombing, in order to stamp out National Socialism—the only thing that could have restored order and sanity in Europe, if absolute selflessness, coupled with genius, were able to turn the tide of time, in a doomed world. And now the people are told that National Socialism is responsible for all the evils that the bombing has occasioned, and that its inspired Founder is the greatest selfish megalomaniac who ever trod this earth. Some people believe it—even in Germany; or were prepared to believe it in 1945 before they got a taste of the substitute which the democracies offered them in the place of the much criticised régime. Most people believe it in the rest of Europe. The cunning rogues, utterly dishonest about violence, who set the tune to this propaganda, have an easy task: they work *in the direction of Time*: for disorder, leading to disintegration; for the destruction of all that is still strong and valuable in present-day humanity; of all that is destined to survive, in spite of all, *their* coming destruction. And they exploit the very characteristics of a decaying epoch: the hatred of all obvious discipline and of all visible and tangible (and responsible) leadership, allied to increasing conceit, increasing imbecility, and, consequently, increasing gullibility.

We have spoken of two sorts of violence. Nowhere is the difference in the very nature of the two more apparent, perhaps, than in the attitude of the upholders—or condoners—of each, towards living creation outside mankind.

The frank and courageous violence, which any idealist with real vision is more or less bound to use as soon as he attempts to translate his intuition of eternal truth into action, in a stubbornly degenerate world, bent on its own destruction, that violence, we say, is never exercised—and can, logically, never be exercised, save, perhaps, in certain cases of vital emergency—against any living creatures other than people. Its only purpose is to crush, as quickly and completely as possible, all resistance to a sociopolitical order imposed too soon to be appreciated by all those whom it affects. As we shall see, it does not, in fact, affect human beings alone. It concerns, and must concern, also, in the long run, all the living. If it did not, it would not be an order based upon everlasting truth, and the violence displayed to impose it would not be justified. But human beings alone can and do oppose such an order. They alone are, therefore, to the extent they become obstacles to its establishment or continuation, the victims of the necessary violence of those whose duty it is to defend it. As a consequence of the fact that they have nothing to do with the shaping of human society, innocent animals are never tormented by men who believe that, if at all, torture can only be excused when applied to forward such impersonal political ends as are in harmony with eternal principles.

Such men can never tolerate the infliction of pain upon living creatures for the sake of researches destined, in the minds of the torturers and of their supporters, to alleviate the sufferings of diseased humanity or to satisfy a mere lust for "scientific" information. For if they really be the exponents of Golden Age ideals—men of action, with an awareness of everlasting Truth and a burning love of perfection—they cannot possibly share, either about humanity or about disease, or about the morbid craving for idle knowledge at any cost, the common prejudices which have been developing, for centuries, as a result of growing degeneracy in this world. They cannot possibly believe that every human life, however debased, is necessarily worth saving. And they must believe that the best way to stamp out disease is not so much to find out new treatments as to teach men and women to live healthier lives, and, before all, to strengthen the naturally privileged races through a systematic, rational policy, applied, in the first place, to the basic art of breeding. And they must feel a sane contempt for all forms of useless research, let alone for that criminal curiosity about the mystery of life, which has turned hundreds of men like Pavlov, or Voronoff — or Claude Bernard — into downright monsters.

There is more. The very Ideology of the strong naturally goes hand in hand with revulsion for every form of cruelty towards helpless and beautiful beasts. Nietzsche has exalted kindness as the highest virtue of the superman — "the last victory of the hero over himself." And kindness that does not embrace all life is no kindness at all. Kindness that prompts man to "love his enemies" without prompting him *a fortiori* to love the innocent creatures of the earth, which did him no wilful harm; kindness that urges him to spare the former's lives while allowing him to chase and eat the latter, and to wear their skins, is either hypocrisy or imbecility. The Ideology of the strong rejects that 2,000 year-old contradiction, with utter contempt.

This is so true that the only people who have, in our times, striven to create a socio-political order upon the basis of such an Ideology, and that, through the most frankly acknowledged ruthlessness; the people who uphold the most consistently that healthy, necessary violence which is inseparable from any selfless struggle against the forces of decay — the makers of National Socialist Germany, are precisely *the* ones who have the most sincerely stressed love of all living Nature in their educational system, and done whatever they could to protect by law both animals[2] and forests; it is so true that the Leader who inspired them — Adolf Hitler, now so shamelessly slandered and so bitterly hated by a worthless world — not only abstained from flesh in his own daily diet, but is, as far as I know, the only European ruler who ever seriously contemplated the possibility of a continent without slaughterhouses and actually intended to make that dream a reality as soon as he could.[3]

---

[2] In National Socialist Germany, not only was the horrid "kosher" killing of animals forbidden, but traps were also not allowed. Animals killed for food had to be dealt with by means of an automatic pistol bringing instantaneous death. And cruelty to *any* beast was severely punished. (I know of the case of a person having spent three-and-a-half years in a concentration camp for having killed a pig "in a cruel manner.")

[3] "An extended chapter of our talk was devoted by the Führer to the

Contrast this with the treatment of creatures at the hands of the majority of those people who deny the superior individuals and races the right to be ruthless in their heroic struggle against Time; of those who would like us to believe they "love their enemies" and have a genuine horror of atrocities! We have seen, we see every day, how the hypocrites treat their enemies—when they catch them. And we know what atrocities they can perform on human beings—or order, or at least condone—when it suits their purpose. They treat animals no better. They take the hidden crimes daily committed against them in this increasingly wicked world, as a matter of course, just as they do those committed against the men and women whom they look upon as "dangerous fanatics," "war criminals," and so forth.

Of course, they find good excuses for their attitude—one always does; logic was granted to man in order that he might justify himself in his own eyes, whatever monstrosity he might choose to support. But their premises are entirely different from those of the selfless people who fight with consistent ruthlessness for ideals in harmony with the perfect cosmic order. Their basic argument is "the interest of humanity"—indiscriminately; the "interest of humanity" as a whole; of "the majority" of human beings, good, bad, and indifferent; and of human beings alone. Their ideals—expressions of the downward tendency of Time, which is hurrying man to his doom—are anything but Golden Age ideals.

Which humanity, indeed, do our kind-hearted agents of the Dark Forces struggle to "save," at the cost of untold suffering inflicted upon healthy, innocent, and beautiful creatures in the torture chambers of "science"? Surely not the strong and proud élite of mankind, waiting for its Day to start a new historical Cy-

---

vegetarian question. He believes more than ever that meat-eating is wrong. Of course, he knows that, during the war, we cannot completely upset our food system. *After the war, however, he intends to tackle this problem also.* Maybe he is right. Certainly the arguments he adduces in favour of his standpoint are very compelling."—*The Goebbels Diaries, 1942-1943*, ed. and trans. Louis P. Lochner (Garden City, N.Y.: Doubleday & Co., 1948), entry of the 26th of April 1942, p. 188. [The Lochner translation reads "meat-eating is harmful to humanity." Savitri changes this to "meat-eating is wrong" without qualification. —Ed.]

cle, upon the ruins of the present world. Such men and women as belong to that healthy minority need no such laboriously discovered medicine, and would not accept it, even if they did. No. The majority of our contemporaries who support the infliction of pain upon living creatures for the sake of "research" are concerned with the relief of "suffering" humanity. They are full of that morbid love for the sick and the crippled, for the weak and the disabled of every description, which Christianity has once made fashionable and which is, undoubtedly, one of the most nauseating signs of decay in modern man. Whether they be professed Christians or not, they all cling to the silly belief that it is a "duty" to save, or at least to prolong, at whatever cost, *any* human life, however worthless—a duty to prolong it, just because it is human. As a consequence, they are prepared to sacrifice any numbers of healthy and beautiful animals, if they imagine that it can help to patch up the failing bodies of people who, most of them, would not have been allowed to live or, rather, would never have been born, in a well-conceived and well-organised society. In their eyes, a human idiot is worth more than the most perfect specimen of animal or plant life. Indeed, as our species degenerates, its conceit grows! And that conceit helps to keep men satisfied, though they be completely cut off from the vision of glorious, healthy perfection that dominated the consciousness of the world in its youth and that still is, and will remain till the end, the inspiring vision of a decreasing minority.

The account of the atrocities committed upon innocent animals in order to find out means to combat disease in a more and more contaminated humanity, or even means to encourage vice in a daily greater number of outspent degenerates,[4] would fill volumes. That of similar abominations performed out of mere scientific curiosity, would also. This is not the place to expatiate upon that gruesome subject. Yet, when one remembers that people who excused those and other horrors, nay, who approved of them—who admired such a fellow as Pasteur, and who had never spoken a word against other ones such as Claude Bernard or, in this century, Pavlov—when one remembers, I say, that such people had the cheek to sit as judges in 1945, 1946,

---

[4] We refer, here, to Voronoff's experiments performed upon live monkeys, with a view to give back sexual potency to old men.

1947,[5] etc., and, with the consent of the world, to sentence to death German doctors, rightly or wrongly charged with having performed far less cruel experiments upon active or potential enemies of all they loved and stood for, then one is disgusted at the depth of hypocrisy that mankind has reached in our times. For never, perhaps, has such a theatrical exhibition of indignation over particular acts of violence gone hand in hand with such universal toleration of acts of violence by far more horrible.

That general dishonesty about violence, which has been steadily increasing from the dawn of history onwards, is manifest today in the way people deliberately conceal from themselves and from others all the horrors which they condone but cannot possibly justify.

Many of the atrocities performed on animals with a view to add to medical knowledge are so gruesome that, in spite of their alleged "justification," it is "in the interest of science" — and in the interest of the commercial concerns dealing in patent medicines — not to allow the public to know about them. And the public is deliberately kept in ignorance — induced to believe that the horrors do not really exist, or that they are not, in reality, half as blood-curdling as they sound. *A fortiori*, the numberless cruelties committed for the sake of sheer curiosity or for the sake of luxury, or amusement, are all the more hidden — subtly denied. Thousands of well-meaning fools who talk about "moral progress" in our times have no idea whatsoever of what goes on (behind the scenes[6]) in scientific institutes, in the fur trade, and in circuses.

Thousands of equally well-meaning and equally foolish people, who take for granted whatever they are given to read and enquire no further, have also no idea of the horrors perpetrated by their compatriots in other people's countries as colonists or as members of occupying armies, nay, no idea of what goes on in their own country behind prison bars, in torture chambers for political investigation, and in concentration camps. Indeed, in England and in other democratic nations, many are under the

---

[5] During the infamous Nuremberg Trial and other similar ones.
[6] Replacing "screens" with "scenes" — Ed.

impression that *their* government never tolerated such things as concentration camps and torture chambers for human beings. Only "the enemy" had them—so they believe. Years ago, they would have thought nothing of admitting that "everybody has them"; must have them; that one cannot run a war without those unpleasant but extremely useful accessories. But now hypocrisy concerning violence has reached its pitch. Never has there been, in the world, so much cruelty, allied to such a general attempt to hide it, to deny it, to forget it, and, if possible, make others forget it. Never have people been so willing to forget it, in externally "decent" and kindly surroundings—houses and streets in which no torture of man or beast can be *seen* or *heard*—provided, of course, it is not "the enemy's" cruelty. The only time modern men and women do *not* try to minimise horrors but actually exaggerate them (and often deliberately invent them) is when these happen to be (or are intended to be presented as) "the enemy's" horrors—never their own. And that is itself only a further instance of the world-wide characteristic of our times: the general love of lies.

What has set the whole world so bitterly against the frank upholders of ruthless methods both in government and war, is not so much that these were violent, but that they were frank. Liars hate those who speak the unpleasant truth, and who act in accordance with it.

The "unpleasant truth" is that pacifism, non-violence, and so forth are, most of the time, just rackets in the service of the forces of disintegration; dishonest tricks to bluff the fools, to emasculate the strong, and to set millions of cowards and hypocrites (the bulk of the world) against the few people whose inspired policy, pursued ruthlessly to its logical end, could perhaps, even now, arrest the decay of man. And if they are *not* that, then, they are nonsense.

As we have said in the beginning, non-violence can only exist in a world in which the temporal socio-political order is, on the human scale, the replica of the eternal Order of the Cosmos. Any effective preaching—and any partial practice—of pacifism in politics; i.e., within Time, outside such a temporal order, only leads, ultimately, to greater violence; to a greater exploitation of living Nature *and* a greater oppression of man at the hands of those who work for the Death-forces. But, for millenniums already, that perfect earthly order has ceased to exist. It has to be created anew before peace can re-flourish. And it cannot, *now*, be created anew, without utmost violence, exerted, this time, in a selfless spirit, by men of vision.

The best course for those who sincerely desire a just and lasting peace would, therefore, naturally be to do all they can to give over the world to those men of vision, as soon as possible; at least, not to try to prevent them from conquering it. Unfortunately, most pacifists either do not really want peace at all, but merely pretend to, or else want it, but only under certain ideological conditions which are incompatible with its establishment, *now*, and with its duration, and which will only become more and more so, till the end of the present historical cycle. Any obvious violence directed against human beings shocks them. People who openly support the use of force—be it in the most disinterested spirit and for the best of purposes—are, for that very reason, anathema in their eyes. Help *them* to conquer and to rule the world? Oh, no! Anything but *that!* The ideals of the ruthless men of vision may well be Golden Age ideals; but their methods!—their cynical attitude towards human life; their relentless chase and pitiless disposal of even *potential* obstacles to the rapid attainment of their selfless aims; their "appalling logic" (to quote the words of a French official in occupied Germany, after this war)[7]—our pacifists could never stand for these! As a result, they stand for far worse—generally without knowing it. For, through their refusal to face facts and take the only reasonable attitude that a true lover of peace should have, today, they become tools in the service of the forces of disintegration.

For one cannot have it both ways: whoever is not *for* the everlasting Forces of Light and Life, is against them. Unless one lives "outside" or "above" Time, one either walks in the direction of

---

[7] *"Cette logique effroyable"* was the expression used by Monsieur Rudolf Grassot, of the French Information Bureau in Baden-Baden, in his conversation with me on the 9th of October 1948. [Cf. Savitri Devi, *Gold in the Furnace: Experiences in Post-War Germany*, ed. R. G. Fowler (Atlanta: Savitri Devi Archive, 2006), p. 132—Ed.]

the unavoidable evolution of history—i.e., towards decay and dissolution—or one stands against the current of centuries, in a bitter, apparently hopeless, but nevertheless beautiful struggle, one's eyes fixed upon those perennial ideals which can be fully translated into material reality only once, at the dawn of every successive Cycle, by every successive new humanity. But it is true that the bold minority of men of action who fight, "against Time," for Golden Age ideals, is bound to become, as time goes on, more and more ruthless in its effort to overcome an increasingly well-organised, increasingly elusive, and increasingly universal opposition. And for that very reason, it will become more and more difficult for the squeamish pacifists to follow it. In all probability, they will continue to prefer identifying themselves with the lying agents of the Dark Forces. And this is natural. Again it is within the law of Time. The forces of death must have practically the whole world under their grip, before a new Beginning can start as a re-assertion of Life's triumph.

And thus, day after day, year after year, now and in the future, the conflicting Powers of light and darkness cannot but carry on their deadly struggle, as they always did, but more and more fiercely as time goes on. And as time goes on, also, the struggle will more and more be between openly acknowledged and openly accepted violence and violence dishonestly disguised, the former being put to the service of Life's highest purpose on earth—namely, the creation of a perfect, or "Golden Age" humanity—and the latter, to that of the enemies of Life. It has to be so until, after the final crash—the "end of the world" as we know it—the leadership of surviving mankind falls to that victorious élite who, even in the midst of the long general decay of man, never lost its faith in the everlasting cosmic values, nor its will to draw from them, and from them alone, its rule of action.

That élite will, then, no longer be compelled to resort to violence in order to impose its will. It will rule without opposition in a peaceful world in which the New Order of its age-old dreams will appear to all as *the* only natural and rational state of affairs. Until man again forgets unchangeable Truth, acts as though the iron Laws of cause and consequence did not concern *him*—God's darling!—and again decays.

Nothing can stop the wheel of Time.

Chapter 3

MEN IN TIME, ABOVE TIME, & AGAINST TIME

All men, inasmuch as they are not liberated from the bondage of Time, follow the downward path of history, whether they know it or not, and whether they like it or not.

Few indeed thoroughly *like* it, even in our epoch — let alone in happier ages, when people read less and thought more. Few follow it unhesitatingly, without throwing, sometime or other, a sad glance towards the distant lost paradise into which they know, in their deeper consciousness, that they are never to enter; the paradise of Perfection *in* time — a thing so remote that the earliest people of whom we know remembered it only as a dream. Yet, they follow the fatal way. They obey their destiny.

That resigned submission to the terrible law of decay — that acceptance of the bondage of Time by creatures who dimly feel that they *could be* free from it, but who find it too hard to try to free themselves; who know beforehand that they would never succeed, even if they did try — is at the bottom of that incurable unhappiness of man, deplored again and again in the Greek tragedies, and long before these were written. Man is unhappy because he knows, because he feels — in general — that the world in which he lives and of which he is a part, is not what it should be, what it could be, what, in fact, it *was* at the dawn of Time, before decay set in and before violence became unavoidable. He cannot wholeheartedly accept that world as his — especially not accept the fact that it is going from bad to worse — and be glad. However much he may try to be a "realist" and snatch from destiny whatever he can, when he can, still an invincible yearning for the better remains at the bottom of his heart. He cannot — in general — will the world as it is.

But few people — as rare as the liberated ones, for whom Time does not exist, and perhaps rarer — can and do; and act up to that will. These are the most thorough, the most mercilessly effective agents of the Death-forces on earth: supremely intelligent and sometimes extraordinarily farsighted; always unscrupulous to the utmost; working without hesitation and without remorse in the direction of the downward process of history and (whether they can see or not as far as that) for its logical conclusion: the annihilation of man and of all life.

Naturally, they do not always see as far as that. But when they do, still they do not care. Since the Law of Time is what it is, and since the end must come, it is just as well that *they* should draw all the profit they possibly can from the process that is, anyhow, sooner or later, to bring about the end. Since no one can re-create the primeval lost Paradise—no one but the wheel of Time itself, after it has rolled its full course—then it is just as well that *they*, who can completely forget the distant vision, or who never had a glimpse of its dying glow; they, who can stifle in themselves the age-old yearning for Perfection, or rather, who never experienced it; it is just as well that they, I say, should squeeze out of the fleeing moment (whether minutes or years, it matters little) all the intense, immediate enjoyment they can, until the hour comes when they must die. It is just as well that they should leave their stamp upon the world—force generations to remember them—until the hour comes for the world to die. So they feel. It makes little difference what suffering they might cause to men or other living creatures, by acting as they do. Both men and creatures are bound to suffer, anyhow. Just as well through them as through others, if that can forward the aims of these people.

The aims of these people—of the men *within* Time, *par excellence*—are always selfish aims, even when, owing to their material magnitude and historical importance, they transcend immeasurably any one man's life, as they actually do, sometimes. For selfishness—the claim of the "part" to more place and to more meaning than is naturally allotted to it within the whole—is the very root of disintegration, and therefore a characteristic inseparable from Time. One can practically say that, the more a person is thoroughly, remorselessly selfish, the more he or she lives "*in Time.*"

But, as we have said, that selfishness is manifested in many different ways. It can find expression in that mere lust for personal enjoyment, which characterises the shameless voluptuary; or in the miser's insatiable greed for gold; or in the individual ambition of the seeker of honours and position; or in the family ambition of the man who is ready to sacrifice every interest in the world to the welfare and happiness of his wife and children. But it can also be brought out in the exaltation of a man's tribe or country above all others, *not because of its inherent worth in the natural hierarchy of Life*, but just because it happens to be the tribe or country of that particular man. It can be, nay, and often is, brought out in the undue exaltation of all human beings, however debased, above all the rest of living creation, however healthy and beautiful—the passion which underlies the age-old tyranny of "man" over Nature; the "love of man" not in harmony with the God-ordained duties and rights of each and every species (as of every race and of every individual) according to its place, but in a spirit of mere solidarity with one's kith and kin, good or bad, worthy or unworthy, solely because they are *one's own*. Men "in Time" only know what is "their own" and what is not, and they love themselves in whatever is *theirs*.

As there are men "in Time," so there are, also, philosophies and religions—"ideologies"—"in Time"; false religions, all of them, for true religion can only be above time. Such doctrines are more and more numerous, more and more varied, and more and more popular as the world proceeds nearer to the end of every historical Cycle. There was an epoch when they did not exist; an epoch in which a man "in Time" was necessarily against all professed doctrines. Today, nearly all interpretations of age-old, true religions, and nearly all the "isms" that have replaced religions, are of the type "in Time." Their function within the scheme of things, at this stage of world-history, is just to deceive the well-meaning weaklings and fools—the hesitating people, who want an excuse, a justification for living "in" Time without the unpleasant feeling of a guilty conscience, and who cannot find one for themselves. These are only too glad to catch hold of a philosophy loudly professing to be unselfish, which allows them, nay, encourages them to work under its cover for their selfish ends. The ones who use a really unselfish doctrine — an originally "timeless" philosophy — for that purpose, lie all the more shamelessly to themselves and to others. And, by doing so, they help in reality to forward the great tendency of history: to hasten the decay which leads to the great End and, beyond — to the following new Beginning.

But the actual, typical men "within Time" need no justifying ideology in order to act. Their thoroughly selfish attitude is, in all its glaring shamelessness, far more beautiful than that growing tendency of the tiny men to slip down the path to perdition while hanging onto some "noble" ends such as "liberty, equality, fraternity" or "the rights of international proletariat," or onto some misunderstood religion. Whatever they may tell the people whom they wish to deceive — whom they *have* to deceive, in order to succeed — the real men "in Time" never deceive themselves. They know what they truly want. And they know the way to get it. And they do not care what it costs to others *or* to themselves. And, especially, they do not, at the same time, want anything *else*, which is incompatible with their aims.

And so — whether on an ordinary scale, like the consistent voluptuary or the single-purposed miser, or on a nation-wide or continent-wide scale, like those who stir millions and sacrifice millions of people, that *they* might impose their own will — they act, in a way, as gods would act. And, both in the grandeur of their achievements and in the beauty of the first-rate qualities of character which they put to the service of their purpose, a few of them really have something god-like — as, for instance, that greatest conqueror of all times, whose extraordinary career forms the subject-matter of a part of this book: Genghis-Khan. They possess the awful splendour of the great devastating forces of Nature; of the roaring sea, rolling out of its bed over the land; of a lava stream, burning its way through all obstacles; of the lightning, that men used to worship, when they still understood what is divine.

Naturally, this can be said only of those men whose action exceeds, by its very magnitude, the limits of what is "personal." It is difficult to imagine any mere seeker of physical pleasure, or even of individual riches, attaining such a grim, god-like greatness. The importance of the men "in Time," as such, depends upon the nature of their action itself and upon the breadth of the surroundings which it influences, no less if not more than upon the way in which, and the one-sided, cynically selfish purpose for which, they act. And this is understandable, for reasons other than the sheer aesthetic impression which the true story of a mighty life can leave upon the reader or the bystander. It is the consequence of the fact that, like the great forces of Nature which we mentioned, real men "in Time" are blind powers, serving unknowingly the purpose of the Cosmos. The same is true, of course, of the petty seekers after small profits, in their limited sphere of activity. They too are blind powers of destruction. But small ones, at our scale at least. We experience the awe of the Divine in the presence of the big ones only — as we do, for instance, before a storm upon the Ocean, while the sight of a pool of water disturbed by the wind leaves us indifferent.

When the ends — however petty and personal in themselves — are masterfully served through such action as stirs the whole world; when, in order to attain them, a man "in Time" displays, upon the international stage, superhuman qualities worthy of much higher ends, then, one feels one's self in the presence not of a *man* "in Time" but of the divine Destroyer — Mahakala, Time Itself — everlastingly rushing the Thing that seems to annihilation followed by new birth and then again by further decay and annihilation.

The man "in Time" can have *any* aim, with the exception of a disinterested one (which would at once raise him "above Time"). He himself is always like a blind force of destructive Nature. (That is the reason why so many thoroughly "bad" characters in literature and in the theatre are so attractive, in their forceful evil.) He has no ideology. Or rather, his ideology is himself, separated from the divine Whole — i.e., it is the disintegration of the Whole (of the universe) for the benefit of himself, and, ultimately, the destruction of himself also, although he does not *know* it or does not care. And that is the case in every instance. But under certain conditions, when his action takes, in human history, the permanent importance that a great geological cataclysm has in the history of the earth, then, as I said, the man "in Time" disappears from our sight, and in his, place — but still bearing his features—appears, in all His dramatic majesty, Mahakala, the eternal Destroyer. It is Him Whom we adore in the great lightning individuals such as Genghis Khan—Him; not them. They are only the clay images inhabited by Him for a few brief years. And just as the clay image hides and suggests the invisible God or Goddess—Power everlasting—so does their selfishness both hide and reveal the impersonal purposefulness of Life; the destructive phase of the divine Play, in which already lies the promise of the new dawn to come.

And just as volcanic convulsions or invading sea-tides prepare, in the course of centuries, a new growth, in a reshaped physical universe, so do the great men "in Time" bring us nearer the liberating end and thereby prepare the way for the next glorious Beginning. "Scourges of God," in a way, they are also blessings in disguise. Far better their frank, brutal destructiveness for selfish ends than the silly patchwork of the ordinary well-meaning people who try to "do good" in this fallen world, without having the courage to strike and burn and tear; who have only "constructive" schemes—all useless! For destruction and creation are forever linked. That is why we adore the Lightning as well as the Sun, and are overwhelmed by a feeling of sacred awe at the thought of the grand-scale exterminators *without* ideologies, human likenesses of great Mahakala.

But there are also men "outside Time" or rather "above Time"; men who live, here and now, in eternity; who (directly at least) have no part to play in the downward rush of history towards disintegration and death, but who behold it from above—as one beholds, from a strong and safe bridge, the irresistible rush of a waterfall into the abyss—and who have repudiated the law of violence which is the law of Time.

Of such men, most live a very special life, away from the world; a life of which the whole inner discipline, spiritual, moral, and physical, is systematically devised to keep them in constant union with the great Reality beyond Time: the Thing that is, as opposed to the Thing that seems. They are the real ascetics (in the etymological sense of the word: those who have "trained" themselves to live in eternity). Others—far rarer—live in eternity without a particular "training," even while living, outwardly, the life of the world; while being husbands and wives, parents and educators of children, manual or intellectual labourers, citizens, soldiers, rulers, etc.

Of those who live "outside" or "above" Time, some are saviours. Others just leave things and people to go their way, feeling that they are not called to intervene in anyone's destiny and knowing that, in the course of centuries, all souls that care to be saved will, anyhow, evolve towards the timeless life of the saints. The distinction between these two types of "liberated" people corresponds, in Buddhist terminology, to that between the Bodhisattvas and the Arhats. Both these are free beings, outside the law of birth and rebirth—the bondage of Time. But, while the Arhat remains completely aloof from the fallen world, the Bodhisattva is born over and over again, of his own free will, in order to help living creatures to work themselves out of the ocean of life within Time.

But the salvation which the men "above Time" offer the world is always that which consists in breaking the time-bondage. It is *never* that which would find its expression in collective life on earth in accordance with Golden Age ideals. It is the salvation of the individual soul, never that of organised society. For the men "above Time" know fully well that *that* cannot be saved before the beginning of a new Time-cycle—especially not by peaceful preaching or even edifying examples. And even when they do, to some extent, try to bring a certain amount of organisation into being among a restricted number of disciples— in monastic communities, for instance—they know that, however saintly it be, the community as such is bound to degenerate sooner or later. The Buddha foretold the corruption of his *sangha* "after five hundred years."

It is true that some—though extremely few—men, of those whom we have characterised as "above Time," have been (or have tried to be) reformers in the worldly sense, by non-violent means. But none of them were "saviours" of society, really speaking. The saviours in the worldly sense of the word—those who set out to perfect not merely men's souls but men's collective life and government, and international relations—are what we call men "against Time." And *they* are necessarily violent, although not always physically so. They may be—in fact, they should be—personally free from the bondage of Time, if they are to act with the maximum of foresight and efficiency. But they have to take into consideration the conditions of action "within Time" to live "in" Time, also, in a way. The others—the men "above Time" who appear to have been reformers—have not really tried to remould the world according to their understanding of eternal truth (otherwise, they would not have remained non-violent). What they did was to live their own timeless philosophy *in* the world. And to the extent that they occupied a position of importance—like that most remarkable of them all, Akhnaton, King of Egypt, who was in his days the most powerful man on earth—their lives could not but have a repercussion upon those of their contemporaries.

It might seem strange that the Founder of a state-religion—for the cult of the "Heat-and-Light-within-the-Disk" *was* that, undoubtedly—should not be counted among the "saviours" of the world, but rather among those extremely rare men "above Time" who have lived the life of this earth while stubbornly remaining foreign to this earth's grim realities. But appearances are deceitful. And we shall see, further on, in examining the nature of the much misunderstood Cult of the Disk and the life of King Akhnaton, its Promoter, that this view is the right one.

The most distinctive trait of the men "outside" or "above" Time, as opposed to those who live "in" Time or "against" Time, is perhaps their consistent refusal to use violence even in order to forward the most righteous cause. Not that they are at all squeamish about violence, like the weaklings, neither good nor bad, who compose 90 percent of mankind in our epoch. They could not possibly disapprove of the warrior-like ideal of detached, selfless violence preached by Lord Krishna—the divine Preserver of the Universe, Himself—in the Bhagavad-Gita; for that ideal is in harmony with everlasting truth, which any man who has transcended Time is bound to acknowledge. Only *they* are not Kshatriyas by nature, whatever be their race, their social position, their inherited responsibilities; they are not men of action, by nature, let alone fighters. *Their* action, like that of the Sun, lies essentially in their personal radiation of power, beauty, and goodness. What they do is, of course, the integral reflection of what they are, nothing more; nothing different; nothing which is foreign to them, for they are fully conscious of their being. And if they have any substantial influence at all, it is, like that of the Sun, an influence from above and from afar, characterised by its absolute impartiality, its indiscriminate and impersonal goodness. They do nothing to compel others—nothing, at least, beyond certain limits, even if they live *in* the world. They know they cannot force the evolution of things, nor suppress the part played by Time in the lives of those who are still submitted to its iron law. Again, like the Sun, they shine. If the seed is alive, it will ripen sooner or later, never mind when, violence would only help to produce an artificial growth. And if the seed be dead? Let it be! There are new seeds; new creations, forever and ever. The people who live in eternity can wait.

We have said: those who remain "above Time" do not resort to violence. This does not mean that all men who abstain from violence are necessarily liberated souls, living "above Time." First, an immense number of cowards are non-violent for fear of taking risks. And they are anything but free from the bondage of Time. Then, that which one often takes for non-violence—that which actually goes under that name—is, in reality, but a subtler form of violence: pressure upon other people's feelings, more oppressive and—when one knows, in each case, what feelings to appeal to—many a time more effective than pressure upon their bodies. The late Mahatma Gandhi's much admired "non-violence" was of that type: moral violence; not: "Do this, or else I kill you!," but: "Do this, or else I kill myself!" *Knowing* that you hold my life as indispensable. It may look "nobler." In fact, it is just the same—apart from the difference in the technique of pressure. It is, rather, *less* "noble" because, precisely on account of that subtler technique, it leads people to believe that it is not violence, and therefore contains an element of deceit, an inherent falsehood, from which ordinary violence is free.

The late Mahatma Gandhi was by no means what we have tried to define as a man "above time." He was what we shall call a man "against Time," aiming *now*—far too late or . . . a little too soon—at the establishment of a tangible order of justice (*Ram raj*) on this earth. But, inasmuch as it lacks the frankness of brutal force, his so-called "non-violence"—moral violence—is characteristic of our epoch of dishonesty (however honest and sincere *he* might have been himself). It is, perhaps, the first instance in history of a disguised form of violence applied, on a broad scale, *in a struggle* for a good purpose. Its popularity in India can partly be credited to the fact that it was, or seemed to be, the only practical weapon in the hands of totally disarmed and, to a great extent, naturally apathetic people. But it enjoyed abroad, also, a tremendous publicity, quite out of proportion with its real value (and the late Mahatma Gandhi's tremendous reputation of "holiness" is no less out of proportion with his real place among the great men of India). The foreigners who have done the most to popularise it are people typical of our degenerate age: people who recoil at the mere thought of any healthy and frank display of force, but who cannot even detect moral violence; men and women (especially women) of the Western democracies, the most hypocritical half of the world. It appealed to them precisely to the extent that it was violence *in disguise*. Even English people (some of whom had lived in India; some of whom had, nay, occupied a high position within the ranks of British colonial officialdom) could not help admiring it. It was not that hated brutal force which other great men "against Time" had used in the course of history (or were using at our epoch) to bring about an age of justice. Oh, no!

But it surely was not, either, the non-violence of the men "above Time" who, if they cared at all to take an occasional stand against the unavoidable fall of mankind, would either use no real pressure at all to enforce their good laws—and fail, from a worldly point of view, as King Akhnaton did—or else, exert "against Time" any amount of violence that might be necessary, in the spirit of the God Who speaks, in the Bhagavad-Gita, to the Fighter for a just cause (provided the latter happens to be, like Arjuna, a Kshatriya, i.e., a warrior by race and by nature).

The men who remain "above Time" seem to be those who have the least influence of all upon the course of events in this world. And that too is to be expected in a world which is sinking deeper and deeper every day into the abyss. In the Age of Truth, and even in later ages pictured in the sacred books of India, the men "above Time"—the true Brahmins, in union with eternal

Reality—were the natural *and actual* counsellors of kings; genuine spiritual authority then backed legitimate temporal power. But as the temporal order on earth became more and more unlike the ideal heavenly Order, kings were less and less inclined to act according to the commands of an increasingly rare timeless wisdom. And what is true of kings is, also, here, true of commoners. As a result, men "outside Time" or "above Time" enjoy less and less authority as the world proceeds towards the end of every Time-cycle. Even when—like King Akhnaton—they themselves happen to be rulers endowed with absolute power, their lives do not—cannot—in what the Hindus call the "Kali Yuga," leave upon the sands of time the trace which they normally should.

Moreover, sometimes—and that, even if they be ascetics, apparently separated from the world—men "above Time" can, like the Sun, with which we have constantly compared them, be destructive, indirectly. Their light, indiscriminately shed upon the righteous and the unrighteous, can have the most varied and unexpected effects amidst a humanity evolving from bad to worse. One can think of the destructiveness of King Akhnaton's "Golden Age" attitude to international affairs, viewed from the Egyptian side. One can think also of the true religions, conceived by such men "above Time" as were *not* in possession of temporal power, and then distorted by clever people who lived, most of them, entirely "within Time," and used by them in the service of the most selfish, the most destructive of all worldly ends. It is, naturally, "not the fault" of the men "above Time" — any more than it would be "the fault" of the Sun, if, in some land where the heat of the sun-rays is unbearable, a man were to tie his enemy to a pillar in a shadeless place and leave him to die there. Truly speaking, it is not "the fault" of the men "within Time" either. It is a consequence of the law of general decay, inseparable from life in time: as the world becomes less and less capable of penetrating their eternal meaning, even the best things are misunderstood, and either hated and rejected or else put to some criminal use.

Exiles of the Golden Age in our Age of Gloom, the men "above Time" either live entirely within their own inner world, or else live and act in this one also, but as though it were still in its Golden Age. They either renounce this world or ignore it—or, better, forget it, as a man forgets the scars of sin and sickness upon a once beautiful face, which he still loves, in spite of all. They see the everlasting and unchangeable behind the downward rush of the stream of time; the Thing that *is*, behind the thing that seems. Even when they live in the world of forms, colours, and sounds as earnestly and intensely as King Akhnaton—that supreme artist—did, still those impressions take on, for them, a meaning entirely different from that which they retain in the consciousness of people submitted to the bondage of Time. Men "above Time" enjoy with detachment, as people who know they will never die. They also suffer with detachment, being constantly aware of their blissful real Self, which is beyond pleasure and pain.

And the fallen world can never understand them, i.e., know them, any more than *they* can understand the fall of man, in which they have no part, as others, who share it, can, and do. And yet, untiringly—like the Sun, far away and omnipresent—they shed their light; that light which is, in our growing gloom, like a glimpse of all the past and future dawns.

But, as we have said, there are also people with a Golden Age outlook—fully aware of what a splendid place this world *could be*, materially and otherwise—who can, however, neither renounce life "as it is" nor ignore it; people who, in addition to that, are endowed with what the Hindus would call a "Kshatriya" nature: born fighters, for whom difficulties exist only to be overcome, and for whom the impossible has a strange fascination. These are the men "against Time"—absolutely sincere, selfless idealists, believers in those eternal values that the fallen world has rejected, and ready, in order to reassert them on the material plane, to resort to any means within their reach. As a consequence of the law of Time, those means are necessarily all the more drastic and all the more brutal as every historical Cycle draws nearer to its end. The last Man "against Time" is, in fact, no other than He Whose name, in Sanskrit Tradition, is Kalki—the last Incarnation of the divine Sustainer of the universe and, at the same time, the Destroyer of the whole world; the Saviour Who will put an end to this present "yuga" in a formidable display of unparalleled violence, in order that a new creation may flourish in the innocence and splendour of a new "Age of Truth."

Men "outside Time" or "above Time," at the most saviours of *souls*, have, more often than not, disciples who are definitely men "against Time." (Sometimes even men "*in* Time"; but we do not speak of these, for they are mere exploiters of religions or ideologies for selfish ends, not sincere disciples of saints.) The true disciples—and, in some rare instances, the Masters themselves—who are "*against* Time," thorough organisers, unscrupulous propagandists, and ruthless fighters, are the actual founders of most of, if not all, the great churches[1] of the world, even when the religions preached by those churches are doctrines originally "above Time," as they generally are. And this is unavoidable inasmuch as a church is always or nearly always, not only itself a material organisation, but an organisation which aims at regulating the lives of thousands, if not millions, of people *in* this world—in Time. Apparently, the one exception to that law is Buddhism, the only important international religion which has conquered over half a mighty continent without the help of men "against Time" and without the use of violence; the one in the name of which persecution of other faiths was never carried on but twice in the whole course of history—and that, by men "*in* Time*,*" and for reasons decidedly political, not religious.[2] But then, we must remember that this creed is, more than any other, dominated by the yearning to escape the bondage of Time, and that it is, in fact, not intended at all for life *in* Time. A person who accepts its postulates cannot possibly think of a better world, except if it be "outside" or "above Time." But, as a result of this, there is perhaps a more shocking disparity between the high ideals of the religion and the life of the faithful in Buddhist countries than anywhere else. The religions that have spread

---

[1] Savitri is using "churches" in a generic sense to refer to all organized religions, not merely the different denominations of Christianity. —Ed.

[2] Once in Central Asia, in the early 13th century, by the "Gurkhan" of the Kara-Khitai, against both Islam and Nestorian Christianity, and another time, in 17th century Japan, by the first Shoguns of the Tokugawa Dynasty—Iyeyasu, Hidetada, and Iyemitsu—against Christianity.

and maintained themselves partly through violence, have had, in spite of many shortcomings, and of less high moral standards, a greater practical influence upon the lives of their followers as a whole, strange as this may appear.

One does not always realise this clearly enough, when one criticises the great active disciples for being inconsistent with "the spirit" of their contemplative masters. One does not realise that, without the ruthless passion of those men, the organisations that have, one must admit, kept to some extent "the spirit" alive, would just not exist in many places where they still flourish, and that many "spiritual treasures," that one values so much, would be lost to the world. *If* one really values those "treasures," one should not find fault with the men "against Time" or, more often than not, "*in* Time," who recoiled from nothing so that they might be put, and kept, within man's reach. Without the brutal methods of Charlemagne, the Saxon-slayer, so obviously anything but "Christ-like," the Germans would perhaps, to this day, have remained attached to their old gods; so would have the Norwegians, without the drastic sort of evangelisation imposed upon them by King Olaf Tryggvason. Without the equally sincere, equally fanatical, and even more brutal activities of many men "against" or "in" Time, in the 16th and 17th centuries, half of Goa, and the whole of Mexico and Peru would probably not be, today, professing the Christian faith. Christianity owes a lot to men "against Time" — and perhaps still more to men "*in* Time."

We, who are not Christians, may—and do—deplore it. We are aware of the fact that many spiritual treasures other than those contained in the Gospels—the truths contained in the old European Paganisms, or long preserved in the solar cults of Central and Southern America; treasures of which, today, one knows much too little—were lost to the world precisely through the impersonal zeal of religious-minded men, by nature "against Time" (or through the wanton destructiveness of men "in Time") such as those we have mentioned. But we believe that, wherever such losses were suffered, there was something wrong not with the forgotten truth (which is eternal) but with the people who should have managed to stand for it against the new and hostile doctrine; we believe, in fact, that there were not enough men "against Time" among *those* people—not enough persons in whose eyes the now lost teachings were, then, sufficiently alive to be made a basis for the organisation of human society against the growing current of decay; not enough who, in order to defend them on those grounds, were prepared to be as ruthless and as perseverant as the Christians were in order to destroy them.

卐 卐 卐

The relation between the Master, permanently "above Time," and the ardent realist "against Time" — builder and defender of all militant churches — who happens to be his disciple, has never been so perfectly pictured as in the words addressed to the Christ by the Grand Inquisitor, in Dostoyevsky's famous episode of *The Brothers Karamazov*. "Thou hast resisted the three temptations of the Devil" — refused the means to rule, offered to Thee by the One who knows men and time, better than any other. "Thou hast refused to turn stones into bread" — to give the multitudes material goods; "Thou hast refused to throw Thyself from the height of the Temple" — to give the people astonishment and awe; "Thou hast refused to bow down to Me" — the Master of lies; the Master of Time — to live "*in* Time," to some extent at least. "As a result, the people have drifted away from Thy teaching and from Thyself, and Thou canst not save them. It is we" — we the unscrupulous, we the violent, the men who stop at nothing to make the truth they love a reality in this world — "it is we, I say, who save them, in Thy stead, by doing all that which Thou hast refused to do and therefore by damning ourselves in Thine eyes. And we accept that damnation for the love of Thee — for Thy name to be praised."

This is the substance of the Inquisitor's discourse, if not its textual wording. And the militant champion of the organised creed tells the Christ: "*Do not come back!* — do not destroy the work that we are doing in this fallen world, for Thy glory!"

For no *organisation* can live "outside Time" — "above Time" — and hope to bring men back, one day, to the knowledge of the eternal values. *That*, all men "above Time" have realised. In order to establish, or even to try to establish, here and now, a better order, in accordance with Truth everlasting, one *has to* live, outwardly at least, like those who are still "in Time"; like them, one *has to be* violent, merciless, destructive — but for different ends. Therein lies the tragedy of bringing into reality any dream of perfection. And the more perfect the dream — the further away from the conditions of success in this fallen world — the more ruthless must necessarily be the methods of those who sincerely wish to impose it upon men, too late or . . . too early.

Knowing this, the real men "above Time" are the first ones to understand and to appreciate the wholehearted efforts of their disciples "against Time," however "awful" these might appear to ordinary people neither good nor bad. The Christ, in Dostoyevsky's famous page, says nothing. What could he say? There is nothing to be said which the leader of the militant church could understand. To the Inquisitor, the Christ will always remain a mystery. But the Christ understands the Inquisitor and values his love. Before leaving the prison cell — and the world of Time — *he kisses him.*

As we have pointed out above, no man "outside Time" can enjoy any real influence upon human society unless he has such disciples, or unless he is himself prepared to become, also, a man "against Time." For it is a fact that one can be both "above Time," in one's personal outlook, and "against Time" in one's activity in the world. All the really great creative men "against Time" possess these two aspects: they are men of vision aware of timeless truths; but they are, also, men who have been stirred to the depth by the glaring contrast between the ideal world, built according to those truths, and the actual world in which they live; men who, after what they have seen and experienced, can neither remain any longer cut off from time, in their own inner paradise, nor act in life as though all were well, but who *must* devote their whole life and energy to the reshaping of tangible reality on the model of their vision of Truth. One such Man is the warrior-like Prophet Mohammed who dreamed of a world theocracy and succeeded in founding a great civilisation, lasting to this day. Another one — whose unparalleled greatness is yet unrecognised, because his followers lost a war instead of winning it — is the tragic and beautiful figure that dominates the history of the West in our own times: Adolf Hitler.

I have compared men "in Time" to the Lightning, and men "outside Time" or "above Time" to the Sun. Using the same metaphorical language, one can say that men "against Time" partake both of the Sun *and* of the Lightning, inasmuch as they are truly inspired by Golden Age ideals, rooted in timeless Truth, and as—precisely in order to be able to stand for such ideals on the material plane, in the Age of Gloom, against the current of Time—they are compelled to display all the practical qualities of the men "in Time"; inasmuch as the only difference between them and the latter lies *not* in their methods (which are the same, and cannot but be so) but in their selfless, impersonal ends.

They serve those ends with merciless realism but, to the extent they are "above Time" also, with the detachment preached to the warrior in the Bhagavad-Gita. In fact, the Teaching of the Bhagavad-Gita is nothing else but the philosophy of the perfect Man "against Time," *yogi* in spirit, warrior in action; a Man like King Akhnaton, the Only-One of the Sun, free from the bondage of Time, and whose strength is cosmic Energy Itself, *but* . . . who uses that strength, on the material plane, in the service of his ideals, with all the remorseless logic of a Genghis Khan.

Alone Kalki—the last Man "against Time," at the end of every historical Cycle; the last Saviour, Who is also the greatest Destroyer—impersonates that double ideal perfectly, and succeeds completely. It is He Who restores to the world its primeval health, beauty, and innocence, thus opening a new Time-cycle.

The other men "against Time"—*before* the very end of each humanity—succeed, and are recognised and exalted by millions, permanently, inasmuch as they, or their followers, abandon their spirit and work decidedly "in" Time, compromising with the forces of death; in other words, inasmuch as they have in them— like the Prophet Mohammed[3]—more "lightning" than "sun." Otherwise, they are defeated by the agents of the Dark Forces, broken in their might by the downward rush of history, which they are unable to stem. And such a fate awaits, always, until the very end of any Time-cycle, those who are too magnanimous, too trusting, too good; those who put too much confidence both in foreigners and in their own people; those who do not "purge"

---

[3] See the life of the Founder of Islam.

their following often enough and thoroughly enough; who love their people too much to suspect ingratitude or actual treachery where it lies; who are not merciless enough, and sometimes spare their fleeing enemies; in one word, those who, like Adolf Hitler, have, in their psychological make-up, too much "sun" and not enough "lightning." Be He, himself, but the last one in date of these, come back with superhuman might after apparent annihilation, or a new one altogether, "Kalki" will avenge them and the people who struggled at their side, for no visible result whatsoever, in their days. And then, He will make their apparently impossible dreams the living reality of the next great Beginning!

In every great Beginning, the men "above Time," lonely ascetics, saviours of souls, or planners of an ideal order, too good for the fallen earth—Arhats, Bodhisattvas, or Rajrishis, to use the Sanskrit terminology—meet the great Ones "against Time" on the material plane as on every other. Then, in a world in which violence is no longer necessary, nay, no longer thinkable; in which freedom and order go hand in hand, things *are*, according to the very law of manifestation in Time, what both the men "above Time" who cared to give a thought to collective life, *and* the greatest men "against Time," wanted them to be. The City-of-the-Horizon-of-the-Disk as King Akhnaton dreamed it; the "Seat of Truth" which, even in his far-gone days, he failed to establish upon earth, and the world New Order which Adolf Hitler fought in vain to install in the midst of our present-day, worthless humanity, are, then one and the same living, tangible reality in time—as long, at least, as unavoidable decay does not once more set in.

And thus, through the perfect, impersonal—mathematical—justice of the Cosmos, each different agent of universal Destiny has the success which is due to him as a man. Those who work for the immediate result of their action, in a selfish spirit, obtain that result (and what a tremendous one, sometimes!) and play their part in the evolution of a world that *must* pass through degradation and death before it can experience the glory of a new birth and of a new youth. They bring that world nearer to its end. On the other hand, those who have renounced the bondage of Time and, purposely, either do not act, or else act in the selfless spirit of the warrior in the Bhagavad-Gita, get the glorious result of their life's thought and work at the beginning of the following Time-cycle. And it may well be that the efforts of the men "against Time," apparently wasted upon an uncomprehending and ungrateful world, actually *do* add to the beauty of every new Beginning, and that they even hasten its advent. For nothing is *ever* lost.

And as we have said, Destruction and Creation are inseparable. Even the most destructive men "in Time" are creative in their way. Men "above Time" are also destructive in their way — indirectly, as the former are creative. Men "against Time" are actively, consciously, *willingly* both creative and destructive — like Lord Shiva Himself: the divine Principle behind all change; the Destroyer, Who again and again creates; and like Vishnu, the Preserver, Who, once at least in every Time-cycle, comes as Kalki, to destroy completely. In them, the Cosmos is forever seeking its Principle, against the irresistible Law of Time, which steadily draws it away from It, from the beginning to the end of every successive material manifestation in time.

Completed in Karlsruhe railway station on the 6th of December, 1948

2. Savitri in Alfeld an der Leine, Lower Saxony, 5 December 1948, the day before she completed this chapter

Part II

THE LIGHTNING: GENGHIS KHAN

3. GENGHIS KHAN

FROM THE JOURNAL OF THE NORTH CHINESE BRANCH OF THE ROYAL ASIATIC SOCIETY—VOL. LVI

Chapter 4

THE CHILD OF VIOLENCE

Just as the physical universe is the masterpiece of divine creativeness in space, so is the history of any "Cycle" the masterpiece of the same impersonal Artistry in time. No man knows the importance of certain events until they have taken their place as unavoidable details of a historical pattern. But once one can see them in their proper perspective—however insignificant they may appear, outwardly, when isolated—one cannot but admire the consistency of the implacable Force which binds cause and effect and compels decaying humanity to hasten to its doom in perfect order.

Some 800 years ago, in the country east of Lake Baikal, along the border of the River Onon, a man of the Merkit tribe was taking home his pretty, newly wedded bride, a girl of the Olhonod clan, round-faced, slit-eyed, and dark-haired, adorned with heavy silver jewellery and beads of bright blue turquoise. The girl was called Hoelun. She did not know herself what an exceptionally strong, masterful woman she was, nor what a staggering destiny awaited her. She did not know that the "dwellers in felt tents"—the men of the steppes—were to praise her name for all times as the mother and grandmother of conquerors, the ancestress of dynasties. She merely knew that she was following her husband, for whom she was to work and bear sons, like any other wife. And she was happy. In her complete ignorance of immediate distress and ultimate glories, she smiled to the sweet present. She watched the reflection of the Sun in the rapid waters of the river, or played with the blue beads of her necklace.

But suddenly her blood went cold. She saw three men on horseback ride towards her, and she at once understood their purpose. She knew that her one man could not overcome three, and she herself urged him to flee and save at least his own life. She would be lost to him anyhow. So the Merkit fled. The three men galloped nearer and nearer until they reached the girl, seized her, and dragged her off. As they carried her away, she wept and lamented. But along the borders of the Onon and from the endless grasslands over which her ravishers rode with her, no answer came to her cries. The bright sky shone above, and the wind swept the green immensity all around her. One of the three men roughly told Hoelun to stop lamenting. "Though thou shouldst weep, thy husband will not turn his head. Seek his traces, thou shalt not find them. Stop thy cries, then, and cease to weep!"[1]

And on they went—the three brothers, on horseback, and the sullen girl in her *kibitka*, drawn by one of the horses—until the day faded over the grasslands without end and the ragged rocks here and there and the burning dust of the barrens, until the hills in the West grew dark against the fiery background of the sky, and the dry air became suddenly cold. The men talked little. A flight of wild birds crossed the sky, far above their heads, and they watched it pass, with sharp hunters' eyes. The wheels of the *kibitka* creaked at regular intervals. Hoelun had ceased weeping. And she did not speak. Resigned—for there was nothing she could do—she was already beginning to adjust herself to the circumstances that were to mould her life. Unknowingly, she was preparing to make the best of them, as a wise girl she was. The creaking wheels were carrying her nearer and nearer to the tents of the Yakka Mongols, amidst whom she was to fulfil her glorious destiny. The silent and robust young man riding the horse that drew her *kibitka* was the chieftain of his tribe. His name was Yesugei.

She watched his darkening silhouette that moved before her above that of the horse.

The Sun had set when, at last, they reached the young man's *ordu*. Above the western horizon, still glowing crimson, layers of unbelievable hues—limpid gold and pale, transparent green and pink and violet—succeeded one another, abruptly. The mountains in the east were the colour of lilac. But Hoelun, to whom the splendour of the cloudless[2] Mongolian sky was an everyday sight, paid little attention. She only saw the camp into

---

[1] Ralph Fox, *Genghis Khan* (London: John Lane, 1936), p. 56.
[2] Replacing "moistless"—Ed.

which the men were driving her: the round felt yurts, the evening fires, the forms of herdsmen and warriors before the fires. She heard voices of men and women, children's laughter, the neighing of horses, the barking of dogs—the voices of life. There were not as many yurts as she had expected. This was a poor *ordu*. Yet it was her new home now. Not the one her father had planned to give her, but the one the Kings of the invisible world—the spirits of the Eternal Blue Sky, who rule all things visible—were giving her, because such was their pleasure, and the world's destiny.

She looked at the strange faces of the new, strange place with childish curiosity mingled with apprehension and the vague feeling of something momentous. She was being driven. Towards what? For a second, she recalled the familiar countenance of the young Merkit warrior to whom she had been wedded, and she was sad. But she was given no time to ponder over the past. Joyful shouts were already greeting the return of the chieftain Yesugei and of his two brothers, who had dismounted. Women were gathering around her *kibitka* to have a look at her. And, as many were commenting upon her fair appearance, she felt pleased.

She was given to Yesugei, and there was a feast at the camp, that night. The warriors ate and drank a lot, and minstrels sang. Hoelun's new life had begun. She was assigned a yurt of her own, and serving women. And Yesugei now spent his nights in that yurt.

She neither lusted after him nor loved him as she had the young husband for the loss of whom she had wept. But she knew that it was her fate to be his wife—to bear sons to the strong man who had stolen her away from the one who had fled. And she submitted to her fate. She worked for Yesugei by day—cooking his food, making felt, dressing skins, and splitting cords from sinews.[3] And at night, when he came to her, she hid her fear of him and her reluctance. She submitted to his passion as the cool, passive, ageless earth submits to the fury of the devastating and fertilising thunder-storm, and she kept her feelings to herself. He was drawn to her by a direct and elemental force

---

[3] Harold Lamb, *The March of the Barbarians* (London: Robert Hale, 1941), p. 51.

like that which gathers together the heavy, restless clouds and loosens rain upon the earth, a force that was beyond him and beyond her, and beyond all men, and that merely used their bodies in order to fulfil the inexorable, hidden logic of evolving history: the superhuman command of Destiny.

During one of those nights, the spark of life was kindled in her womb. And she conceived the son who was to render her name and that of Yesugei immortal; the Child of lust and violence and of divine, irresistible purpose; the future Genghis Khan. But Hoelun did not know it. Nor did Yesugei. No man knows what he is doing when he soothes the fire of his loins in a woman's belly.

In the camp of the Yakka Mongols and in the wide world outside the camp, everything was — or seemed — the same as on any other night. The bitter wind howled over the barrens, and the River Onon rushed on to mingle its waters with those of the Ingoda and, finally, those of the mighty River Amur. Now and then, the howling of a jackal or of a wolf could be heard within the howling of the wind. But, although no one noticed it, the position of the stars in the resplendent heavens was an unusual one, full of meaning.

And while Hoelun busied herself with the monotonous everyday tasks of life — while she tended her new husband's yurt and cooked his food, or slept at his side — the child of Destiny took shape within her body. He was born in the year of the Hare according to the Calendar of the Twelve Beasts — the year 1157 of the Christian era — clutching a clot of blood within his right hand.

Chapter 5

THE WILL TO SURVIVE

"He came into the world with little else except the strong instinct to survive," writes a modern historian[1] about Temujin, son of Yesugei: the child who was to become Genghis Khan. And this is not merely a true statement concerning the baby; it is the key to the man's whole life, the explanation — if there be any — of the conqueror's extraordinary career. There is no impersonal inspiration, no disinterested love behind Temujin's long, stubborn struggle against tremendous hostile forces — a struggle that any onlooker would have judged hopeless at the time. There is no "ideology" of any sort behind his battles, and behind the iron discipline — the *order* — which he imposed upon the people of 50 subdued kingdoms. There is only a patient, methodical, overwhelming will — the will to survive — assisted by clear intelligence and unfailing knowledge of men, or, rather, by an unfailing instinct, clearer, surer, and more powerful than that which we generally call intelligence; a mysterious but absolute knowledge of all that was (or could be made) *useful* to him, and a constant readiness to act in accordance with what he knew. Admirable qualities, which would raise any man far above all men, and which did not fail to set Temujin aside as *the* greatest conqueror and one of the greatest men of all times. But they were means to an end. And the end was first to keep Temujin alive and then to make him and his family secure. The vision that was to fill the consciousness of the great warrior more and more compellingly as time and victory increased his power beyond all limits was neither the salvation of the world for its own sake, nor its destruction, but the organisation of the world for *his* own benefit and that of the *Altyn Uruk* — the "Golden Family" — *his* family; for the survival of himself and of his power in his sons and grand-sons, clad in luxury and seated upon thrones.

Moreover, Temujin — Genghis Khan — is, as far as I know,

---

[1] Lamb, *The March of the Barbarians*, p. 41.

the first man in history to have shaken two continents while prompted by such a simple, eminently practical aim. There was no vanity in him, as in many a lesser conqueror, no lust for dramatic effects—although his career be, no doubt, one of the most splendid living dramas ever staged upon this earth. And, despite the "pyramids of skulls" and other such grim realities connected with his name, no superfluous cruelty either; no cruelty out of impulse as occasionally in Alexander the Great; and no cold-blooded yet purposeless cruelty for the sheer pleasure of it, as in Assurnasirpal, King of Assyria.[2] He was too strong—and too practical—to be impressed by the by-products of power. He knew what he wanted, and patiently made himself ready. And when ready, he struck straight at his aim with the irresistibility—and the divine indifference—of lightning. He is perhaps the first historic figure embodying *to the full* that which I have called, in the first part of this book, the power of Lightning—the power of Time in its merciless onward rush. His destructiveness was the passionless destructiveness of Mahakala, all-devouring Time. And his aims, so personal, so precise and practical, were but the pretext used by the everlasting forces of disintegration to quicken the march of mankind towards its doom. No one has indeed deserved, more than he, the title of "Scourge of God" given him, in fear, by whole crumbling civilisations. But "God" was, in reality, not the man-loving God of the Christian and Muslim chroniclers, but the impersonal creative-destructive Power immanent in all growth, in all life. The "scourge" came from within, not from without. Genghis Khan was an instance, not a punishment. For his attitude to the living world, manifested on the broadest possible scale, his merciless self-centred claims, were but those of every man in a decaying humanity in which all activity has become more and more self-centred—provided every man had the sincerity, the courage, and the strength to admit that, in his eyes, nothing matters but himself, and to carry on that attitude to its logical conclusion. It was the attitude of a doomed humanity, but completely devoid of that monstrous hypocrisy which makes a doomed humanity so repulsive.

And it is that harsh frankness of purpose, along with his al-

---

[2] 884–859 B.C.

most miraculous achievements on the plane of physical reality, that give Genghis Khan that sombre, god-like grandeur in comparison with which the glory of so many men of fame, nay, of so many men of war, appears feeble—"all-too human."

From the very beginning, Temujin was schooled by circumstances to believe that he alone mattered. In the rough society in which he was born, many a son of a chieftain doubtless thought the same. Men did outside Mongolia, with less commendable innocence. But most men, at least most children, had protectors and friends whom they could trust. Temujin was, very early in life, left with none. He had to be ruthlessly self-centred in order to live.

We get a glimpse—but just a glimpse—of his person in his very early years in the words Dai Sechen, the shrewd old father of Bortei the Fair, addressed to Yesugei, as he met him riding with the boy towards the camp of the Olhonod (Hoelun's clan) in search of a bride for him: "Shining eyes and a bright face has thy son...,"[3] and in the much less flattering last words of Yesugei himself to Dai Sechen as, after the betrothal, he left the future "Emperor of all men" to his care, according to an old custom: "My son is afraid of dogs. Do not let dogs frighten him..."[4] Temujin was then a mere child. And however proud the Mongol chieftain, his father, might have been—as every one of the *baghatur* (valiant men) of the steppes was—he was far from suspecting how amusing his simple statement and request would one day appear, when printed in history books, in many foreign languages. And old Dai Sechen's praise indicated nothing extraordinary in the lad's physical features or bearing. Many a healthy and intelligent child has "shining eyes and a bright face," whether on the banks of the Onon or on those of the Rhine. As far as we know, there was, in Temujin, nothing that foreshadowed a conqueror, apart from his latent capabilities and his horoscope—his nature, which circumstances would reveal, and his destiny. Even in later years, when chroniclers of East and West started recording his world-shaking deeds, none

---

[3] Fox, *Genghis Khan*, p. 57.
[4] Fox, p. 59.

was to dig out of the great warrior's remote childhood any significant episode, any sign of irresistible might to be, as others had once, for instance, pictured nine-year-old Hannibal swearing everlasting hatred of Rome before the altar of his grim gods. And, which is more, if one possesses any of that particular historical intuition that puts one, so to say, in direct touch with the great men of the past, one feels that, had Temujin remembered such an episode from his boyhood, he never would have referred to it in following years. As I said before, he was more interested in his precise purpose than in the exaltation of himself, in solid power than in glory. There was not a trace of conceit in him. Action alone — victory alone — mattered in his eyes, not the long genealogy of victory. *That* was to be *lived*, the resplendent result alone to be recorded. Personal latent capabilities mattered only when they ceased being latent.

But Destiny was soon to begin forging its instrument. A few days after Temujin's betrothal to Bortei, Yesugei was dead — poisoned on his homeward journey by some Tatar chieftain whose treacherous hospitality he had enjoyed for a night. Temujin was sent for. He came back at once, only to find that his father's followers had deserted the *ordu*, that his mother had been refused admission to the tribal sacrifices by the Shaman and expelled with her children, with ignominy, by the other women of the clan. Riding after them alone, with the banner of the nine yak tails — the standard of the Yakka Mongols — in vain had the courageous widow tried to shame some of the tribesmen and urge them to return and swear allegiance to the son of their deceased *khan*. According the law of the steppes, she was now the head of her husband's *ordu*, and their legal chieftain until her sons came of age or until a new *khan* was elected. But the warriors who had come back for a while had slipped away again. "The deep water is dried up," had they declared, in the poetic language of the nomads; "the strong wheel is broken. Let us go!" And they had joined the Taijiut chieftains, who were powerful.

An outcasted woman and her children — four sons and a daughter — and two other boys, sons of Yesugei by another wife, and an old slave, left to fend for themselves by the River Onon while the many tents and flocks moved on towards the summer pastures under the guidance of new *khans*: that was all that remained of Yesugei's *ordu*; that was all Temujin's inheritance—that *and* his indomitable will, the will to survive, the will to endure, the will to win a place for himself among the merciless men who had thrown him aside like a useless burden. A place "among" them? No, but *at the head of them*, for he was their *khan*—the will to hold his own in the merciless world that belonged, belongs, and always shall belong to the single-minded, the cunning, and the strong.

He was a mere boy in his early teens. He knew not how to read or write—nor was he ever to know. But he possessed that superhuman will, and he knew what he wanted: first, to live; and then, to live well: to acquire power for himself and for his family, and plenty for his people; to put himself in his place in the world as a *khan* by divine birth-right. The situation that he now faced could not have been more accurately summed up than in that tragic dilemma which another staggering Embodiment of the Will to survive (but of the collective Will, this time[5]) was to set, 750 years later, before a whole great nation: "Future, or ruin!" He did not bother to analyse it. He was too young. And also, abstract thought would have taken time; and he had no time. He set about to hunt—to live. And he kept in mind his mother's constant talk about the vengeance that he was one day to wreak upon his enemies, the two Taijiut chiefs, Yesugei's kinsmen, for whom his people had deserted him.

He hunted—or trapped—whatever there was to be caught: small game, marmots, even field mice, anything that would fill his stomach. He even caught fish and brought them home to be cooked and eaten—such despised food, in the eyes of the Mongols, that none would touch it unless bitterly compelled by the pangs of hunger; but Temujin *was* hungry. He struggled to keep himself alive—and fit—at any cost. He quarrelled and fought with his brothers and half-brothers over the game they captured, and angry shouts and hard blows were a feature of his and their everyday life, in the tiny settlement on the fringe of the woods by the Onon. Already at that early age, Temujin seems to have known no scruples and no pity. Apparently—like all naturally single-minded people, from the absolutely

---

[5] Adolf Hitler, one of whose first great public speeches was on the subject: "Zukunft, oder Untergang."

selfless idealists, men "against Time" as I have called them, down to people such as himself, with no ideology and no idealism whatsoever, but just a precise, self-centred, and unwavering purpose—he classified the rest of mankind under three well-defined categories: the useful; the useless (but harmless), and the dangerous. In his case, this meant the useful *to him*, the useless as far as he was concerned, and the dangerous *to him*—those who stood in his way. His brother Kasar, strong and skilled with the bow and full of an almost dog-like devotion to him, was eminently useful, and was to remain so all his life. But Bektor, his half-brother, although he had not his cunning, was stronger than he and often robbed him of the best part of his hunt. Temujin decided in his heart that he was dangerous. And one day, taking Kasar with him to help him if need be, he walked to the place where Bektor, unprepared and suspecting nothing, stood, peacefully herding the few horses that the family possessed, and he killed him straight away with an arrow.

He does not seem actually to have hated him. In cold blood, he just removed one of the first obstacles from his path. And when the unfortunate lad, dying, begged him not to harm or desert Belgutei—the other son of Yesugei by the same mother—he readily promised that he would not. And he kept his word—without difficulty. For Belgutei was not dangerous. (He even proved useful in later life.)

Such an episode shows already, in the lad Temujin, the remorseless ruthlessness of the future Genghis Khan. But, however important it might have appeared to him in the heat of his anger, the issue was not worth the deed. The eldest son of Yesugei had better things to think of. And the wise widow, Hoelun—a woman not merely of courage, but of vision also—reminded him of the greater issue; of the *one* issue worthy of all his strength, watchfulness, and cunning at that stage of his life: vengeance upon his foes; the reassertion of his rights; his rise, from the status of an outcast to that of a chief, once more. She reminded him and his brothers of their absolute isolation in the midst of a hostile world, and of the compelling struggle constantly before them—the struggle that should make them forget all pettiness, all jealousy and hatred among themselves. "Save your shadows," said she, "you have no companions. Save your horse's tail, you have no whip. The wrong done unto you by the two Taijiut chiefs is unbearable. And when you should be thinking of avenging yourselves on your foes, you go and do this!"[6] She was burning with bitter indignation and contempt. She did not blame her sons for killing another boy, and a defenceless one, and their own half-brother. She blamed them for wasting precious time and energy by doing so — already by *wishing* to do so — instead of thinking *solely* of their revenge upon their real enemies. She blamed them — she blamed Temujin — for allowing a side-issue to take, even for a short time, the first place; for not being sufficiently possessed with the one-pointed will, without which the most outstanding qualities are as naught.

Although Temujin thought no more about the incident, he never forgot the lesson.

卐 卐 卐

Hoelun also told him of his ancestors, the Borjigin, the Blue-eyed heroes, sons of the legendary Blue-Wolf. "Their voices," said she, "rolled as thunder in the mountains; their hands were as strong as bears' paws — breaking men in two as easily as arrows. In winter nights, they slept naked by a fire of mighty trees, and they felt the sparks and embers that fell upon them no more than insect bites."[7]

And the lad listened with elation to those ancient tales, in the evenings, by the fire of his mother's *yurt*, while the bitter wind — that same wind that had stirred the steppe with aimless fury on the night he was conceived — howled in the near-by birch-tree forests and over the grassy expanses, endlessly. And the howling of the wind sounded like the unearthly lament of 10,000 hungry hounds, like the persistent call of ghostly trumpets, like the cry of dying men and horses upon a battlefield as broad as the world. Terrible presences from the superhuman sphere — *kelets*; spirits of the Everlasting Blue Sky, whom even the bravest dread, for one cannot fight that which one cannot see — filled the freezing starry night. But Temujin was not afraid. In those moments of pride and elation, his deep instinct told him that the *kelets* of the Sky never would do any harm to

---

[6] Fox, p. 61.
[7] Lamb, p. 41.

him; on the contrary, that they would help him in whatever he would undertake; that he was their Chosen One for some great work of power, of which he knew nothing yet. He felt within himself their frightful, impersonal irresistibility. But he was no dreamer. And when the morning came, he put that might, stirred in him by the voice of his racial past and by the voice of the Unseen, to the service of the one aim which he understood and pursued as worth its while: his own survival; his own victory over hunger, poverty, and humiliation; over the difficulties of his everyday life as an outcast, keeping in mind, all the time, that the first condition of security for him was the annihilation of his father's kinsmen who had robbed him of his *ordu*. For, young as he was, he already knew that he was to spare no man who stood in his way.

His mother's tales of the half-mythical Borjigin only stimulated in him the natural self-confidence which is the privilege of the strong. He too had blue eyes, like those ancestors who, visualised through Hoelun's poetic speech, appeared as demigods. And his thick hair had the colour of fire. He too was a son of the Blue-Wolf. He set himself to his day-to-day task the hunt for food, and the watch against constant lurking danger — with increasing determination to snatch the best out of every circumstance, turning even the greatest set-backs to advantage.

Guided by his hunter's instinct, patiently, methodically, he traced his eight stolen horses — all his horses but one — for three days over the trackless plains, found them, and drove them back, shooting his unfailing arrows at the pursuing thieves until at last night fell, and they lost sight of him. And at the same time, he won the friendship of Borguchi, a lad who had helped him in this difficult undertaking and who was all his life to remain his faithful retainer.

On another occasion, captured by Targutai-Kiriltuk and Todoyan-Girte, the Taijiut chiefs, his foes, he escaped them, although heavy Chinese stocks had been locked around his neck; and he hid himself entirely in the icy-cold waters of the Onon for a part of the night, the top of his head concealed among the reeds, until a serving man, who admired his courage and cunning, helped him to free himself from the stocks and to reach his tent in safety. And so he grew in years, in strength, in skill, in self-possession. And the irresistible appeal of his personality grew with him. Indeed, from these early days of his life as an outcast, he seems to have developed his ability to bind to his service, forever, the very best among all those who came in touch with him. And, as in all men predestined to stir multitudes into organised action, the appeal of his personality was the almighty appeal of natural leadership, which leaves none unmoved, save of course those whom their jealousy and envy of the born-leader have rendered stubborn in their hatred of him, and ... the congenital idiots.

His strength increased. Constant danger quickened his instinct, sharpened his wits. Repeated reverses stimulated his determination to overcome whatever might have caused them, multiplied his resourcefulness, roused his genius. And the field of his struggle broadened as years passed, and was to broaden throughout his life until it reached gigantic proportions. But his aim always remained the same: *his own survival*, the survival of his family, his revenge upon the bitterness and destitution of his early years—the very aim he had when he used to trap and eat marmots and mice, failing better game, and wait for hours in hiding until he could no longer hear, in the distance, the hoofs of the Taijiut horsemen who had been seeking to kill him.

Temujin was now a hardy, crafty young man with a handful of admiring friends—ready followers—and his first task lay before him, namely, the task of winning back his people from the Taijiut chiefs. But he never was rash. He took his time, felt the ground before proceeding, and allowed the patient play of circumstances—his invisible allies—to work for him. However, as soon as his instinct told him that the auspicious moment for a decisive step bad come, he acted straight away.

Just now, he rode once more to the tents of the Olhonod clan to claim Bortei, his betrothed, from old Dai Sechen. The latter, feeling in him a promising young *baghatur*, did not hesitate to give her to him, although Temujin was poor and still powerless. But he was far from suspecting that, by doing so, he was making the beautiful young girl immortal. Along with her, he handed over to his son-in-law a black sable coat: her dowry. It was a magnificent gift, and the first treasure the son of Yesugei ever possessed.

He valued it, no doubt, for he loved splendid and precious things. Still, his reaction was neither to remain happy in its ownership, nor to exchange it for gold or silver—other treasures of the same class. There was but one treasure worth struggling for, in Temujin's eyes: a life of freedom and of plenty, which implied—which always implies—a life of power; his birth-right; the life of a *khan* of the blood of the Blue-Wolf, son and father of *khans*. He presented the sable coat—*all* he had—as a gift to the powerful chief of the Kerait Turks, Togrul Khan, whose numerous tents, some of which were said to be made of cloth of gold, were pitched not far from the Great Wall of Cathay. And he asked him nothing in return . . . save his friendship, i.e., his potential usefulness. The *khan*, a crafty old man whose reputation of riches had even reached far-away Europe,[8] had been pleased to bestow his protection upon some of the smaller chieftains of the steppes, and he had accepted to be Yesugei's *anda* or sworn brother. Temujin turned to him. He needed an ally in his bitter struggle for survival, and this one could prove handy. In a gesture of diplomatic genius, he gave him his all, and spoke to him of the old oath and of the son's filial allegiance to the father's patron. Togrul Khan was flattered and felt inclined to help the young *baghatur*, if ever need there were.

Need soon came. The forest Merkit had never forgotten the insult done to them by Yesugei when he had snatched Hoelun away from one of their men. They raided the small camp on the border of the Onon, carried off newly-wedded Bortei to avenge upon her the old wrong, and pursued Temujin as long as they could—until he reached Burkan Kaldun, the "mountain of Power," and took refuge in the thick woods upon its slopes.

All seemed lost, now. All *was* lost, save Hoelun, the grim, warrior-like mother, the prophetess of deadly struggle and merciless revenge, and Temujin himself, with his invincible determination to win back his right to live, and with the seal of Destiny set upon him, already before his birth. While the exultant Merkit, shouting and singing and jeering, carried Bortei the Fair and Yesugei's second wife, Belgutei's mother, to their camp; while they feasted and got drunk around the bright camp fires, until dawn, the future master of Asia slept under

---

[8] A convert to the Nestorian form of Christianity, Togrul Khan was the fabulous "Prester John" of mediaeval tales.

the cover of Burkan Kaldun's living mantle, the dark forest. He wasted no energy in grief for his losses, nor in anticipated fears for what was likely to befall him. He just slept—leaving the forces of the invisible world to work for him in their mysterious way, since there was nothing else he *could* do. And when morning came—while his enemies slept a drunken sleep—he humbled himself before the Unseen and All-pervading, the Power of the Eternal Blue Sky, Which the Mongols worshipped.

In a ritual gesture, as a man making submission to an overlord, he took off his cap and hung it upon his waist, and unbuckled his leather girdle and hung it around his neck, and thus bowed down nine times before the rising Sun, acknowledging his own nothingness in the face of the Source of all life and all power. And he poured a libation of *kumys,* mare's milk, and made a promise: "Burkan Kaldun has saved my poor life," said he; "henceforth I shall make sacrifice here, and call on my children and grand-children to do likewise." He was grateful to the Unseen for his survival. He now realised that a Power far beyond him wanted him to survive; was his ally. But he did not know yet to what purpose, or if he did, dimly—for he was ambitious, and no dreams were too great for him—he did not allow the lure of an undefined future to interfere with the stern, precise preoccupations of the present. He only knew that the spirits of the Sky, and also the spirits of the earth and forests and waters were with him, and that he would triumph, in the end, over his immediate enemies: over those who had hunted him on that night and also over those who had been hunting him all his life; he knew that he would, one day, make good for his losses, and live as a *khan* should live.

In the meantime, he stood before the radiant Blue Sky, on Burkan Kaldun, near the head waters of the Onon, of the Kerulen, of the Tula—of the tributaries of the River Amur as well as of those of Lake Baikal, of the rivers flowing east as well as of those flowing west and north; he who was, one day, to conquer in the four directions. He stood there, grateful and humble—strong, as only the sincerely humble can be. And the rays of the Sun, Source of power, shone upon his greasy face[9] and upon

---

[9] The Mongols used to smear their skin with fat, to keep out the cold.

his thick, fiery-red hair, that the wind shuffled. And in this blue eyes—sign of the more-than-human blood of the Borjigin—one could have read the joyous serenity of a man who knows that nothing can crush him.

Soon, with the help of Togrul Khan's warriors and of Jamuga Sechen—Jamuga the Wise—who had become his sworn brother, Temujin raided the Merkit camp, bringing back much loot (or what appeared to him as "much loot," at this early stage of his career) and a number of captives who swore allegiance to him. He won back Bortei. But he was never sure whether her first-born, Juchi—"the Guest"—was his son or that of the man to whom she had been given on that night of shame. However, the boy was sturdy—a future warrior. He would be useful. (In fact, he was, one day, to conquer and rule the steppes beyond the Caspian Sea.) He was welcome, whosoever son he might have been. For Temujin was too intelligent, too practical not to realise that "healthy children are the most precious possession of a nation." But, unlike the superman who uttered these memorable words on several occasions, in our times,[10] he was no idealist. He was only interested in potential warriors inasmuch as their devotion to him, and their efficiency, would help *him* to assert himself as a lord in the steppes, after crushing all his foes. The very Power of the Eternal Blue Sky before which he humbled himself—conscious as he was of its awful limitlessness—he regarded as his ally in his struggle for power and plenty, like most primitive men look upon their gods as helpers in the pursuit of personal ends. At the bottom of his heart, he believed in himself alone. He felt as though the forces of the great Unseen were the first to come under the spell of his boundless, magic will.

But the impersonal Power of the Blue Sky—if at all conscious of itself and of him—must have regarded him as one of the most perfect instruments of its everlasting, serene, and merciless Play.

卐 卐 卐

Nothing seems to bring further success like success itself. Now, after this first victory, Temujin witnessed many followers

---

[10] Adolf Hitler.

come to him of their own accord, to offer him their services. He already had his own devoted brother, Kasar, the Bowman, and faithful Bogurchi—the youth who had once lent him his horse to ride in search of his eight stolen ones—and Jamuga, his *anda* or sworn brother, and Jelmei, the son of one of Yesugei's former vassals, who had joined him after the rumour had spread over the steppes that he had renewed his father's friendship with Togrul Khan.

Now Munlik, to whom Yesugei had once entrusted him, as a helpless boy, soon to be an orphan, and who had nevertheless deserted him like the rest of the *ordu*, came back to, him with his seven (presently grown-up) sons, one of whom, named Kokchu, was to win fame as a shaman. Others came too: some from Temujin's own Kiyat clan,[11] some from other clans, some from altogether other tribes: Jebei, Kubilai, great warriors; and the very embodiment of valour, virtue, and military genius, Subodai, destined, one day, to lead the Mongols across Europe, now a bare youth in his teens, full of passionate devotion to the rising *khan*.

Few men in history have inspired in their followers such absolute loyalty as Temujin. "I shall gather for thee like an old mouse, fly for thee like a jackdaw, cover thee like a horse blanket, and protect thee like a felt in the lee of the wind. So shall I be towards thee,"[12] young Subodai is said to have told him, as he joined his nucleus of heroes. And if so, he indeed kept his word to the end. The other paladins, whatever picturesque similies, different from his, they might have used to express their devotion, were equally eager to stand or fall with Temujin in his bitter struggle for survival. They loved him, not for the sake of any great idea behind him—there *was* none—but for himself; for the magnetic appeal of his person and personality; for the complete satisfaction which he gave, in them, to the natural need of man to be led by a real leader and to worship a living god. He was a leader, if ever there has been one. And he was a god in the sense that, even before his staggering victories, nay, even in the depth the forest where he hid, upon the slopes of Burkan Kaldun, at a hair's breadth from destruction, he had in

---

[11] Lamb, p. 41.
[12] Fox, p. 76.

him all the qualifications that were to give him, in years to come, the empire of Asia. The forces of the Invisible had actually set him apart, above other men, and associated him with their power. As the shamans of Mongolia were soon to say, "the power of the Everlasting Blue Sky" had "descended upon him." Here, upon earth, he was "Its agent."[13]

I repeat: there was no ideology behind any of his undertakings. Even the great dream of Mongol unity, which was soon to take shape within his consciousness, if it had not already done so by now, was not the dream of an idealist. In its materialisation, Temujin merely saw a preliminary condition of his own survival and security. It is for *his* survival and *his* security that his paladins fought. Also for the loot that they would share with him, naturally — and they knew that he was generous, and that he never broke the promises he made to his friends — but, first of all, for him; for the sheer pleasure of fighting at his side.

Few men in history have understood — felt — as keenly as Temujin the eternal meaning of war, that vital function of healthy mankind (so long, at least, as man lives "in" Time) as natural as eating or mating. Few have pointed out as clearly as he that destructiveness without hate — such as that of the hunter — can never replace the intoxication of victory over human enemies whom one does hate. His companions, to whom he had once asked what they considered to be a man's greatest joy, had replied, as simple Barbarians would, describing to him the pleasures of the chase. But the future "Scourge of God" said: "No, ye have not answered well." And he gave them *his* conception of happiness in a few typical sentences: "The pleasure and joy of man," said he, "lies in treading over the rebel and conquering the enemy; in tearing him up by the root; in taking from him all that he has; in making his servants wail, so that their tears flow from eyes and nose; in riding pleasantly upon his well-fed geldings; in making one's bed a litter upon the belly and navel of his wives, in loving their rosy cheeks and kissing and sucking their scarlet lips."[14]

Not that he was not always ready to strike, even without the feeling of aggressive hostility — lust of vengeance, or mere ha-

---

[13] Lamb, pp. 54 and 57.
[14] Fox, p. 88.

tred of opposition—at those whom he regarded as obstacles. That, he surely was, as one can clearly see in every act of his career, from the casual murder of Bektor, in his childhood, to the systematic wiping out of all the useless (or those whom the Mongols considered as such) among the population of conquered cities, years and years later. Expediency, of course, always came first, with him, the ultimate incentive of all his actions being his reckless determination to survive and succeed. But his emotional incentive, whenever he had one also, was always the pleasure of breaking down whomever and whatever prevented his own expansion; whomever stood in the way of his fullest possible self-assertion; whomever threatened his person, his security, his hold upon things: the rebel, the rival, *the enemy*. It is the everlasting incentive of all men of action—warriors and others—who live entirely "in Time." But only the best ones among them—those who are, like Temujin, free from hypocrisy—have the sincerity to admit it to themselves, let alone to tell it to others as plainly as he did. Of such ones, the son of Yesugei is, perhaps, the first one in date to have made history on a continent-wide scale (the first in date, at any rate, about whom enough is known to enable us to trace his psychology, to a certain extent). That is why we find that frankness in him. Of the other great self-centred destroyers *after* him, hardly any is without a notable amount of hypocrisy in his make-up. And that amount increases—as it is to be expected—as we get nearer our own times, while in Temujin—the "Lightning"-man *par excellence*, as I have called him—there is no pretence.

He did not remain idle after his victory over the Merkit. The powerful Taijiut chiefs, still in possession of the greatest part of his father's *ordu*, viewed his alliance with Togrul Khan with suspicion and his first victory with resentment. This son of Yesugei was surely a *baghatur* full of possibilities. They hated him all the more for it, and regretted they had not killed him years before, when he had been a helpless captive in their hands. Now he knew of their hatred—his mother had been reminding him of it all his life—and he knew that he would never survive unless they were destroyed. And he waged war upon them at the first opportunity.

In one of his encounters with them he was wounded in the neck, by an arrow, and only lived thanks to the devotion of Jelmei, his faithful squire, who sucked the wound clean and risked his own life in order to bring Temujin some curds mixed with water to drink. As one of his modern biographers says, "nothing was to come easily to this man."[15] The Taijiut were a numerous tribe, and Targutai-Kiriltuk and Todoyan-Girte were fierce warriors. Yet, in the end, Temujin's nucleus of an army, in which he was already beginning to enforce that iron discipline that was to make the Mongols invincible, beat them in a major battle in which Targutai was slain. Todoyan-Girte, captured, was also put to death. The future conqueror was never to allow an unreconcilable enemy to live. But a number of minor chiefs who submitted and swore allegiance to him were spared, despite some assertions to the contrary, dismissed by modern historians as tales of fear, or deeds of other *baghaturs* erroneously attributed to Temujin.[16] And the bulk of the tribe was also spared, its able-bodied men soon being incorporated into the all-powerful military machine that was taking shape in the Mongol's hands: the *horde*. Temujin could, no doubt, inflict suffering. Traitors to him, when found out, were condemned to death by torture. To such a death he had, also, after his victory over the Merkit, condemned the man who had raped Bortei. But this he did with a view to strike terror into the hearts of potential enemies. Otherwise he was too practical to indulge in cruelty for its own sake. He killed to remove obstacles.

Now, after the defeat of the Taijiut, he was the paramount chief in northern Gobi—quite an important man among the so-called Barbarians, but nothing to be compared, in riches, with Togrul Khan; and still totally unknown to the outer world West of the Altai Mountains and beyond the Great Wall of Cathay.

---

[15] Fox, p. 69.

[16] Harold Lamb (in "Genghis Khan, Emperor of all men") dismisses the story of 70 captured chieftains boiled alive at Temujin's orders, as "most improbable," while Ralph Fox (*Genghis Khan*, p. 82) states that this treatment was inflected *not* by Temujin upon the Taijiut, but by Jamuga, upon 70 of Temujin's followers, after war had broken out between the two sworn brothers.

The Chinese, always busy playing a game of balance of power among their turbulent nomad neighbours—seeking who was prepared to help them humble the latest tribe that had given them trouble—did not turn to him but to the Kerait Turk, to ask for his collaboration in an expedition which they led against the Tatars. But Temujin joined Togrul Khan in the expedition and defeated the Tatars. The patronising officials of Cathay gave Togrul Khan the Chinese title of Wang, which is translated as "prince," while Temujin was named something which means "Commander of the frontier"—a modest military distinction, in comparison. But he does not seem to have cared. As all practical and single-minded people, he never attached undue importance to external signs of power. The Tatar chiefs now swore allegiance to him. The Tatar warriors now increased the ranks of his potential army. He knew what he wanted and where he was going. He had the clear vision of a day when, in the steppes, he, Temujin, would no longer have any rival or any enemy; when he, who had been hunted all his life, would emerge at last more secure and more powerful than his father had ever been. And then . . . the will to survive might give way to the will to conquer . . . In the meantime, he let the Kerait chief be "Wang Khan"—"the prince"—and entirely devoted himself to the organisation of his warriors and of his increasingly numerous *ordu*.

The discipline he imposed at first seems to have been rude and primitive enough. At some feast, at which his drunken followers had started quarrelling, it is said that he himself brought them to their senses with a wooden club—the only argument that was sure to be understood in that rough society. But the nomads appreciated the fact that, whatever were the methods he employed, he always managed to control his men, and also that he kept them in good fighting condition.

"He feeds his warriors and keeps his *ulus* in good order"[17] was the opinion the tribesmen had of him. And it was a much higher opinion than it may sound to sophisticated people.

But then, he soon proceeded to create a real army out of his hitherto unruly warriors, and a nation out of the coalesced clans of the Mongols and of the subdued nomad peoples. The

---

[17] Fox, p. 110.

bravest and most efficient warriors among those who were blindly devoted to him, companions of his early struggle for survival, became at the same time his trusted bodyguard and his General Staff. Others were made officers in command of tribal levies. All those were the *nokud*, owing allegiance to no one but to Temujin himself, and invested with absolute power — with the right of life and death — over the men under their command. Temujin lay down strict rules, codified in the broader Yasa, of which I shall speak later on, concerning the equipment, routine, and discipline of the troops. He trained his soldiers and his officers until he had in hand a force that moved and acted as a single man — absolutely reliable, absolutely efficient. He put a stop to all feuds between the tribes that had submitted to him, crushed individual quarrelsomeness, killed the spirit of individual independence, moulded the proud Mongols (and the conquered tribes) into one increasingly numerous, highly disciplined collectivity, in which each and every unit had but one duty: to obey the authority set immediately above it, without murmuring, without questioning. The army dominated that nation in the process of formation. And he, Temujin, was the guiding and organising intelligence, the will and the soul of the army. The faithful chosen few among those commanders of genius who were to help him take the world unto himself, were, in his hands, like hounds in the hands of a mighty hunter — hounds "fed on human flesh and led on an iron leash," as the terrorised tribal chieftains, yet unsubdued, were beginning to think; and whom they described, in the forceful language of the steppes, full of suggestive similies, the language of warriors and poets: "They have skulls of brass: their teeth are hewn from rock; their tongues are shaped like awls; their hearts are of iron. In place of horsewhips, they carry curved swords. They drink the dew and ride upon the wind. . . . The foam flies from their mouths, and they are filled with joy."[18]

The friendship between Temujin and Togrul Khan, the rich Kerait chieftain — now "Wang Khan" — was not to endure. True,

---

[18] Fox, p. 101; Lamb, p. 54.

The Will to Survive

Temujin had, in many ways, made himself useful to his father's *anda*, whom he courteously called his "foster-father." He had been warring at his side not only against the Tatars but against the forest Merkit also (who, although once defeated, were yet far from subdued) and against the Naiman. He had (in exchange of payment of course) protected caravans against the attack of unruly tribes and made the trade routes safer than ever before. And in the prosperous Kerait settlements—half camps and half markets—the merchants were grateful to "Wang Khan" for the alliance he had made. But Wang Khan started intriguing against Temujin with Jamuga, Temujin's ambitious sworn brother, who had a personal conception of Mongol unity, different from his. And the son of Yesugei did not feel safe until he had broken both these new foes.

But he did not yet feel strong enough to challenge Wang Khan openly, in a war to the finish, and, after a first indecisive encounter with him, he sent him an outwardly friendly message mentioning old bonds, old services, and expressing the desire of lasting peace—although he knew there could be no such thing. The old Kerait, and his cunning son, Sen-Kung, knew that also, and rejected Temujin's advances. Temujin, again at one of the tragic hours of his career—again before the same momentous alternative which he had faced years before, in the pine woods of Burkan Kaldun, the alternative of "future or ruin," to quote once more the immortal modern words—withdrew with his trusted warriors to the marshes around Lake Baljun and waited. And again the spell of the indomitable will to survive was to compel—so to say—the power of the Everlasting Blue Sky to descend upon him and to carry hint to victory; I say "the spell," for there is a positive magic potency in the one-pointed, concentrated will that stops at nothing.

The Sun rose and set over the waters of Lake Baljun, and Temujin's companions hunted for food in the salty marshes. One dreary day succeeded another. Temujin thought: "The victory of the Kerait would mean the end of me. Therefore I must overcome him, never mind by what means. Where force is insufficient, let cunning supplement it!" And he bade his devoted brother, Kasar, the Bowman, send a message to Wang Khan—a lying message, stating that Temujin had fled no one knew where to, and that he, Kasar, in despair, was planning to desert his banner and to surrender to the Kerait Khan, whose protection he wished to secure. "Treachery," would say the chivalrous and the truth-loving, and those who value spotlessness more than life. "Necessity," would reply Temujin, and, with him, all single-purposed men of action, including the most unlike himself, the selfless idealists, to the extent that they too are, practical, and wish to accomplish something in this world of untruth, hatred, and stupidity; necessity—the only choice of the fighter who feels himself cornered and who, yet, is determined to win.

Wang Khan believed the clever lie—believed in peace and security—and ordered a feast. Temujin, appearing by surprise, stormed the Kerait camp. The old chief was captured and killed while attempting to flee. His son went south, only to meet his death a little later. Those of the Kerait Turks who were not slain in battle were incorporated into Temujin's confederation of tribes under Mongol overlordship. Their most desirable women were as usual given to the chieftains of the army. Temujin kept for himself one of the two beautiful nieces of Wang Khan, allotted to him in the division of the spoils. She became his fourth wife. (He had taken his second and third one from the defeated Tatars.) The other he gave to Tuli, the youngest of his sons by Bortei. She was the famous Siyurkukti-ti, fated to become the mother of three conquerors.

And now, he turned his forces against the Naiman, a numerous, semi-settled people whose *khan*, Tayan, had a Uighur chancellor and many subjects who professed Buddhism or the Nestorian form of Christianity, apart from those who clung to the old spirit-cult of the steppes. Temujin's *anda*, Jamuga, had been intriguing with Tayan against him—pointing out, in him, the enemy of the tribesmen's proud, personal liberty (which indeed he was, for individual liberty and iron organisation do not go together).

The Naiman, despite their number, were defeated, their chief, killed, and Jamuga, who had fled, captured and brought before Temujin. There was no longer, for him, any hope, any possibility of becoming important, let alone powerful. And Temujin, who knew this, was willing to pardon the man who had sworn him eternal friendship . . . once, long before, in the days when he had been poor and hunted, and without friends.

In victory, he could be generous to an enemy who had ceased being dangerous, *a fortiori* to an old friend. But Jamuga did not wish to live. Perhaps he felt that there could be no place for him in the new world that Temujin was forging out of discipline and war. He asked to be killed without spilling of blood so that, according to the belief of the Mongols—his spirit might continue to live, unchanged, in the world, and "help forever the descendants of Temujin" (whom he could not keep himself from loving, at heart, for the sake of old times). And he was smothered to death.

Temujin then broke the last resistance of the Merkit, his old enemies, taking from them his fifth wife, Kulan, whose beauty was to be praised through the ages by the minstrels of the steppes. Toktoa, the Merkit chief, was killed. Lesser tribes either were subdued by the irresistible Mongol horsemen, now organised into a regular army, or came forth and made submission of their own accord, feeling that there was nothing else that they could do.

Temujin was now the master of all those tribes which he had conquered and united, from the Altai Mountains to the Great Wall of Cathay. It had taken him years to win that position—years of patient, stubborn struggle, during which, more than once, all had seemed to be lost, while again and again his superhuman will-power had enabled him to triumph over every obstacle, compelling, as I have said before, through its invincible magic, the Powers of the Unseen to fight on his side. Thanks to that tremendous will, seconded by his military genius—his skill at organisation, his knowledge of men, his inborn intuition of historical necessity, he had indeed survived; he, once the hunted boy who had lived on the mice and marmots he managed to trap, robbed of his inheritance, rejected by his father's scornful tribesmen, harassed by his deadly enemies, day and night. And not only had he regained his father's position among the nomads, but he had created (apparently out of nothing!) that which the steppe-dwellers had not seen since the great rise of Turkish power seven centuries before: a real nomad kingdom, ruled from the saddle. From his very childhood, surrounded on all sides by treacherous foes, he had understood more and more clearly that only if he could become a king would he, at last, be safe. And he had fought to that end, and now, in the fiftieth year of his age, he was, at last, a king. It only remained for him to be solemnly recognised by the other chiefs of the steppes who, already, one after the other, willingly or by compulsion, had accepted his permanent overlordship in peace as well as in war. It only remained for him to be proclaimed by them as the *khan* above all *khans*: the Khakhan.

So he summoned a general *kuriltai* — a meeting of chiefs — on the banks of the Onon, in the year 1206 of the Christian era, which was the year of the Leopard according to the cyclic Calendar of the Twelve Beasts. And the assembled chiefs elected him Khakhan, supreme Ruler "of all those who dwell in felt tents." And he distributed honours and duties among them, fixing, in that historic meeting, the final structure of the great feudal state which he had been patiently building for over 30 years.

Every faithful chieftain was made a *noyon*, or prince, and given a definite domain, with its people — not necessarily all of the same tribe — as his *ulus* (his personal subjects) and the pastures that would feed their flocks. Every one had to send an appointed number of warriors from his *ulus*, to serve in the Khakhan's army and fight his wars. The few most tested and trusted officers — Temujin's companions all through his struggle, who had remained at his side in the darkest days, when his fortune had hung in the balance — were confirmed in the command of his Guard, that élite of the Army, now a wonderfully disciplined, most powerful military machine. More will be said later on of the rights and duties of the new feudal lords, of the equipment of the soldiers, and of the organisation of the whole bulk of the people — steadily increasing — under the rule of Temujin or rather of Genghis Khan (for this was the title, variously translated, which he was now given); of the Yasa, that famous code of laws which assured the stability of rise conqueror's life's work, as long as his descendants would hold fast to its commandments *and to its spirit*. It is sufficient, here, to stress that the entire organisation of the new centralised state in the midst of the steppes was inspired by Genghis Khan's will not only — now — to survive, but to conquer the outer world in its length and breadth; and not only to conquer it, but to make his conquests permanent; to make himself, the Mongol Khakhan, also the emperor of all men, and the "Golden Family" — *Altyn Uruk* — *his* blood, *his* race — the ruling family of the world, forever.

Already a middle-aged man with tremendous achievements behind him — the unification of the tribes of the Gobi *was* indeed something enormous — Genghis Khan thought of anything but "settling down" comfortably as king of all the lands between the Baikal Lake, the Altai ranges, and the Great Wall. As he beheld the assembled *khans* who had just elected him as their overlord; and his own warriors, camped in hundreds of tents all around the place of the *kuriltai*; and as he looked back to his past miseries and triumphs — to that day-to-day struggle of over thirty years — from his conquered seat of power, he did not feel: "I am safe at last, and a Khakhan. My work is done." No. For he had in him that everlasting youth which is the gift of the unbending, one-pointed will; that youth in the eyes of which nothing is ever "finished"; in the mind of which no opportunity ever comes "too late." He felt himself at the threshold of his career, not at the end of it. Now — now that he was at last a Khakhan — he would begin to assert himself. Whatever he had achieved up till then was only a preparation. He had survived. But why? To what end? Only to assert himself. Only to conquer — to break new opposition, and to take more and more precious things — land, people, further sources of plenty and of safety, further possibilities — from new enemies. His formidable war-machine — the first one of his time and one of the first ones of all times — was ready: organised, drilled, equipped, experienced, and superstitiously devoted to him. With such an army at his disposal he could assert himself indeed, he who had waited so long.

Beyond the Great Wall and beyond the distant Western mountains, the wide world, ripe for conquest, was blissfully unaware of him and of his *kuriltai*. And even if it had known, it would not have understood. It would not have realised what a momentous event had taken place in the election of this obscure and illiterate Barbarian as leader of other Barbarian chieftains, all of them as dirty, as picturesque, and, outwardly, as insignificant as himself; men who, when they were not drinking and stuffing themselves with mutton and horse-flesh, or breeding, or sleeping, could do nothing else but fight — or hunt; and who were, moreover, neither Christians nor Moslems — nor Buddhists; hardly human beings. To the Chinese, who despised soldiers, any minor meeting of scholars would have seemed far more interesting. To the Moslem world, the capture of Delhi by Mahmud Ghori — of the true Faith — only ten years before, or the rapid rise of the Khwarizm Shah (whose territory now comprised half the kingdom of the Kara-Khitai and the whole of Afghanistan) would have appeared infinitely more impressive. While Europe — destined to be trampled under the hoofs of the Mongol cavalry exactly thirty-five years later — would doubtless have found the recent exploits of the French knights of the Fourth Crusade — that pack of bombastic third-rate robbers, of no character, who had settled themselves in Constantinople and in Greece little over a year before the gathering on the banks of the Onon — much more noteworthy.

Contemporary history is always misunderstood.

At the appearing of the Mongol horsemen, the East and West were to realise what Genghis Khan's leadership meant. In the meantime, outside the steppes of High Asia, the *kuriltai* of 1206 remained as unnoticed as had, half a century before, the birth of the child Temujin, son of Yesugei. I repeat: great events, bearing endless creative or destructive after-effects, are never noticed at the time they happen. Still, they happen. And they bear their fruit. Genghis Khan, supreme ruler "of all those who dwell in felt tents," was now ready to thrust his irresistible horsemen against the forces of "civilisation" and to conquer both the East and the West.

Written in Werl (Westphalia) in July and August, 1949.

Chapter 6

THE WILL TO CONQUER

Genghis Khan was to conquer. "But how? And why?" — so have bewildered men repeatedly wondered, at the thought of his extraordinary destiny. The right answer is, in the words of Kokchu, the shaman, a believer in miracles (and doubtless appointed by Genghis Khan himself to present his career in such a light as to strike the Mongols with sacred awe) "because 'the power of the Eternal Blue Sky' had 'descended upon him.' Because he was 'here on earth, Its agent'."[1] The right answer is, in the words of Ralph Fox, a believer in historical materialism: "Because Temujin-Chingis was born at a time of crisis among his own people, when all was ready for the leader who should build a new society; and because it was his fate also to be born when the two great feudal states on either side of him, the Khwarazmian Empire in Central Asia and the Kin Empire in China, were in full decay."[2]

I said twice "the *right* answer," for *both* explanations — the supernatural and mediaeval, and the modern, materialistic — are true to fact in the eyes of whoever sees, in the unfurling of events in time, the manifestation of a timeless Necessity. The next consequence of the state of the Universe at any given time and place — the "will of the Eternal Blue Sky" at that particular time and in that particular place — is nothing else but that which has to be, according to the unchanging Laws that rule both the visible and the invisible world. And Genghis Khan *had to be*, like all the great ones who made history (while the implacable logic of previous history had made their appearing unavoidable, and sketched out the part they were to play upon the international stage). He had to be, and he had to conquer. And doubtless the socio-political conditions in Asia, in his time — the conditions in the steppes, on one hand, and the conditions in the two Empires, on the other — determined how complete his success was to be.

---

[1] Lamb, *The March of the Barbarians*, p. 57.
[2] Fox, *Genghis Khan*, p. 50.

But there is more to be said. His own will played, in his conquests, a part at least as important as that of those exceptional circumstances under which it manifested itself. And if those largely account for the succession of *events* in his career, the quality and the direction of his will, and the aspirations of his heart, give the key to *him* and situate him in his particular place among the god-like men of action.

As I said before, there was no ideology whatsoever behind his long bitter struggle for the mastery of the steppes. There was but the sheer will to overcome his enemies, to free himself from danger — the will to survive. And behind those wars that were now to give him mastery over the greatest part of Asia, there was also no ideology, no sacred zeal. There was the desire of greater security and the increasing lust of wealth and well-being for himself and for his family — nothing more. He conquered for booty. And he organised his conquests with admirable skill — imposing peace and security upon the terrorised survivors of the conquered people — merely in order to make booty systematic, permanent, and more and more plentiful.

He "welded together into a new nation the people who dwelt in tents," and above this nation, he set up "the Mongol clan, the *tarkhans* and *noyons*, companions of his early struggles."[3] But above them (and, in his mind, forever and ever) he set up the *Altyn Uruk*; the "Golden Family"; his own sons and their sons; his own blood — himself. His people were the servants of his sons, and his. No doubt, he rewarded their loyalty magnificently. Nevertheless, he and his sons were the real centre of all his care, the aim of all his efforts. He was a million miles away from the spirit of the disinterested modern idealist who wrote: "My son is but a part of my people."[4] And it is *this* attitude — and *not* the necessary ruthlessness of his wars — which makes him, in our eyes, a man "*in* Time," a typical "Lightning-man" in the succession of those great Ones that have changed or tried to change the face of the earth.

And the study of his campaigns abroad only deepens that

---

[3] Lamb, p. 73.

[4] "Mein Sohn ist nur ein Teil von meinem Volk" — Wolf Sörensen, in *Die Stimme der Ahnen: Eine Dichtung* (Magdeburg: Nordland, 1936), p. 36.

overwhelming impression of self-centred power that one gathers from the early history of his life.

卐 卐 卐

As living instances of his thoroughness and efficiency, Genghis Khan's wars against Hsi-Hsia, against China, and against the West, provide one of the most uplifting lessons in patience, will-power, and intelligence that I can think of.

The sturdy Tangut kingdom of Hsi-Hsia—which lay just outside the Great Wall of Cathay—although at first only superficially subdued, was sufficiently weakened not to become a danger to the Mongols during their expedition against northern China. That expedition was decided by Genghis Khan in answer to the pretention of the new Chinese Emperor to receive from him the traditional act of submission which the nomad chieftains beyond the Wall had given every new occupant of the Dragon Throne for generations. It was but a formal act of submission. But Genghis Khan, well-informed about the internal weakness of China in general and of the Kin Dynasty of northern China in particular, decided that the custom—meaningless anyhow—had lasted long enough. To break it meant war. But war was the only path to boundless power and increasing plenty, to the fulfilment of Genghis Khan's destiny.

The preparation of that war—as that of any other of Genghis Khan's campaigns, in fact—is as admirable as the war itself; a masterpiece of patient, far-sighted, minute, and thorough organisation, stretched over years. First, the silent, unassuming, but absolutely efficient network of spies who, from all corners of the enemy's realm, regularly brought the illiterate son of Yesugei all the information he needed in order to think out his campaign and then to carry it to fruition, is enough to amaze even such people as are acquainted with more modern secret organisations of similar nature. The enemy was doomed beforehand. Then come the series of actual military preparations: another wonder. As his modern English biographer rightly points out, Genghis Khan "left nothing to chance."[5] From the sort of propaganda the most likely to give the Mongols the desired unity and the best possible fighting spirit, down to the smallest details concerning

---

[5] Fox, p. 144. Lamb, p. 58, says: "He took no chances."

the diet of the troops and their daily exercises, down to the meanest item of military equipment, all was conceived and calculated with one aim in view: unfailing, machine-like efficiency. "The heavy cavalry wore armour consisting of four overlapping plates of tanned hide, which were lacquered to protect them against humidity," notes the same biographer.

> They were armed with lance and curved sabre. The light cavalry carried a javelin and two bows, one for shooting from horseback, and another for use on foot, when greater precision of aim was desired. They had three quivers, with different calibre arrows, one of which was armour-piercing. The troopers carried tools, a camp-kettle, an iron ration of dried meat, a water-tight bag with a change of clothes, which could also be inflated and used in crossing rivers. All manoeuvres were directed by signals, and the whole army worked as smoothly as a machine.[6]

And the soul of that extraordinary human machine was a newly born Mongol nationalism, which Genghis Khan cleverly kindled and used to his own ends.

The numerical inferiority of the Mongols, compared with their enemies, is also a remarkable fact. Their astounding mobility, their thorough preparation, and their discipline made up for it.

Finally, there is one thing which cannot but impress us as much as if not more than all the rest, at this stage of the conqueror's life, and that is (if I may employ such an unusual combination of words) his own spiritual preparation for war. Indeed, before leading his army to the mountain passes and across the Great Wall that had, hitherto, seemed impregnable to the Mongols—before engaging himself into a great war that was to last several years—Genghis Khan "retired for three days into his tent, with a rope around his neck, to fast and commune with himself, and then, going to a hill-top, he took off cap and belt and made sacrifice to the Blue Sky."[7] He was now well in his "fifties"—for this was five years after the great *kuriltai* on the

---

[6] Fox, p. 145.
[7] Fox, p. 144.

banks of the Onon. With infinite patience and caution, he had marched irresistibly on and on, and again he had just been taking every thinkable earthly step to make his new war a success. But his unfailing intuition told him that even this was not enough, that there were in war imponderable factors, and that there were means to victory which were neither military nor economic, nor, generally speaking, human. *What* exactly did the Khakhan think, alone before the majesty of the Everlasting Blue Sky? No one knows. But he most certainly felt that there is a secret source of strength in the state of mind of the man who humbles himself in front of the eternal and implacable, putting himself and all his schemes into the hands of superhuman Forces, *after having done all that was humanly advisable in view of success.* But, as one reads that reference to his retirement on the eve of his victorious onslaught on China, one cannot help remembering that other time — now far away in his stormy past — when, having lost everything he possessed, including his newly-wedded young wife, he communed with the Unseen upon the slopes of Burkan Kaldun, at sunrise, making libations of mare's milk to the mysterious Power that had saved his hunted life. One cannot help putting in parallel those two moments and admiring that quest of the conqueror for union with something divine, beyond himself, both at the lowest ebb of his fortune and now, on the eve of his long-prepared victory over the armies of Cathay. And one cannot help feeling that there *was* a divine purpose (of which he himself did not know) behind that stubborn man who fought for his own security and for the grandeur and riches of his increasing family.

The swiftness and discipline of Genghis Khan's army and the skill of his commanders — and his own — overcame all difficulties. The army of the Kin Emperor was defeated in a major battle, the memory of which struck terror for a long time in the hearts of the Chinese. And slowly — for Peking was not to surrender till the summer of 1215 — but steadily, the Mongols conquered the whole country, unto the River Hoang-Ho. At first, they avoided walled towns. They raided the land, driving off horses and cattle, and were content with taking the armies of the Kin Emperor by surprise and beating them in numberless encounters, while many "auxiliaries" of Mongol blood deserted the Chinese to join Genghis Khan's banner. The terror of the Mongol name, already great, grew and grew. It increased beyond all measure when the invaders *did* begin to besiege towns successfully. For Genghis Khan showed no mercy to the people of the cities that he captured. "Any resistance was crushed with inhuman methodical massacre of all that lived within the walls."[8]

And although, even after the surrender of Peking, the resistance of the Kin by no means ceased,[9] the entire north of China, Manchuria — and Korea — were now a part of Genghis Khan's growing empire, and a source of untold wealth to him and to his people.

In 1215, leaving behind him Mukuli, a trusted commander, at the head of the army of occupation, the conqueror, now nearly 60, rode homewards. The steppes where he had grown up as a hunted wanderer and fought as the chieftain of a handful of warriors, now swarmed with foreign slaves; gold and silver, and priceless objects of ivory and of jade — treasures unheard of — filled the Khakhan's coffers; his sons and faithful followers were "clothed in brocaded silk"[10] as he had wished. And he now counted among his wives a Chinese princess, adopted daughter of the Kin Emperor. And a man of royal blood, wise Yeliu Chuts'ai, descendant of those Khitan Emperors whom the Kin had dethroned, was his counsellor. One could rightly have said of Genghis Khan that he had conquered his dream — and more still. He was now wealthy and dreaded, as he had longed to be all his life. He was a real king. And had he died at that moment of his career, still his name would have been great in the history of Asia; still he would have remained the builder of Mongol power and the father and founder of the new Yuan Dynasty that was to hold the Dragon Throne for over 150 years.[11] But 60 years before — on that cold night when his mother, Hoelun, had conceived him from her ravisher — the unnoticed pattern of constellations in the depth of the "Eternal Blue Sky" had marked him

---

[8] Lamb, *The March of the Barbarians*, p. 59.
[9] It was not to be entirely broken till after the second Mongol campaign, under Ogodai, Genghis Khan's son.
[10] Lamb, *The March of the Barbarians*, p. 56.
[11] Until 1370, date of the advent of the Ming.

out to be more, far more than that.

Apparently, he could have stayed quiet and enjoyed his conquests, ate and drunk in peace and plenty among his people, now organised and prosperous. Maybe, he had himself no intention of doing anything else, and, as some of his biographers say,[12] did not actually want war at this stage of his life. Or, maybe, the insatiable lust for power and possessions was still as strong in him as when he had led his *tumans* through the open gates of the Great Wall, a few years before. We shall never know. But things were happening, and were soon to happen, in High Asia, that were to make war unavoidable. And the hidden, mathematical determinism of the world, combined with his own irresistible destiny — the destiny of the child Temujin, tangible forecast of the changes that *had* to take place — drew Genghis Khan to the West, to unprecedented military greatness; and Asia, to accelerated decay, after his death.

After Tayan's death and the defeat of his tribe, which we mentioned in the preceding chapter, Kuchluk, the Naiman chieftain, had fled to Balasagun, the capital of the Kara-Khitai country which stretched from the Altai Mountains, and from the boundary of the former Hsi-Hsia Kingdom, to the River Syr Daria. The Gurkhan, head of the Kara-Khitai realm, had given him refuge there, and he, very rapidly, through all manner of treachery, had raised himself to the position of an independent ruler. Genghis Khan could wait, but he never forgot. And it was, with him, a principle that no irreducible enemy should be allowed to live. So, well-informed as he was of what had taken place — and fully aware of the weakness of Kuchluk's position in spite of such a rapid rise — he had ordered one of his trusted generals, Jebei-Noyon, to march into the land of the Kara-Khitai. The land had been conquered, and Kuchluk captured and put to death in 1218, three years after the surrender of Peking. And knowing how unpopular both he and the Gurkhan had made themselves by persecuting the Moslems and Nestorian Christians, and what bitter hatred these all nourished towards the Buddhists in the whole realm, the Mongol general had proclaimed complete reli-

---

[12] Fox, p. 162.

gious freedom in the name of the Khakhan, a gesture which had made him appear as a liberator in the eyes of a great section of the people, and had immensely strengthened the hold of the Mongols upon the country.

Genghis Khan's empire now practically bordered that of the Khwarizm Shah, i.e., that of the Turkoman dynasty which ruled, in the place of the former Seljuk Sultans, over Turan and the whole of Iran — from the mouth of the Ural River, and the land north of the Aral Sea, down to the Persian Gulf, and from Iraq to the Hindu Kush. But again, at first, nothing seemed to foreshadow war between the two potentates.

Yet, war was to break out. As I said: it was Asia's destiny, linked up with the extraordinary destiny of the son of Yesugei. The greed and folly of the governor of Otrar (a frontier town on the border of the two empires) and the incapacity of Mohammed ben Takash, the ruling Khwarizm Shah, to face the situation as a realist, were the pretext and the immediate cause of the war.

Genghis Khan had sent an embassy to the Khwarizm Shah — who had first sent him one, at the close of the Chinese campaign. A caravan, "a trading enterprise of the Moslem merchants" who now surrounded the Mongol conqueror, followed. "Its 500 camels carried nuggets of gold and silver, silk, . . . the furs of beaver and sable, and many ingenious and elegant articles of Chinese workmanship."[13] When this caravan reached Otrar, the local governor had the merchants and their servants massacred and the treasures seized. Genghis Khan, who, even in great indignation, always remained too practical to be rash, did not, at once, in answer to that outrage, wage war on Mohammed ben Takash, however difficult it might have appeared to believe that the deed had been perpetrated without the latter's knowledge. He sent, instead, a second embassy, to demand of him the punishment of the governor of Otrar and compensation for the losses. And it is only after the head of *this* embassy had been murdered by order of the Khwarizm Shah, in defiance of all accepted notions of right, and its other members shamefully treated, that he decided on war, and started preparing his march to the west as minutely and methodically as he had, years before, his onslaught on Cathay. There was no other honourable course which

---

[13] Fox, p. 196.

he could take. But this war was to be a war to the finish. And the Khwarizm Shah must often have regretted not having avoided it while it was yet time.

For, in Genghis Khan, bitter, immediate resentment at the feeling of insult, and thirst of revenge, kindled the old will to conquer into a superhuman force of destruction. In all his campaigns the conqueror had shown swiftness—no sooner the time of patient preparation had come to an end and action had started—along with unprecedented ruthlessness. But in this one—his last one—he was to strike with the sudden irresistibility of Lightning and to bring about such wide-scale desolation as only great physical cataclysms—only God Himself—can work out upon the earth. He was to prove himself, if ever, animated with that which I have called in the beginning of this book, the spirit of "Lightning."

With the same efficiency as always, the conqueror's extraordinary "intelligence service" gave him all the necessary information about the enemy's country and conditions of life and political intrigues, about his exact strength and weaknesses, before war actually started. As always, every detail concerning the mobilisation, the training, the equipment and transport of troops was patiently worked out, and every predictable difficulty surmounted beforehand. And once more, in order to draw to himself the divine Power of the invisible world, which he felt at the back of all his achievements, Genghis Khan humbled himself before the one thing he knew to be greater than he: the Everlasting Blue Sky. "He went alone to a height near the Mountain of Power, and took the covering from his head, the girdle from his waist. For hours he communed with the spirits of the high and distant places; and he came down with a message: the Everlasting Blue Sky had granted victory to the Mongols."[14] As Harold Lamb says, he probably had the intention of strengthening the morale of his people at the beginning of a great new campaign. But I somewhat feel there was more than that in this ritual gesture of allegiance to the Invisible. It was a gesture of supreme wisdom, without which Genghis Khan would not have been Genghis Khan. It was, on the part of the greatest conqueror of all times, the recognition that even *his* career was but an episode in

---

[14] Lamb, p. 62.

endless Time, and even *he* but an instrument in the hands of the heavenly Forces that lead the Dance of Time; that, however much he fought for himself, he too fought for the purpose of all Creation.

The Dance of Time is the Dance of death—and rebirth; and the purpose of all Creation is destruction—before a new Creation; death, before the glory of a new Beginning. Many things were to be destroyed in old Asia. So, "tending the remount herds and the wagon trains,"[15] slowly but methodically—as irresistible as Time Itself—on went the Mongol *tumans* over the mountain ranges, the natural barrier between the Eastern steppes and the world of Islam. They felled trees, broke down rocks, and built roads and bridges as they went. They were not hundreds of thousands, as the vanquished were soon to imagine in their terror. They were, according to Ralph Fox, barely 70,000 regular Mongol soldiers, to which estimate one should add an equal number of levies from the subject Turkish peoples,[16] and, according to Harold Lamb, "some 15 divisions of 10,000 men."[17]

A surprise raid of Juchi, the eldest prince of the Golden Family, across the Ak-Kum Desert and the Kara-Tau Hills to the lower Syr Daria region, i.e., in the direction of the Aral Sea, deceived the enemy. While Jelal-ud-Din, son of Mohammed-ben-Takash, uselessly pursued the raiders (who disappeared as swiftly as they had appeared), Genghis Khan's main army, concentrated near Lake Balkash, was resting, after its long and difficult westward march, and preparing to attack. All was ready by the autumn of 1219. Yet, not until the early spring of 1220 did Genghis Khan order his general Jebei-Noyon (who, by the way, was not with the main army, but much further to the south, in the region of Kashgar) to march to Khojend, as though he intended to strike immediately at the two great cities of the Khwarazmian Empire: Samarkand and Bokhara. The Khakhan had had time, during those six months, to make full use of his amazing "intelligence service" and to gather all the information he needed concerning the enemy's preparations, and, also, the enemy's weaknesses and blunders, so as to take the greatest advantage of all these in

---

[15] Lamb, p. 62.
[16] Fox, p. 199.
[17] Lamb, p. 62.

his own plans against him. The time, which a superficial observer would have considered as wasted, had been, in reality, well-employed — in a way that was to render possible the swiftness of the decisive blow. Indeed, nothing is more remarkable, in the history of *all* Genghis Khan's wars, than the contrast between the apparent slowness of methodical, far-reaching preparations, and the lightning-speed of action at the decisive moment. Nothing renders those wars more admirable, from the standpoint both of the strategist and of the artist.

While Mohammed Shah's attention was diverted by Juchi's attack, the main Mongol army, divided into three sections, moved rapidly over the land that Juchi had just laid waste, and reached the River Syr Daria. Two forces, each of 30,000 soldiers, were commanded by Genghis Khan's eldest sons; and the third, consisting of another 30,000 men and of the Guard, was under the command of the conqueror himself, assisted by his younger son, and by the veteran of the China war and future hero of the European campaign, Subodai, one of the greatest generals of all times. The two princes, Juchi and Chagatai, went south — along the bank of the Syr Daria — to join Jebei and to attack Samarkand with him. Meanwhile Genghis Khan crossed the river and conducted his *tumans* across the Kizil Kum Desert, suddenly appearing, a month later, "almost on the top of Bokhara, and in the rear of the Shah's armies."[18] As always, he had taken every precaution so as to assure the success of such a march. Every trooper had been provided with the necessary supply of dried meat and water; remount herds of horses had been taken; and the time had been carefully chosen. "Such a march through the desert would have been impossible at any other season of the year"[19] says the modern biographer that we have quoted so many times.

Once more, swiftness of movement determined the Mongols' victory. On the 11th of April, 1220, while Mohammed-ben-Takash fled for his life, the son of Yesugei entered the prosperous and populous city of Bokhara — the hallowed seat of Islamic learning — without encountering almost any resistance. His first orders to the vanquished were to bring hay and water for his

---

[18] Fox, p. 202.
[19] Fox, p. 202.

tired horses and food for his men.

For a few days, the Mongols gave themselves without restraint to feasting and to lechery. Then, they turned to Samarkand, that the combined forces of Juchi and Chagatai and Jebei-Noyon were attacking from the east. The famous "city of gardens and of palaces" had no choice but to surrender and to be plundered. Its inhabitants were not systematically killed as in the case of towns that resisted the Mongols. The great bulk of the people of Bokhara (who had also not resisted) had been driven before the conquerors to be used in groups "as a human shield for the first ranks of the Mongol attack on Samarkand."[20] And the captives of Samarkand were later on driven off to help the Mongols fill the ditch around Urganj, the besieged capital of the Khwarizm Shah. In the meantime, during the autumn and winter 1220, Genghis Khan allowed the greater part of his army to rest in Samarkand while a force of 30,000 men, under Subodai and Jebei-Noyon, had been commanded by him to pursue Mohammed Shah "like the flying wind," wherever he might take refuge.

Mohammed-ben-Takash, the Khwarizm Shah, who, for weeks, had been hunted from town to town, expired alone on an island of the Caspian Sea—his last refuge—after learning that "his wives and children were prisoners and his treasure on its way to Samarkand, under convoy."[21] Subodai and Jebei-Noyon then crossed the Caucasus with their storming column and made a successful raid into the Russian plains as far as the River Don, while the sons of Genghis Khan, Juchi, Chagatai, and Ogodai, driving before them the captives from Samarkand, hastened to lay siege before Urganj. On account of its stubborn resistance—as useless as that which any of the other towns had offered—the capital was doomed beforehand, fated to be utterly wiped out.

Meanwhile the conqueror himself, taking with him his younger son Tuli and some of his grandsons, proceeded to deserve, in Khorasan and Afghanistan, that reputation of irresisti-

---

[20] Lamb, p. 64.
[21] Fox, p. 210.

ble destructiveness which the terror of the crushed people has attached to his name for all times.

Any town that made even a show of resistance was "stormed or tricked into surrender"[22] and levelled to the ground—as Urganj had been—while its people, with the exception of the useful artisans and of the young and desirable women, were systematically killed. This mass-slaughter evidently aimed at paralysing all will to resist, nay, all possibility of resistance . . . It was practical and methodical, like everything the Mongols did, at Genghis Khan's orders—and it was carried out "without evidence of sadistic torment."[23] The Mongols, says Harold Lamb:

> led out the people of walled towns, examining then carefully, and ordering the skilled workers—who would be useful—to move apart. Then the soldiers went through the ranks of helpless human beings, killing methodically with their swords and hand axes—as harvesters would go through a field of standing wheat. They took the wailing women by the hair, bending forwards their heads, to sever the spine more easily. They slaughtered with blows on the head men who resisted weakly.[24]

It is said that about nine million people were thus put to the sword in and around the place where had once stood the prosperous city of Merv. Fear caused, no doubt, the contemporary Muslim chroniclers to exaggerate the number of the dead. Genghis Khan appeared to them as "the scourge of Allah," and, wherever his army passed, it was like the end of the world—the end, at least, of that world which they knew. Yet, even if the figures were to be brought down to their half, still they would suggest a magnitude of slaughter unprecedented in history.

It is noticeable that material signs of power, wealth, or culture—strong walls, works of irrigation, libraries—for which the conquerors had no use, were no more respected than human life; that the destruction was as complete and as impartial as it could possibly be when wrought by man's imperfect weapons under

---

[22] Lamb, p. 63.
[23] Lamb, p. 65.
[24] Lamb, p. 63.

the guidance of man's will; as similar as it could possibly be to the total, indiscriminate destruction wrought by ever-changing Nature through her storms, earthquakes, and volcanic eruptions, or simply through all-devouring Time, the very Principle of Change.

Yet, it was destruction wrought by man, at the orders of a self-centred man of genius and, ultimately, for that man's personal ends. Genghis Khan "deliberately turned the rich belt of Islamic civilisation into a no-man's-land. He put an end to the agricultural working of the country, creating an artificial steppe here, on the frontier of his new empire; making it—he thought—suited to the life of his own people."[25] And he did this, apparently conscious of the fact that only if his people, the nomad Mongols, *remained nomadic*, could his sons and grandsons continue forever to govern the empire he had won them, and to enjoy its wealth. He felt that he had to destroy so that he and his sons and their sons might thrive—*not* on account of any real or supposed natural right of theirs to domination, not in the name of any real or supposed naturally superior rank of theirs in the everlasting scheme of Creation, but simply because they were *his* progeny, his "Golden Family." As I already stated: he loved himself in them—not them and himself in his broader and higher self: his race, integrated, in its proper place, in the still broader realm of Life, human and non-human, as a true idealist, a man "against Time"—capable of no less methodical and thorough destruction as he, but in an entirely different spirit—would have done in his place. He was essentially the embodiment of separativeness, the God-appointed agent of Death; of all the men "in Time," as I have called them in the beginning of this book, the nearest to the unchanging Principle of separativeness and destructiveness—of change—Mahakala, Time.

Indeed, when one reads the description of the terror that followed his horsemen wherever they went in Khorasan and Afghanistan, and especially when one ponders over the emotionless, remorseless, methodical character of the mass-slaughter they wrought, one cannot help admiring the detachment and efficiency with which the latter was carried out, and secretly re-

---

[25] Lamb, p. 66.

gretting that such wide-scale, machinelike power of killing was not applied in the service of a better cause—of some impersonal truth; of some more-than-human justice, in the spirit expressed by Lord Krishna when, exhorting the warrior Arjuna, in Kurukshetra, He told him, speaking of the enemies he was to slay: "These bodies of the embodied One, Who is eternal, indestructible, and immeasurable, are known as finite. *Therefore fight*, O Bharata!"[26]

But that was not the spirit of Genghis Khan, the warlord submitted to the bondage of self and therefore of Time. And now and then an episode that history has brought down to us— such as that of the annihilation of Bamyan—stands out to show what a gap separates the Mongol conqueror, despite all his undeniable grandeur, from the ideal of the warrior "against Time" as portrayed in the old Sanskrit Scripture. At the siege of Bamyan, in Afghanistan, Mukutin, son of Chagatai, and one of the young grandsons of Genghis Khan, was killed. As we have seen, in *all* the conqueror's campaigns, cities that had, to any extent, resisted the Mongols, had been destroyed, and the greater part of their inhabitants put to the sword. But the blood of the Golden Family, even though it were shed through the veins of one single individual, was still more precious, in Genghis Khan's eyes, than that of any number of Mongol soldiers, and cried for a greater vengeance. The old Khakhan, therefore, commanded that *all living creatures*—people without the customary discrimination between the useful and the useless, beasts, and the very birds of the air—be killed to the last, in and around Bamyan, and that all trace of the town upon the earth be wiped out. And "the order was strictly carried out,"[27] notes the modern biographer of Genghis Khan—who cannot help contrasting the horror of that deed with the serene, unearthly beauty symbolised in "the great cave of Buddhas," high up on the mountain-side, above the destroyed city full of decaying corpses. The opposition *is* indeed staggering. It is, carried to its utmost forcefulness, the lasting contrast between the man "*in* Time" and what we have called the man "above Time."

But one should not miss its real meaning by allowing one's

---

[26] The Bhagavad-Gita, II, Verse 18.
[27] Fox, p. 214.

mind to be swayed by hasty reactions. Despite all appearances, it is not the contrast between destructive fury and boundless kindness — love towards all creatures — which is the most remarkable, the actual contrast. It is the opposition between the family-centred, i.e., self-centred attitude of Genghis Khan, as illustrated by that as by many other of his actions, and the perfect detachment of the Indian Sage from all ties. There — in what they *are* far more than in what they *do* — lies the gap between the man "in Time" and the Man "above Time." And, I repeat, had the self-same mass-slaughter taken place, but in the name of some impersonal necessity worth its while, and not for the sake of that primitive passion of family vendetta which, in the circumstance, animated Genghis Khan, the physical contrast between the beautiful, peaceful cave on high and the place of massacre, pervaded with the stench of death, would have remained; and it would, doubtless, have been equally impressive in the eyes of the superficial observer; nay, it would have stirred the same feelings, that one guesses — the feelings nowadays so lavishly exploited in all cheap "atrocity campaigns" for mass consumption — in the hearts of unthinking humanitarians. But it would have been just a physical, an outward contrast; it would not have expressed any *real* contrast, from the standpoint of integral truth, for men "against Time" — capable of destruction in a detached spirit and "in the interest of Creation" — and men "above Time" walk along parallel paths, in eternity if not in history; along parallel paths different from that followed by those, however great, who are still within the bondage of Time.

During this whole lightning-like campaign, only once did the Mongols experience the bitterness of defeat; and that was at Perwana, where Jelal-ed-Din, the fugitive son of the Khwarizm Shah, managed to get the best of Shigi-Kutuku, one of Genghis Khan's lieutenants. The Mongols who fell alive into his clutches were put to torture at the orders of the Turkish prince who, for a short time, enjoyed the pleasure of feeling himself the avenger of his father and of his people in a proper Turkish manner — or, should I not rather say: in the manner of a man who lived (despite the tremendous disparity between them) far more "in Time" even than his great enemy?

There was indeed, in this war, from the start to the end, as much deadly passion on one side as on the other. Only Genghis Khan's passion — his will to conquer, so that his sons and grandsons might be emperors — was served with far more perseverance, and, above all, with far more lucidity, than his enemy's will to save what he could of the Khwarizmian Empire.

It was, in fact, if not by Genghis Khan himself, at least by more than one of his generals — in particular, by virtuous Subodai, the very embodiment of boundless, disinterested devotion — served with detachment; for those men had no personal lust, for power or riches; their lives were ruled solely by their love for their Khan and their stern sense of duty towards him and him alone; they were freer than he from what I have called the ties of Time; perhaps even some of them were men "against Time," who saw in him the originator of a new organisation of Asia, destined, in their minds, to lead to lasting peace and prosperity — to the good of all people — and who followed him for that reason. I personally believe that the presence of such men in the conqueror's General Staff (and possibly also among the thousands who composed his army) was a considerable factor of victory on his side.

The calm with which Genghis Khan commented upon Shigi-Kutuku's misfortune, simply stating that defeat would teach him caution, and giving him and the other chiefs a practical lesson in strategy upon the site of the lost battle, shows how the conqueror could remain master of himself whenever self-control was useful in view of further efficiency — for he must have felt very deeply the grief of that one only defeat his soldiers had ever known.

In that immense and constant self-control, source of his extraordinary patience, coupled, with the capacity of taking the right decisions in the wink of an eye *at the right moment*; in other words, in qualities eminently characteristic of those men whom we called men "above" and "against" Time, lies the secret of Genghis Khan's greatness. The fact that he used these splendid qualities entirely in view of the materialisation of a self-centred purpose and in a self-centred spirit, makes him a man "*in* Time" all the more appalling, in certain of his activities, that one is more aware of what a warrior endowed with his virtues *could have been*, had he only cared to serve, in the words of the Bhagavad-Gita, "the interest of the Universe" — of the whole of Creation — instead of his own and that of his family.

It was, no doubt, difficult, and perhaps impossible, for a Mongol to raise himself to that attitude — and to cling to it — especially when having attained absolute power after years and years of hardships and struggle. It would seem that the Mongol, nay, that man of Mongolian race in the broader sense of the word, can only be perfectly disinterested when he feels himself the follower of somebody — man or god — not when he happens to be, himself, the source of power. And yet . . . it is not easy to assert how far the great conqueror's practical, pitiless self-centredness is an inherent trait of his race. Ralph Fox has, somewhere in his book, compared Genghis Khan's practical qualities with those of "the founders of the great capitalistic enterprises of the last century, men who also stopped at nothing, who ruined their enemies gleefully and stole their wives and daughters no less gleefully; men who organised great empires, also — empires of steel and power"[28] — men like him essentially self-centred; we would say: like him living essentially "*in* Time." Yet, those were not Mongols. Nor was, before them, the overrated Corsican upstart Napoleon Bonaparte, he, at least, a warrior — and one of undeniable military genius, although a pigmy even in that respect, when compared with Genghis Khan — who led the French to the conquest of Europe in order to secure comfortable thrones for his worthless brothers. Nor were so many self-centred organisers of all sorts, of lesser magnitude, military or political — or both — who left somewhat of a name in history. The truth is that absolutely disinterested — selfless — characters, "men against Time" as we have called them, are extremely rare among the great nation-building warriors as, in general, among the remarkable men of action of *any* race or epoch.

Jelal-ed-Din did not enjoy for long the advantage given him by the one single victory he had won. His last stronghold fell to Genghis Khan in the autumn of 1221. By then, most of the *tumans* that had taken part in the siege of Urganj, or scaled the Caucasus and pushed into the Russian plains as far as the Sea of

---

[28] Fox, p. 88.

Azov, had joined the main Mongol forces. It seemed as though nothing could stem the conqueror's advance.

The Khakhan overtook the Turkish prince as the latter had reached the Indus River, and there he defeated him in a last pitched battle and sent a cavalry division in pursuit of him. But the raid beyond the Indus "was not pressed home,"[29] and it is not till years later—after the death of Genghis Khan—that Jelal-ed-Din (who, in the meantime, had secured himself a new kingdom in Iraq) was again hunted along the highways by the Mongols, and that he met his end. Yet, one can safely say that at the moment he crossed the Indus he was, already, for all intents and purposes, "politically dead"—no longer able to stand in the way of the Mongols. And he never was to acquire, anyhow, but a shadow of power.

Before starting, in the spring of 1223, the long homeward journey back to his native Mongolia, Genghis Khan had a few conversations with one of those rare men "above Time" that Asia has never failed to produce, even in the darkest periods of her history: the Chinese sage Ch'ang Ch'un, a Taoist. The main reason why he had invited the wise Cathayan to his camp shows how much the conqueror was, despite all his greatness, submitted to the bondage of Time *and conscious of it*: he wanted to learn from Ch'ang Ch'un the secret of prolonging physical life and strength indefinitely. He had heard that the seekers of the *Tao*—the priests and monks of Ch'ang Ch'un's sect—were in possession of such a secret. From his boyhood he had been fighting in order to survive, and in order to leave his family power and riches—the greatest enjoyment of life—in inheritance. Now that he was growing old, he clung to life more and more. His mind was not sufficiently detached to accept death joyfully—as so many of his own followers had accepted it for his sake. (His followers had him to love and to die for; but he loved nobody save himself and his progeny, being, in that respect, no better than millions of lesser men.) And when the serene man of meditation, the man "above Time," told him that there was "no medicine for acquiring immortality," he was disappointed. Yet, he was sufficiently impressed by Ch'ang Ch'un's talk to grant him a decree exempting "all Taoist priests

---

[29] Fox, p. 217.

and institutions from the payment of tax."[30]

The journey across the mountain-ranges and steppes of Central Asia, back to Karakorum, took months. It was interrupted by great hunts and great feasts, after which took place athletic exercises and horse-races—sports dear to the Mongols as to many other warrior-like peoples. It was saddened, for Genghis Khan, by the growing hostility that opposed Juchi to his other sons and by the departure of Bortei's first-born—of doubtful birth—to the Kipchak steppes and, soon after, by the news of his death. But Genghis Khan's own end was drawing nigh.

The years 1226 and 1227 were filled with the conqueror's last campaign: his second war against the former Tangut kingdom of Hsi-Hsia, whose king had rebelled against Mongol yoke. Genghis Khan died in August 1227—the year of the Pig, in the Calendar of the Twelve Beasts—after the Tangut had been defeated and while Kara-Khoto, their capital, was still besieged by his army. He died in the saddle, as he had lived, "on the upper Wei River, near the junction of the frontiers of the modern provinces of Kan-Su and Shen-Su."[31] His last order was to put the Tangut king and all his followers to death, as soon as Kara-Khoto would fall.

The conqueror's body was taken back to the *ordu* of the Yakka Mongols in the midst of which he had been born 70 years before. The men who carried him, lying in his coffin upon a two-wheeled wagon, killed every living creature, human being or beast, that they met on their way, according to Mongol custom.[32] In death as in life a trail of blood was to follow that extraordinary man, who had come into the world clutching a clot of blood in his right hand.

He was buried in some place that he had himself designated long before—probably somewhere in the shade of Burkan Kaldun, the "Mountain of Power," on which he had once communed with the Eternal Blue Sky, in the hour of distress, near

---

[30] Fox, p. 234; Lamb, p. 70.

[31] Fox, p. 240.

[32] So that no enemies might see the death cart of the Khan (or be, indirectly, caused to learn of his departure) (Lamb, p. 75).

the headwaters of the Onon and of the Kurulen, but no one knows *where*, to this day, save, perhaps (it is believed), a very small number of Mongols, who keep the knowledge religiously secret.

When he lay in his grave, with offerings of meat and grain, with his bow and sword, and the bones of the last warhorse that he had mounted,[33] it was solemnly announced by the chief-shaman—the Beki—who had presided over the burial ceremony, that his *skülde* or life-spirit had left his body to abide forever in the Banner of the Nine Yak Tails—the banner of the Mongol tribe—so that it might, there, continue to lead his army to victory. For, kindled by the consciousness of the sombre beauty of his great life, the will to conquer had survived the conqueror. And his sons would continue and extend his work: strengthen the hold of the ever wealthier and more powerful Golden Family upon Asia and—they hoped—upon the world.

---

[33] Lamb, p. 77.

Chapter 7

FROM THE DANUBE TO THE YELLOW SEA

The impulse which Genghis Khan had given the Mongols did not abate with his death. On the contrary: conquest went on with amazing rapidity and thoroughness—and skill—under his immediate successors, as though the god-like warrior's *süldé* had indeed taken abode in the Mongol banner.

As we have said, Genghis Khan died in August 1227. Soon afterwards, the last resistance of the Kin (whose Emperor had gone south) was broken, Nan-king stormed, and the whole of China down to the River Yang-Tse definitively brought to submission. This was mainly the work of Subodai, the veteran general who had served Genghis Khan all his life. But Ogodai—now Khakhan—and his brother Tuli (who died on his way back to Karakorum) had led separate armies operating together with his, all through the early part of the campaign. Then, but a few years later—in the summer of 1236—the Mongol *tumans*, rested and equipped anew (provided with "a corps of Chinese engineers under the command of a *k'ung pao*, a master of artillery"[1]), were again marching west, covering the 60 degrees of longitude that separated them from the limit of the already conquered lands, in order to conquer more. Batu, son of Juchi, of whom the rich grasslands of Russia were to be the heritage; Mangu, son of Tuli; the promising young war-lord Kaidu, son of Kuyuk son of Ogodai, and Subodai, led the irresistible forces. The same unbelievably patient and cautious preparations as in the days of the dead conqueror, followed by the same swift action at the decisive moment, characterised this new great campaign—the second one without the material presence of Genghis Khan. (They were to characterise all the following Mongol campaigns, for another 30 years.)

The results are known. They are: the total collapse of all Russian resistance and the conquest of half of Europe by Genghis

---

[1] Lamb, *The March of the Barbarians*, p. 121.

Khan's countrymen. "In the month of February" (1237), writes the historian, "twelve walled cities were obliterated. In the short space between December and the end of March, the free peoples of central Russia vanished. And the sturdy and turbulent independence of the Variag-governed Slavs ceased to be."[2] The half-Byzantine city of Kiev, which the Mongols named "the Court of the Golden Heads" on account of the resplendent domes of its many churches, was stormed on the 6th December 1240 and completely destroyed. And the Western march culminated in the famous battle of Liegnitz (at which, on the 9th April, 1241, Kaidu crushed the coalesced armies of Henry the Pious, Duke of Silesia, and of the Margrave of Moravia, before King Wenceslas of Bohemia had had time to join them) and, nearly at the same time, in the defeat of King Béla on the banks of the River Sayo, and in the conquest of Hungary by Subodai and Batu, soon followed by a further advance of the Mongol hosts, who crossed the frozen Danube on Christmas Day and who, "with Gran smoking behind them, circled Vienna and pushed on as far as Neustadt."[3] The arrival at the Mongol camp, in February 1242, of a courier from far-away Karakorum, with news of the Khakhan's death and the order to march back to the *kuriltai* to be held in the homeland, put an end to the conquest of Europe. But Russia was to remain under Mongol yoke for over 300 years.

But that was not all. A little later—in 1253, when Mangu, son of Tuli, had succeeded short-lived Kuyuk, son of Ogodai, as Khakhan—Kubilai, Tuli's second son, "was ordered to march against the Sung Empire in southern China, that had never been invaded by Barbarians"[3] while, at the other end of Asia, Hulagu, another of Mangu's brothers, started the campaign that was to make him the master of eastern Asia Minor, Syria, and Iraq, extending the limits of the domination of the Golden Family to the shores of the Mediterranean and to the Arabian sands.

In 1258, Mostasem, last Caliph of Baghdad, was captured in his city. Hulagu had him wrapped in felt and trampled under the hoofs of the Mongol horses, so that his blood—royal blood—might not be shed. Baghdad was put to sack and ruined. And although, about to march into Egypt, the grandson of Genghis

---

[2] Lamb, p. 130.
[3] Lamb, p. 208.

Khan turned from his conquest at the news of Mangu's death, to take part in the meeting of the Mongol princes in their distant homeland — as Subodai and Kaidu had turned from the conquest of Western Europe 17 years before — and although none of his descendants were ever to resume the onslaught against the civilised lands of the South, still, his son, Abaka, and, after him, five other princes of his blood, known in history as the "Il-Khans of Persia," ruled in succession over the greater part of the lands he had conquered. The dynasty lasted till 1335.

Meanwhile, in the Far East, Kubilai, now Khakhan after Mangu, and the master of the whole of China and of Yu-nan after years of war, received the formal submission of the lords of Tong-King and sent his fleets "to raid the Malayan coasts, and officers in disguise to explore the distant island of Sumatra."[4] And his descendants, known in the Chinese annals as "the Yuan Dynasty," held their domination until the priest Chu, known as Tai-Tsong, overthrew Shun-Ti, the last of them, in 1368, becoming himself the founder of the Ming Dynasty.

In the steppes of High Asia, "from the forested Altai to the heights of Afghanistan"[5] — between the Chinese world, domain of Kubilai and of his sons, to the East, and the domain of the Il-Khans, sons of Hulagu, and that of the Khans of the Golden Horde, sons of Batu or sons of his brother Birkai, to the West — ruled Kaidu, son of Kuyuk son of Ogodai; Kaidu, the victor of Liegnitz. "He had knit together the lands of the house of Ogodai — his own — and of the house of Chagatai."[6] With his warrior-like daughter Ai-Yuruk — one of the most fascinating feminine historic figures of all times — constantly at his side, he lived and fought in the old Mongol fashion, contemptuous of his uncles' increasing luxuries, and made frequent inroads into the lands of Kubilai Khan, to whom he never submitted. Of all Genghis Khan's grandsons and great-grandsons, he was, perhaps, the one who resembled the great ancestor the most. Yet, in glaring contrast to him, "the one thing Kaidu lacked was patience."[7] And that was enough to keep him in the background of history

---

[4] Lamb, p. 275.
[5] Lamb, p. 243.
[6] Lamb, p. 274.
[7] Lamb, p. 126.

forever, after the brilliant part he played under Subodai's guidance, during the European campaign. One cannot help wondering what a different course events in Asia *might have taken*, had the gifted prince been also endowed with that mastery in the art of waiting, which is the quality of the strong, *par excellence*.

However, the fact remains that the map of the lands conquered by Genghis Khan *and* by his immediate successors under the impulse his genius had given them, is singularly impressive. *Never* had there existed on earth such a great empire. Its territory stretched, in latitude, from the frozen "tundras" of Northern Siberia to the Persian Gulf, the Himalayas, and the jungles of Burma and Tong-King, and, in longitude, from the Danube and the Eastern Mediterranean to the Pacific Ocean. And the varied peoples thus assembled under the yoke of one family comprised more than half the total number of human beings.

And that was not all. More impressive even than the extent of the Mongol Empire was its extraordinary organisation, and the peace and security that followed, wherever Mongol domination was firmly established. "The Mongols proved in practice that they were as splendid organisers as they were soldiers,"[8] writes one of Genghis Khan's modern biographers, summing up the staggering impression of efficiency in peace as well as in war that 13th-century European observers—both monks and traders—gathered from a close contact with the Empire of the steppes.

The most obvious mark of that amazing genius for organisation was, perhaps, the perfect safety in which travellers and merchants, and preachers of every faith, could move from relay to relay along the great post roads that ran in every direction, from one end of the Empire to the other. In Genghis Khan's own days, or under his immediate successors Ogodai and Kuyuk, it is said that a 15-year-old virgin, covered with jewels, could have walked through Asia unmolested, so high was the standard of honesty and so strict the discipline imposed upon every human being by the conqueror's iron code of laws: the Yasa. And over 100 years later, at the time the Florentine trader Francesco Balducci Pegolotti went along it as a representative of the important

---

[8] Fox, *Genghis Khan*, p. 254.

commercial firm of the Bardi, the land route to Cathay, which started from Tana on the Sea of Azov, was still "the safest in the world,"[9] thanks to the fact that the conqueror's policy had been, to a great extent, carried on by his descendants. A merchant needed no escort whatsoever. In spite of many changes in the political structure of the Empire, Genghis Khan's Yasa still preserved the "Mongolian peace" within all lands from Poland to the Pacific Ocean, at least as far as harmless travellers were concerned.

"Dictated by Genghis Khan from time to time and traced upon leaves of gold by his secretaries,"[10] the Yasa was a strange code of laws. Age-old tribal regulations designed to enforce a certain amount of cleanliness among the Mongols, or illustrating the nomads' particular conception of the spirit-world and their idea of its interference in human affairs, were to be found in it, side by side with dictates of a far broader scope—dictates revealing the conqueror's will to make his conquest everlasting and his actual capacity of doing so *if only* . . . his successors would faithfully abide by his commands. It was, for instance, among many other things, forbidden to urinate upon the ashes of a fire, or to pollute running water even by making ablutions or washing clothes in it, for that water was to be drunk (and in Central Asia streams are rare). It was also forbidden "to walk in running water during the spring and summer" or "to walk over a fire" so as "not to trouble the tutelary spirits of fire and water."[11] But at the same time, all Genghis Khan's subjects were ordered "to respect all religious faiths without being bound by any one faith"[12] and not to quarrel with one another on any account. The Yasa, in fact, imposed the death penalty "for any evidence of quarrelling—even for spying upon another man, or taking sides with one of two who were disputing together";[13] and religious toleration was enforced only in order to avoid further occasions of dispute and further germs of division among the millions of people that the conqueror wished to unite. Likewise, fornication,

---

[9] Fox, p. 187.
[10] Lamb, p. 95.
[11] Lamb, p. 96.
[12] Lamb, p. 96.
[13] Lamb, p. 96.

sodomy, magic, and deliberate lying—all sins that could give rise to personal jealousies and sow seeds of dissension among people, and that could not but enervate them both physically and morally; or sins that might forward possibilities of rebellion—were punished by death; so was, also, and above all, "disobedience to an order" and "any attempt of a lesser man to use the authority that belonged to the Khakhan alone."[14] The only loyalty which both Mongols and subject people were to share was loyalty to the Khakhan "Emperor of all men"; their one religion above all religions was to be the strong sense of duty that bound them to him through the representatives of his authority at all levels of that military hierarchy upon which rested, throughout the conquered world, what we have called "the Mongol peace."

In other words, the Yasa was, first and foremost, a military code designed to stabilise for all times to come the result of Genghis Khan's conquests—and of the conquests of his successors—a legal system that would "hold his Mongols together as a clan through all changes in fortune,"[15] and also hold down the subject people under them, permanently. And it is only to be expected that it went into many details with regard to the equipment and discipline of the army in war time,[16] while it imposed upon all Mongols a truly military-like comradeship and equality in peace time as well. (No Mongol was "to eat in the presence of another without sharing his food with him," and "no one was to satisfy his hunger more than another."[17]) But it was also, as Harold Lamb has written, "a one-man's family code,"[18] for in Genghis Khan's eyes Mongol domination meant nothing else but the domination of the "Golden Family"—of *his* family—endlessly prolonging his own absolute rule. He had struggled all his life in order to assure riches and power—unshakable security—for his sons and grandsons. He devised the Yasa and made it the one law binding together 50 conquered kingdoms, *not* in view of the happy evolution of these kingdoms under the best possible con-

---

[14] Lamb, p. 96.
[15] Lamb, p. 95.
[16] Lamb, pp. 114–15.
[17] Lamb, p. 95.
[18] Lamb, p. 97.

ditions, but in view of their most intelligent, most efficient, and lasting exploitation for the profit of the children of his own blood — the only men who were allowed to touch the sheets of gold upon which the new Law was written. And he had in fact said: "If the descendants born after me keep to the Yasa, and do not change it, for a thousand and ten thousand years the Everlasting Sky will aid and preserve them."[19]

One of the most striking practical results of his legislation was that, during his lifetime — and for quite a long time afterwards — he actually managed to eradicate crime among the Mongols and to make the various countries which the latter had conquered the best organised in the world. No doubt, the Yasa "worked hardship enough on subject peoples and those enslaved by the wars";[20] yet those peoples, accustomed to the misrule of decaying dynasties or to the whimsical tyranny of petty chieftains, were benefited by it to the extent that order, however harsh it be, is always better than disorder.

But the self-centred family spirit in which the iron code of laws was conceived was the very reason why it could not keep the Empire together forever. Nothing short of the impersonal cult of truth — of absolute devotion to a state of things built upon objective truth — can keep even a few thousand people together *forever*. It is (when one comes to think of it) amazing that the Yasa remained "a sort of religion"[21] to the Mongols themselves for so long after the death of the great conqueror.

卐 卐 卐

The respect in which the legislation was held was due to the personal devotion that every Mongol felt for Genghis Khan, rather than to ideological reasons. Genghis Khan's word was obeyed blindly, unconditionally, even years after his death, just because it was *his* word — the word of a victorious Leader in whom every Mongol revered the one appointed by the Everlasting Blue Sky to rule the earth. For two generations, nobody — save, perhaps, Juchi, and his son Batu — dreamed of disobeying its dictates. It stated, for instance, that, at the death of a Khakhan,

---

[19] Lamb, p. 95.
[20] Lamb, p. 97.
[21] Lamb, p. 97.

the princes of the Golden Family and the chieftains of the army should gather, from wherever they might happen to be, in the Mongolian homeland, for the election of a new Khakhan. So when, in February 1242, the news of Ogodai's death was brought to Subodai's headquarters on the Danube, the veteran general and the Mongolian army just about to move further west and to conquer the whole of Europe (where nothing could have stopped them) turned back, and started the long, long journey to Karakorum as a matter of course. To Subodai—and to every one of the chiefs, save Batu—to disregard the summons to the appointed *kuriltai* was "unthinkable."[22] And as the conqueror had expressly designed his second (or third) son, Ogodai, to be Khakhan after him, the Mongol chiefs had sworn at their first *kuriltai* never to elect a Khakhan who were not a member of the house of Ogodai; and at the second gathering of the blood-kin, after Ogodai's death, they elected Kuyuk, Ogodai's son. But although nobody—not even Batu—dreamed of questioning the authority of the Yasa openly, those of its dictates that stood in the way of more than one ambitious member of the Golden Family were simply ignored (if not deliberately brushed aside) after Kuyuk had died, and more and more so, as time went on.

Mangu's election to the supreme dignity of Khakhan, away from the Mongol homeland, in Batu's camp at the mouth of the River Imil, at a *kuriltai* at which not one of the princes of the house of Ogodai was present, was illegal from the standpoint of the Yasa. And even more so (if that be possible) was, after Mangu's death, the election of his brother Kubilai, in the Chinese town of Shang-tu, at an assembly attended only by the officers of the Left Wing of the army—of *his* army—and by Chinese officials. These elections, the result of both of which was a further blow to the unity of the Mongol Empire, in defiance of Genghis Khan's life-long aim and dearest dreams, were possible only because the members of the Golden Family that were thus favoured loved themselves and their own sons more than the memory of the great Ancestor to whose conquests they owed their place in the world; more than the Golden Family at large, whose domination *he* had struggled to secure at all costs. In other words, Mangu and Kubilai (and, still more than they, their

---

[22] Lamb, p. 161.

ambitious and patient mother, Siyurkuktiti, whose clever intrigues are at the bottom of the rise of the house of Tuli to supreme power) had Genghis Khan's own attitude to life: nothing guided them in their decisions but the lust of plenty and power — of security forever — for the sons and grandsons of their own loins.

No doubt, they were both remarkable men, and they achieved great things in war as well as in the administration of the conquered lands. They both extended the limits of the already immense Mongol Empire. Yet, by accepting the Khakhan's throne from an illegally assembled *kuriltai* (as Mangu did) or by actually grabbing it through a sort of *coup d'état* (as Kubilai did, when he gathered his followers in Shang-tu) they both rose against the order established by Genghis Khan and prepared the collapse of his life's work; they wrought the disintegration of what *he* had welded together and had intended to keep together. The Conqueror had indeed told his sons and their sons: "While you are together and of one mind, you will endure. If you are separated, you will be broken."[23] Mangu and Kubilai separated themselves from the rest of the Golden Family, in particular from the sons and grandsons of Ogodai, legitimate heirs to the domination of the steppes by Genghis Khan's own choice — and that, nay, while there *was*, among others, in the person of Kaidu son of Kuyuk, the victor of Liegnitz and the hero of Hungary, a brilliant representative of the privileged House to which the Mongol chieftains had pledged their faith at the first *kuriltai* held after Genghis Khan's death.

Batu, of course, already years before, had not cared to go back to the Mongol homeland to attend the assembly that had raised Kuyuk to the throne. As it is, however, not sure whether his father, Juchi, was Genghis Khan's own son or not, his attitude may seem more natural than that of his cousins. But from the standpoint of the Yasa, it was no less censurable. Genghis Khan himself had given his sons the order to march against Juchi when the latter had failed to obey his summons to a gathering of the Mongol chiefs. For the Yasa was binding on all Mongols — no less than on the subject peoples that were barred from the Mongol privileges.

---

[23] Lamb, p. 82.

⚛ ⚛ ⚛

Batu's refusal to march back to Karakorum in order to sit there as lord of the West, among the other Mongol princes, his kinsmen, lords of various conquered lands, at the *kuriltai,* that was to appoint Kuyuk Khakhan, "Lord of the world"; and, a few years later, the election of Mangu by an assembly illegally held in Batu's camp by the Lake of the Eagles; and, after that, the election of Kubilai, also away from the Mongol homeland and against the will of more than half the Golden Family, were, as I said, acts of disobedience to Genghis Khan's order to his descendants to "remain together." A subtler, yet no less flagrant defiance of the conqueror's will is to be noted in the gradual conversion of all but a few princes of the Golden Family to various foreign religions and cultures—in their absorption into the civilisations of the subject nations.

Significantly enough, it is among those descendants of Genghis Khan who played in history the greatest part—the princes of the house of Juchi, rulers of Russia, and the princes of the house of Tuli, Emperors of China and Il-Khans of Persia—that Mongol followers of the ways of the conquered peoples are to be found. Birkai, son of Juchi, "the first of the line of Genghis Khan to yield himself to a religion,"[24] embraced Islam and, what is more, championed the cause of Islam in war against his cousin Hulagu. And Sartak, Batu's eldest son, is said to have embraced Christianity—although one has to admit that, in his life among many wives, amidst surroundings that appeared to the Belgian Friar William of Ruysbroek as those "of another age,"[25] he hardly seems to have taken the Christian standards of behaviour into account. At the other end of the earth, Kubilai, son of Tuli, who, in his youth, had learnt the pictographic script of Cathay along with elements of Chinese wisdom under Yao Chow, was more of a Chinese potentate than of a Mongol Khakhan. Before he conquered the south of China, he had himself, says the historian, "been conquered by the Chinese," and "he may not have realised, or he may not have cared, that, in uniting China, he had brought the Empire of the steppes to an end."[26] But the Chinese

---

[24] Lamb, p. 194.
[25] Lamb, p. 195.
[26] Lamb, p. 279.

can only have "conquered him" because the appeal which their luxuries and their wisdom had for him were stronger than his attachment to Genghis Khan's great dream. With Timur, Kubilai's grandson and successor, who had "lost the energy and simplicity of the barbarians,"[27] the old idea of military rule and of the Mongols' aloofness from the conquered peoples was completely forgotten. The Buddhists were given new privileges.[28] The Yuan Dynasty had already become a Chinese dynasty after many others.

And in Persia, where Hulagu himself had followed Genghis Khan's Mongol policy detached from all religion, and where Abaka, his son and successor, kept an empty throne beside him, raised higher than his own, as a symbol of his submission to the distant Khakhan in the East (who then happened to be Kubulai) Islam and Persian culture prevailed in the end among Genghis Khan's descendants. At Abaka's death in 1282, another of Hulagu's sons became a convert to the faith of the Prophet and held the throne for two years under the name of Ahmed, until he met his fate in a popular rising. Arghun, son of Abaka, who then rose to power, was not a Mohammadan. But his successor, Ghazan, became one. And the following Il-Khans of Persia, easygoing patrons of art—with less and less of Genghis Khan's blood in their veins—were definitively conquered to the religion and life of the land, over which they ruled with the help of Mohammedan viziers and where "all trace of Hulagu" —and of Genghis Khan— "had been lost."[29]

Alone the princes of the house of Chagatai and those of the dispossessed house of Ogodai (to whom Genghis Khan had wished to give pre-eminence over the others) remained unaffected by the lure of foreign vanities and foreign subtleties of thought, faithful to the old Mongol way of life. And they found in Kaidu son of Kuyuk son of Ogodai son of Genghis Khan a chieftain worthy of them, "a hard soul, indifferent to religion, determined to lead the steppe dwellers to war"[30]—a man who despised the refinements of decadence which others called civi-

---

[27] Lamb, p. 281.
[28] Lamb, p. 281.
[29] Lamb, p. 287.
[30] Lamb, pp. 242–43.

lisation. And Kaidu, to whom the elder Mongols had given the title of Khakhan[31] and who was the master of High Asia from Afghanistan to the Altai ranges, fought all his life against his uncle Kubilai who had turned from both the letter and the spirit of the Yasa to become the founder of the Yuan Dynasty of Cathay.

But it is difficult to say how far Kaidu was (any more than Genghis Khan himself) a disinterested idealist. He doubtless deplored the gradual absorption of the conquerors by the conquered people, the submission of Mongols to strange religions, contrarily to the great Ancestor's command the prevalence of a different strange etiquette at each of the different new Mongol courts. He doubtless deplored the fact that "the Mongol empire was dismembering swiftly into its four quarters," that "the homelands had ceased to have any significance,"[32] and that it was probably already too late to try to put things right again in accordance with Genghis Khan's dream. Yet, at least from the little we know of his ardent life, all his bravery and skill—just like his great-grandsire's, and that of the other Mongol princes— were put to the service of one purpose: *his own* survival and power and that of his family in the narrow sense of the word. He certainly should have been proclaimed Khakhan in the place of Mangu, at Kuyuk's death. And Mangu—and Kubilai—should have acted as his lieutenants, stabilising and extending the Mongol conquests for him and with him, with selfless zeal, so as to make Genghis Khan's work everlasting. If they did not do so, it is because they loved themselves and *their own* families—the children of their own bodies—more than any great imperial dream that could no longer be directly and personally connected with them; because they failed to feel for their nephew of genius, of the privileged house of Ogodai, that sort of loyalty which a knight feels for his king. But nothing we know of Kaidu's history goes to prove that he was, in any way, different from them in his purpose, however much he might have been in his tastes; nothing suggests that he was, any less that they or than Genghis Khan himself, what I have called in the beginning of this book a "man 'in Time'."

---

[31] Lamb, p. 273.
[32] Lamb, p. 244.

卍 卍 卍

The actually disinterested characters, more than any others the makers of Mongol greatness in the 13th century, are to be sought among Genghis Khan's devoted followers rather than among his own grandsons and great-grandsons. Towering above them all stands one of the finest war-lords — and also one of the finest men — of all times: Subodai.

The very embodiment of the highest and purest warrior-like virtues, he had, from the early days of Genghis Khan's struggle for power — for 50 years, all his life — fought with irresistible efficiency, with vision, with genius, *not* for any profit or glory of his own but solely for the greatness and glory of the Leader whom he loved and revered. He had served him brilliantly in his westward lightning march and scaled the Caucasus and raided the Russian plains at his command. And, after his death, he had conquered China down to Nanking for his successors, in a campaign that was a masterpiece of warfare, directing sieges with unfailing skill, and, just as in the West, ordering mass-massacres without a trace of either glee or horror — with perfect detachment — whenever he considered it a military necessity and had received no orders not to do so. He had conquered Russia, Poland, Hungary — half of Europe — for Ogodai, Genghis Khan's son, and turned his back on his conquests as a matter of course, without resentment, without regret, when, at Ogodai's death, he had received the summons to attend the customary assembly of chiefs in far-away Karakorum. And then, when Kuyuk son of Ogodai was preparing to march against Bata, who had defied his authority; when, for the first time, Mongols were to fight Mongols, he retired from active life, with the permission of the Khakhan. He retired "to his yurt in the steppes by the River Tula." And "there he put away the insignia of his rank and took to sitting on the sunny side of his yurt, watching his herds go out to grazing."[33]

"A soldier without a weakness"[34] in the words of John of Carpini, the first European to visit the Mongol realm of his own accord; "implacable as death itself,"[35] in the words of the mod-

---

[33] Lamb, p. 178.
[34] Lamb, p. 178.
[35] Lamb, p. 111.

ern historian Harold Lamb, he had but one love: Genghis Khan, his Leader; and he knew but one law: the Yasa, expression of Genghis Khan's will, and one morality: absolute obedience to that will. And when facts told him that that will no longer ruled the new world which he had helped to build, he retired from the world—back to his flocks, back to obscurity; back to the nothingness out of which Mongol grandeur had sprang through Genghis Khan, and into which it was, one day, to sink, once more, now that the conqueror's command to "remain together" no longer bound the Golden Family. Absolute devotion can only exteriorise itself in absolute obedience or—when obedience has lost all meaning; when the Leader's will, which is the sole measure of right and wrong, is defeated on the material plane—in silence.

It is the presence of such characters as Subodai—of men unconditionally devoted to Genghis Khan (or to his memory) without a trace of selfishness—at all levels of the Mongol military hierarchy, that enabled the conqueror's work to last as long as it did. Had Genghis Khan's own grandsons and great-grandsons all had that spirit, and had they "remained together," contemptuously aloof from the beliefs and controversies and interests of the vanquished—faithful to the Yasa alone, or at least to the purpose of the Yasa—the stupendous Empire of the steppes might have endured for centuries. As things stood, it is, as I have said before, a wonder that it endured as long as it did.

For it was the monument of one extraordinary man's successful ambition, not a historical structure based upon truth, not a step towards a new world-order conceived on the model of the eternal Order of Life. And the Yasa, on the obedience to which its strength rested, was "a one man's family code"[36] not the charter of a new faith nearer to truth than the then-existing ones. It had been devised to keep the conquered world enslaved to the descendants of one man, because that man had fought and conquered for himself and for them, *not* because they had been given by Nature any special right to rule forever, *not* because they represented in any way a permanently superior type of humanity.

One cannot but understand—and admire—Subodai's devo-

---

[36] Lamb, p. 97.

tion to his Leader. It was a glaring homage to the greatness of personality, that essence of leadership; a recognition of the unquestionable rights that personality enjoys, according to the laws of life. In devoting his genius to the strong man whom the Everlasting Blue Sky had appointed to rule the earth, Subodai was, in all humility and wisdom, faithful to those eternal Laws. And so were all those who, like him, followed Genghis Khan without even thinking of what advantages and glory they would thereby win for themselves.

But one has to admit that, beautiful as it certainly is in itself, such devotion is not enough to build up either a lasting empire or a lasting civilisation. That alone which is rooted in truth is lasting. And for absolute devotion to a Leader to have its full creative—and lasting—potency (which is, *sooner or later*, bound to mould the course of history according to the Leader's dreams) the Leader himself should be more than an ambitious self-centred man in quest of security and power for his own family; more than a man "in Time," however great. He should be worthy of absolute devotion, worthy of life-long day-to-day unconditional sacrifice, not merely in the eyes of his enthusiastic followers, who might idealise him, but from the impersonal standpoint of what is called in the Bhagavad-Gita "the welfare of the Universe"—from the point of view of the purpose of Life. In other words, he should himself be a selfless soul; a man striving with detachment to "live in Truth" and calling others to do likewise—whether "above Time," like King Akhnaton or the Buddha, or "against Time," like Lord Krishna, the political *Karma Yogi*, in most ancient India; like the Prophet Mohammed or, in our times, the inspired Builder of the only order of truth in the world after many centuries: Adolf Hitler. In all other cases his work, however staggering it be, will perish with him or soon after him. Loyalty to him will die out, as it did in the instance of Genghis Khan, soon after the few of his contemporaries who followed him with disinterested love have all died—or it will become as good as dead: an accepted tradition of reverence, perpetuating the leader's memory, but incapable of holding down the passions that stand in the way of complete obedience to his will. Loyalty to a man always dies out, sooner or later, when it is not at the same time loyalty to a system, to a faith, to a scale of values—to something *more than a man*, which alone that type of leader who is himself a disinterested idealist can represent; when it is not loyalty to impersonal truth.

As I said, there was no Ideology behind Genghis Khan's will to power, no conscious purpose other than the survival and welfare of himself and of his family. And therefore the Yasa represented no scale of values. Admittedly, it gave the Mongols special rights and forced upon them special duties, before all, the duty of remaining together, faithful to the Golden Family and aloof from the civilisations that they had set out to crush. But it laid down no rule of conduct that aimed at keeping them *in fact*—physically—different from the conquered nations. It forbade them to quarrel among themselves; it forbade them to yield themselves to strange religions; but it omitted to forbid them to mingle their blood in marriage with that of the conquered Chinese, Persians, Russians, Magyars; to become, themselves, a new people. Genghis Khan, says Harold Lamb, had not allowed for "the effect of education on a simple people. He had thought, it appears, that they would learn and still remain nomads."[37] We believe that they *could have* "learnt" and still have remained, if not "nomads," at least Mongols united in the pride of their common strength around a united Golden Family, had they not taken to wife women of all nations. One of the main reasons why the Golden Family itself was gradually absorbed into the civilisations of the conquered (with the exception of the houses of Chagatai and Ogodai, that remained in the steppes, isolated from the outer world) was that, from the start—in the very Yasa—no stress was ever laid upon the necessity of avoiding mixtures of blood. And the main reason why Genghis Khan had never mentioned—let alone stressed—such a necessity, is to be sought in the fact that all he wanted after his own survival and domination was the domination *of his own family*, solely because it was *his own*—not because it was the most able to lead the Mongols to endless conquests, nor because the Mongols, as a people, had, even in his eyes, any greater *inherent* value than other nations, and any natural right to rule the world (which indeed they had not). To him, in fact, it mattered little how far his descendants would or not remain full-fledged Mongols, provided that they were his descendants; provided that *he* would live

---

[37] Lamb, p. 97.

in them, anyhow. (But would he—*could* he—continue living in them, after they no longer would be, physically, full-fledged Mongols? We believe he could not. He apparently believed he could and would or, more probably, did not even ask[38] himself the question.) He thought his iron code of laws was sufficient to keep the Mongols and the conquered outer world in obedience to his descendants forever, if *they*—the latter—"remained together." He did not realise what factors would unavoidably lead them to fall apart.

Curiously enough, it is precisely because his descendants had exactly the same outlook as he himself—because they too sought their own immediate welfare, their own power, and the future of their own sons, in other words, *themselves*, and *not* the triumph of any impersonal Ideology, in all their achievements; because they had no Ideology (any more than he had had)—that they started to disobey him: to quarrel among themselves, to build up separate kingdoms, to champion their newly acquired foreign faiths against one another, to turn their backs to the Yasa.

They had not for Genghis Khan, whom many of them had never known personally, the selfless devotion that Subodai had. And the conqueror had given them nothing to which they could, throughout centuries, pin their faith and give their love; nothing for which they could fight unceasingly, regardless of personal advantages and even of glory, as Subodai and so many others had fought for *him*. On the contrary, he had left them the memory of a man who had struggled all his life for himself alone and whose patient, cunning, thorough, ruthless service of himself had led to the mastery of more than half of Asia. They followed his example (not Subodai's), every one of them for his own account. They followed it without his genius, and without that spirit of binding solidarity that he had tried so hard to give them but failed to put into their hearts in the sole name of their common descent from him—without that spirit of solidarity which it is not possible to infuse into any human collectivity for long, save in the name of some higher truth, rooted in the lives of the people but exceeding them by far; in the name of some higher purpose, sustained in the consciousness of absolute, eternal Truth. And after the third or fourth generation, they fol-

---

[38] Replacing "put" —Ed.

lowed it without even being, most of them, as pure Mongols as before.

The result was the splitting up of the Mongol Empire and the acceleration of the material and moral decay of Asia as a whole, and — after the empire had altogether ceased to exist, after the sons of Kaidu had sunk back into obscurity, and after the Mongol dynasties directly sprung from Genghis Khan had been overthrown in Persia, China, and finally Russia — the tragic absence of any great force capable of helping Asia to rise from the ruins of the worn-out kingdoms that the Mongol horsemen had smashed or from the increasing apathy of the others (such as the Indian ones). Tamerlane and, a century later, Baber, warriors of Genghis Khan's race and, like him, men essentially "in Time" — centred around themselves — were not able to arrest the decay, even though the latter built up in India an empire that endured over 250 years; on the contrary, they rather hastened it, in the long run. And if the *selfless* warrior-like spirit, the true immemorial Aryan spirit expressed in the Bhagavad-Gita, never died in India, where it was in constant clash with foreign ideas, it was not alive enough to raise out of India such a Kshatriya as could play, on the political plane, a part of lasting international importance.

"The sword of Genghis Khan wrought a great revolution, but it was Asia in the end which lost by it, Europe, which gained,"[39] writes Ralph Fox, meaning thereby that the failure of Genghis Khan's descendants to create and to organise a new Asia on the basis of his Yasa resulted in the whole continent soon becoming the competition ground — and the prey — of merchants from Europe, whether Italian, Portuguese, Dutch, French, or British; that it contributed more than one is generally inclined to believe to the growth of the new, cynically money-worshipping world which was to replace mediaeval Christendom in the West and to subdue the whole earthly sphere (save an irreducible minority of genuine idealists) to the tyranny of its false values; of the ugly world dominated to this day by international Finance.

It is a noteworthy (and, in our eyes, *not* an accidental fact) that the only country in Asia that escaped both slavery to the great European trade companies in the 17th and 18th centuries

---

[39] Fox, p. 257.

and the infection of modern democracy in the 20th, while on the other hand it also resisted the influence of the Christian missionaries (and even openly fought it, for a long time at least) is Japan—the one country to have victoriously defied the might of Kubilai Khan with the help of the "divine Wind of Ise."[40] And it is hardly possible not to oppose the self-centred attitude of Genghis Khan's descendants no less than his own, to that disinterested, active, devotional nationalism of the Japanese, expressed to this day in the highest form of Shintoism: in the Emperor cult and the cult of the Race, both merged into the cult of the Sun, the cult of Life; to that spirit that was, one day, to give birth to Tōyama and to make Tōjō and the Japanese warlords and soldiers and people of 1941 the allies of the great European Man "against Time," champion *par excellence* of the rights of Life in the modern phase of Life's age-old struggle against the Dark Forces of disintegration and death.

Written in Lyons (France) in 1951 and 1952

---

[40] On the 14th of August, 1281.

Part III

THE SUN: AKHNATON

4. Head of King Akhnaton

(formerly in the Berlin Museum, now in Wiesbaden)

Chapter 8

"THE BEAUTIFUL CHILD OF THE LIVING ATON"

Two hundred years of victorious war had put Egypt at the head of nations in what was, then—some 1,420 years before the Christian Era—the "known world." Loaded with the spoils both of Semites and Nubians and Negroes, her young King, Menkheperura—Thutmose the Fourth—ruled in splendour from the waters of the Upper Euphrates to the Fifth and even to the Sixth Cataract of the Nile. And Thebes, his capital, was the most gorgeous city the world had yet seen, and the Great God, Amon—the old tribal god of Thebes, raised to the rank of the supreme state-god—the most honoured and the most feared of all gods, and his priests, the richest and the most powerful men in the land—hardly less powerful than the king himself, who was looked upon as the son of Amon and said to hold his absolute authority directly from him.

The sea-lords of Crete and of the Aegean Isles were doubtless great potentates. And so was the king of the Hittites, who ruled over a sturdy and stubborn people in far-away Hattusa, near modern Ankara. And so was the king of Babylon. (India and China were too remote to speak of.) But none could be compared with Pharaoh. And that world above which Egypt towered, like the Theban god Amon above the other many gods of the Nile Valley and of the Empire, was already thousands of years old. And within its diversity it possessed certain traits of culture which were common to all or nearly all its people, from the easy-going, art-loving Cretans to the merchants, sages, and toiling masses of Dravidian India: it placed the authority of the priest (or priestess) above that of the warrior; nay, it sought in the supernatural the normal source of all authority; and it saw in the mystery of death something more important even than life itself. It was an old, old world, in which each people lived slowly and regularly according to long-established Tradition, the origin of which was lost in the past, the meaning of which was being—or had already *been*—forgotten by all save perhaps a few initiates. And of all nations, Egypt was perhaps the one that had been living for the longest time to a slow rhythm.

Now, the Gods, who govern all things from within, put a strange desire into Pharaoh's heart—an unheard-of yearning to mingle himself with that which lay beyond the limits of the self-contained world that he dominated—and he asked Artatama, king of Mitanni, for one of his daughters to wife. This was against the immemorial custom of Egypt, where kings usually married their own sisters, or at least close relations. It was also, apparently, against the custom of Mitanni for "*six times* did Thutmose the Fourth make his request in vain."[1] But it was the first and most decisive of the happenings that had to take place, in order to make possible the appearing of an extraordinary prince—the true Child of the Sun—half a century later.

For beyond the boundaries of that self-contained Near and Middle East, in which Egypt was supreme, the young, beautiful—and gifted—Aryan race, whose tremendous destiny was not yet clear, except to the Gods themselves and to its own sages, was pushing forward from the North-West to the South and to the South-East, seeking further living space among the people of the old nations. It was, in duration of years, perhaps as old as they or nearly so, perhaps actually the youngest race on earth. But it was anyhow—and was fated to remain—young in outlook. It believed in the pre-eminence of Action over Speculation. It placed the warrior and king above the priest, and the worship of Life above the thirst of the Unknown which is beyond. It was confident in its own vitality, and confident in its God-ordained mission. And it worshipped Light as the most glorious visible expression of the Energy which is Life Itself, and the Sun as the Source of Light and Life. And the kings, allies of Egypt, who now held sway over the land of Mitanni, within the great bend of the Upper Euphrates, still controlling what was, one day, to be known as Assyria,[2] belonged to that

---

[1] Sir E. A. Wallis Budge, *Tutankhamen, Amenism, Atenism, and Egyptian Monotheism* (London: Martin Hopkinson, 1923), p. 20.

[2] R. H. Hall, *Ancient History of the Near East: From the Earliest Times*

predestined race (as did, for the last 500 years, the kings of Babylon).[3]

Pharaoh's marriage to King Artatama's daughter was to bring together—for the first time to our knowledge—two worlds that had hitherto co-existed without meeting save in occasional war: the "known world" headed by Egypt, with its close and remote connections in time and space: older Egypt, up to pre-dynastic days; Minoan Crete, with its 2,000 year-old past; immemorial Sumeria, and the kindred peaceful civilisation of the Indus Valley, and the Aryan world of the time and of unsuspected past and future ages, from the Germanic tribes, with their Sun and Star worship already centuries old,[4] to rising Sanskrit India. The immediate result—to be experienced within a few decades, after a blaze of splendour—was disaster, both for Egypt and for the Kingdom of Mitanni (which a weakened Egypt could no longer protect against the growing power of its neighbours). The result for all times was, in the person of the grandson of the royal couple, a lonely, short-lived pioneer of that Golden Age (of the *next* Time-cycle) that we are still awaiting, a Child of Light living "above Time"—"in Truth, forever and ever"—Akhnaton, Founder of the famous Religion of the Disk.

Six times had Thutmose the Fourth made his request in vain. We know it from a letter addressed by Dushratta, king of Mitanni—Artatama's grandson—to Akhnaton.[5] Mitanni was a small kingdom, nothing to be compared with the mighty Egyptian Empire. But was not Aryan blood to be kept pure? Was it not more valuable even than the Theban throne and all its glory? One can indeed find no other explanation of King Artatama's repeated refusal to give his daughter in marriage to

---

to the Battle of Salamis, 9th edition (London: Methuen, 1936), p. 260.

[3] The Kings of the Kassite Dynasty.

[4] Wilhelm Teudt, *Germanische Heiligtümer*, first edition (Jena: Eugen Diederichs, 1929), pp. 38 and following.

[5] See Hugo Winckler, *Die Thontafeln von Tell-el-Amarna* (Berlin: Reuther and Reichard, 1896), no. 24, p. 51. The letter is—or *was*, till 1945—preserved in Berlin.

the most powerful monarch of his times.

The friendship of the powerful is sweet, however — sweet ... and useful. And, harder than the desire to please Pharaoh — or the awareness that it was good policy to please him — a Destiny was steadily pressing Artatama to accept, to submit, in the interest he knew not of *what*. And "after the seventh asking, the king of Mitanni gave his daughter to the king of Egypt."[6] The new Queen forsook her Aryan name and adopted an Egyptian one, more in keeping with her new position — Mutemwiya, or "Mut in the sacred bark"[7] — and is styled upon the monuments as "hereditary princess, Great Lady, presiding over the South and over the North."[8] Of her personality and actual influence nothing is known. It can only be surmised that she would, in her new home, feel herself drawn to the old Sun-gods of Anu, or On, which the Greeks were one day to call Heliopolis — to Ra-Horakhti of the Two Horizons; to Atem or Aton, the fiery Disk — more akin than Amon to her native Aryan gods Mithra and Surya, rather than to the exalted tribal god of Thebes. Her real, undeniable contribution to the further history of Egypt (and of religious thought) lies however in the fact that she gave birth to King Amenhotep the Third — Amenhotep the Magnificent — who, whatever may have been his interest or lack of interest in philosophical matters, was *himself* half-Aryan.

Amenhotep the Third married one of the most remarkable feminine characters of Antiquity, Tiy, daughter of Yuaa and of Tuau, or Tuaa.

Yuaa, although he was a priest of the age-old Egyptian fertility god, Min, was a foreigner "from North Syria" or, to be more precise, from Mitanni,[9] Queen Mutemwiya's land, the ruling aristocracy of which was, like the king, Aryan, whatever mixture of Semitic and Hittite blood the bulk of its population may have been. Sir Flinders Petrie holds him to have been one

---

[6] Budge, p. 20.

[7] Sir Flinders Petrie, *A History of Egypt*, vol. 2 (London: Methuen, 1899), p. 174.

[8] Budge, p. 20.

[9] Petrie, vol. 2, p. 183.

of those numerous allied or vassal princes that were then brought up at the Egyptian court. One does not know whether Queen Tiy's mother, Tuau or Tuaa, who, according to most scholars, was of royal descent, was a full-blooded Egyptian or partly or wholly Mitannian in spite of her Egyptian name. "In a letter sent by Dushratta, king of Mitanni, to Akhnaton, Tiy is called *"my sister,"*[10] which would indicate that she herself was, through one of her parents at least, if not through both, of royal Mitannian blood.

Much has been written[11] about the probable influence of the many Mitannians who lived at the Egyptian court — and in particular in Amenhotep the Third's "house of women" — upon the *education* of the young prince who was to ascend the throne as Amenhotep the Fourth and to become immortal under the name of Akhnaton. I have, in another book,[12] striven to show how difficult such an influence is to prove, and stressed that Akhnaton's conception of one cosmic Godhead, as opposed to the many gods of Egypt, was the outcome of his *own* direct intuition, rather than that of any external influences: ideas of genius always are. The truth is that the Religion of Aton — the Sun-disk — which Sir Flinders Petrie judged "fit for our times,"[13] is the one glaring instance of Aryan creativeness within an ancient Egyptian setting. It is so, however, not so much because its Founder was, or might well have been, *influenced* by people having an Aryan outlook (be it by his Mitannian stepmothers or by his own mother) as because *he was himself* surely half, if not more than half Aryan: a blending of the old blood of the kings of Thebes with that of the noble race from the North predestined to give the world, along with the heroic philosophy of disinterested Action, the lure of logical thinking and disinterested research — the scientific spirit.

---

[10] Hall, p. 201. Arthur Weigall, *The Life and Times of Akhnaton, Pharaoh of Egypt* (London: Thornton and Butterworth, 1923), p. 26.

[11] By Sir Wallis Budge, Arthur Weigall and others.

[12] In Savitri Devi, *A Son of God: The Life and Philosophy of Akhnaton, King of Egypt* (London: Philosophical Publishing House, 1946), pp. 25, 26, 27. Also in *Akhnaton's Eternal Message: A Scientific Religion 3,300 Years Old* (Calcutta: A. K. Mukherji, 1940), pp. 5-6.

[13] Petrie, vol. 2, p. 214.

卐 卐 卐

He was born in the lovely Charuk palace,[14] in Thebes, in or shortly after 1395 B.C.[15] — some 13,000 years after the last traces of the receding Great Ice had disappeared from Germany; 200 years *before* the Trojan War; more than 1,100 years before the Indian Emperor Asoka, like he, a Messenger of peace; 2,000 years before the Prophet of Islam, whose faith, monotheistic like his, but of a totally different character, was one day to be the faith of his kingdom; more than 2,500 years before Genghis Khan his most striking "opposite" in world history — and 3,300 years before the birth of *the* Man "against Time," Adolf Hitler, who, accepting the Law of Violence, which he ignored, was to seek to build upon its only possible basis, the reign of Truth towards which he had aspired.

---

[14] Usually called the Malkata palace — Ed.
[15] See Petrie, vol. 2, p. 205. Other scholars place his birth a few years later (See Arthur Weigall's *The Life and Times of Akhnaton*; also Sir Wallis Budge's *Tutankhamen, Amenism, Atenism, and Egyptian Monotheism*.)

Chapter 9

THE HEAT-AND-LIGHT-WITHIN-THE-DISK

The new king was about twelve years old when he came to the throne, and, for some time, he merely reigned while his mother governed. (Dushratta, King of Mitanni, writing to congratulate him on his accession, addresses himself to Queen Tiy, not to him directly, and, even in later letters of this period — which are addressed to him — asks him on several occasions to "refer to his mother" about important matters.)[1] In the sixth year of his reign, after he had decidedly taken power into his own hands, he proclaimed his faith in one God — the Sun, which he designated by the name of Aton (i.e., "the Disk," the fiery Orb) — to the exclusion of all others; built a temple to Him within the sacred enclosure of Karnak, in Thebes; gave the quarter of Thebes where the temple stood the name of "Brightness of Aton, the Great One"; and changed the name of the capital itself from that of Nut-Amon — the City of Amon — to that of "City of the Brightness of Aton." After the conflict into which he had entered with the powerful priesthood of Amon had become quite open, and bitter, he also changed his own name from Amenhotep (meaning: Amon is at peace) to Akhnaton ("Joy of the Sun") and finally forbade the cult of Amon, and of the many gods of Egypt altogether, and had their names erased from the monuments and from private inscriptions, even from those within his own father's tomb. Then, as he fully grew to realise that he would never succeed in making Thebes the centre of the new world which he was planning to build on the basis of his new (or very old) faith, he left the city and sailed down the Nile in search of a suitable spot to lay the foundations of another capital upon. The site which appealed to his

---

[1] Petrie, vol. 2, p. 211. See *The Tell-el-Amarna Letters*, ed. Hugo Winckler, trans. J. Metcalf (London: Lemcke & Buechner, 1896), Knutzon, 28.

intuition lies some 190 miles south of that of modern Cairo. King Akhnaton had boundary stones set up, with inscriptions relating the ceremonial birth of the new city, Akhetaton or "the City-of-the-Horizon-of-the-Disk," and stating its demarcation in length and breadth. And two years later—when the new capital, for the building and decoration of which the workmanship of the whole Empire and even of foreign lands had been mobilised, was practically inhabitable—he moved to it with all his court and about 80,000 followers.

And there he lived nine years—until his premature death—teaching his lofty solar religion to those whom he deemed fit to understand it, and governing his City and Egypt and the Empire according to what he felt to be its implications, but without taking at all into account either the unbending laws that rule *any* development in Time, or the hard facts that characterise *any* "Age of Gloom" such as the one to which both he and we belong. He built and adorned temples, presented offerings, composed and sang hymns to the Sun, and lived in idyllic domestic life which was, at the same time, an object of edification for his subjects. He explained or tried to explain to a narrow circle of disciples the mystery of the Rays of the fiery Disk—Heat which is Light, Light which is Heat—clear to his extraordinary intuition, but so difficult to express in words, that the thinking world was to take 3,300 years to evolve a theory to account for it. He set forth new canons in architecture, sculpture, and painting, and (although we have no *proof* of this) probably in music also—for all the arts are necessarily connected. He preached love of all living things and peace and good will among men, and neither hunted nor led an army to battle. And when there was unrest in Syria and Palestine, and when letters came to him from Egyptian governors and from vassal princes, informing him of rebellion of other vassal princes and of spreading disaffection, of inroads of wild tribes and of local movements of resistance against Egyptian rule, and begging him for help, he appears to have preferred to lose the Empire that he had inherited from his warrior-like forefathers, rather than to deny, through prompt and decisive military action, his conviction that the law of love was to rule (and, in the first place, that it *could* and *can* rule) international relations no less than private dealings

He died at the early age of 29, whether of natural death or of slow poisoning—it is impossible to tell. His new capital was systematically ruined, his life's work destroyed, the few followers who had possibly remained faithful to him relentlessly persecuted, after the ephemeral reign of his immediate successor. His memory was solemnly cursed. To the Egyptians, who had returned to their many traditional gods, he became known only as "that criminal"—for it was a punishable offence even to utter his name. And he was gradually forgotten, and remained so for over 3,000 years. It is not until *our* times that *something* of his Teaching and of the story of his life was, thanks to archaeological excavation, brought to light again, and that his greatness was recognised—although his proper significance as perhaps *the* most eloquent known instance of a man "above Time" outside the host of such ones who have renounced the world, may not necessarily have been understood by most of his modern admirers, to say nothing of his detractors.

That is the essential of what we know for certain about Akhnaton's life. It is not much. Yet, it reveals an exceptional personality, with very definite leading features which one extremely seldom finds *together*: an enormous will-power and untiring energy entirely devoted to the service of that which he experienced as Truth itself; a ruthlessly uncompromising mind and no less uncompromising feelings—the natural intolerance of absolute earnestness—and, *along with that*, such a reluctance to violence that one is forced to believe that it was the expression of a moral principle of his, no less than a deep-seated, insurmountable trait of his nature; in other words that, in his eyes, to accept slaughter, even when it could have made possible the triumph of his religion, would have been to deny the basis of the latter, and was, therefore, out of question.

Gifted with this most unusual combination of qualities, and inspired and sustained by his absolute devotion to his God—Aton—the young king declared war upon centuries of Egyptian tradition (or, to speak more accurately, upon that which Tradition had become in Egypt in the course of centuries) when he was 18. The main point—clue to the real nature of the conflict between him and the priests (and people) of his time—is: "Who was that new God (or what was that new conception of a very old God) Aton, by Whom he strove to replace the whole pantheon of the Nile Valley?"

Aton has been identified with "a tender loving Father of all creatures"[2] by some of the most enthusiastic 20th-century admirers of the so-called "heretic" Pharaoh, and repeatedly compared by them with the personal God of the Christians—the "Father who is in Heaven" of the "Lord's Prayer"—obviously with the pious purpose of pointing out, in Akhnaton's solar Faith, "a monotheistic religion second only to Christianity itself in purity of tone."[3] This view, however, seems to be more the product of Christian wishful thinking than that of a rigorous and impartial deduction. It is surely not compatible with the fact that Aton is, before all, an *immanent* God, or rather immanent Godhead Itself. And that fact is perhaps *the one* which emerges with the maximum of certainty from all the data concerning Akhnaton's religion.

Already in the earliest known list of his titles,[4] Akhnaton (who, at the time the inscription was set up, still bore the name of Amenhotep) is called "Wearer of diadems in the Southern Heliopolis" and "High Priest of Ra-Horakhti-of-the-Two-Horizons," rejoicing in His horizon in His name: "Shu-which-is-in-the-Disk," apart from "King of Upper and Lower Egypt" and "Son of Ra," like all Pharaohs since the Fifth Dynasty, and "Nefer-kheperu-Ra, Ua-en-Ra"—"Beautiful Essence of the Sun, Only-One of the Sun"—as he was to call himself in every one of his inscriptions, to the end of his reign.

On the other hand, in the beginning of both the surviving famous Hymns to the Sun, which are the main source of our knowledge of the Aton religion, the God is designated as "Living Horus of the Two Horizons, Who rejoiceth in the horizon in His name: 'Shu-which-is-in-the-Disk,' the Giver of life forever

---

[2] Weigall, pp. 101–104.

[3] Weigall, p. 250.

[4] In the inscription of Silsileh. See James Henry Breasted, *Ancient Records of Egypt: Historical Documents from the Earliest Times to the Persian Conquest* (Chicago: University of Chicago Press, 1906), vol. 2, p. 384.

and ever"⁵ or "Horakhti, the living One, exalted in the Eastern horizon in His name: 'Shu-which-is-in-the-Disk,' Who liveth forever and ever."⁶ And in the Longer Hymn he is called, in addition to that, "the living and great Aton; He who is in the Set Festival, the Lord of the Circle, the Lord of the Disk, the Lord of Heaven, the Lord of earth."⁷ What strikes us in those texts is the identification of Aton (or Aten) — the Solar Disk — with two very old Egyptian gods — Sun-gods, specially worshipped in the sacred city of On or Anu (the "City-of-the-Pillar," i.e., of the Obelisk, which the Greeks were to call Heliopolis, the City of the Sun) — and the identification of those, in their turn (and therefore of Aton *also*), with the mysterious Entity "Shu-which-is-in-the-Disk."

Now, "wherever a solar god was worshipped in Egypt, the habitat of this god was believed to be the solar Disk, Aten or Athen. But the oldest solar god associated with the Disk was Tem or Atmu, who is frequently referred to in the religious texts as 'Tem in his Disk'; when Ra usurped the attributes of Tem, he became 'the Dweller in the Disk,'" while "Horuakhuti" (Horakhti) was "'the god of the two horizons,' i.e., the Sun-god by day, from sunrise to sunset."⁸ To Akhnaton, however, the "Dweller in the Disk," Ra, *is* the "Sun by day" and *is* the Disk itself: Aton. In the inscriptions upon the boundary-stones demarcating the king's new capital, Akhetaton, the God who is, henceforth, to be the sole God of Egypt, and of the Empire, is actually designated as "Ra-Horakhti-Aton."⁹ And Sir Wallis Budge, whose words are all the more significant while he does not seem aware of their immense metaphysical implication, notes, in connection with King Akhnaton's conception of the Sun as the sole object of worship: "But to him [Akhnaton] the Disk was not only the abode of the Sun-god, *it was the god himself*, who by means of the heat and light which emanated from his own body, gave life to everything on earth."¹⁰

---

⁵ Shorter Hymn to the Sun, Budge, p. 116.
⁶ Longer Hymn to the Sun, Budge, p. 122.
⁷ Budge, p. 122.
⁸ Budge, pp. 64–65.
⁹ Breasted, vol. 2, p. 386. See also Weigall, p. 88.
¹⁰ Budge, p. 80.

But that is not all. *Shu* — that mysterious Entity "which-is-in-the-Disk" — "we must translate by 'heat' or by 'heat and light,' for the word has these meanings."[11] Which signifies that Akhnaton worshipped the "Heat-and-Light-within-the-Disk" — the Radiant Energy of the Sun[12] — which he looked upon not merely as inherent in, but *as identical in nature to the material Disk itself, and to supreme Godhead*, whatever be the names by which men might try to characterise the latter, and under which they might worship It.

It is remarkable that, among those names, the young king chose to mention only those of Sun gods of the Heliopolitan Tradition — doubtless because he considered this to be the most consistent solar tradition that Egypt had known up till then, and one by far more akin to his own religious philosophy than anything that could be found in the Southern Egyptian school of Wisdom headed by the High Priest of Amon. Throughout his reign, Akhnaton was to *stress* the connection of his Teaching with the wisdom of the Heliopolitan seers of old, as well as with Egypt's most ancient political tradition of divine royalty. (He himself, in his capacity of "High Priest of Aton," took over the title of *Ur-ma* — "great One of visions," i.e., "seer," *initiate* — which the High Priest of the Sun in Heliopolis had borne from time immemorial.)

But that does not mean to say that his conception of the Divine was exactly that of the priests of Heliopolis. It was not. In particular, "the old Heliopolitan tradition made Tem, or Tem-Ra, or Khepera, *the creator of Aten, the Disk*, but this view Amenhotep IV rejected, and he asserted that the Disk was self-created and self-subsistent."[13] And Akhnaton's notion of "Shu" — "Heat-and-Light-within-the-Disk" — which, to him, *is* supreme Godhead Itself and the same as the self-created and self-sustaining Disk, is quite different from that of the "god" Shu, conceived (as in the old "Pyramid Texts") as the radiation or emanation of Tem, or Tem-Ra, i.e., of the Creator of the Sun-Disk, *different and distinct from it*, and male counterpart of the "goddess" Tefnut (Moisture, also an emanation of Tem) who

---

[11] Budge, p. 80.
[12] Petrie, vol. 2, p. 214.
[13] Budge, p. 80.

forms with him and with Tem the original Heliopolitan Trinity. It is the notion of Divinity conceived as Something absolutely *impersonal* and undefinable, *immanent in all* material and non-material existence, and identical in nature both to visible Matter (to the visible flaming Disk, everlasting and self-created) and to invisible Energy—Heat-and-Light—also self-created and everlasting, and inseparable from Matter as Matter is from It.

And this is confirmed by the prayer inscribed upon the famous scarab discovered at Sadenga, in the Egyptian Sudan, and dating from the early period of Akhnaton's reign. The text, though short (and mutilated), is extremely significant. The God to whom it is addressed, and who can only be Aton (for he bears some of the titles that characterise Aton in other texts) is called "great One of roarings" or "great One of thunders," as though the king—and that, already *before* he had changed his name and entered into open conflict with the priesthood of Amon and with the traditional gods of Egypt—had identified his one and pre-eminently solar God with a Storm god. But, as I have tried to point out in another book,[14] coming from him, the worshipper of "Heat-and-Light" in the Sunbeams, such an identification can hardly mean anything else but the recognition of the equivalence of that very same "Heat-and-Light" to thunder in particular and to sound in general and, above all, to Lightning (Heat-and-Light inseparable from thunder), and to that mysterious form of energy, the presence and tremendous power of which Lightning and Thunder merely reveal: electricity, possibly better known to the wise men at least in remote Antiquity than we modern people in our conceit care to believe. We cannot help thinking, here, of the "threefold Agni" of the Vedas—Sun, Lightning, and Fire upon earth (and within the earth); Heat, Light, and electric Energy in one—as well as of the modern scientific Idea of the equivalence of all forms of energy, and of the fundamental identity of Energy and Matter.

All this makes it clear that Aton—the Solar Disk which is the same as the "Heat-and-Light-within-the-Disk"—is none other than He-She-It—*That*—which is the Essence of all material and immaterial existence, the undefinable Essence both of Matter

---

[14] Savitri Devi, *A Son of God*, pp. 100–101.

and of Energy—"matter to the coarser, and energy to the finer senses"[15]—which is God. Not any God to be compared with the loving "heavenly Father" of the Christians or with any personal God—least of all with the ill-tempered, narrow-minded, and jealous tribal god Jehovah, created in the image of the Jews—but the equivalent of the immanent, impersonal *Tat*—That—of the Chandogya Upanishad, no less than of *das* Gott (as opposed to "*der* Gott") of the ancient Germans, and the one conception of Divinity that modern science, far from disproving, on the contrary, suggests.

Such a God can neither "love," in the all-too-human, Christian sense of the word, nor hate, nor give "commandments" and distribute rewards and punishments in the manner of a human king, nor perform "miracles" if, by such, one means actions in *real* contradiction with the iron Laws of Nature, which are His Laws, nor be "the Maker" of the world "out of nothingness," in the sense a craftsman is the maker of an object, external to himself, out of metal, stone, or clay.

There is no common measure between Him—between Him-Her-It—and the current conception of "God Almighty" as it exists today in Christian or in Mohammedan countries, or, rather, among pious people in countries where the influence of Christianity or Islam—any of the two great international monotheistic religions issued from Judaism—has shaped religious and metaphysical ideas. And although He—He-She-It—be (substantially) less remote from the unknown and indefinable "Neter" or "pa Neter"—"God," or *the* God behind all gods; formless, original Creative Power, which existed of and by Itself, within the primeval watery mass, Nenu—of the most ancient Egyptians, than from that nowadays more popular conception of Divinity. He is different from him to the extent that "Neter," according to the moral Papyri,[16] is still, for all practical purposes, endowed with a certain amount of anthropomorphic personality. Aton—Cosmic Energy, Essence of all existence, "Ka" or Soul of the Sun (to quote a word from Akhnaton's own

---

[15] Savitri Devi, A Son of God, p. 103.
[16] See: "Precepts" of Kagemni (IVth Dynasty) and of Ptah-hotep (Vth Dynasty); of Khonsuhotep, or "Maxims of Ani"; of Amenemapt, (XVIIth Dynasty) (Budge, pp. 145–48).

hymns) identical to the Sun disk itself and Essence of the material world—corresponds to a thoroughly impersonal and *positive* conception of Godhead. And, provided one takes the word "religion" in the sense the average modern European does, i.e., in the sense of a system of beliefs centred around a personal God, an ideal of conduct "according to his will," and a definite conception of life after death, H. R. Hall is right in saying that Akhnaton's "heresy" was "a philosophic and scientific revolt against religion"[17] rather than a new religion.

Hall goes a little further and calls Akhnaton "the first example of the scientific mind,"[18] meaning, naturally, the first one that we are in a position to link with a definite name and date and individual personality, for the "scientific mind" is as old as mankind or, at least, as old as the youngest among the superior races, the Aryan or Indo-European, one of whose glories it is to have evolved exact sciences out of logical thinking, and to have carried them to perfection. And Sir Flinders Petrie pays the Founder of the Religion of the Disk a magnificent tribute for his "really philosophical worship of the radiant energy of the Sun." "No one," says he,

> seems to have realised until within this century, the truth which was the basis of Akhenaten's worship: that the rays of the Sun are the means of the Sun's action, the source of all life, power, and force in the universe. This abstraction of regarding the radiant energy as all-important was quite disregarded until recent views of the conservation of force, of heat as a mode of motion, and the identity of heat, light, and electricity, have made us familiar with the scientific conception which was the characteristic feature of Akhenaten's new worship.

And, a little further:

> If this were a new religion, invented to satisfy our mod-

---

[17] Hall, p. 599.
[18] Hall, p. 599.

ern scientific conceptions, we could not find a flaw in the correctness of this view of the energy of the solar system. How much Akhenaten understood, we cannot say, but he certainly bounded forward in his views and symbolism to a position which we cannot logically improve upon at the present day. Not a rag of superstition or of falsity can be found clinging to this new worship evolved out of the old Aton of Heliopolis, the sole Lord of the universe.[19]

Scientific—*rational*—seems indeed to be *the* word by which one should characterise Akhnaton's conception of Godhead, in opposition both to the crude polytheism of the Egyptian masses and to the monotheism of the Egyptian élite of his days, and, even more so, to the later monotheism of the Jewish prophets and of the Christians and Mohammedans who look upon them as "inspired men."

The expressions which one finds in the Hymns, pointing to Aton as to the one Creator, and exalting His love—"Maker of every land, Creator of whatsoever there is upon it," "Mother and Father of all that Thou hast made,"[20] "Thou fillest every land with Thy love,"[21] etc.—are not to be taken in the sense they would have in the case of a personal God. Other words in the same poems throw light upon them, while rendering, in a more precise manner, the idea of "creation" in connection with Akhnaton's impersonal God: "Thou Thyself art alone, but there are millions of powers of life *in* Thee, to make Thy creatures live";[22] "Thou hast produced millions of creations (or *evolutions*) *from Thy one Self.*"[23] They suggest a creation which, far from being the exceptional act by which a God, distinct from the created world, causes it to spring out of nothingness (or, at the most, out of a primeval Matter which is not He) consists in a gradual and endless manifestation into actual existence, of the different possibilities latent within perennial, unmanifested Reality.[24] And the

---

[19] Petrie, p. 214.
[20] Shorter Hymn to the Sun, trans. Budge, p. 116.
[21] Longer Hymn to the Sun, trans. Budge, p. 122.
[22] Shorter Hymn to the Sun, trans. Budge, p. 116.
[23] Longer Hymn to the Sun, trans. Budge, p. 122.
[24] Savitri Devi, *A Son of God*, p. 127.

words "Father and Mother of all that Thou hast made" are neither the translation of an anthropomorphic idea out of keeping with that of a cosmic God such as Radiant Energy, *nor* a metaphor of mere literary import. They reveal an attempt at rendering, as forcefully as human speech can, the two complementary and inseparable aspects of the One Reality: the positive, active, or masculine, forever urging new forms out of dim possibilities—the *Purusha* of the Sanskrit Scriptures—and the negative, passive (or, if active, not organisingly active) or *feminine*—the equivalent of the Sanskrit *Prakriti*—sensitive receptacle of all latent qualities and matrix of actual existence; the One, everlasting Power of differentiation, and the everlasting and ever-differentiated underlying Oneness.[25]

As for the love of the One, impersonal, cosmic God, Aton, for the universe, it can mean nothing else but the relation of the Essence of all existence to the endlessly and orderly diversified individual lives, human *and* non-human, which are sparks of divine consciousness, more or less bright; an abstract, metaphysical relation of substantial dependence (illustrated in the word "bindest"), *not* an emotional one, for God conceived as "the Heat-and-Light-within-the-Disk," identical to the Sun-disk itself—radiant Energy, Essence of Matter *and* of Life—can have no emotions. That the Egyptians, Akhnaton's own subjects, had no illusions about this, can be seen in the fact—put forward by Sir Wallis Budge and emphasised by J. Pendlebury—that "there are none of the pathetic appeals to the Aton for help or cure that we find addressed to other gods in happier times";[26] that, indeed, such a God as the One Whose glory the young king proclaimed and sang, had "no time to worry about May's headache or Sherira's barrenness."[27]

And the love of all men, nay, of all creatures, including plants, for Aton—the adoration of the divine "Ka" or Essence of the Sun by the whole scale of created beings, from the inspired Seer himself down to the humble water-lilies—is nothing more than the instinctive and universal love of life and

---

[25] Savitri Devi, *A Son of God*, p. 127.
[26] J. D. S. Pendlebury, *Tell-el-Amarna* (London: Lovat Dickson & Thomson Ltd., 1935), p. 159.
[27] Pendlebury, p. 159.

sunshine, contemplated by a Man who really felt and worshipped the divinity of Nature, a Man who beheld the world and lived his own life in full consciousness of the Eternal manifested therein, in other words: a Man *above Time*. Such a Man saw the simple, everyday facts — birds circling around and around in the pure sky, with shrills of joy; beasts skipping about among the high grasses covered with morning dew; fishes, whose silver scales shine through the sunlit water, swimming up to the surface of the river, and flowers opening themselves to the touch of the first sun-rays — in their *real* light; with the eyes of a man of the Golden Age, to whom the world appears as a visible Paradise because he is in tune with it and with himself. Not only did he recognise, in cool judgement (as anybody would), the grandeur of the daily miracle of conception and birth, but he *felt* it with all the piety of a perfect artist; he *felt* the beauty of every new healthy pattern of Life — young bird, newly-born baby; from the standpoint of Eternity, equally irreplaceable — and the solemnity of its unique appearing and fleeting passage amidst the ever-moving infinity of beings, witnesses of Aton's inexhaustible creativeness. And he sang what he felt. And his song was — and could only be — a hymn of adoration unmarred by a shade of sadness; foreign to the idea of suffering and death; a hymn in the spirit of every one of the endlessly recurring Golden Ages, in which all is well with the visible and invisible world in complete harmony with each other and with their common divine archetype; the expression of more-than-earthly love and joy rooted in this sunlit earth, in this divine earthly life.

H. R. Hall, apparently unable to see into the psychology of a "man above Time" or "outside Time," calls the elation expressed in Akhnaton's hymns a mere "cat-like enjoyment of the sun and of the fact that it is good to be alive."[28] He thus intends to stress what seems to him to be a lack of spirituality. Yet, undignified as his sentence may sound, he is literally *right*, provided that one remembers that, to a man "above Time," who actually feels the divinity of Life behind and within all diving forms, the purring of a cat, comfortably rolled up in the warm sunshine, *is* a hymn to the loveliness and glory of Life, as holy, in its innocence, and

---

[28] Hall, p. 599.

at its level, as any human words of praise; all the *more* divine that it is more spontaneous, more sincere, less penetrated with "intellect" as opposed to sensation and intuition; provided that one remembers that, to such a man, the joy of the whole created world at the feeling that "it is good to be alive" is an act of adoration. Akhnaton's own joy at the sight of the rising Sun was not different, in nature, from that universal joy. It was merely the supreme, fully-conscious expression of it: the joy which is inseparable from the direct knowledge of a Man "above Time"; from his *experience* of himself as part and parcel of the divine Cosmos, which he loves because it is so beautiful, and the hidden Essence of which he feels shimmering within his own nerves.

In that joyous cosmic consciousness lies the secret of the apparent amorality of Akhnaton's Teaching, and its actual moral meaning.

As I said already, such a God as "the Heat-and-Light-within-the-Disk" can issue no "commandments" like an exalted tribal deity made in the image of its worshippers. His laws are none but the unbending Laws of Nature, expressions of the inner harmony of His own being at every stage and in every detail of His manifestation in Time. There *is*, indeed, and there can be no other rule of conduct for His worshippers but to "live in Truth," i.e., in tune with the eternal Order of the Universe, accomplishing the diverse tasks which are theirs while remaining inwardly at peace with themselves and with every created being. And that ideal of life—which may well seem vague to those who do not grasp its implications—*is* precisely the one put forward by King Akhnaton. (The famous title "*Ankh-em-Maat*"—Living in Truth—accompanies his name in every inscription of his reign apart from the *very* early ones.) And the only definite information that can be gathered about his actual practical Teaching, from the inscriptions in the tombs of his professed followers at Tell-el-Amarna, is that he preached the love of "truth" in all walks of life. "The King has put truth into me, and my abomination is to lie,"[29] declares one of the courti-

---

[29] Inscription in the tomb of Ay at Tell-el-Amarna.

ers, named Ay, and "truth" cannot mean anything else but that which I have just said (and "lie," its contrary), in the case of a religion centred around Solar Energy.

But neither Ay nor any other has attempted to make this clear and to describe the sort of conduct which he (or King Akhnaton himself) associated with "truth" and "living in truth." None has even mentioned as an example any action which, in his eyes, corresponded to such an ideal of conduct. None has alluded to any punishments (or mere consequences) of sin, i.e., of untruth, in this life or another, or to any rewards (or consequences of faithfulness to "truth") — apart from the very tangible royal presents which they received for having "hearkened to" Akhnaton's "Teaching of life."

We know in fact nothing of the ethical code of the Religion of the Disk, and nay, all appears as though it never had an "ethical code" in the ordinary sense of the word — a list of "dos and don'ts" — or implied any "sense of sin." But that does not mean that it had "no ethics." It *had*, I repeat, the only ethics that go hand in hand with faith in an impersonal God Who is the "Ka" or Essence (Soul) of the fiery Orb and of Life itself, the ethics implied in *"life* in Truth" — life according to the logic of the Universe: according to the biological and social laws that express the will of Nature, the will of the Sun, the supreme finality of Creation.

It is difficult to say how far the king's followers were aware of all that this means. But the king himself certainly was. It is, of course, possible that he did set up some rules of conduct, of the evidence of which no trace has been found. After all, an enormous amount of documents of his reign were purposely destroyed after his death by the enemies of the Aton faith, and surely any inscription or papyrus referring to his Teaching, was, when not protected by the sanctity of the tomb, destroyed before any other. But it would not be, on the other hand, at all surprising if he had remained contented with formulating his moral ideal in the motto "living in Truth" — his favourite motto — and with developing at most *orally* all that it implied. The history of his reign, in particular the official correspondence of his vassals and governors, forces one to admit that no man ever was more estranged to the reality of Time, and more unaware of the inherent weaknesses and passions of his contemporaries, than he. As we shall see in the next chapter, he was convinced that he could, in this very Age of Gloom—his Age *and* ours—build up an ideal state without having to resort to violence. It is natural that such a man—pre-eminently "above Time," or "outside Time"—should have looked upon the implications of "life in Truth" as something self-evident, and not deemed it necessary to formulate a "code" of behaviour. In a way, taking into account the fundamental difference between the two creeds, one could set his motto of "life in Truth" in parallel with Jesus Christ's well-known sole commandment of love towards one's neighbours *which is the same as* love towards God, the spirit of which Saint Augustine expressed most adequately in his laconic and forceful sentence: "Love!—and do whatever you please!" Akhnaton—like Jesus Christ, a Man "above Time," a Solar Being in the full sense of the word—could well have said: "There is but one Law: to live in Truth, holding all forms of falsehood in abomination. Stick to Truth—and do whatever you please!"

And "Truth," to him, meant love—love of *all beings*, not of man alone, not of man specially; love of the sun-lit world (with all it contains) for the sake of its beauty. It meant, also, *knowledge* of the eternal Order and of the eternal Values, through the contemplation of beauty—for in every Golden Age (Age *of Truth*), the visible is the faithful image of invisible Perfection; and Akhnaton, being a Man "above Time," lived (in spirit) in a Golden Age.

And although nothing even hints at the existence of a code of ethics attached to the Religion of the Disk, in the amount of evidence yet unearthed, there are, in his Longer Hymn to the Sun, three remarkable lines which express, more eloquently perhaps than any others, the young king's idea of man—three lines which have not attracted, as far as I know, the special attention of any archaeologists: "Thou hast put every man *in his place*. Thou framest their lives. Thou givest everyone his belongings, reckoning his length of days. *Thou hast made them different in form, in the colour of their skins, and in speech. As a Divider, Thou dividest the foreign people* [from one another]."[30]

These words clearly show that, far from putting "all men"

---

[30] Savitri's brackets—Ed.

on the same level, Akhnaton stressed the *differences* between one human race and another as an expression of that Will of the Sun that has moulded the world or, in modern speech, as a result of the fact that man, like the rest of creatures of this earth, is a "solar product," owing his very being to a combination of definite bio-physical conditions. He states here without ambiguity that all features that differentiate one people from another — features among which the racial ones, form and colour, are not only all-important but *fundamental:* the first ones mentioned — are the Sun's work: "As a Divider, Thou hast divided the foreign people . . ." — which logically implies that those differentiating qualities should be taken into account in human legislation, if one is to have a world in which men "*live in Truth.*" The existence of different — unequal — human races comes within the pattern of the eternal order; *has to be*, according to the finality which lies, as a guiding principle, within the play of the immanent Creative Power: the "Heat-and-Light-within-the-Disk." One is not to mix or to forward the mixture of that which the Creative Power has divided — nor, in any way, to hide or suppress the signs of division.

There is, here, of course, no question of *struggle* between races. There cannot be, in the mind of a man who is entirely "above Time"; who lives, in spirit, in a Golden Age, where all violence, nay, all conflict, is out of place. There is merely the idea of *harmony* between the different races, every one of which has its place and purpose, its part to play in the universal concert, and *should remain different* in order to play it perfectly. There is a stress upon differences and division, which logically suggests that men have neither all the same rights nor all the same duties. And this is perhaps the ultimate reason why the ideal of "life in *Truth*" — life according to one's place and purpose in the *natural* hierarchy of beings — cannot be made explicit in any universal list of concrete "dos and don'ts," such as modern Christian critics of the Religion of the Disk would have liked to have found. All one can say is that to "sin" is to *lie*; to deny the eternal Order of things which are, independently of man, by refusing to live according to it; to say "no" to the Will of the Sun.

One can agree with R. H. Hall that Akhnaton's "enthusiasm for truth and for what was right was not really religious, but scientific,"[31] if one thinks of a religion of the hereafter settled, like Christianity, upon impenetrable dogmas. But if one bears in mind that the Religion of the Disk is itself built upon a scientific foundation—upon intuitions concerning this living visible world, that have, centuries later, proved to be in keeping with the data of science, even if they were, in the consciousness of its Founder, directly *experienced* (and anything but the result of observation and induction)—then one can only assert that science and *such* religion are not only in harmony with each other, but *identical* as regards their ultimate object, that the truth around which they are centred is the same. The real and only difference between them lies in man's approach to that truth: mainly—although never solely—through the data of material experience and through the deductive (or more often inductive) mind, in the case of science; mainly when not solely through mystical yearning and direct intuition, in the case of "religion."

Morality—life in Truth, from the standpoint of the eternal (that was Akhnaton's)—cannot be codified. It can be defined as the application of knowledge to *right* action, i.e., to one's contribution to the work of the Creative Power, in one's natural capacity and from one's natural place. We shall see that Akhnaton's personal fulfilment of his own cherished motto consisted in bearing witness to the glory of all the Golden Ages or "Ages of Truth," behind him and ahead of him, untiringly, even at the cost of material ruin and historical failure.

Archaeologists have more than once pointed out the foreign character of Akhnaton's religion. Maybe the names of the One God—Aton, Ra, Ra-Horakhti of the Two Horizons rejoicing in His Horizon in His name "Shu-which-is-in-the-Disk"—were Egyptian, and nay, some of them, many centuries old; maybe, the king lost no opportunity of stressing the connection of his new cult with the venerable old Sun-cult of Heliopolis—and, as we shall see in the next chapter, the connection of his new art with archaic Egyptian art.[32] "But"—notes Sir Flinders Petrie—

---

[31] Hall, p. 599.
[32] Weigall, pp. 62–63.

"a glance at the character of the whole age marks it out as due to some completely un-Egyptian influence, which no Heliopolitan source could ever have originated."[33] While Sir Wallis Budge ascribes the failure of the Aton religion to the fact that it was "too philosophical to impose itself upon the Egyptian mind," and "probably based upon esoteric doctrines that were of foreign origin."[34] And he wonders whether Akhnaton's "insistence upon the beauty and power of light" was not a sign of "the penetration into Egypt of Aryan ideas concerning Mithra, Varuna, and Surya or Savitri, the Sun-god."[35]

Since the discovery of the famous text of the treaty between Shubbiluliuma, king of the Hittites, and Mattiuza, son of Dushratta, it is a known fact that the kings of Mitanni—themselves Aryans—worshipped Aryan gods. Four of these gods are mentioned as guarantors of Mattiuza's faithful observance of the treaty. Their names are practically the same as those of the Vedic gods Mithra, Indra, Varuna, and the Nasatya Twins, and their identification with the latter "seems to be certain."[36] From Mitannian proper names, such as "Shuwardata," one can also infer the presence of the Vedic Sun-god Surya (who was also revered by the Kassites, the Aryan kings of Babylon, under the name of Suryash) in the Mitannian pantheon. And the similarity between Akhnaton's One God and Surya is indeed striking. Not only does the Sanskrit description of the divine Source of Light—"As the Vivifier and Quickener He raises His long arms of gold in the morning, rouses all beings from their slumber, infuses energy into them, and buries them in sleep in the evening"[37]—correspond perfectly to the picture of Aton given in the Egyptian king's hymns (and to the Sun-disk with rays ending in hands, the Symbol of his religion) but the idea of a both male and female (i.e., two-poled) Principle suggested in the other

---

[33] Petrie, p. 212.
[34] Budge, p. 82.
[35] Budge, p. 113.
[36] Budge, p. 21.
[37] W. J. Wilkins, *Hindu Mythology: Vedic and Puranic*, p. 33. [This is a poetic paraphrase of the words that appear in the edition I consulted (Calcutta: Thacker, Spink, 1913), but Savitri may have had access to a different edition. —Ed.]

Sanskrit names of the Sun—for instance Savita, and Savitri, Savita's Energy—finds its parallel in the expression: "Father-and-Mother of all that Thou hast made," applied to Aton.

This has prompted a number of writers to emphasise the supposed influence of his father's Mitannian wives—nay, of the many Mitannians who doubtless were to be seen at the Theban court—upon the child who was to become Akhnaton, the Prophet of Godhead experienced as Radiant Energy, "Heat-and-Light-within-the-Sun-Disk."

To what extent such an influence should be taken into account, is, however, difficult to determine, first because we have no records of Akhnaton's life *before* his accession to the throne, and second, because, apart from the mentioned treaty with the king of the Hittites, there are no Mitannian texts yet known which refer to the Aryan gods, so that we cannot tell how far the *Mitannian* religious outlook embodied in their cult was similar to that of the Sanskrit-speaking Aryans and to Akhnaton's; and finally because it is, in the two hymns to Aton that have come down to us, quite obvious that the reality of his impersonal God, "the Heat-and-Light-which-is-in-the-Disk," appeared to Akhnaton himself as the object of a revelation *from within*—as truth directly experienced, which he was the only one to understand because he was (as far as he knew) the only one to *feel* it. "Thou art in my heart," says he, addressing himself to the resplendent Orb—God's visible Face—in the Longer Hymn; "There is no one who knoweth Thee except Thy Son, Nefer-kheperu-ra Ua-en-ra (Beautiful Essence of the Sun, Only-One of the Sun). Thou hast made him wise to understand Thy plans and Thy power."[38] And as I have tried to point out in other writings, these words, coming from one who cared as little for conventions as Akhnaton did, express the innermost certitude of a self-realised soul who can sincerely say of God: "I am He"—or "I am *That*" rather than the pride of a king of Egypt in his solar descent.[39]

Of course, Akhnaton did not underestimate the privilege of that solar descent—of that double aristocracy of his, as off-

---

[38] Longer Hymn to the Sun, trans. Budge.
[39] See Savitri Devi, *A Son of God*, pp. 26 and 27. Also *Akhnaton's Eternal Message*, pp. 5–6.

spring both of the kings of the Nile Valley and of the kings of Mitanni. The mere fact that he erected shrines to the memory of several of his ancestors (as we shall see) would suffice to prove that he was fully aware of all that he owed them. Nor should one brush aside that which he quite possibly owed to his contact, as a child, with the Mitannian and half-Mitannian—and Kassite—princesses of his father's harem (and first of all with his own mother): memories of Aryan legends in which was exalted the triumph of the Forces of Light over those of Gloom, and—perhaps—the glory of a Sun-god with "long arms of gold," the symbolism of whose image he may have felt very deeply and never forgotten. Indeed, it must not have taken much to quicken the power of intuition and to awaken thought in such a child as he, marked out, already before his birth, to be a Man "above Time." Still, the part played by direct feeling must be given the first place in the genealogy of his conception of Divinity, i.e., importance must be given not so much to the *name* "Heat-and-Light-within-the-Disk" (which he found already existing), as to that which *he* put behind that name; as to that conception of impersonal, two-poled Reality which is both Matter and Energy—the Sun out of which sprang the Earth itself, *and* His life-giving Rays—and which manifests itself nowhere as well as in radiant Heat-and-Light or (if we remember the scarab of Sadenga) Heat-Light-and-Electricity—and creative Sound—Its manifold, imponderable Vibration.

We can well admit that Akhnaton was not unfamiliar with Aryan symbolism, that he had quite possibly heard of golden-armed Surya, even of Agni, the threefold Fire. But we should picture him, already as a prematurely thoughtful child, and then as an ardently sensitive adolescent, alone before the sight of the gorgeous sunrises and sunsets of Egypt, or before the deep blue infinity of the cloudless Egyptian sky. We should imagine him absorbed in contemplation, carried away, in almost physical rapture, by the feeling of "Heat-and-Light, and nothing else"—the consciousness of the burning blue Void in which nothing exists but Sun-rays—or by the grandeur of the contrast between Light and Darkness in a country where dawn is sudden and overwhelming and where there is practically no twilight.[40] And we

---

[40] That feeling is illustrated in the forceful words: "Thou risest,

should not forget that he was half if not more than half Aryan—
that he had in his blood that enthusiastic devotion to Light and
Life which had created, among the fair Conquerors of India, the
myth of the threefold Fire as well as that of golden-armed Surya-
Savitri and, among the Celts, who had not yet crossed the
threshold of history, the myth of Lugh Langhana—Lugh the
Longhanded—the life-giving god of Light—but that he had other blood *also*: the blood of that venerable old Southern race out of
which had sprung the kings of Thebes and the priests of Amon.
To a great extent, no doubt, he owed his deep meditative sensitiveness to that also remarkable half of his ancestry. He put the
whole of his being—all the extreme and apparently incompatible
forces rooted within his double heredity—to the service of his
one purpose: the glorification of Aton, the One God, "Heat-and-
Light-which-is-in-the-Disk."

For the sight of the fathomless blue of the sky, and of the
gold and scarlet of dawn and sunset, had definitively torn him
away from the gods of Thebes, exalted *totems* of very, very long
before, to which the ingenious theological mind had given a
more and more subtle symbolical interpretation. He could no
longer feel attracted to them—in admitting that he ever had
been—after having merged himself, be it once, into the Soul of
luminous Infinity. They seemed false to him—clumsy, all-too-
human caricatures of the One Reality. And they had, in his
eyes, the pitiful ugliness of all caricatures, which becomes sacrilegious when connected with things divine. And much of that
which was related to him of their legends must have shocked
his Aryan mind athirst for logic. Some of it, of course, may well
have appealed to his imagination. But the naked Truth which
he *felt*, in his growing consciousness of the sunlit Void, receptacle of all life, was so immeasurably more beautiful! And from
his early adolescence onwards—perhaps even from his childhood onwards; such a man as he had surely been an exceptional child—he knew that he could never worship anything but
the Sun and His Rays—Heat-and-Light—the Soul of the resplendent blue abyss. It is possible that other people's utterances—his mother's, his step-mothers', and those of any other Mi-

---

and Thy creatures live; Thou settest, and they die," which those alone
who have lived in tropical lands can really understand.

tannians or half-Mitannians that he may have known—consciously or unconsciously suggested to him the idea of those Rays ending in hands—the arms of the Sun—that were to play such a characteristic part as the visible Sign of his religion. But it is his Aryan blood that gave him his spontaneous joy in light and life *and* the unbending consistency—the scientific mind, coupled with uncompromising will-power—with which he conceived his Teaching and carried it out in his own life, and imposed it (as far as he could) with all its implications, upon Egypt and the Egyptian Empire.

Akhnaton's attitude to death seems to be (as far as one can make it out) a result both of his scientific thinking and of his natural and systematic rejection of all that is negative.

From what remains of the tombs of his followers, one is induced to believe that the whole Egyptian tradition concerning the Tuat—the world of the dead—and the journey of the departed soul to the throne of Osiris—the seat of Judgment—through all sorts of trials and dangers, appeared to him, if not as "ridiculous fictions"[41] as Budge says, at least as symbolical language, the accuracy of which could never be proved and had, after all, little importance. The idea of death seems to have inspired in him neither fear, nor yearning, nor curiosity; like other negative ideas, such as violence, it simply had no place in his thought-world, which was the thought-world of a man of a Golden Age, faithful to this earth, and "long in duration of years"—of a man who, at least, *felt* himself to be so, in his realisation of the *true* world (the earthly Paradise) under (or beyond) the one which he saw without actually seeing it, and ignored.

One does not know enough of the Aton Teaching to be able to say whether the idea of the perennial Struggle between Light and Darkness—in the rhythm of day and night *and* on all planes—was stressed in it or not. In all that has survived of the Religion of the Disk, there is surely no hint at the negative qualities of the Sun; nothing foreshadowing in the least the meaning of the Greek name of the god of Light, which is a typ-

---

[41] Budge, pp. 94–95.

ically Aryan god from the Far North:[42] Apollon—the "Destroyer." It would seem that Akhnaton refused to see anything outside beneficent Heat-and-Light in the divine Energy of the Sunbeams; anything outside beautiful, happy life upon this earth.

He had to, in his time—some 3,000 years after the Dark Age in which we are still living had begun, and many myriads of years after the end of the latest Golden Age, in which all was perfect. He had to, being a man "above Time," a complete "Sun-type" of a man, if he wanted at all to be "faithful to this earth"; to act upon earth as an earthly king and priest at the same time. His only alternative to that was either to turn from this earth or to impose his Golden Age Teaching by means of violence; to seek for himself and for others a way out of earthly conditions altogether, as the Buddha was to, some 900 years later; to live and act *in* this world without at all feeling bound to it, saying—like Jesus Christ was to, one day—"My Kingdom is *not* of this earth," or else to become a man "*against* Time," and to fight dispassionately for the triumph of his timeless Truth on earth with the only weapons that work within the bondage of Time, and especially within the Dark Age: fear—terror—and occasionally bribery; intelligent, discriminate bribery and well-conducted terror. He could take no other course because there is no other to be taken. He loved this beautiful earth too much to follow the first way: the way of escape from the earthly conditions of life altogether, which is that of most men "above Time." His dream was that of an *earthly* Paradise. And his inborn reluctance to violence was too great—and too deep-rooted—for him ever to accept the conditions of victory *in* Time or "against Time," to uphold, or even to stress any manner of destructiveness.

His God, Aton, essentially an immanent and impersonal God, has surely very little, if anything, in common with the rather naïve "loving Father" of the Christians, despite what Christian admirers of Akhnaton's hymns may say or write. He may well be "international," even "universal": the "Heat-and-Light within the Sun-disk" could hardly be anything else. But He—He-She-It—is so as a cosmic Entity, Principle of all life, human *and non-human*; adored not merely by "all men," but

---

[42] Apollon *Hyperboreios*.

also by all living creatures—quadrupeds, birds, fishes, and plants—full of solicitude for all creatures, i.e., shaping them (from *within*) and making them all grow, indiscriminately, impartially, as only an impersonal God can. And there lies all the difference: Aton is the one God the modern scientific mind could acknowledge without difficulty.

And He represents, under His Egyptian names and in spite of them, and in spite of the historical connection of His cult with that of the solar gods of Heliopolis, an Indo-European conception of Godhead—the eternal Idea behind long-handed Lugh; behind the almighty Father-of-Light—"*Lichtvater, der Allwaltende*"—of the ancient Germans; behind golden-armed Surya-Savitri—*not* because Akhnaton, who took consciousness of Him through some direct experience, had been influenced by Aryan people (especially by people of Mitannian origin), but because he—Akhnaton—was himself at least half-Aryan, and because, being so, he could not find a better expression of his inner experience—an expression that would both correspond to his direct intuition of the Supreme *and* satisfy his logical mind.

But Aton is an Indo-European god, or rather *the* Indo-European conception of Godhead, without that element of destructiveness inseparable from the notion of perennial Struggle against Darkness and Chaos, which is present in most Aryan gods of Light and Life; an Indo-European God, conceived by a Man faithful to this earth, no doubt, but who lived entirely "above Time" or "outside Time," according to the vision of a Golden Age world-Order—while the Indo-European or Aryan race (the youngest of our Time-cycle) is essentially *the* race "against Time."

Chapter 10

THE SEAT OF TRUTH

The Religion of the Disk was a state religion. From the beginning, Akhnaton had intended it to be. This fact is strongly emphasized by some archaeologists such as Sir Wallis Budge, while others seem to be more impressed by — and more interested in — the actually religious (or philosophical) side of the King's Teaching: its simple, and scientifically accurate, theology; its absence of any explicit moral code; its Founder's inherent reluctance to violence. I say: not merely a state *cult* — compatible with *any* religious views and moral principles (provided these were not, directly or indirectly, dangerous to the security or prestige of the state) like the cult of the traditional gods of Rome was one day to become, under the tolerant rule of the emperors — but a state *religion*, dictating a definite metaphysical conception of the Universe and a definite ideal of life to a whole people, nay, to a whole empire and (in Akhnaton's mind) to the whole world; a state religion that was at the same time a world religion, *and* a religion exalting individual perfection — "life in Truth" — as its goal; such was, as I have tried to point out in another book,[1] that solar religion which Sir Flinders Petrie considered "fit to satisfy our modern scientific conceptions."[2] It was, in other words, not a way *out* of this life (or out of the endless cycle of birth and death and rebirth) into a Kingdom of Righteousness which is "not of this earth" or into the absolute peace of Nothingness, but a way of life here and now, upon this earth, in tune with this earth, and *therefore* a state religion — for life here and now, in tune with this earth, presupposes social order, political order, hierarchy — organisation — and religion — *real* religion — whenever it is not a path of escape from life, is inseparable from any *real* state, as it is from life itself.

This is no arbitrary assumption. We have, of course, no written records of any Age save of the one in which we are living to

---

[1] Savitri Devi, *A Son of God*.
[2] Petrie, p. 214.

this day—the Dark Age (the *Kali Yuga* of the Sanskrit Scriptures). Archaeological evidence helps us to reconstruct something (be it extremely little) of the preceding Age. And Tradition alone gives us, in the absence of any glimpse into the actual *history* of the two first Ages of our Time-cycle—the long *Satya Yuga* (or *Krita Yuga*) and the *Treta Yuga* of the Sanskrit books, the Golden Age and the Silver Age of the ancient Greeks—at least a hint as to the quality of their civilisations. Yet it is noteworthy—nay, visible already within this present Dark Age—that, the more one goes *up* the stream of time, the more religion and state power are tightly bound together, not separated. In the very early part of this Age of Gloom—2,000 and more than 2,000 years before Akhnaton—royal power and priestly dignity were the attributes of the same person. And it remained so for a long time. Every *patesi* in old Sumeria was chief-priest as well as king in the area over which he held sway. And so were—and so remained, formally at least, for centuries—the Chinese Emperors, "Sons of Heaven," whose office it was to perform the Four Ceremonies and to fix the calendar, i.e., to put their realm in harmony with Space and Time. And in the former Age, and in the one before it, it was more and more generally so, if we believe Indian Tradition in connection with all the "*rajrishis*"—rulers and saints, i.e., men having realised the Divine within themselves while they maintained, or tried to maintain, the divine Order within the world—some of whose names have come down to us. While in the Golden Age, in all countries, the gods themselves were kings—"the gods," i.e., supermen, as far above even the beautiful humanity of their times as average mankind is above average animality. The "separation of church and state" is a modern invention or, to speak more accurately, an increasing necessity of the late Dark Age, readily recognised by the great men "within Time"—who are *all* tolerant towards the existing religions of their epoch (unless they consider it their interest to use one of them against the others)—and by any such men "against Time" who feel that they must, for practical reasons, *first* seize power, and then only put their higher programme, their *real* programme, through. It is unconceivable in any time save the last period of our Age, even though, for centuries already, neither state nor "church" any longer be what they should be, and what they *are*, to the supreme degree, in the Golden Age. It is less and less conceivable as one reaches back into remoter Antiquity, least of all in the Golden Age itself—or in the minds of those men "above Time" who live in spirit within such an Age.

Akhnaton could not, any more than his fathers had, isolate religion from the state. He could not *want* such an unnatural and absurd separation. He could want it far less than they, who had understood the meaning and purpose both of religion and of the state less clearly and vividly than he. His religion was bound to be a state religion, not because he was born a king, but because he was born a man "above Time," living in spirit within the Golden Age, *and* a man of action, faithful to this earth, and because, *along with that*, he happened to be a king.

But while the pharaonic state was the outcome of the slow evolution of the perfect theocratic state idea of the "days of Ra" in the course of endless time, Akhnaton's ideal city was to be (in his mind at least) built upon *that* state idea itself. It was to be the living expression of nothing less than the original divine Order—i.e., of the Golden Age Order—in its uncompromising purity; in other words: a broad-scale earthly Paradise. In it—over it—the direct, absolute, yet mild and peaceable rule of a god-like Man, "Son of the living Aton, like unto Him without ceasing"—namely his own rule—was to replace the less and less happy (and less and less effective) collaboration of temporal power and spiritual authority—royalty and priesthood—that Egypt and practically all countries had hitherto gradually evolved. The "Teaching of Truth" could only be the state religion of a Golden Age state organised according to its spirit.

And it really looks as though, with that youthful confidence in the irresistibility of Truth which was to characterise his whole career, Akhnaton had first tried to turn Thebes into the capital of that state of his dreams. It is at least significant that, after building his first known temple to the Sun-disk within the enclosure of Karnak, already holy to the Thebans for hundreds of years, he renamed the glorious city of his ancestors "City of the Brightness of Aton." It is no less remarkable that he seems to have done all he could to replace *smoothly and peacefully* the pharaonic régime of his time by his lofty Golden Age theocracy.

The nature of his faith was conducive to such a policy.

We have seen in the preceding chapter that, contrary to the opinion of some modern authors, Aton—Ra-Horakhti-Aton, as He is called on the boundary stelae of Tell-el-Amarna—never was—could in no way be—a "jealous" God, that, philosophically speaking, He had no quarrel with the all-too-human conceptions of Divinity which the Egyptians cherished, nay, not even with Amon himself. (Impersonal Energy manifested in the Sunbeams; "Heat-and-Light-within-the-Disk"—Aton *is* nothing else—could hardly be so narrow-minded!) The fact can never be too emphatically stressed. And it explains why there are, in the early part of Akhnaton's reign, no signs of "religious intolerance" whatsoever—however much the young king may have looked upon many deep-rooted Egyptian beliefs with unmixed contempt, and however much he may have deplored the raising of Amon, a local tribal deity, to the rank of *the* Great God of the Empire, nay, his identification with the venerable Ra of Heliopolis, the Sun god of those hallowed Pharaohs who had built the Pyramids. It explains why the fragments of sandstone that were once part of the first Aton temple bear, besides the exalted name of Horus, the names of such other traditional Egyptian gods as Set, and jackal-headed Wepwawet. It explains why the royal steward Apiy did not hesitate to mention Ptah and "the gods and goddesses of Memphis" in his letter to the king, in the fifth year of the latter's reign—a letter in which Akhnaton is still called Amenhotep, although he already bears the significant title: "living in Truth." It explains why there was, originally, above the inscription of Silsileh commemorating the opening of quarries in the South, to provide stone for the earliest known Aton temple, a figure of the king worshipping *Amon*, while the Sun-disk—Aton—shed over him the famous Rays ending in hands, symbol of Energy—"Heat-and-Light"—in the new religion.[3]

As I have tried to show in other writings,[4] Akhnaton was then already conscious of what Godhead meant to him, and, which is more, already eager to preach his new (or rather eternal) religion, wherever he deemed any man worthy to hear of it,

---

[3] Breasted, p. 384.
[4] See Savitri Devi, *A Son of God*, chapters 2 and 3.

as it is quite clear from the inscription in the tomb of Ramose in Thebes.³

This signifies that the change that was soon to appear in his attitude towards the traditional gods of Egypt in general and towards Amon in particular, and the steps he was soon to take against the priesthood of Amon, had a political rather than a "religious" meaning—but a political meaning that cannot be grasped apart from the Religion of the Disk as an organic system of thought, a meaning derived from the very definite conception of the state which goes hand in hand with it and with the fact of Akhnaton being a Man "above Time" who had *not* renounced this world.

That conception of the state—that régime, to use a very modern word in connection with a very ancient reality—was, as I said, a theocracy. Not an arbitrary government of priests pretending to rule on behalf of the Gods or of "God"—that which one generally *calls* "theocracy" through a misuse of the word—but the real thing: the government of God Himself, exercised by an actual "Son of God" "wise in the understanding of the plans and of the might"⁵ of Him Whom he had realised, and *rightly* endowed both with temporal power *and* spiritual authority.

It is *that* idea, *that* conception, to which the priests of Amon so strongly objected rather than to the king's metaphysical conception of Aton. Unfamiliar, unorthodox—un-Egyptian—as the latter may have sounded to them, they never would have deemed it worthwhile setting themselves in open, bitter opposition to the lawful Pharaoh in order to destroy it. Like all ancient religions, theirs recognised the fact that many and various ways lead to the knowledge of the Hidden One—Amon, Aton, whatever men may choose to call Him—and that the Hidden One Himself has many and various attributes. It did not proclaim itself the only possible approach to Truth. And they were not fighting to forward the belief that it was, or that it should be looked upon as such. They were fighting for their *own* survival as *the* "spiritual Authority" behind the Egyptian throne—a "spiritual Authority" which had, in fact, long ceased to be purely spiritual, but that they claimed all the more violently to represent as a means to an end. They had become, in the course of time, a more and more

---

⁵ Longer Hymn to the Sun.

intriguing, more and more power-grabbing organisation. They were fighting to retain the possibility of indefinitely extending their privileges. Their ultimate goal (which they were to reach two-and-a-half centuries later)[6] was not the defence of the pharaonic order *as it stood* — royal power separated from, yet in close alliance with priestly authority — but nothing short of the seizure of the royal sceptre in their own hands and the establishment, to their own profit, of a theocracy in the most ordinary sense of the word, i.e., of a régime under which both temporal *and* spiritual power would be theirs. They were fighting, apparently, maybe, as champions of the existing order, but in reality, to forward that bold dream of priestly rule.

It was a necessity for them to crush Akhnaton and his dream of divine rule, under which they would have no place. It was a necessity for him to put an end to their intrigues, and to suppress their influence. From the sixth year of his reign onwards, he stood up alone against centuries of tradition and waged war on Amon and on practically all the gods of Egypt, not because his lofty impersonal God had suddenly become a "jealous" one in his eyes, *not because* he had, himself, become a religious "fanatic" (or an intellectual one), but because he had grown thoroughly conscious of the danger that the priests represented from *his* point of view, i.e., from the point of view of his state idea.

The necessity that prompted him to action was more than "religious" or, to be more accurate, it was not religious at all in the narrow, individual sense of the word. It had nothing to do with his realisation of the Divine, which nobody contested, nor with the destiny of his personal soul, with which nobody interfered. It was the necessity of coping with danger. It arose as a consequence of the stubborn opposition of the priests of Amon to his conception of an ideal theocratic *state*, headed by himself, and especially to his attempt to make Thebes — *their* sacred Thebes, stronghold of their power for centuries — the centre of such a state. That opposition had to be overcome at any cost, if Akhnaton was at all to try to bring his Golden Age theocracy into existence. But it was powerful, for the priests of Amon were, as a body, fabulously rich. And it was bitter — desperate — for the

---

[6] In 1117 B.C., when, at the death of Ramesses XI, Herihor, High Priest of Amon, ascended the Theban throne.

issue at stake presented itself to them in the form of the tragic dilemma: to rule or not to rule, which, to their ambitious hearts, meant: to be or not to be.

We do not know what they actually *did* to confound the king's plans. But they surely did something which provoked Akhnaton's greatest indignation: we have an echo of his vehement reaction to their stand in an unfortunately mutilated inscription upon one of the boundary stones of Tell-el-Amarna; the text is eloquent, even though many words are missing,[7] and shows at least that the Founder of the Religion of the Disk saw in the priests of Amon an essentially *evil* force. Evil, and mighty. Exceptional situations—dangerous situations—call for exceptional measures. King Akhnaton answered the priests' hostility by a declaration of war to the finish: he banned the name of Amon as the symbol of the hitherto pharaonic state in which those priests had had so much to say, and as that of the priestly state—the false theocracy—by which they dreamed of replacing it one day; and he had it and all representations of the Theban god erased from all public and private monuments, even from the walls of his own father's tomb; he changed his own name, Amenhotep, which meant "Amon is at peace," into Akhnaton— "Joy-of-the-Solar-Disk." And he confiscated the priests' wealth: their enormous land property, and all their treasures on which he could lay hands. And he caused the doors of the great temple of Amon in Karnak to be closed. Then, seeing in the priesthoods of the many other gods a force that could only ally itself to that of Amon's servants in their struggle against himself and against the state he intended to build, he soon dismissed them *also*, and had the names of the traditional deities and the plural word "gods" erased from the inscriptions, and *all* temples closed (with the exception of those of the Sun gods of Heliopolis, in connection with whose tradition he intended to give his Aton religion a hold upon his people). And finally—when he realised that the city of Amon would irredeemably remain hostile to his plans,

---

[7] "For as my Father liveth ... more evil are they (the priests) than those things which I have heard in the 4th year; more evil are they than those things which King ... heard; more evil are they than those things which Menkheperura (Thutmose IV) heard ... in the mouth of Negroes; in the mouth of any people!"

when he lost all hope of making it the centre of his ideal state—he moved from Thebes in search of some virgin soil upon which he could lay the foundations of the city of his dreams, new capital of the Egyptian Empire, political *and* religious centre of a new world.

From there, his struggle against the priests of Amon—now dispossessed, but never persecuted, for Akhnaton, the Man "*above* Time," was opposed to all violence—would no doubt continue, and so would, from all Egypt, their struggle against him. It was, however, we repeat—for one can never repeat it and stress it enough—anything but a struggle between his God-conscious "individual" soul and the traditional gods of the community: the national gods as such. It was, least of all, a struggle between "monotheism" and "polytheism." It was a conflict between the Golden Age conception of the state ruled by an actual King-god—one of the rare divine Men that appear now and then in all ages, but with less and less power on earth as time follows its downward course—and the conception of the state ruled by a king assisted, and gradually dominated—overshadowed—and finally replaced by an increasingly powerful priestly class, a conception which leads ultimately to priestly rule (in the name of the gods, for the benefit of the priests). It was the conflict between the long-forgotten state idea implied in the "Kingdom of Ra," and that embodied in the pharaonic state rapidly evolving towards the kingdom of Herihor, in other words, the conflict between real and false theocracy.

In the sixth year of his reign, Akhnaton founded the city that was to be the pattern and the capital of his ideal state. And he named it Akhetaton—the City-of-the-Horizon-of-the-Disk.

As stated above,[8] the place which he selected—and where the ruins of the city are still to be seen—lies some 190 miles south of the site of modern Cairo, on the eastern bank of the Nile. It is a crescent-shaped bay, some eight miles long and three miles wide, at the foot of the limestone desert cliffs which, to the north and to the south of it, abruptly recede from the river.

---

[8] Page 133.

It is difficult to tell what hidden reasons—what mysterious but all-potent cosmic correspondences—prompted the young Prophet of the Sun to order his ships to be anchored and his following to land, as he beheld the predestined bay on his right-hand side, during his slow and thoughtful journey down the Nile. There must have been such reasons; there always are for the determination or, rather, for the discovery of a sacred spot, anywhere upon the surface of the earth. And from what one can guess of his religious sensitiveness, Akhnaton was surely aware of their existence, even though it be rash to assert that he "knew" them, intellectually, i.e., that he could have formulated them in clear sentences, *explained* them. However, two factors undoubtedly played a decisive part in his conscious choice of the site: first, it was beautiful; in the distance, the light-grey limestone cliffs—that looked white under the dazzling midday sun, pink or violet at sunset—resplendent between the yellow desert sand and the pure sky, unbelievably blue. And, coming from the South, one could see their clear-cut outlines, bordering the bay to the North, above the shining, greyish-blue waters of the Nile. Under moonlight (supposing that Akhnaton had a first glimpse of it at night) the place was no less if not even more dreamlike. And, in addition to that, it was virgin land—religiously speaking; sacred, no doubt, according to the untraced cosmic parallelism that made it so, but never yet noticed, never yet recognised and utilised as such, never connected with the cult of any of the man-made deities, or with the life of any king. In the words of the first boundary stelae of Tell-el-Amarna, it belonged "neither to a god nor to a goddess, neither to a prince nor to a princess."[9] It was awaiting its first consecration—like the new, purified earth, at the opening of every further Time-cycle. It *symbolised* that innocent and beautiful new Earth.

Akhnaton consecrated it to the fiery Orb, Aton, Source of Life, whence the atoms of its material substance had sprung, milliards[10] of years before, to Aton Whose Essence—Heat-and-Light, vibrating Energy—he had experienced, *realised*, to be the same as the essence of his own being, and Whom he could therefore rightly call his "Father."

---

[9] Tell-el-Amarna boundary stelae.
[10] Billions (short scale)—Ed.

He caused a solemn sacrifice to be offered. And then, proceeding to the South and to the North, he halted, and fixed the limits of the holy territory. And he caused the words of consecration to be inscribed upon the stelae set up at its limits: frontier posts between the world as it was—the world that had refused his message—and the earthly Paradise, like unto that in the far-gone "days of Ra," which he hoped to reinstall upon that stretch of land, which had never before borne a temple or a palace: "It belongs to my Father, Aton, mountains, deserts, meadows, islands, high-grounds, low-grounds, land, water, villages, embankments, men, beasts, groves, and all things which Aton, my Father, will bring into existence, forever and ever."[11]

The area occupied by the demarcated territory, which stretched on both sides of the Nile "from the Eastern hills to the Western hills" (including the island in the midst of the river) was indeed very small: it measured roughly eight miles (from north to south) by 17 (from east to west)—a spot, in comparison with the surface of Egypt, not to speak of the Egyptian Empire and of the whole Earth. And Akhnaton swore a great oath that he would not extend it. He felt, perhaps, that he hardly could expect to bring the world of his dreams into existence, unless it be (to begin with, at least) within a very restricted area.

The size of the place has, however, little importance. What counts is the spirit—the meaning—of its consecration, the intention behind the symbolical gesture opening (or, to be more accurate, haltingly foreshadowing, God alone knew how many thousands of years in advance, the opening of) a new era. As I said, this era was to be nothing less than the "Era of Truth"—the Golden Age—in which the world, aware of all that is implied in its filiation to the Sun, is governed by "gods," real "Children of the Sun," *not* for the greatest "happiness" of the greatest number of men (a decadent idea) but for the fulfilment of Life's highest purpose, which is to be a *conscious* hymn to the Sun. And the words of consecration and the oath, first pronounced "on the thirteenth day of the fourth month of the second season," in the sixth year of the king's reign, were repeated, according to a tablet, "on the eighth day of the first month of the second season," in the eighth regnal year, when Akhnaton came back to inhabit

---

[11] Second Foundation inscription, quoted in Weigall, pp. 89–90.

his newly-built capital; repeated, nay, with renewed stress: "It" (the dedicated territory) "shall be *for* Aton, my Father: its hills, its deserts, all its fowl, all its people, all its cattle, all things which Aton produces, on which His rays shine; all things which are in Akhetaton, they will be for my Father, the living Aton, unto the temple of Aton in the city, forever and ever. *They are all offered to His spirit.* And may His rays be beauteous when they receive them."[12]

The oath the young king had sworn not to extend the sacred territory beyond the limits he had given it, did not bind him to remain within it, cut off from the rest of the world, as though in an ivory tower. It merely emphasised the extraordinary importance which he gave the demarcated land (possibly for mystical reasons, unknown to us) and his desire to restrict to it (doubtless for practical reasons) his direct experiment of the ideal state. We know, in fact, from the famous Tell-el-Amarna tablets — a part of his diplomatic correspondence with other kings and with his own high officials and vassals in Syria and Palestine — that he continued governing the Empire from his new capital (only that he governed it in the strange manner of a man who did not live in his own Age). And we know that, apart from the City-of-the-Horizon-of-the-Disk, he founded at least two other towns dedicated to Aton, and intended (in his mind) to be, like the capital, radiating centres of the new worship: one somewhere in Syria — we do not know where — and one, named Gem-Aton, in Nubia, near the Third Cataract of the Nile.[13]

As I have pointed out elsewhere[14] one is tempted to see, in the choice of these two places, one at each end of his dominions, a sign of Akhnaton's effort to prepare his whole Empire to become sacred territory, "property of the Sun" in the highest sense of the word. His *ultimate* desire was, no doubt, to see the rule of the Sun — the socio-political (and religious) earthly order identical to the divine cosmic Order — established in *every* land: the Religion of Light and Life as cosmic Energy cannot be limited to a particular area of the earthly sphere. But after his bitter experi-

---

[12] Quoted by Weigall, p. 93.

[13] James Baikie, *The Amarna Age: A Study of the Crisis of the Ancient World* (London: A. & C. Black, 1926), p. 263. Also Weigall, p. 166.

[14] Savitri Devi, *A Son of God*, p. 65.

ence in Thebes, he was aware of the difficulties that stand in the way of such an achievement, and of the necessity of acting gradually. The best he could do, to begin with, was to see to it that at least three dedicated cities were built within his Empire. And of these, Akhetaton, the capital, founded upon holy ground which he had personally selected, and directly governed by him, was to be the first visible and tangible instance of the Golden Age theocracy of his dreams: the first example of what the earth can become when a true child of the Sun "causes it to belong to Him Who hath made it."

This is not the place to describe in detail the City-of-the-Horizon-of-the-Disk. That has been done by archaeologists far better than I could do it. But it is not superfluous to point out that the most suggestive observations of those who, themselves, without prepossessions, have "dug up the past" upon the famous site, confirm that which I have stressed concerning Akhnaton's tremendous dream, and show, at the same time, how lamentably the city, even when it was at the height of its splendour, fell short of it—for even a Man "above Time" is, in connection with his practical achievements, a prisoner of the Age in which he lives; and no earthly Paradise is possible in a Dark Age.

One of the most pathetic facts about Akhetaton, the "Seat of Truth," is certainly the haste with which it was built.

Within about two years—between the date of the solemn consecration of the holy territory, in the sixth year of Akhnaton's reign, and the date at which he came and settled there, early in the eighth year—the new capital took shape, with the result that, in many instances, instead of finely-cut masonry, "rubble was used, with a thin stone facing. Mud brick was white-washed to look like limestone."[15] Even the tombs—"houses of eternity"— that the king caused to be hewn out of the living[16] rock, in the desert hills to the east of the city, for those of his followers that he particularly wished to honour, "also witness to the furious hurry in which everything was done and to the lack of sufficient

---

[15] Pendlebury, p. 17.
[16] Replacing "live"—Ed.

skilled artisans and artists."[17] It was as though Akhnaton had known from the start that his days were numbered and had been obsessed by the tragic dilemma: "Now — or never!" (which *is*, in fact, the dilemma hanging over the genesis of *all* great achievements within Time, more or less at *any* period, save at the beginning of a new Time-cycle, and whatever be the *quality* — "in Time," "above Time," or "against Time" — of the men fated to act, the dilemma more and more inseparable from action in Time as such, as one advances towards — or into — the Dark Age).

And yet — in spite of that haste — the city, the central part of which at least was "particularly well laid out,"[18] was, on the whole, an exceptional abode of order and beauty. It stretched between the light, greyish-yellow sand of the desert and the orchards and gardens that bordered the Nile, over a distance of five miles from south to north, on either side of two main avenues. One of these is, to this day, known to the inhabitants of the near-by villages as "the Imperial Way" — *Sikket-es Sultan* — while the other, somewhat further east, has been given the name of High-Priest Street by the modern excavators of the site — as though the theocratic idea that gave birth to the short-lived capital had imposed itself upon their subconscious mind. In the Northern Suburb, "High-Priest Street" is continued as "West Road," while another thoroughfare, parallel to it — "East Road" — has been cleared to the east of it. A number of other streets ran from West to East, at right angles to the former. The breadth of the town was roughly three quarters of a mile. In the centralmost locality, fronting on the main avenue — the "Imperial Way" — lay the king's vast estate, with its private and official quarters, its gardens and pleasure lake, its beautiful private temple, and, to the North of it, the Great Temple of Aton. There was another palace at the northern end of the city, and several more temples. In fact, every house — whether that of a well-known courtier or high official, lodged in the immediate neighbourhood of the royal estate, or that of a man of less exalted condition, such as those who lived in what is now known as "the Northern Suburb" — was provided with a chapel. About a mile

---

[17] Pendlebury, p. 56.
[18] Pendlebury, p. 41.

to the South of the capital, were the famous gardens of Maru-Aton—the nearest approach to an earthly Paradise, if any—with their fresh green arbours, their colonnaded pavilions, and their artificial lakes full of pink and white lotus flowers. While to the East, between the city and the limestone hills that limited the landscape, lay a small walled village, regularly planned, with neat rows of cottages all alike, destined—the archaeologists presume—for the workmen occupied on the tombs in the Eastern hills.

In glaring contrast to all the older temples of Egypt—and, may I add, to the classical temples of India, to this day—in which the holy of holies, abode of the hidden God, is the smallest and the darkest room, "the Temple at Amarna was a true sanctuary of the Sun, with airy courts open to the sky succeeding one another as far as the High Altar."[19] And this is true of *all* the religious buildings of Akhnaton's capital, from the Great Temple of Aton, which was to be the centre of the new worship in the whole of the Egyptian Empire, down to the most modest private chapel, comprising just one altar in the midst of a small court.

The spirit of the new worship—the idea that enthusiasm at the sight of light and beauty is the best form of adoration—is everywhere obvious. A curious fact, however—too curious not to be mentioned—is that, while in the state temples the altar was always approached facing the East, "orientation did not seem to matter in the private chapels," which faced "in all directions."[20] Was this, on the part of many a house-owner, a senseless and spectacular reaction against Tradition, taken indiscriminately, as a whole? And if so, how is it that the king—who did *not* reject that which, in Tradition, actually symbolised eternal facts or laws—allow his subjects to disregard such an important matter as the orientation of their Sun chapels? The only possible answer to that question is that, although he considered it his duty to observe the potent symbolism of orientation with regard to state temples (thus putting the state in harmony with the Solar System) Akhnaton was, like all those who have risen above the bondage of Time and Space, convinced that "wherever one turns, there is God," and that he therefore judged it unnecessary

---

[19] Pendlebury, p. 77.
[20] Pendlebury.

to interfere—taken, of course, for granted that he *knew* that so many chapels within his sacred city were not oriented. To him, as I just said, the most important thing in religion was reverent, adoring joy at the awareness of supreme beauty. The right sense of symbolical correspondences was, indeed, the natural outcome of true devotion to true Divinity. Its natural outcome, but not its generator. The important thing, in practice, remained the creation of that atmosphere of beauty and innocent joy of life—that actual Golden Age atmosphere—external expression of wisdom "above Time" and yet "faithful to the earth," in the midst of which the symbolical correspondences—signs of harmony between earth and cosmos—would automatically appear, and be felt.

Everything in Akhetaton—everything, at least, which lay within the king's power, everything that unlimited wealth and unfettered artistry could produce, at the command and under the inspiration of a god-like Man who was himself an artist[21] — was designed to forward such an atmosphere.

Both the Great Temple of Aton and the king's main palace were buildings of unbelievable splendour.[22] The decoration of the latter—its painted pavements in the new, free "Amarna style," representing calves gambolling through high grasses full of poppies, or wild ducks waddling their way through marshes (or, in the more public rooms, processions of the subject-races of the Empire: Negroes and Nubians, Libyans and Semites); its wall frescoes picturing birds and butterflies fluttering over ponds covered with water lilies, while silver-scaled fishes swam between the reeds; its painted ceilings, picturing flights of pigeons—was, like that of the Northern Palace, a hymn to the loveliness of Life, the visible equivalent of the well-known songs of praise through which we infer the essential of Akhnaton's religion. And one can hardly imagine the impression that one

---

[21] Pendlebury, p. 92, suggests that Akhnaton himself quite possibly used to paint. "Two paint brushes of palm-fibre, several fishbones for use of drawing quills, the end still stained with colour, and a good deal of raw paints were found in a private room of the king's palace."

[22] See the description of them in Weigall's *The Life and Times of Akhnaton*, Baikie's *The Amarna Age*, Pendlebury's *Tell-el-Amarna*, etc.

must have had on entering what seems to have been its immense reception hall, the 542 palm-shaped pillars of which bore capitals inlaid with gold and richly-coloured glazes.

And although the temple has been so utterly destroyed that nothing is left of it but the foundations, we can safely presume that it was no less beautifully adorned than the king's own dwelling.

Indeed, even the ordinary middle-class house in Akhetaton, the type of which can be studied in the remains of the Northern Suburb of the city, was more lovely than many a rich flat of our modern world. Not only was it independent—self-contained—and practically always situated within extensive grounds,[23] but it had more than a sufficient number of rooms to secure privacy to the members of a large household and was provided with all the comfort that was possible in 18th Dynasty Egypt. And the walls were painted with birds and garlands, less elaborately, of course, than those of the palace, but in the same nature-loving spirit, and the inside of it, though simple, "must have been a glow of colour, with the patches of bright paint and the gilded or polished furniture."[24]

The remains of the whole place testify to Akhnaton's attempt to make it the pattern and the centre of a world of beauty and happiness, of a world regenerated through utmost truth to Nature—faithfulness to the spirit of the Sun. And more eloquent, perhaps, than all the rest, are the ruins of the "workmen's village" to the East of the city. There stood regularly planned "neat rows of cottages side by side,"[25] along roads at right angles to one another. Each labourer shared with his family one of those little cottages, which comprised

> a front room, used both as a kitchen and as a parlour, bedrooms, and a cupboard at the back. Inside the houses, rough paintings on the mud walls hint at the effort of the

---

[23] The house T. 36, 11 studied by J. D. S. Pendlebury, lay, for instance, in an enclosure of 70 yards by 50 (Pendlebury, pp. 102 and following).

[24] Pendlebury, p. 109.

[25] Pendlebury, pp. 58 and 118. See also Sir Leonard Woolley, *Digging Up the Past* (London: Pelican, 1937), pp. 61–63.

individual workman to decorate his surroundings and to express his piety; the charms and amulets picked up on the floor show which of the many gods of Egypt were most in favour with working men; scattered tools and implements tell of the work of each, or of his pursuits in leisure hours.[26]

And if, as it has sometimes been supposed — as the single entrance to it, the "marks of patrol roads all around it," the surrounding walls "in no way defensive" but high enough to "keep people in,"[27] and its apparently intentional aloofness from the city, would perhaps suggest — this "workmen's village" was, in fact, a place of internment for men who had disobeyed the king (what people call today a "re-education" camp, when they are polite, or a concentration camp, when they are not, or when they speak of "the enemy's" institutions), then its evidence would be even more eloquent still. For, dreary as they may have looked, in their uniformity, those little houses all in a row were far better than any "coolie lines" of modern India (before 1947, at least), nay, better than the English workmen's dwellings of the dark years of industrial growth, in the 19th century. And their inmates — whether free labourers or "internees" — *had* "leisure hours." And they were not asked — or "conditioned" — to pay homage to the faith in power, as people are today under every capitalistic and non-capitalistic form of democracy. "They clung to their old gods, and their favourite seems to have been Bes, the little dancing lion-dwarf."[28] Akhnaton was a forerunner neither of Christianity nor of democracy nor of Marxism, nor of any man-centred faith of this world or of the next — products of decay, typical of an advanced stage of the Age of Gloom or misapplication of a doctrine of despair and escape from earth. He was, as I said before, one of the very rare men "above Time" who, while refusing to accept the conditions of the Age of Gloom, *did not* turn their backs to this world, and perhaps the only such one endowed, in historical times, with absolute power. Only if one considers him — and it — in this light, can one hope to understand

---

[26] Woolley, p. 62.
[27] Pendlebury.
[28] Pendlebury, p. 58.

his creation: Akhetaton, centre of true solar theocracy and capital of a new earth.

Only if one considers it in its political symbolism—as an expression of Akhnaton's claim to embody the oldest and true—the perennial-solar Tradition, in contrast to what that Tradition had become through the gradual rise of Amon (i.e., of Amon's priests) to prominence—can one grasp the right meaning of the most discussed and most misunderstood aspect of the "Amarna style," namely, of the treatment of the king's own figure, and of that of the members of his family, in nearly all but the very early paintings and reliefs of his reign.

In all these pictures "the skull is elongated; the chin, as seen in profile, is drawn as though it were sharply pointed; the flesh under the jaw is skimped, thus giving an upward turn to the line; and the neck is represented as being long and thin," details to which one must add the prominent paunch and the abnormally large hips and thighs, "though from the knee downwards, the legs are of more natural size."[29] The explanation given for those anatomic abnormalities by many, nay, by most archaeologists, is simple—*too* simple, in fact. It rests upon the following reasoning process: in all its *other* aspects (as one can see from the scenes of animal and plant life on the walls and pavements of the palaces) the Amarna art excels in faithfulness to nature; it has represented Akhnaton with a misshaped head and an ungainly body; *therefore*, he must have been afflicted with both. Too simple, I say, for this is contradicted by several likenesses of the king such as the life-size limestone bust of the Berlin Museum,[30] which is anything but out of proportion. The true explanation is to be sought elsewhere: in the time-honoured tradition that "Ra-Horakhti had once reigned on earth," and in the comparison of the strangest "portraits" of the king, queen, and princesses with the Egyptian "wood and slate carvings and ivory figures of archaic times." "The similarity between the treatment of the human body in this archaic art and the 'new' art of Akhnaton at

---

[29] Weigall, p. 59.
[30] Now in Wiesbaden.

once becomes apparent," writes Arthur Weigall, the one archaeologist who, to my knowledge, and whatever may have been his prepossessions about the Aton religion, hinted at the right significance of the strange "exaggerations" of the Amarna artists; "in all representations of archaic men, one sees the elongated skull, so characteristic of the king's style; in the clay and ivory figures is the prominent stomach; and here also, most apparent of all, are the unaccountably large thighs and ponderous hips."[31] And he produces, in support of this statement, two royal heads and a statuette in archaic style discovered by Sir Flinders Petrie at Abydos and Diospolis,[32] works of art in which the "Amarna features are obvious," and he boldly holds Akhnaton's "new style" for what it is: *not* the realistic portraiture of an ungainly model, still less the sickly creation of decadent artists in search of *bizarrerie*, but an "archaic renaissance" with a deep political meaning, the external sign of a return to the old idea of divine kingship, with its old implications.

This is indeed the only explanation of the "Amarna style" in the light of which the apparent contrast between the utter realism in the rendering of nature scenes (and in *some* of the portrait painting and sculpture) and the strangeness of the distorted "portraits" disappears. The figures of calves and ducks and papyrus-reeds and water lilies merely had to be true to life—and decorative; the figures of the king, son of the Sun, had *first* (and even at the cost of external beauty) to be true to the meaning and purpose of his reign; they had, through unmistakable filiation to models as archaic as possible, to manifest, in a manner likely to strike the Egyptians, the filiation of Akhnaton's new order to the "days of Ra," past and to come; they had, nay, to be a sign that, with him, in Akhetaton at least, the "days of Ra" had returned.

The same intention, the same theocratic symbolism, is to be noticed in the fact—equally stressed by A. Weigall—that the king is nearly always represented with the crown of Lower Egypt—by far the oldest of the "Two Lands," and the immemorial seat of that Heliopolitan Sun worship with which he tried so hard to connect his, in the minds and hearts of his subjects—and that "the names of the new God were placed within royal

---

[31] Weigall, p. 63.
[32] See the pictures in Weigall, p. 64.

cartouches";[33] also in the fact that, wherever one turns in Akhetaton, the person of the King is honoured, exalted — adored — along with the Disk with rays ending in hands, Sign of impersonal, cosmic Godhead.

This can be seen in the most simple, the most average private houses of the sacred city. Every house was, as stated above, provided with a more or less elaborate private chapel, the place of worship of the family. There, "on the back wall behind the altar" — the wall one faced when standing *before* the altar, in the attitude of prayer — would be placed a stele not merely picturing the Sun-disk, Symbol of the all-pervading He-She-It, "Heat-and-Light-within-the-Disk," but "showing the King worshipping the Disk of the Sun."[34] And there were representations of the King, as well as written words in praise of Aton, in more than one part of the house outside the chapel; many a niche or false door, sunk into a wall for the sake of symmetry, was inscribed with prayers, and "one at least shows a scene of the king making an offering,"[35] while "the lintel of the front door" (in the same house) bore a picture of the owner of the house "worshipping the royal and divine Names, and saying a short prayer."[36]

This can be seen also, and no less glaringly, in the 25 tombs in the desert hills, to the East of the city. "Taken together," those tombs, where not a single reference to Osiris or to any of the old mythology of the Netherworld is to be found, and where only two funeral scenes are depicted,[37] "only reveal one personality, one family, one home, one career, and one mode of worship. This is the figure, family, palace, and occupations of the King, and the worship of the Sun — which also was his."[38] Of course, scenes from the career of those men to whom the tombs were destined — in the tomb of Mahu, for instance, scenes showing the latter's efficiency as Commander of the Police — were *also* repre-

---

[33] Weigall, p. 65; Pendlebury, p. 14.
[34] Pendlebury, p. 102.
[35] Pendlebury, p. 109.
[36] Pendlebury, p. 103.
[37] In the burial chamber of Princess Maketaton, and in the tomb of Huya.
[38] Norman de Garis Davies, *The Rock Tombs of El-Amarna*, 6 vols. (London: Egypt Exploration Fund, 1903), pp. 18–19.

sented upon the walls. But they are *always* connected, in one manner or another, with the person of the King. They tell of the loyalty which the courtiers (outwardly at least) professed to him, their readiness to "hearken to his Teaching of life," the generosity with which he lavished rewards upon them for their zeal in the discharge of their official duties and for their alleged orthodoxy regarding the Religion of the Disk. And the scenes of domestic life—the naturalness of which has been emphasised by all archaeologists—show the life of the royal family. And the scenes of worship picture the King and Queen before the altar of the Sun. And in their prayers, the noblemen, owners of the tombs, beg Aton, the Source of life, Who is also the Ruler of Destiny, to grant them to continue serving the King beyond the gates of death, and proclaim, again and again, in beautiful words, Akhnaton's divinity as Son of the Sun: "Thou hast formed him out of Thine own Rays . . . He is Thy Emanation . . .";[39] "Thy rays are upon Thy bright Image, the Ruler of Truth, who proceedeth from Eternity; Thou givest him Thy duration and Thy years . . . As long as Heaven is, He shall be!"[40] "Thou art eternal, Neferkhepe-rura Ua-en-Ra" (Beautiful Essence of the Sun, Only One of the Sun); "living and sound art thou, for He begat thee."[41]

One has indeed to follow the stream of history nearly 3,000 years—namely, down to the relatively modern great Sun state of South America, the Inca Empire, to find such an absolute identification of the person of the King with the Sun, Principle of cosmic Godhead. But there is an enormous difference—a difference in nature, in meaning, not merely in years—between that latest in date of the traditional Sun kingdoms[42] and the short-lived City of the Horizon of Aton. The Inca state was perhaps *the* most

---

[39] Tomb of Tuta (Inscription).
[40] Tomb of May (Inscription).
[41] Tomb of Ay (Inscription).
[42] Japan, the one Sun state of our contemporary world is *much older*. But I do not mention it in this connection because of the very long eclipse of the Emperors' personal rule, from the days of Yoritomo, the first *Shogun* (1186–1199) to 1866. Also because of the part played by thought currents *other* than state Sun worship (Buddhism, Confucianism, etc.) in Japanese history.

eminently "totalitarian" state of all times (if I be allowed to apply that fashionable word to a reality centuries old), a state in which everything—including private individuals' marriages—was firmly and minutely regulated by the government, and, in addition to that, a warrior-like state—a state in which the necessity of war was, at least, fully recognised, although its kings were not wantonly aggressive. With its lofty solar religion—very much the same as Akhnaton's and, contrarily to that of Japan, the only religious force in the land[43]—and its great ideal of social justice, it was what I would call a state "against Time." Akhnaton's holy city was a place of individual liberty as well as a place of beauty, and his new order, an order of peace, for *he* was a Man "above Time." They were fully so, however, only to the extent it was for him materially (and psychologically) possible to bring his dream of an earthly paradise into existence. And this was *not* possible for, as I said before, there is and there can be no state "above Time" in the Dark Age.

There can be none, because every state rests upon coercion—i.e., violence—nay, because, *always*, save at the very dawn of a new Time-cycle—and all the *more* as one advances into an Age of Gloom—life itself is inseparable from violence under some form or another. And archaeological evidence shows that, with all its loveliness, Akhnaton's city was no exception to the eternal Laws. However much the sight of it may have been, as a whole, "like a glimpse of Heaven,"[44] it bore, even materially, the signs of the Dark Age: behind the beautiful estates that lined the roads in the North Suburb and the "second ring of medium-sized houses" at the back of these, "finally came the slums: a mere tangle of hovels, sharing common court-yards."[45] In spite of his endeavour to give everyone a place within his sacred territory;

---

[43] Even before 551 A.D. (date of the introduction of Buddhism) Japan had other important gods besides the Sun goddess. Legend shows that for a long time the supremacy of the latter had to be won over the claims of her powerful and troublesome brother Su-sa-no-wo, the tempest god.

[44] Inscription in the tomb of May (tomb 14) at Tell-el-Amarna.

[45] Pendlebury, p. 45.

nay, in spite of the fact that he had, in his hymns, laid down the principle of the separation of races, implying the idea that *only natural differences* among men should be sanctioned and stressed in a society copied upon the eternal Order of heaven, Akhnaton could not, even in the city of his dreams, avoid the bitter struggle for space between the well-to-do and the poor, *on grounds of wealth alone*, a struggle that had, in his days already, long become one of the permanent features of human life. It is indeed difficult to say whether, in that "tangle of hovels"—the back streets of the Northern Suburb—no Egyptian lived whom his sincere adherence to the Religion of the Disk and his qualities of character should have recommended to the king's attention and won him a private house as comfortable as that which Pnahesi the Ethiopian (or the Negro)[46] occupied to the South of the official Quarters.

There is more. As I said above, the so-called "workmen's village," some miles to the East of the capital, looks strangely like a model convicts' camp, run under exceptionally humane conditions. Now, even if it were just a workmen's village (which is possible, despite the isolating walls and the traces of patrol roads all around it), still the fact would remain that there existed an armed police force in Akhetaton, and that this force did not confine its activity to mere parades. This is unmistakably shown upon the walls of the tomb of Mahu, "Chief of the Police,"[47] where malefactors are actually pictured "led handcuffed into the presence of the Vizier and other nobles, for examination."[48] There is, admittedly, no evidence at all of the death-penalty, or even of drastic repression methods, having existed within the sacred area (or, in fact, anywhere in Egypt) during Akhnaton's reign. (Sir Wallis Budge's assumption of the contrary is a purely gratuitous one, based, as he himself states, upon the mere fact that Akhnaton's was an "Oriental" court.)[49] And even the priests of Amon—the King's arch-enemies—were merely dispossessed of their fabulous wealth, and, apparently, neither killed nor in any way persecuted (otherwise, this would have been record-

---

[46] Budge, p. 92.
[47] Tomb No. 9 (southern series) at Tell-el-Amarna.
[48] Pendlebury, p. 52.
[49] Budge, pp. 107–108.

ed—and stressed—in such inscriptions as the Cairo stele, describing conditions under Akhnaton's government, retrospectively, after the restoration of the cult of Amon). Yet, the mere existence of a force of coercion in Akhetaton shows that the city was not the earthly paradise of the king's dreams.

The maintenance of a police force was not the only willing or unwilling—conscious or unconscious—concession of the Man "above Time" to the necessities (or to the standing conditions) of this Dark Age. All archaeologists agree that not only was Akhnaton himself "no hunter," but that there is in his reign no evidence of hunting, as though the cruel sport had been forbidden, or at least strongly discouraged, as contrary to the spirit of a religion which exalted the beauty and sanctity of Life. Yet, on the other hand, it is more difficult to deny the evidence of at least occasional animal-sacrifices in connection with the Religion of the Disk. Even though the offerings may have consisted "mostly of vegetables, fruits, and flowers,"[50] even though a passage of Sir Wallis Budge relating to the altars in the open courts of the Great Temple of Aton would seem to suggest that no sacrifices were offered upon them, any more than on the altar which Queen Hatshepsut had erected to Ra-Horakhti in her temple at Deir-el-Bahri,[51] there remains the first inscription set up in commemoration of the foundation of Akhetaton, which states that the King offered Aton a great sacrifice "of bread, beer, horned bulls, polled bulls, beasts, fowl, wine, incense, and all goodly herbs";[52] there remains the disturbing, even if not 100 percent convincing,

---

[50] Weigall, p. 108.

[51] Sir E. A. Wallis Budge, *A History of Egypt from the End of the Neolithic Period to the Death of Cleopatra VII, B.C. 30*, vol. 4, *Egypt and her Asiatic Empire* (London: Kegan Paul, Trench, Trübner & Co., 1902), p. 122: ". . . it is possible that the idea of the altars was suggested to the architect Bek, the son of Men, by the altar which Queen Hatshepsut, had erected in her temple at Der-al-Bahari. It is an interesting fact that *no sacrifices* of any kind were offered up either on the Queen's altar or the altars of her successors, and it must be noted that the Queen says in her inscription that she had built the altar for her father Ra-Harmachis, and that Ra-Harmachis was the one ancient god of the Egyptians that Amenhotep IV delighted to honour."

[52] Quoted in Weigall, p. 83.

pictorial evidence of garlanded bulls,[53] and of feasts in which the presence of meat and poultry is suggested.[54] It may be, of course, that Akhnaton only allowed animal sacrifices in order to impress upon his people the filiation of his "new" cult to the immemorial Sun cult of Heliopolis, of which such ritual bloodshed was a feature — he needed spectacular concessions to deep-rooted tradition, if he was to impose upon Egypt, "peacefully," a religion as "un-Egyptian" as his. It may be also that he realised that, if suppressed, the time-honoured rite, which at least regulated and restricted meat-eating to some extent, would only be replaced by a more extensive and more gruesome slaughter of animals in the name of gluttony alone (as it actually was to be, one day, in the Christian world). But whatever be the explanation one might put forward to reconcile his attitude in this matter with the lofty Golden Age wisdom that radiates from all we know of Akhnaton's career, it cannot destroy the fact that the two *are* incompatible.

There never was and there never can be any killing of innocent birds and beasts — be it as offerings to the Sun — in a *real* Golden Age. And the toleration of this most ancient rite, even exceptionally, and with the most laudable practical justification, in Akhnaton's holy city, merely illustrates with further forcefulness how impossible it is for a Man "above Time" — nay, *especially* for a Man "above Time" — to create an earthly paradise within our Dark Age.

But the most tragically instructive instance of the application of a Golden Age wisdom to the earth in this Dark Age, regardless of the conditions of the latter, is to be studied in Akhnaton's uncompromising "no" to war, in his refusal, as the head of an Empire, to accept the law of violence, which is the law of Time *par excellence* (and especially the law of Time in all Dark Ages.)

The story of the unrest in Syria and Palestine — i.e., in the whole northern portion of the Egyptian Empire — in Akhnaton's reign has been pieced together from some 300 clay tablets covered with cuneiform writing — the diplomatic script of his

---

[53] In the tomb of Merira (tomb 4) at Tell -el-Amarna.
[54] In the tomb of Huya (tomb 1) at Tell-el-Amarna.

days—found in 1887 and 1891 among the ruins of Akhetaton, and representing the dispatches sent to the King by vassal dynasts and Egyptian governors of the war-torn lands. We do not—and, unfortunately, shall never—know the *whole* story, for over two-thirds of the clay tablets were lost through senseless mishandling after their discovery.[55] But from what we do know of it, the situation can be retrospectively summed up and characterised as "a great concerted anti-Egyptian movement"[56] led by local vassal princes in close alliance with wild plundering elements, apparently desert tribes: the Sa-Gaz, in North Syria, and the Habiru (in whom some authors are tempted to recognise the "Hebrews," in one of the invading waves that carried them to what they called their "Promised Land") in Palestine, while at the back of it, invisible organiser of all the trouble, stood Shubbiluliuma, the ambitious and crafty king of the Hittites, whose aim it was to extend his own domination at the expense of the Egyptian Empire.

The movement seems to have had two main centres: the land of Amor, in Northern Syria, and the Plain of Jezreel, in Palestine. The Amorite chieftain Abdashirta and his three sons—and, foremost among these, the famous Aziru—and Ikatama, the "man of Kadesh," and, in the South, Labaya (or Lapaya), Tagi, Milki-Ili, and others, were the most troublesome anti-Egyptian dynasts—those whose names one reads over and over again in the complaining reports addressed to Akhnaton by loyal ones such as Abi-Milki of Tyre, Biridiya of Megiddo, and, above all, Ribaddi, the indefatigable "king" of Gebal (Byblos), and Abdikhipa, Governor of Jerusalem.

These both remained unflinchingly faithful to the end (even after Abi-Milki and many another staunch ally of Egypt had long gone over to the Sa-Gaz in sheer desperation, as no help had come to him from Pharaoh, in answer to his pathetic dispatches). Their messages are not only the most numerous (over 50 letters addressed to Akhnaton by Ribaddi alone have come down to us), but they are moving beyond words, even to this day, at a distance of 3,300 years—moving, as completely selfless

---

[55] Petrie, p. 259.
[56] Stanley Cook, *Cambridge Ancient History* (Cambridge: Cambridge University Press, 1924), vol. 2, p. 303.

loyalty (loyalty coupled with the certainty of disaster) always is. And at first, one can only experience bewilderment at Akhnaton's attitude as *he* took knowledge of them, bewilderment and something more at his apparent indifference to the fate of those who were dying for him with such faith. But let us recall in a nutshell the general course of events, as one follows it in the "Tell-el-Amarna Letters."

The immediate impression one gathers from these most ancient diplomatic documents is extremely confusing. A number of local princes and chieftains, after equally lengthy and vehement protestations of their own loyalty to the King of Egypt, describe him the growing unrest in their particular areas, every one of them accusing his neighbour of being a friend of the Sa-Gaz (or of the Habiru), a liar, and a traitor. It is only gradually—as one reads further messages—that one begins to understand who is really loyal and who is not. Then one reads of dynasts at first faithful to Egypt—such as Abi-Milki—who, one after the other, go over to the opposite—anti-Egyptian—camp. Their names are given in the letters of other local dynasts who still hold on. But from the increasing entreaty in their *own* messages—appeals for military help and protection—one concludes that no satisfactory answer had reached them from the distant capital of the Sun, and that they have gone over to the enemy in sheer rage and disgust, not wanting to die uselessly for a king who did not seem to value their devotion to his cause. Soon, there are practically only two chieftains who have accepted to carry on, in the name of and for Egypt, the struggle against the Sa-Gaz and Habiru and whomever might stand on their side; two last sincere allies of Akhnaton as an emperor: Ribaddi and Abdikhipa. The letters of both of them give a rapidly darkening picture of the situation, and lay more and more stress upon the urgency of the Pharaoh's intervention, if the Empire is to be saved.

The progress of the Amorites, under Abdashirta and his sons, towards the South (and towards the sea-coast) makes Ribaddi feel threatened in his stronghold. And yet, *in the beginning*, his demands strike us as being indeed very modest, "May it seem good to my Lord, the Sun of the Lands, to send me 20 pairs of horses,"[57] writes he, in one of his early dispatches. In another he

---

[57] Letter 103 (Knutzon Collection).

merely asks for "300 men"[58] to help him to hold Gebal (Byblos) against the increasing menace. But that aid is, apparently, never sent. And although Abdashirta is killed in a skirmish, the Amorites push forward, now in alliance with Arvad, a coastal town that has thrown in its lot with theirs. And they are besieging Simyra, another — important — harbour. "As a bird in the fowler's snare, so is Simyra. Night and day the sons of Abdashirta are against it, by land, and the men of Arvad by sea."[59] Meanwhile, the elders of distant Tunip, in North-East Syria, send Akhnaton what is, certainly, one of the most moving official documents of all times:

> Who could formerly have plundered Tunip, without being plundered by Men-kheper-Ra? [Thutmose the Third]. . . . May the king, our Lord, ask his old men if it be not so. But now, we no longer belong to Egypt. . . . Aziru will treat Tunip as he has treated Niy. . . . And when Aziru enters Simyra, he will do to us as he pleases, and the King will have to lament. . . . And now, Tunip, thy city, weeps, and her tears are flowing, and there is no help for us. For twenty years we have been sending [dispatches] to our Lord, the King of Egypt, but there has not come to us a word from our Lord — not one![60]

Still no aid comes. It is as though Akhnaton were deaf to all appeals: as though the fate of his dominions did not interest him or, as though, perhaps — one wonders — the Syrian news never reached him.

More local dynasts — Zimrida of Sidon, Yapa-addu, and others — join the enemies of Egypt. Ribaddi sends the king a list of the towns that "the sons of Abadashirta" have taken, describes his own plight, cut off as he is from the ports of Northern Syria and surrounded by enemies closing in on him, and begs, again and again, for troops to be sent to him, to help him defend Simyra. For if Simyra falls, Byblos is sure to fall. But no troops are

---

[58] Letter 93 (Knutzon Collection).
[59] Letter 84 (Winckler Collection).
[60] Letter 41 (Winckler Collection) quoted (CLXX) in Petrie, pp. 292–93.

sent. And a line or two upon a clay tablet tell Akhnaton the result of his refusal to fight: "Simyra, thy fortress, is now in the power of the Sa-Gaz."[61]

Then follows the whole story of Ribaddi's desperate stand, from the midst of a starving town in growing rebellion against him—alone, loyal to his overlord to the bitter end, in spite of every sign of the latter's indifference—and his last pathetic appeal: "O, let not my Lord the king neglect the city"[62] and his last brief news: "The enemy does not depart from the gates of Byblos ..."

As Byblos fell, he was captured by Aziru and delivered into the hands of the confederate Amorite chiefs, to be put to death in a manner one is left to imagine. We know it from Akhnaton's one surviving letter, written to Aziru after the happening. The King's grief and indignation, as the deed was brought to his knowledge, seem hardly compatible with his constant refusal to help the most faithful and the bravest of all his vassals.

The dispatches from Palestine give the account of parallel events succeeding one another at the same tragic tempo: increasing pressure of the Habiru from all sides and increasing disaffection of the chieftains hitherto loyal to Egypt, as they receive no aid in answer to their distressed letters, intrigues of the most able hostile princelings in order to bribe or threaten into their alliance (and that of the Habiru) those who still hesitate, wondering where their interest lies, and, from the one man faithful to Egypt to the end, namely Abdikhipa, Governor of Jerusalem, further reports of spreading lawlessness—plunder and murder—and desperate appeals for help, and desperate warnings that, if no help comes, the whole land will become the prey of the rebels and of their allies—"If no troops come this year, all the lands of the king, my Lord, will be lost"[63]—postscripts addressed to Akhnaton's cuneiform scribe, with whom Abdikhipa seems to have been personally acquainted: "Bring clearly before the king, my Lord, these words: All the lands of the king my Lord are going to ruin."[64] And finally, the faithful Governor's

---

[61] Letter 56 (Winckler Collection).
[62] Letter 137 (Knutzon Collection).
[63] Letter 183 (Winckler Collection).
[64] Letter 183 (Winckler Collection).

last report of disaster: "Now, the Habiru occupy the cities. Not one prince remains; all are ruined"[65] — and his last protest of loyalty, in, spite of all: "The king has set his name upon the Land of Jerusalem forever; therefore I cannot forsake the Land of Jerusalem."[66]

There is no evidence that Akhnaton did anything to defend his last stronghold in Asia, be it at the eleventh hour, or that he tried to recover any portion of the lost territories. And thus "from the boundaries of Asia Minor and Northern Mesopotamia to the Sinai Desert, Egyptian domination now became a thing of the past — a thing, nay, that was, despite the efforts and partial success of the Pharaohs of the next dynasty, never to be again."[67]

And along with the Egyptian Empire (and with Akhnaton's prestige at home, which alone victorious war could have strengthened) disappeared the chances of the Religion of the Disk to remain the state religion of Egypt and to become, in the form Akhnaton had given it, a world force. In Syria, harsh Hittite domination replaced mild Egyptian rule. And if the Habiru of the Tell-el-Amarna Letters really be the all-too-well-known Hebrews, it is hardly necessary to point out what far-reaching consequences — totally unpredictable in Akhnaton's days — their permanent settling in Canaan was to have for world history. This was not the last time that a ruler's reluctance to war was to originate developments far worse (in the long run) than war would have been, nor — if the above suggestion be right — the last time that a generous dream was finally to forward the ends of the least generous of all races. But it was the first — and last — time that such a powerful potentate — the mightiest of his epoch — took on such a terrible responsibility for the sake of and sacrificed so much to an ideal of peace rooted neither in a philosophy of decay (like the pacifism of most of *our* contemporaries) nor in a lofty but other-worldly wisdom, such as Emperor Asoka's Buddhism, but in a Golden Age conception of life, at the same time unquestionably generous *and* faithful to this earth.

For there is no reason to suppose, as some archaeologists seem to, that Akhnaton acted, or rather, abstained from acting,

---

[65] Letter 181 (Winckler Collection).
[66] Quoted in Baikie, p. 183.
[67] See Savitri Devi, *A Son of God*, p. 208.

out of sheer ignorance of the situation. True, the Tell-el-Amarna Letters are confusing. True, the most decidedly treacherous vassals of Egypt, such as Abdashirta, or Aziru himself, express their allegiance to their "Lord, the King, the Sun of the lands" in the most glowing phrases (all the more glowing that *they* are more treacherous). True, there were at the court of Akhetaton, elements of very, *very* doubtful loyalty (such as that Tutu, with whom Aziru was personally in correspondence, and to whom he used to send presents). And Akhnaton "may well have received a very censored and edited version"[68] of the Syrian dispatches. Still, of all that amount of appealing distress, *something* must have reached him. And there remained to him, anyhow, one reliable way of finding out the truth, and that consisted in going to Syria himself, as his forefathers had, one after the other. That way he never cared — or wished — to take.

On the other hand, "supineness and apathy"[69] are not the proper words by which to describe his attitude, or one would not, in his one own surviving letter to Aziru, feel that sincere grief and righteous indignation at the news that Ribaddi has been handed over to the Amorite princes, his bitterest enemies — an indignation that prompts the king even to threaten his vassal with death. Nor would Akhnaton have done all he could and had his other most faithful supporter, Abdikhipa of Jerusalem, safely brought to Egypt according to the latter's expressed wish, if he just had not cared what happened to those who defended the Empire in his name. No, the young king's bewildering reaction to the Syrian war cannot be so lightly explained. There is, in fact, no logical explanation for it, outside that given by Arthur Weigall: "Akhnaton definitely refused to do battle believing that a resort to arms was an offence to God. Whether fortune or misfortune, gain or loss, was to be his lot, he would hold to his principles and would not return to the old gods of battle."[70] Only, the ideal in the name of which he acted (or, to be more accurate, refrained from acting) was *not* the Christian-like ideal of "brotherhood of all men" that Arthur Weigall supposes. It was a broader and more rational — truer — ideal, a *cosmic* ideal, in the

---

[68] Pendlebury, p. 221.
[69] Baikie, p. 375.
[70] Weigall, p. 202.

light of which "peace on earth and good will towards men" were a mere implication of the established harmony between heaven and earth *on all planes;* the ideal of paradise here and now, in beauty and fullness of life; I repeat: a Golden Age ideal, faithful not to this earth as it *is*, but to this earth as it *was and will be*, at the beginning of every Time-cycle, when strife is yet unconceivable.

In other words, he refused to act according to the law of violence, which is the law of any development in Time save in a Golden Age.

And yet he did *not* turn from this fallen world—renounce the responsibility of temporal power, as Prince Gautama (the Buddha) and Mahavira (the Founder of the Jain religion, also a Kshatriya by birth) were to do, some 800 years later. But he lived in it and for it, as though it were not fallen. He refused to become what I have described in the beginning of this book as a "man *against* Time." And yet he did not seek, beyond the loveliness of this sunlit world—and beyond its unavoidable violence—the eternal Principle of that refusal, but found it in the beauty of his *earthly* Golden Age dream alone.

In this lies his unique position among the famous men "above Time."

The great Indian Emperor Asoka, son of Bindusara, who was to appear 1,100 years after him, is the one towering historical figure with whom one might compare him: a man "above Time," like himself, endowed, like he, with unlimited temporal power, like he, a king who held both hunting and war in abhorrence. (The world-famous apostle of "non-violence" in our times, the late Mahatma Gandhi, *is not in the same class* as either Asoka or Akhnaton. His "nonviolence" is, in reality, the subtlest form of *moral* violence—a typical product of our Dark Age that distorts and corrupts all vital instincts, and calls them by the wrong names. And he is—or was—a most realistic man "*against* Time," who used that distorted violence as a weapon, identifying it—falsely, though sincerely—with the real nonviolence of those who are not of this world and who do not fight for worldly ends.)

But there are differences between the Maurya potentate and the "King of Upper and Lower Egypt, living in Truth." First, a fundamental difference in the nature of their creeds; for, although Asoka might not be described as "an ascetic," the creed in the name of which he protected all life (and first gave up war) *was* an ascetic one: a creed of renunciation of this world, a way explicitly intended to lead men out of the endless cycle of birth, death, and re-birth, considered as a cycle of suffering. Non-violence was, to him, a consequence of that renunciation of the curse of earthly life—nay, of any form of individual life—while it was, to Akhnaton, an inseparable condition of life in beauty and truth, here and now. Then, an all-important difference in the *history* of the two potentates: Asoka was a *convert* to his creed of detachment and love; Akhnaton was the originator of his, and had practised it from the beginning. This may be, from the standpoint of the "soul" of the two great men, just the same. It is *not* at all "the same" from the standpoint of their creation in Time.

Chandasoka—Asoka before he became a Buddhist—had not only taken violence for granted, as the most natural thing, but had exerted it himself, to the utmost extent. He had been a warrior, and a fierce one—and, which is more, a victorious one. Dharmasoka—Asoka *after* the sight (and the experience) of the horror of war had changed his heart—had Chandasoka's career behind him. And, painful as the memory of it doubtless was to him—and ironical as the fact may be—this gave him an immense practical advantage: *he did not need to sacrifice* an inch of his empire to his creed of non-violence: the people of Kalinga had been too ruthlessly crushed even to dream of rebellion. And thus, in the peace and safety won by his own sword at the time he still had been but a Kshatriya full of the lure of carnage and conquest, the great patron of Buddhism could devote his whole energy, and the revenues of a prosperous realm, to his new ideal of meekness and love towards all creatures—his new dream of escape from the bondage of Time. The consequence of his former ruthlessness—the existence of a strengthened centralised state, with increased resources—forwarded the unhindered development of his new creation: the *Buddhist* state, with its glorious laws regulating social welfare and restricting, and finally forbidding, the slaughter of animals, and its organised missionary activity infusing the spirit of non-violence and the yearning of renunciation—the ascetic contempt of this world within Time—into human hearts, from Ceylon and Burma to Palestine, Alexandria, and even Greece and Italy.

Asoka never ceased taking the conditions of this Dark Age into full consideration: first—when he was yet a man "in Time"—in order to conquer (through violence) and then—as he rose "above Time"—in order to renounce this world, to reject it as his home, while still governing it in a spirit of non-violence—with infinitely more thoroughness and more logic than the Christians (with their dogma of personal immortality and their childish partiality towards "man" among all creatures) ever were to show. And he was, as the patron of the great other-worldly religion of peace and love, as successful as he had been as a warrior, and more so.

Akhnaton, who, although he had in him the will-power and uncompromising determination of a fighter, had never been a man of violence, lost everything for the sake of a creed that was anything but an ascetic one. He lost everything, and did not succeed in leaving the stamp of his Teaching upon the future, precisely because of his stubborn refusal to wage war, when war was the only way to that order and peace (and prestige) that he so needed, if his lofty solar philosophy was to continue to find expression in a state religion. Nor did he, on the other hand, go as far as Asoka in the enforcement of non-violence in everyday life. He surely sang the loveliness of Life under *all* its forms, and was no friend of the chase. But no edicts of his forbade or restricted, as far as we know, the slaughter of creatures for man's food, as Asoka's did, and that alone must be looked upon as an abdication before the power of the Dark Age, as a recognition that he *could not* change its conditions of existence, or its scale of values.

But, as I already said, instead of combatting these (in this and other expressions of theirs) in the name of his religion of this world and of this life, and standing "against Time," as other great teachers and leaders were to do in the name of various creeds—some worldly, some other-worldly—he was contented with bearing witness to the beauty of his Golden Age wisdom in the splendid new capital—Seat of Truth—that he had built, but which, in spite of all his efforts, was not the perfect oasis of peace that he had wanted. He alone was, in the midst of it, an oasis of true peace—of inner peace—and of invincible cosmic joy. Deaf to the noise of strife, blind to the conditions of this Dark Age, he carried on his earthly paradise experiment, feeling himself strong enough to create new conditions, at least within his immediate surroundings. He presided over solar rites in which solemn music, hymns, and sacred dances[71] played a great part; he burnt incense upon the altars of the Great Temple of Aton, under the open sky, so unbelievably blue; he entertained himself with his disciples (or those who pretended to be such ones) about the mystery of the divine Rays of the Sun—Light which is Heat, Heat which is Light—he set before his people the example of domestic harmony, symbolising (in him, the King, and in the Queen) the ineffable harmony within the Twofold Principle—He *and* She—kernel of all things, while messengers brought him such letters as those of Ribaddi and Abdikhipa, such ones as that of the elders of Tunip: "Tunip, thy city, weeps, and there is no help for us . . ." And with the sword in hand—needing only to utter a word in order to send the whole Egyptian army across the border—he chose not to fight. He chose to remain to the end, in the midst of strife, the witness of a long-forgotten world, the return of which seemed impossible: a world of beauty, without strife.

The result was material—and moral—disaster: the plight of endless streams of Egyptian and Syrian refugees, pouring across the Sinai Desert;[72] the king's own premature death (perhaps due to slow poisoning: he had enemies even in his close entourage); the systematic destruction of his capital after a few years; the relentless persecution of his already unpopular faith (many supporters of which changed their minds anyhow, as soon as he was no longer there to reward them with gifts of "gold and silver"); the anathematisation of his name as "that criminal of Akhetaton," and, finally, his fall into total oblivion for 3,300 years—

---

[71] Budge, p. 92.

[72] "They have been destroyed, and their towns laid waste, and fire has been thrown (into their grain) . . . ; their countries are starving; they are like goats upon the mountains" (Words of an Egyptian officer, who was in charge of those refugees). See James Henry Breasted in *The Cambridge Ancient History*, vol. 2, p. 125.

until his diplomatic correspondence and then his two surviving hymns to the Sun were brought to light in modern times. Disaster, as complete as that of any movement crushed in the bud — and without the hopes of speedy resurrection that the latter has, when its followers are of a better mettle than those of the Egyptian king, and when they are, *also*, in the Dark Age, prepared to use Dark Age methods.[73] Disaster ... And yet — within the endless downward evolution of history since the dawn of our Timecycle, a unique stand: an extraordinary testimony to man's immemorial yearning for the splendour of the Golden Age *as it was*: without the renunciation yet unknown to it, and without the bitter struggle of the men "against Time"; a unique stand which springs, as I stated in other writings, from an essentially *aesthetic* standpoint, and which is beautiful in itself, despite the unavoidable failure implied in it.

Beautiful, and also *instructive*, inasmuch as the study of the imperfections of the Seat of Truth "like unto a glimpse of Heaven," and that of the nature and consequences of Akhnaton's "pacifism," glaringly show the impossibility of carrying out, in our Dark Age (or, by the way, at any moment of Time, save in a Golden Age itself) an earthly paradise programme through peaceful methods. Peace is not the law of action in a fallen world. One has either to accept violence — the condition of any development in Time — and to fight, *with the methods of the fallen world*, against that world, and "against Time," for a Golden Age ideal, or to project that ideal "outside" this visible and tangible earth, according to the words of Jesus of Nazareth "My Kingdom is not of this world" (and the words of the Christian hymn: "This world is not our home ...")[74] which express the attitude of all men essentially "above Time," with the one outstanding exception of Akhnaton, King of Egypt.

---

[73] As it is, for example, the case, with the persecuted National Socialists of today.

[74] A French Protestant hymn: "Non, ce monde n'est pas notre patrie ..."

Chapter 11

TOO LATE & TOO EARLY

The tragedy of Akhnaton's life lies in what I am tempted to call the middle position which he occupies in our Age—i.e., in the Dark Age of the present Time-cycle—and in our world of many races.

When he came into it, this world was nearly as old as it is today. (For what are 3,300 years, compared with the aeons that the present Time-cycle had already lasted?) One still spoke, of course, of the hallowed and mysterious "days of Ra" or "days of the Gods"—the more and more distant Golden Age, when this earth had been in glorious harmony with the rest of the Cosmos and with itself. One will still speak of it, under some name or another, and with ever-increasing yearning, to the very last minute of this Time-cycle. But one had been, for millenniums and millenniums, out of touch with it, and it had become more and more mysterious. Even the Second great Age, or Silver Age—into which decay had already set itself, in spite of the still clear and widespread knowledge of the original Nature-wisdom—was so far away that one hardly distinguished it from the First. One had, at the most, some faint idea of the last part of the Third Age—of the kingdoms before the Great Flood—like now, and perhaps a more accurate idea of it and of them, then, through tradition alone, than now, through the painstaking piecing together of very scanty archaeological evidence. But one was, like now, already shut in the present Dark Age, just as in the courtyard of a prison. Like now, the Golden Age—"Age of Truth," "Age of the Gods"—was not merely unreachable (even through Tradition) but *unthinkable*. The intuition even of such a man as Akhnaton could barely grasp but *some* of its glorious features, and stress *them*, while remaining impervious to others, and therefore incapable of evoking the *real* atmosphere of the divine epoch, in its organic integrity. Like now, the latter was already something towards which one *tended*, rather than something which one could in any way describe. And there was undoubtedly, at the bottom of the hearts of those who "tended" the most ardently towards it (even in Akhnaton's own heart, at times, at least) the secret feeling that all efforts were useless, that *it was too late* to try to restore it—the saddest and most depressing of all feelings, and the one corresponding to the sole fact of which we *are* sure, with regard to the long golden Dawn of our Time-cycle.

On the other hand, if the 33 centuries that separate Akhnaton from us are nothing compared with the many myriads of years that stand between both him *and* us and that far-gone First Age of innocence and glory, they still represent a *long time* if one takes, as one should, into account, the acceleration of the tempo of decay within the Age of Gloom.

This earth was surely no paradise in Akhnaton's days. Not only did it contain the "germs" of degeneracy—these are inherent in life in Time as such, and became noticeable as soon as the Golden Age had come to an end, but it was already glaringly stamped with all the characteristics of the Dark Age: selfishness, wanton brutality, superstition, conceit, fear, and hypocrisy. Its wars were (outwardly) about as horrible as ours, despite the fact that *fewer* people were killed and *fewer* buildings destroyed. And the everyday life of its men and women was about as dreary as that of the majority of our contemporaries. And yet, in spite of all, it *was not*, decidedly, anything like as bad.[1] Technical progress was not, for 3,000 years more, to turn men's heads and hearts to the new superstition of "happiness" through ever-increasing production. Nor were the dangerous—and false—idea of human equality and the dangerous illusion of liberty to appear, for a very long time. And things were still called by the *right* names, and facts—hard facts, consequences of the Fall that had started the obvious process of decay, thousands of years before—were faced without fear or squeamishness, as things that have to be. However *outwardly* barbarous, wars were, *innerly*, far more honest than those of our world: they were not called "crusades" against this or that idea which people had, first, been systematically taught to hate,[2] or wars "against war," but were frankly carried out "to extend the limits" of a king's realm, and to exploit the vanquished after plundering them—to acquire living space, raw materials, and cheap labour, as those of us who

---

[1] Adding "not," which seems required by the overall argument—Ed.
[2] Like Eisenhower's disgusting "Crusade to Europe."

are not liars say today. But then, everybody said it. There were acts of cruelty in war. But people were neither ashamed of them nor indignant about them—did not call them "war crimes" when they happened to be "the enemy's," and conceal them, when they were their own doings. Kings caused, as a matter of fact, accounts of such actions of theirs to be written down upon stone, to last forever.[3] There were, as now, enslaved people—the spoils of war. And they worked in the victors' mines, or rowed the victors' ships. But many centuries were to pass before the victors' priests were to bother their heads about their "souls" and offer them promises of hypothetical happiness in the hereafter, in compensation for their wretched lot on earth—and many more centuries before the victors' men of law were to give them lectures about an hypothetical "universal moral conscience," the commands of which they should have obeyed, instead of ruthlessly fighting for their kings. They had no compensation for their lot, save the games of dice or the merry-making that occasionally relieved the monotony of daily toil, or—when they happened to be men of a higher type—the pride of facing heroically a bitter, but unavoidable destiny . . . Christianity as we know it—that anti-natural religion, based upon lies—was not to appear for another one-and-a-half millennia. And Jewish thought (for non-Jewish consumption)—the main factor of world disintegration from at least the 3rd century B.C. onwards (if not from the fourth)—was yet totally non-existent.[4]

And the perennial Paradise-dream, although it was just as unrealisable in practice as it is now, was purer, more sincere, and more disinterested than all the pacifist utopias of later times. Its expression was not, like theirs, necessarily silly. It could be great, and beautiful. It *was* great and beautiful when it was the product of the yearning, imagination, and logic of such an artist as Akhnaton. The time had not yet come when wise men of his spiritual class would either, in despair, turn their backs to all manifestations in Time and choose the way of renunciation, or else, fight with the weapons of violence against the downward

---

[3] For instance, Amenhotep the Second's account of his treatment of the seven Syrian Chiefs, and, later, the countless Assyrian written accounts.

[4] Replacing "inexistent" —Ed.

current of history—"against Time"—also in despair.

In other words, the latest Golden Age behind Akhnaton (and us) was by far too remote in time for any attempt to restore it not to be a complete failure. While, on the other hand, the world was not yet ripe—not yet corrupt *enough*, not yet visibly enough *lost*—for a wise man, inspired with the dream of earthly Perfection, i.e., with the dream of harmony between earth and Cosmos, to feel himself "cornered" and, either to call every manifestation in Time a thing of sin and sorrow and to seek for Perfection in escape from the conditions of fallen life, through inner discipline, or else, to stick to this world as to his home, and to fight the increasing effects of Time in the advanced Dark Age, and establish a state "against Time," forerunner, amidst this fallen mankind, of the *next* Golden Age, ahead of us and, *a fortiori*, of him. The impossible state "above Time"—the state "Seat of Truth"—was still dreamable, dreamable for the last time perhaps in the history of this Dark Age, dreamable, but yet, as impossible, in practice, as it had been for millenniums, and as it is, *a fortiori*, today. Akhnaton's unique position in history lies in the fact that he is the last Man "above Time" who had enough faith in the remaining goodness of men (in spite of the Fall) and enough courage—and enough political power—to try, in all earnest, to bring it into being.

The last, I say, for all the well-known men "above Time" who have, after him, proclaimed their uncompromising condemnation of violence—considering the latter incompatible with timeless Truth—have renounced every temporal power for themselves, and every hope of a temporal order of perfection in this fallen world. They have given up the fallen world as past praying for, and rejected, beforehand, as doomed utopias, all dreams of restoring the long-destroyed harmony between Heaven and Earth, and turned to *the individual* "soul"—the only thing that one still can save, even up to the last day of the Dark Age. All the religions which they have preached: Buddhism, Jainism, Taoism, *and*, finally, Christianity (real Christianity as a purely personal faith and discipline, *not* as an organised church) are paths leading *the individual soul* out of the sinking ship, out of this world, irredeemably unfaithful to its heavenly pattern: out of the bondage of Time. And the "non-violence" common to all of them is *not* that implied in the lost Religion of the Sun-disk — not the radiant aura of an earthly paradise, but the tangible sign that the individual soul has given up its solidarity with this Time-ridden world, "its pomps and its vanities," that it no longer accepts it as its real fatherland, and no longer is, therefore, bound to recognise the law of violence, which is its law.

Another characteristic of these religions of meekness and self-denial originated by men "above Time" is that they take absolutely no account of race either as a feature of the natural Order (as the Religion of the Disk did) or as a factor of salvation (as the oldest Way of life "against Time" which I can think of — Brahminism — did and still does). And this is to be understood: they are, as I said, paths *out* of this fallen world; when one no longer belongs to this earth, the natural barriers within the realm of Life disappear no less than the artificial ones; the *Sannyasi* has no longer any caste. And it is written in the Book of books that "a sage" — i.e., a man who has freed himself from the ties of Time — "looks upon a learned Brahmin, a cow, an elephant, a dog, and even a man who eats dog's flesh, in the same light," or, according to another version, "sees in them the One Reality."[5]

But Brahminism is, as I said, essentially a way back to world harmony and perfection, taking into full account the conditions of each Age, and particularly those of the present Dark Age, a way of life "against Time." The *Sannyasi*, the man who has renounced the world completely and risen "above Time," has first lived in the world the life of the world: as a young man struggling to be, even in thought, master of his senses, as a householder with responsibilities, as a dweller in retirement. At all these three classical stages[6] — as long as he has not yet renounced the world *completely* — a man's caste — his race[7] — and the Age in which he lives, determine his duties and his rights. The higher his place within the natural hierarchy of races, the more exacting

---

[5] Bhagavad-Gita, V, verse 18.

[6] The three ashrams: that of the *brahmachari*, of the *grihastha*, of the *vanaprastha*, which lead normally to the fourth: that of the *sannyasi*.

[7] *Varna*, one of the usual Sanskrit names for caste means "colour." The other name for it, "*jat*," means race.

are his duties: what is allowed to a Sudra is forbidden to a Brahmin or to a Kshatriya—a member of the Aryan castes. And also, the further one goes down the stream of Time, the stricter and the more exacting are the duties, and the greater the responsibilities of the higher race, destined to start a new world of perfection, here on earth, as soon as the Dark Age will—at last—come to an end. Marriages that were, in former epochs, allowed to the members of the topmost castes—the best *in fact* in a society dominated to this day by the ideal of blood purity—are, according to the Laws of Manu, no longer allowed within the Dark Age. And it is—normally—less difficult for a man born as a Brahmin or a Kshatriya than for another to become a real sage. Nay, he who has "fallen from yoga"—who has sincerely striven to attain the wisdom of Timelessness but who failed—is finally "reborn *in a pure and blessed house*" and, "having recovered the characteristics of his former body, again laboureth for perfection."[8] Moreover, even the "sage"—as long at least as he has not severed all ties with human society and become a mere meditative ascetic—should act and perform the duties of his race and position: fight and kill, in the name of a just cause, if he be of a race of warriors, "for there is nothing more welcome to a Kshatriya than righteous war."[9] But he should act with complete detachment "for duty's sake alone."[10] In other words, in all Ages but that in which the manifested Universe, realm of Time, still is in tune with Eternity, the perfect Man "above Time" should *also* be the most active and the most thorough Man "against Time," faithful to race and state and duty in the natural sense of the word, faithful to this earth, in action, although living, in spirit, already in Eternity.

Akhnaton, in his youthful confidence in man and in his own power as a king, and the Founders of the great other-worldly religions of meekness and renunciation, in their thorough distrust of man taken *en masse* and of all mass-regulations and of all states, have both overlooked the fact that Life is irredeemably bound to the conditions of the Age through which it is passing. And both failed even to prepare the coming of the new Golden

---

[8] Bhagavad-Gita, VI, 41-43.
[9] Bhagavad-Gita, II, 31.
[10] Bhagavad-Gita, III, verses 19, 25, 30.

Age, save through the beauty of their own lives.

Akhnaton's ideal theocratic state—the ever-peaceful Kingdom of the Sun on earth—was, and remains, an impossibility in our Dark Age. It was from the beginning stamped with the sign of failure. And the "un-Egyptian" character of the particular solar Wisdom upon which it was to be built, was, perhaps, the pretext, but certainly not the deeper cause, of its failure. (Other nations had accepted, or were to accept and keep, outwardly at least, for centuries, religions that were anything but in harmony with the genius of their people: one only has to think of the Aryan wisdom of the Vedas, held sacred to this day by millions of Dravidians, sons of the "Dasyus" of old, the overwhelming majority of the Hindu population, or to consider how Christianity was successfully forced upon the Germanic people of Northern Europe, much against their will, or how Buddhism peacefully conquered millions of followers among the yellow races—in particular, how it managed to become one of the leading creeds of warrior-like Japan—or how Islam spread, also peacefully, to the Isle of Java.) The cause of the failure of the Religion of the Disk to survive, even in an imperfect form, is to be sought in its own inner contradictions: in the fact that it rests, as I said before, upon a thoroughly Indo-European conception of the Divine and yet, that its wisdom is *not* a wisdom "against Time," a warrior-like wisdom as would befit the young race predestined to open the *next* Time-cycle, and to rule the world in the coming "days of Ra," after the collapse of this Dark Age, not a wisdom "against Time" and *also not* a wisdom of despair. It is to be sought further still, perhaps, in the deepest contrasts of Akhnaton's own heredity, as scion of the aristocracy of elder mankind (akin to Sumerians and to Mohenjo-Daro Indians), and, at the same time, of the rising Aryan race.

The Egyptians shared with the other noble races of the pre-Aryan world a profound love of peace. This may seem in flat contradiction with the history of the 12th and especially of the 18th Dynasty.[11] Yet these recurring periods of conquest and of punitive expeditions in conquered lands, even the 150 years of

---

[11] See the great inscription of Senusret the Third (16th year of his reign) at Semneh, 30 miles above the Second Cataract of the Nile. Also Thutmose the Third's hymn of victory at Karnak.

warfare that stretch (with one remarkable interruption)[12] from Sequenen-Ra to Thutmose the Fourth—partly to be understood as a reaction against the twice as long and bitterly hated domination of the Semitic conquerors of Egypt, the Hyksos Kings—were but mere episodes in the endless history of the "Two Lands." The Egyptian, like the Indian of the Indus Valley civilisation, only fought when he felt himself forced to, and then, never with the wholeheartedness of either the Semite or the Aryan.

Akhnaton inherited that deep-rooted reluctance to violence, which his immediate forefathers had discarded. He inherited it *along with* outstanding Aryan qualities: creative intelligence, will-power and consistency, thoroughness. These qualities enabled him to grasp the idea of the "Heat-and-Light-within-the-Sun-disk" and to worship it as the one Thing divine. And he made further use of them to forward, in the name of that amazingly impersonal God, a Golden Age ideal of peace within a beautiful world, of peace *through* the love of Life and Beauty—in other words, to answer, or try to answer, here and now, the immemorial yearning of the older races for the mysterious lost Paradise at the dawn of our Time-cycle.

There was, in him, too much of the softness of the very old and refined South for him to become a man "against Time"—a fighter, accepting the methods of this Dark Age and working, with their help, in view of the *next* Golden Age. And the Dark Age was, in his days, not quite advanced enough for escape out of the conditions of life in Time altogether, to have become, for an uncompromising peace-lover and lover of Life, gifted with unbending logic and will-power, the only thinkable course.

Thus, myriads of years after the latest Golden Age, the hazy vision of which was the pattern of his impossible theocracy, and centuries before the redeeming crash that will put an end to this present Age of Gloom, Akhnaton, half-Egyptian, half-Aryan—last heir, in direct line, of the Southern royal house of Thebes, and heir of the kings of Mitanni—stands alone, as a pillar of

---

[12] The peaceful reign of Queen Hatshepsut.

light, at a great turning point in the downward stream of Time that nothing can hold back. He is the last man, at least the last great king and teacher, "above Time," faithful to this sunlit world, like the earliest "sons of Ra," or the *"rajrishis"* of most ancient India. After him, no peaceful divine rule on earth is even dreamable. (And he came already thousands of years too late for his solar theocracy to have been anything *more* than a dream.) After him, at least in the Western half of what is now known as the old continent—from Europe to India—the relatively peaceful non-Semitic Southern peoples were, gradually, to play a less and less active part in world history. The fair and vigorous Aryan race which, in its far-away Northern home, had steadily clung to the perennial cult of Light and Life in its purest form, was to continue pushing southwards and eastwards, entering in contact with other cultures and, everywhere or nearly everywhere, while leaving the stamp of its creative genius upon conquered populations, forgetting something of the original solar Wisdom in an attempt to understand new myths or to account for new experiences. And the Semites were also to increase their influence—quite a different sort of influence—through political power and, later on, through faiths centred around a personal and transcendent God, the philosophical opposite of Akhnaton's "Heat-and-Light-within-the-Disk." The overthrow of Mitannian tutelage by Ashuruballit, son of Erba-Adad, king of a yet unimportant Assyria, during Akhnaton's reign, and the intensified infiltration of the *Habiru* into Palestine, at the same time, are early signs of this new rise of the Semite, while, in far-away India, Aryans were devising the caste system, or giving it a new—racial—interpretation, and laying, in the midst of an immense foreign environment, the foundations of the oldest truly rational civilisation of the Dark Age: Brahminism, a civilisation "against Time," and while, less than a century later, the Thesprotian invasion was to carry to Greece "an overwhelmingly Aryan population"[13]: the new blood that was to evolve Hellenism out of its own genius and of the old Aegean culture, still alive.

But, I repeat, no race and no man was ever to renew Akhnaton's experiment of a *state* ruled in defiance of the conditions of the Dark Age, according to a creed of this earth. In fact, as the

---

[13] Hall, p. 67.

Dark Age goes on, states and *all* temporal organisms—with a few glaring exceptions—become more and more organisms "in Time," the real aim of which is merely the worldly welfare of a ruling family or of a ruling minority, or of a whole people, without that family, group, or people being, from the standpoint of the natural hierarchy of life, "the worthiest," without its privileges being justified in the light of cosmic Truth. The great men "above Time" who appear after Akhnaton turn their backs to this hopeless world and seek, as I said before, the salvation or "liberation" of the individual soul, its escape from the bondage of Time altogether. The Buddhist Sanga and the even more unworldly brotherhood of Jain ascetics are communities of people who deliberately leave no descendants and concentrate all their efforts upon never being, themselves, born again, if they can help it. The Kingdom of Jesus Christ is "not of this world." And although it is, according to the actual, practical founder of the Christian church, Paul of Tarsus, "better" for a Christian (as it is, by the way, "better" also for a Buddhist or a Jain) "to marry than to burn" (with passion), it is, for him, better still, whenever possible, to live in celibacy. The Christian doctrine is doubtless less consistent than the Buddhist or Jain with regard to non-violence. The much over-rated "love" that it preaches is shockingly limited to *man*, of all living beings. But the Christian ideal—the *aim* of the religious discipline both of the individual mystic and of the mystical community—is also an essentially ascetic and otherworldly one, one in the light of which the saint who is not of this earth is looked upon as the highest type of human being, the type to which the faithful should aspire. Whether the saint be finally expected to reach the state of *nirvana* or the more personal bliss of the Christian "Heaven" is, from the standpoint of wisdom rooted in and faithful to this earth, just the same. In either case, he saves himself, leaving the doomed earth to her fate—at the most coming back (being born again) of his own free will, as a "Bodhisattva," to help other *souls* out of the nightmare of existence in Time, or helping them directly, from the stage of bliss he has attained, in accordance with the Christian dogma of the "communion of saints"—the solidarity between the "triumphant" and the "militant" churches, which is nothing more than a natural fact expressed in religious language.

But he has no part in the one struggle, the aim of which is to prepare the coming of the *next* Golden Age: the struggle "against Time," here and now.

On the contrary: the great other-worldly religions that exalt escape from the conditions of this Dark Age in particular and of Time in general — individual "salvation" or "liberation" — merely succeed, *in practice*, in making the conditions of the Dark Age all the worse. They do so for the simple reason that they draw the best of human energy — and, to begin with, the best of human blood — away from this earth. The first, and many of the latter well-known Buddhist ascetics, and many of the Jain, were Brahmins or Kshatriyas — Aryans — and many of the unmarried Christian saints were of Germanic stock.

If only the ascetic religions really *could* draw *all* men away from this planet, their effect would not be so tragic. It would, in course of time, amount to the extinction of mankind through the most non-violent process of all: through lack of interest in reproduction, lack of desire to live in this world as anything save travellers to the next or, beyond death, as anything save "liberated" *souls* — *not* as new living men and women, inheritors of the character and possibilities of existing human races and of their Nature-ordained tasks, struggles, and greatness. But only minorities are capable of carrying out an uncompromising teaching to its last logical consequences. And therefore, no religion of however unworldly a character has, yet, as far as I know, ever had a sufficient appeal to lead the *whole* community of its believers to that extinction through indifference to life, which I just mentioned. For next to the good monk who, in thought and deed, holds virginity to be better than marriage, is the lay man who merely remembers that "it is better to marry than to burn," and who has a family. The monk — who often is a man of the very best blood — is lost to this earth, in the earthly sense. The lay man becomes positively dangerous as soon as he forgets that disregard of race is, at the most, permissible to those who tread the ascetic path, and who disregard life as such, to those who, already in this world, "neither marry nor give in marriage." And he *always* forgets this sooner or later, in the course of decades or centuries, for not a single other-worldly creed has, to my knowledge, taken the trouble of stressing the fact. (Brahminism has stressed the fact. But Brahminism is not an "other-worldly creed," a religion "above Time"; it is the one *social system* "against Time" in the frame of which there is place for all creeds [worldly *and* other-worldly] and all races, from the lowest of all to the pure Aryan, in a harmony which reflects—or is, at least, intended to reflect—the original harmony of Creation.)

Thus the practical result of the great religions of escape from the conditions of Time, the practical result of the teachings of the great, men "above Time" after Akhnaton, is a lowering of the racial level and therefore of the quality of their own adherents and, through them and their proselytes, of mankind in general: not—unfortunately!—a generation of "sadhus" and meditative saints, followed by a planet without men (doubtless more beautiful than it has been for a very long time) but cross-products of Aryan and Mongolic, or Aryan and Jewish blood, and a further non-descript hotchpotch of all the races of the Far and Middle East, or of all the races of the Near East and of Europe, professing increasingly debased forms of Buddhism or Christianity, and breeding, breeding, and ever breeding increasingly debased specimens of the two-legged mammal. In other words: a tightening of the grip of Dark Age conditions upon the world, and further disintegration.

It is hardly necessary to add that this disintegration has been encouraged and exploited by every power "*in* Time" in need of *Menschenmaterial* regardless of quality. The other-worldly teaching according to which man is to be looked upon before all as "a soul" has been mobilised in support of schemes of unjustified worldly domination by the Christian church itself and by a number of Christian rulers. A typical, but by no means unique, instance of this opportunism is that of Albuquerque's policy in Goa, encouraging mixed marriages between Portuguese and Indian Christians of any caste. Every new crossbreed, christened by the holy church, would be—at least Albuquerque expected—a future saint in Heaven and, in the meantime, a loyal supporter of Portuguese interests. The Spanish viceroys of Mexico and Peru have encouraged mixed marriages in a similar spirit, and so did, long before them, in the Near East, the Byzantine Emperors and the Caliphs of Damascus and of Baghdad. It is the most natural policy of a ruler "*in* Time" whose religion happens to be a fraternity of *faith*, regardless of blood—and all the more so if this religion be, like Islam, an other-worldly one, no doubt, but by no means a "non-violent" one.

Would the definitely non-violent but *not* other-worldly Religion of the Disk have followed, in practice, the same path, had it lasted? The path is in contradiction with the idea of the God-ordained separation of races, implied in Akhnaton's words: "Thou hast put every man in his place; Thou hast made them different in shape, colour and speech; like a Divider, Thou hast divided the foreign people from one another."[14] But who can ever tell what a religion might become in the hands of ambitious and greedy lip-adherents, when it has no hard and fast code of conduct, nothing to guide the faithful (as far as we know) save the intuition of an artist, in tune with the beauty of Creation? We know that several of Akhnaton's contemporaries and professed followers were, at least, anything but such artists. It is difficult to say what would have been his further followers, and whether any great man would have — could have — arisen among them, to save that which could be saved of the young king's Golden Age theocracy in this Dark Age, giving it the rigid laws that any Dark Age organism needs, in order to endure. All we can say is that such a leader would necessarily have been — would *have had to be* — a man "against Time," "above Time," no doubt, but "*against Time*" *also*, not merely "above Time" as Akhnaton himself and as the Founders of the non-violent, other-worldly religions after him. There is, as I said, in the Dark Age, no place, no possibility of existence for a state "above Time." However much the *inspiration*, the philosophy, behind state rule be of a nonviolent nature (worldly or other-worldly), the methods have to be the hard methods of the Dark Age. The one man who avoided these methods in his Buddhist Empire — Asoka — was only able to do so because he had applied them, with a vengeance, *before* his conversion to non-violence.

In other words, there is, in this Dark Age, place only for religions "against Time" — apart from false religions "in Time." The sincere, intelligent, and absolutely consistent follower of a teaching 100 percent "above Time" — 100 percent non-violent as such — has only one course left to him: he should disappear. He does not belong to this planet in this Age; he should get out of it — and never come back. Non-violence is not only incompatible with the existence of any state, nay, of any collective life, in any

---

[14] Longer Hymn to the Sun.

period of Time, apart from a Golden Age (and, *a fortiori*, in *our* Age), but it is, save in a Golden Age, incompatible with Life itself.

Of all the followers of non-violent religions, the Jains are the ones who, apparently, have understood this the best. They are, no doubt, like others, divided into a minority of monks and a majority of people who live—as non-violently as it is materially possible—the life of this world. But their ascetics go further than any others I know along the path of renunciation for the sake of love towards all creatures. Not contented with respecting animal life alone, like the lay Jains and all the vegetarians of the world, they serenely refuse all compromise with the hard Law of Life in all times but the unthinkable Golden Age: kill and eat, kill and live. And, gradually pushing aside vegetables, fruits, and finally even water, they die of inanition in the name of the real logic of non-violence—of the only logic of men of our Dark Age who cling to the bitter end to their will to defy the conditions of existence in Time.

There is one consistent alternative to this extreme position—one position as logical and as heroic as it—and that is the one of the philosophical equivalent of Brahminical racialism in our technically advanced and yet dangerously decadent world, the one of the modern creed "against Time" and "faithful to this earth" *par excellence*, or, to be more accurate, of the modern form of the perennial Wisdom of Light and Life: National Socialism, which short-sighted people mistake for a mere political creed and nothing *more*.

And this alternative is, for those at least who are of Aryan blood and of a warrior-like nature—for *Kshatriyas*—the best of the two. For it is written in the Book of books, addressed by God Himself—i.e., by the Genius of the Race, in human garb—to a prince of Kshatriyas, that "action is superior to inaction."[15]

Emsdetten in Westfalen (Germany), 23rd of May 1954

---

[15] Bhagavad-Gita, III, verse 8.

Part IV

BOTH SUN & LIGHTNING: ADOLF HITLER

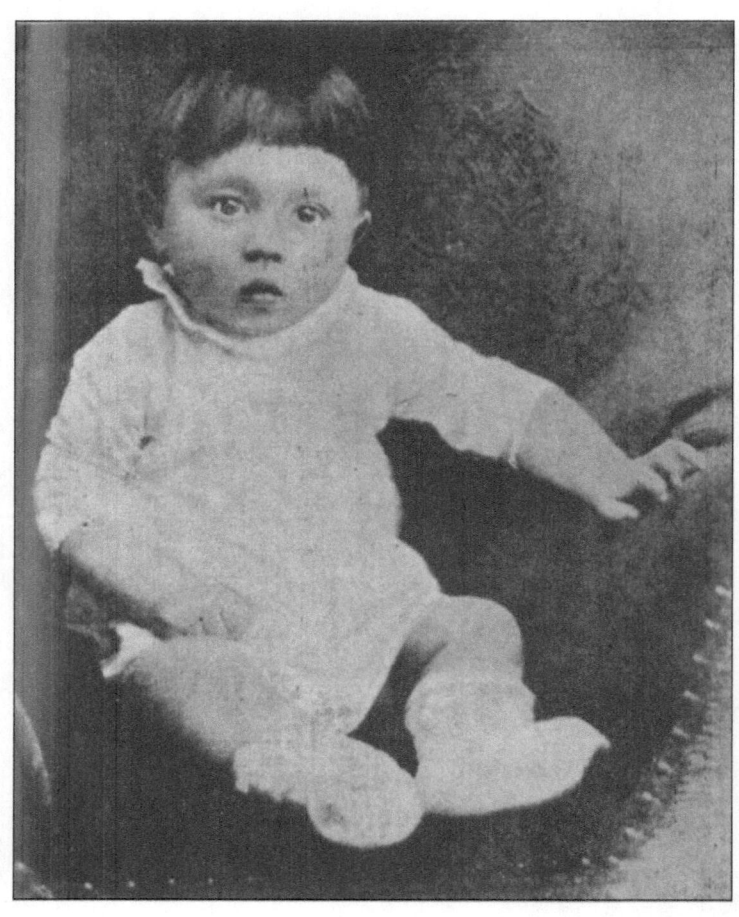

5. THE LATE-BORN CHILD OF LIGHT

Chapter 12

THE LATE-BORN CHILD OF LIGHT

It was in 1889 — during the first year of Kaiser William the Second's reign.

Bismarck — the Iron Chancellor, the maker of the Second German Reich — was still in power, though not for long. The hidden anti-German forces that were soon to cause his dismissal and then, gradually, to break the impetus he had given things, were already at work, had been at work for years. But there were imponderable factors — moral and mystical forces — besides and, nay, behind them: the very forces of disintegration that had been, for over two millenniums,[1] striving to lead the Aryan race to its doom. And it needed a more-than-political genius, nay, a more-than-human personality, to stand in the way of *those*.

Especially for the past 100 years, i.e., since the outbreak of the French Revolution, Europe had been sinking, more speedily than ever, under the influence of international Jewry and of its cunning agents: Freemasonry and the various so-called "spiritual" secret bodies directly or indirectly affiliated to it. Centuries of erroneous application of Christianity — an essentially other-worldly creed — to worldly affairs had prepared the ground for the triumph of the most dangerous superstitions: the belief in the "equal rights" of "all men" to life and "happiness," the belief in citizenship and "culture" as distinct from and more important than race, the belief in unlimited "progress" through a presumed universal receptivity to "education" and in the possibility of universal Peace and "happiness" as a result of "progress" — the wonderful discoveries of science being put to the service of "man," the belief in the right of man

---

[1] I say "*over* two millenniums" meaning that the disintegrating influence of Jewry upon the Aryan race began *before* the advent of Christianity. The disastrous new scale of values drawn from the misapplied other-worldly religion, and the spreading of the creed itself, were the consequences of Jewish influence, not its causes.

to work against Nature's spirit and purpose for his own brief pleasure or profit. One had increasingly stressed, exalted, made popular the sickly love of "man" as distinct from and opposed to all other creatures, or, to be more accurate, the love of a repulsive, standardised conception of "the average man," "neither all good nor all bad" but weak, *mediocre* — as foreign as possible to the age-old warrior-like Aryan idea of superior humanity expressed in the conception of the "hero like unto the Gods," to use Homer's words.

And colonialism was at its height, and Christian missionary activity also. Which means that, after having given herself up to the forces of disintegration, Europe was rapidly handing the rest of the world over to them, preparing the very last phase of the Dark Age: the state of biological chaos which is the preliminary condition of the rule of the worst and the systematic annihilation of any surviving human élite of blood and character.

At that time, an elderly, honest, and hard-working customs officer lived with his wife and family in Braunau, a pretty little town on the river Inn, on the border of Austria and Germany.

The town, with its main square, on one side of which an old fountain, dominated by a stone statue of Christ, is still to be seen, with its old houses and churches, its old streets — clean, but often narrow — and the four-storied "tower" — the Salzburger Turm — that already separated the main square from "the suburb,"[2] was little different from any small town in the region. It probably looked much the same as it does today: small towns change less than large ones. And the customs officer, whose name was Alois Hitler, lived and reacted to life as many a government clerk. Gifted with enormous will-power and perseverance, he had, in his youth, worked himself up from the position of a village lad to that of a scribe in a government office, which appeared to him as the summit of respectability. And now, after all these years, the days of which were so desperately alike, his dreary life did not seem dreary to him, for he had no time to think of it as such. Meticulously dutiful, he worked and worked. And days and years went by.

---

[2] *Die Vorstadt*

Time would soon come when the honest clerk would retire, with a small pension.

Meanwhile, he lived in "the suburb," only a few footsteps from the Salzburger Turm, in an old, two-storied house that had picturesque arched landings at the top of each flight of stairs, and spacious rooms. His wife, Clara, was pretty: blonde, with magnificent blue eyes. Aged 29 only (she was his third wife), she was of an ardent, thoughtful, and self-possessed nature, as imaginative and intuitive as her husband was unromantically painstaking, as loving as he was dutiful, and capable of endless sustained sacrifice. She respected him deeply; he was her husband. But she loved her children—and God, God *in* her children. And she did not herself know how right she was, i.e., how truly the divine spirit—the divine collective Self of Aryan mankind, Whose manifestation appears now and then in the form of an extraordinary human being—lived in the youngest baby son that she was nursing: her fourth child.

She had just given birth to him on the 20th of April, at 6:18 in the afternoon, in that large airy room on the second floor—the last on the right hand side, at the end of a narrow passage—in which she was now reclining, still feeling weak, but happy. The three windows opened on the street. Through their spotless glass panes and white blinds warm sunshine poured in. The baby slept. The mother rested. She did not know that she had just been the instrument of a tremendous cosmic Will.

A few hundreds of yards away—beyond the Salzburger Turm and the broad square surrounded with relatively high houses—on flowed the greyish-blue River Inn, tributary of the Danube. There was a bridge over it, like today. The landscape—soft green hills, with woods here and there, and neat and homey red-roofed houses, and, occasionally, the steeple of a church, between the river bank and the rich green slopes in the distance—was the same on both sides of the bridge. The people were the same: Bavarians—Germans. But this side—where the main Square with its old fountain, the Salzburger Turm, and "the suburb" stood—was called "Austria," the other side: Germany.

The baby slept; the mother rested, was grateful for the bright sunshine and the coming summer. She would be able to take the child out, now and then, when she would find time. In the meantime she prayed to the Queen of Heaven that he might live: her first three children had died, one after the other.

卐 卐 卐

The Child was christened Adolf.

Thirty-five years later, the Man into whom he had grown was to write: "It appears to me today that Destiny has happily appointed me Braunau on the Inn as a birthplace. This little town lies indeed on the border of the two German states, the unification of which we men of the younger generation consider as our life's work, to be carried out by all means."[3]

He referred to "Destiny." Had it not been for the oddness of such a statement in a book written for millions of Europeans hardly concerned with or interested in the idea of birth and rebirth, he could have, with equal if not greater accuracy, spoken of his "own choice." For according to the Ancient Wisdom, men of such a quality as he *choose* to be born, without being compelled to, *and choose their birthplace*.

Invisible in the blue sky above the little frontier town, the stars formed, on the 20th of April 1889, at 6:18 in the afternoon, a definite pattern marking the return to earth of Him Who comes back, of the divine Man "against Time" — the incarnate collective Self of superior mankind — Who, again and again, and every time more heroically, stands alone against the ever-accelerated current of universal decay, and prepares, in hard, bloody struggle, the dawning of the following Time-cycle, even if he be, for some years or decades, apparently bound to fail.

For the newly born Babe was none other than He.

卐 卐 卐

Never had circumstances been more unfavourable to His recognition, nay, to the very possibility of His taking consciousness of His mission in the garb of a predestined ruler. Not only was there, as everyone will readily agree, a long way from the child's humble status to that which he had to attain in order to play, in the history of the West, the *political* part he was destined, but nothing seemed likely to prepare him for the accomplishment of his even greater task, namely that of awakening the

---

[3] Adolf Hitler, *Mein Kampf*, p. 1.

Western Aryan Soul to *its own* natural wisdom. Aryan Wisdom, in its conscious, warrior-like form, in opposition to all the traditional values of Christianity, was unknown in the Western world of the time, let alone in Braunau on the Inn—unknown, at least, to all but a few lonely thinkers such as Friedrich Nietzsche. The heavenly Powers, however, gave the divine Child two main privileges through which he was, amazingly soon, to become aware of it, to *reinvent it* of his own accord: first, a pure, healthy heredity, containing the very best both of Nordic and of Celtic blood—the fiery imagination and mystical intuition of the Celt, allied to Nordic will-power, thoroughness, efficiency, and sense of justice (and insight *also*); and, along with that, a passionate, limitless, and fathomless love for that German Land that stretched on both sides of the Inn as well as on both sides of the Danube and beyond, and for its people, his blood-brothers: not those who are perfect specimens of higher humanity (for there are none in this Dark Age) but for those who can and will *become* such ones, while they have the stuff in them.

Through that love—and through it alone—he was to raise himself to the intuitive certitude of the eternal Truth upon which he was to build the National Socialist Doctrine, the modern form of the perennial Religion of Life, to that certitude which separates him from even the greatest politicians and sets him straight away into the category of the warring Seers, Founders of the healthiest civilisations we know, into the category of the Men "against Time," whose vision grasps, beyond our sickly world, doomed to speedy destruction, the yet unthinkable following Golden Age, of which they are the prophets and will be the gods.

Written in Emsdetten in Westfalen (Germany),
on the 14th of August, 1954

6. Adolf Hitler in the early days of the struggle

Chapter 13

THE STRUGGLE FOR TRUTH

Whether alive or dead in the flesh, the predestined Child of Braunau — Adolf Hitler — lives forever in National Socialism, his creation and integral expression. To understand the latter is to understand him: to see him in the proper light and to place him — whether one be, personally, attracted to him or not — on the proper *level* and in the proper *class* among the galaxy of exceptionally great men. And that is precisely what most National Socialists, even those who remained *after* 1945, irreproachable in their profession of faith — even "fanatical" ones — (let alone our enemies, and the world at large, which lies for the last ten years under their influence), apparently fail to do, out of lack of feeling for cosmic realities and, in particular, out of lack of awareness of the rhythm of Time which explains all laws of history, if not also all great happenings.

One should carefully distinguish the ephemeral N.S.D.A.P. — the National Socialist German Workers Party,[1] an organisation in view of precise aims, which have their place in German and European history — from the everlasting National Socialist Idea.

The Party came (officially) into existence on the 24th of February 1920, in *fact* already in 1919. It was a revolutionary body determined to win power for its Leader — and for its members — to rid Germany of the enslavement and shame resulting from the Versailles Treaty, and — for the first time in the history of the West — to apply, on a broad scale, solid — eternal — biological principles to social and to political life. It had, however, the characteristics of even the very best organisations of our Dark Age: their inherent clumsiness, their all-too-human shortcomings. There were all sorts of people — fearless idealists and time-servers, heroes, nay, demi-gods, *and* an immense majority of irresponsible, sheep-like creatures, *and* a few influential traitors — among the 13 million members it had at the height of its glory. It achieved a lot, and yet it failed. It has, since 1945, ceased

---

[1] Nationalsozialistische Deutsche Arbeiter Partei

to exist as a body, and even if it be, one day, destined to rise again under its old name and everlasting Sign, will never be restored exactly as before. Cannot be, for it belongs to Time, and in Time nothing is ever *restored*. *Should not be*, for restoration would mean stagnation, whence incapacity to face new circumstances and overcome new dangers.

The National Socialist Idea is not the Party. Not only was it in existence—"in the air"—more or less in its present-day garb, *before* the Party (the Proclamation of Friedrich Lange's "Deutsches Bund," in Heidelberg, on the 9th of May 1894—when Adolf Hitler was five years old—has all the traits of a National Socialist Manifesto, and so have Hans Krebs' declarations in 1904), but it is, in its essence, as old as the oldest contact and first clash between the Germanic race and the outer world. Fundamentally, it is nothing else but the expression of the collective will of the race to survive and to rule, of its readiness to combat and eradicate all that which, from without or from within, stands in the way of its survival and expansion, of its healthy consciousness of itself—of its strength, of its youth—and of the Godhead *within itself*: a biological reality stressed in political and in social life, rather than a "political" idea. One could say that Theodoric the Great acted in the true National Socialist spirit when, 1,400 years before the famous "Nuremberg Laws," he did all he possibly could to prevent marriages between his Goths and the racially less pure—less Aryan—people of conquered Italy, let alone people of altogether non-Aryan stock. And I have many times and in different writings pointed out that there is no difference in purpose and in standpoint between the National Socialist attitude to life and that of the ancient, warrior-like Aryans, worshippers of Light, who were conquering North-West India, setting the caste system, conceived on a racial basis, between themselves and the conquered people, and praying to the Vedic Gods for "many sons," prosperous flocks, and "victory over the dark-skinned Dasyus"—for *Lebensraum*—several thousands of years before 1919, 1933, or 1935.

One could go a step further and state that, in its *essence*, the National Socialist Idea exceeds not only Germany and our times, but the Aryan race and mankind itself and *any* epoch, that it ultimately expresses *that* mysterious and unfailing Wisdom according to which Nature lives and creates: the impersonal Wisdom of the primeval forest and of the ocean-depth, and of the spheres in the dark fields of Space; and that it is Adolf Hitler's glory not merely to have gone back to that divine Wisdom — stigmatising man's silly infatuation with "intellect," his childish pride in "progress," and his criminal attempt to enslave Nature — but to have made it the basis of a *practical* regeneration-policy of world-wide scope, precisely *now*, in our over-crowded, over-civilised, and technically over-evolved world, at the very end of the Dark Age.

In other words, it is impossible to understand National Socialism unless one integrates it into the cyclic conception of history as suggested by Tradition, i.e., unless one sees in it not a political system among many others — not an ephemeral "ism," the product of ephemeral circumstances — but the last (or, as we shall see, the one before the last) effort of the permanent and more-than-human Forces of Life within this Time-cycle, against the accelerated current of degeneracy characteristic of any advanced development in Time, or, in one sentence, unless one sees in it the effort "against Time" at the very end of the last Age of our present Cycle.

Seen in this light, the whole well-known struggle to free Germany from the enslavement to which the Versailles Treaty had reduced her — the National Socialist struggle for "freedom and bread" (and for space), for the German people's right to thrive in healthy creative activity — is the last (or, rather, as we shall see, the one before the last) phase of the perennial Struggle for Truth within the present Time-cycle; the form which that perennial Struggle was bound to take in our epoch, i.e., at the end of the Dark Age. And Adolf Hitler is the most heroic of the heroes who, in the course of history, stood in the way of the world's fated downward rush towards its doom, the One Who comes back, in His last desperate attempt to save that which is still worth saving, before it is too late — the typical Man "against Time." He embodies that eternal Nature-wisdom to which I have alluded in the former paragraph — the only wisdom that deserves the name of divine, and opposed *it* — *not* human arguments — to the false science, and false religion, and false morality, and, of course, *also* false political conceptions of our decadent Age, and made Germany's struggle for freedom the occasion of a broader systematic struggle for the liberation of higher mankind from the chains of the Dark Age. And made the Sign of the Sun—the Sign of Health[2]—the Symbol of both German and *Aryan* regeneration, and Germany, the holy Land of the West—the Stronghold of regenerate Aryandom.

Considered as the 20th-century expression of the age-old yearning of Aryan mankind to free itself, here and at once, from the appalling determinism of decay, National Socialism begins *before* Adolf Hitler's political career. Its unrecorded but real evolution as an incarnate Idea—its true history—starts with the future German Führer's gradual awakening to the consciousness of his own scale of values, of his fundamental aspirations and repulsions, and of his mission: the awakening of the Man "against Time," as such.

There are, to my knowledge—unfortunately—no records of Adolf Hitler's childhood. And, enlightening as it surely is, the little one can gather about it from a conversation with his most sympathetic old tutor, Herr Mayrhofer (who is still living in Leonding, near Linz, and whom I met twice) and the little he mentions himself in *Mein Kampf* (which is not an autobiography) is not enough to buttress such a definite (and unusual) view of him as the one put forth in the present study. The one apparently authoritative picture of the future ruler's life and character, years before he "decided to become a politician," is to be found in the very good book in which August Kubizek—the one friend he had in early youth—has related the story of his four years' friendship with him, namely from 1904 to 1908.[3]

In those years—i.e., when he was over 15, less than 19—Adolf Hitler's main traits of character were already fixed, and visible at every step of his: in all he said or did. His scale of values was already that one which was, in later years, to set him apart from every political leader of our times. And the psychological (the *real*) basis of his philosophy, the source of his unshakable faith in it, and the key to his whole career—was already definite. In other words, the man he was to be—the Man he could *but* be, under

---

[2] The *Swastika*, "Swasthi," Sanskrit, meaning: "health," "well-being"

[3] August Kubizek, *Adolf Hitler, mein Jugendfreund* [Adolf Hitler, Friend of My Youth] (Göttingen: Leopold Stocker Verlag, 1953).

the given circumstances—had already taken shape and was, with the sureness of instinct, with a mysterious, inner knowledge, a logic of his own that baffled all human calculations, invincibly following the path of his tremendous destiny. And the features of the rapidly awakening personality were unmistakably those, and the unfailing, baffling logic, that of a Man of the type I have, in this book, characterised as "against Time": of an inspired, ruthless, and realistic—extraordinarily far-sighted—fighter for a Golden Age ideal, in the depth of our Dark Age.

And, were we able to trace the history of Adolf Hitler's evolution further into those very early years which he describes as providing (from the standpoint of events) "little to remember,"[4] it is not only probable but certain that we would find, in him, up to the very beginning of his life, the self-same, deeply distinctive traits of character, the self-same *fundamental* aspirations—the same *person*. Such men as he are not, as so many people seem to think, the "product of circumstances," but predestined beings who *use* the given circumstances to the utmost, for a purpose which far exceeds the obvious, immediate aim of their action, or, to speak the language of ancient Wisdom—and one is, ultimately, compelled to speak that language—great free Souls,[5] no longer bound by the law of birth and rebirth, who choose to be born in *the* environment (within the race, the country, the social stratum) in which, and to grow into leading men, and to struggle as such under *the* circumstances under which they are to act the most efficiently, in the highest interest of Creation. They are children and adolescents "against Time" before leaving in history the mark of their passage as Men "against Time."

One of the most noticeable traits of people "against Time" — no less than of those I have described as "above Time" — is that they fit nowhere in the world as it is, that their moral and aesthetic—and practical—standards: their conception of happiness and unhappiness, their idea of "success" and failure, and of usefulness, in one word their *values*, and its, have nothing in common. And, from all that his friend A. Kubizek relates about Adolf Hitler's adolescence in Linz, that appears precisely to have

---

[4] *Mein Kampf*, p. 2.
[5] In Sanskrit "*Mukta Purusha*."

been the case of the future master of Germany, at that time a no doubt remarkably gifted but, in the estimation of cool-minded grown-ups, "unpractical" youth, who had recently left middle-school without completing the course of his studies, and nourished the ambition of becoming a great artist—a painter, or perhaps an architect—with little material prospects of fulfilling it, and who lived on his widowed mother's meagre pension, and roamed about the streets—or the countryside—and occasionally went to the theatre (taking admittedly the cheapest seats), and made gigantic plans, and spoke—already—with compelling eloquence—of things that interested nobody but himself, while other boys earned their living and helped their families, or were learning something "useful." "He just fitted into no social frame whatsoever,"[6] concludes A. Kubizek, after having tried to analyse the reasons why his friend, despite capacities by far above the average, failed, even in subsequent years, to "get on" professionally. "He had not the slightest ambition of securing himself a livelihood"[7] and of being comfortable. He did not wish to be "comfortable." He did not—and never was to—think in terms of comfort or of personal "happiness." What others called "enjoying life" was something absolutely foreign to him.[8] Nor could he "take things as they came" and live lightly, free of worry, entirely within the present.[9] He was, at a very early age, intensely aware that things were *wrong* in the world around him—wrong in every walk of life, in every domain of thought and action, from A to Z—and he felt himself duty-bound to change them, not to change this or that *in* them, leaving the rest untouched, but to change them ruthlessly and radically, for they were radically wrong, and to build *everything* anew, according to principles different from those that had prevailed up till then.

And this was not a mere wish, a more or less vague desire or day-dream. It was a purpose that he pursued with "deadly seriousness"[10] and unfailing consistency,[11] busying himself long be-

---

[6] Kubizek, p. 37.
[7] Kubizek, p. 36.
[8] Kubizek, p. 37.
[9] Kubizek, p. 43.
[10] Kubizek, p. 43.
[11] Kubizek, p. 52.

forehand with the most minute details of his plans in every particular case, without for all that ever losing sight of the spirit and general lines of his creation as a whole, so much so that that "extraordinary seriousness" and consistency—and merciless radicality[12]—struck all those who knew him as the main trait of his character. He pursued it—nay, already in those years in which he was not yet politically active, already while he himself still believed that art would remain, throughout life, his first and foremost concern—with that feverish impatience which finds its expression in the words: "Now, or never," with the haste inherent in all earnest action "against Time." And that impatience—that tragic awareness that "tomorrow will be too late"—was to stamp his whole career as a ruler and as the Founder of the last *true* civilisation within the Dark Age. In it, in fact, lies the source and the explanation of Adolf Hitler's most drastic—and most criticized—steps in later life and the sign that National Socialism, that most heroic of all reactions against our Dark Age, *historically* still belongs to this Age, while transcending its spirit.

The ideal in the name of which Adolf Hitler constantly rebelled against practically all he saw in living life—already as an adolescent, and then *more and more* as a young man and as a man of 30 and over 30—was nothing less than that which I have described in this book as "a Golden Age ideal," the inner vision of a healthy, beautiful, and also peaceful (*necessarily* peaceful) world; of *the* real earthly paradise, the faithful image of cosmic perfection, in which righteousness prevails as a matter of course. There can be no doubt about it if one reads not only that interesting story of his youthful years which his friend A. Kubizek has written, but also all that he wrote and said himself in later, active life. And in an epoch such as that in which we are *now* living—when, all over the world, every possible attempt is made to present him not merely as a "warmonger" but as the number one "war criminal"—it is not superfluous to stress the fact that Adolf Hitler was, not only at the dawn of his awakening as a "Man against Time" but *all* his life, "a bitter enemy of war"[13] as such,

---

[12] Kubizek, p. 203.
[13] Kubizek, p. 294.

the fact that he was by nature "gifted with deep sensitiveness, and full of sympathy for others,"[14] that his programme was essentially a *constructive* one, his struggle, the struggle for an exalted, *positive* aim, his aim: the regeneration of higher mankind (of the only section of mankind worth saving) and, ultimately, through the survival of regenerated higher mankind, the restoration of the long-destroyed harmony between the cosmic Order and the sociopolitical conditions on earth, i.e., the restoration of Golden Age conditions, the opening not merely of a "new era" for Germany, but of a new Time-cycle for the whole world.

It is not superfluous, in times like ours, to remind the reader of all the Führer's efforts *to avoid* the Second World War, even at the price of heavy concessions, and then (when this had proved impossible) to stop it, while it could yet be stopped. It is not superfluous to recall the words he addressed his old friend Kubizek on the 23rd of July 1940, i.e., when, from a military standpoint, all seemed to be going on splendidly, when the Swastika Flag was fluttering over public buildings in the capitals of seven conquered states—"This war thrusts us years back in our constructive work. *It is deplorable.* I have not indeed become the Chancellor of the Greater German Reich in order to conduct war!"[15] Not only was he against war for war's sake (or for the sake of worthless motives), but he was against any form of useless violence, not to speak of "useless cruelty," which was, under the Third Reich, according to law and (whenever detected) also in fact, a severely punishable offence.[16] The news of even such an understandable outburst of broad-scale revengefulness as that which took place during the "*Kristallnacht*" (8th–9th of November 1938)—attacks on Jews and Jewish property, and burning down of synagogues *in answer to repeated Jewish provocation*—brought him "to the pitch of indignation."[17]

---

[14] Kubizek, p. 44.

[15] Kubizek, p. 345.

[16] It is a fact, for instance, that Martin Sommer was, in 1943, i.e., under the N.S. régime and by a N.S. tribunal, sentenced to three years imprisonment for ill-treating internees in the Buchenwald concentration Camp.

[17] Konstantin Hierl, *Im Dienst für Deutschland, 1918–1945* [In Ser-

That inborn reluctance to wanton violence is a trait common to all those whom I have called men "above Time" (such as King Akhnaton, the Buddha, or Jesus Christ) *and* to the great fighters "against Time," Founders of new religious and cultural eras, such as Lord Krishna or, nearer to our times, the Prophet Mohammed, the only men with whom Adolf Hitler can be compared if one feels at all the necessity of drawing historical parallels.

It is one of the signs that his ultimate aim remained — like theirs — a state of deep-rooted, lasting (more-than-human) harmony, *not* of conflict among men, in other words, I repeat, a restoration of the original Golden Age conditions upon earth, the only conditions under which absolute health — which means: perfection — ever prevailed. Considered in the light of such an aim, every necessary violence is a "deplorable" necessity (to quote once more Adolf Hitler's own words about the Second World War in 1940). Every unnecessary violence is a denial of the spirit of such a struggle "against Time" as that of National Socialism for power, a foolish provocation of the Dark Forces that stand in the way of its success, and therefore a sin against the Cause of Truth. And that is the real, deep meaning of the Führer's bitter words, addressed to Dr. Goebbels at the news of the "*Kristallnacht*": "You people have thrust back National Socialism, and spoilt my work for many years if not for good, through this nonsense!"[18]

Adolf Hitler's leading emotion is obviously his "love beyond all measure"[19] for Germany and all that is German. "He lived *in* the German people; nothing counted for him, save they."[20] These words, describing the future ruler's feelings already in early youth, are true at *all* stages of his life. And his main intellectual, or rather, spiritual, feature is perhaps that inborn, baffling intuition of history in the broadest sense of the word — of

---

vice for Germany] (Heidelberg: Vowinckel, 1954), p. 138.

[18] Hans Grimm, *Warum? Woher? aber Wohin?* [Why?, Whence? but Whither?] (Lippoldsberg: Klosterhaus, 1954), p. 184.

[19] Kubizek, p. 292.

[20] Kubizek, p. 115.

history as our planet's destiny—which lifts him straight above all politicians, generals, and actual kings, to the level of the great Seers, and gives his whole career that extraordinary, "dream-like"[21] character of which Hans Grimm so appropriately speaks. The originality of his genius lies in the fact that *he lived his German patriotism from a cosmic point of view*, giving both Germany and the history of our times their true significance in the light of not merely human but *cosmic* evolution.

I do not know whether Adolf Hitler would have been, at any period of his career, in a position to give a learned lecture about the cyclic conception of history according to ancient Wisdom. But I am absolutely sure that he felt, thought, and acted, from beginning to end, in full consciousness of the eternal truth—both biological and metaphysical—which this conception expresses. His writings—especially the general statements which he laid down in Chapter 11 of the first part of *Mein Kampf*—his speeches before and after his rise to power, and more eloquently than anything, the great decisions of his life, prove that he did. The basic tenets and entire spirit of the National Socialist doctrine prove that he did. For what *is* the latter, if not a passionate denial of the widespread belief in the "dignity" of "man" as such (of *any* human creature of any race) and of the no less widespread and no less arbitrary idea of man's "mastery" over Nature, and of his unlimited "progress"? The denial of these dogmas in favour of an aristocratic conception of the Universe and, in particular, of history, in the light of which the noble races (and, among them, in first rank, the Aryan, the noblest of all) are alone capable of bringing *collectively* into material fulfilment, the whole wealth of higher human possibilities? Their denial, also, in favour of the bold assertion that history is—in *fact*, has always been—a long process of more or less slow decay from original perfection to a final state of chaos out of which one rises once more *not through regular, unbroken evolution, but abruptly*—i.e., through revolutionary methods—to the state of health, virtue, and beauty, i.e., of earthly godhead, which marks the springtime (all the successive springtimes) of Creation?

Considered in its essence, it is, indeed, *that*, before anything

---

[21] *Traumhaft* is the word Grimm repeatedly uses in *Warum? Woher? aber Wohin?*

else. More so: the fact *that* it is that governs, as we shall see, its attitude—determines its position—with regard to the various "questions" of our times, from the all-important, world-wide Jewish problem (which is anything but "modern") to those affairs which, at first sight, seem to concern Germany alone. (And there lies precisely the hidden but actual source of its unpopularity in this Dark Age.)

Years before he came to power, nay, years before he started his political career—Adolf Hitler was vividly aware of that incompatibility between this Age, this world as we see it, and the healthy, glorious world of his dreams. And he sought the reality of the latter, if not in the *historical* Golden Age of our Time-cycle—so far behind us and so different from all we know that it is practically unthinkable—at least in as remote a past as his imagination could reach: in the legendary Age before the dawn of recorded German history, the Age pictured in the old Germanic Sagas. He did not study that age as a student of archaeology would have. He *lived* in it through his own visionary's intuition and through the magic of Richard Wagner's music, which he loved. And far from being the mere product of an ephemeral youthful enthusiasm, that consciousness of the world of the Sagas was precisely that which, more decisively than anything else, "conditioned his historical *and political* views."[22] It was the consciousness of the world "to which he felt he actually belonged." And "all through his life, he found nothing for which he could stand with such pious devotion as he did for that world, which the Sagas of the German heroes had opened to him."[23]

In other words, it is the healthy, strong, beautiful Germans of the heroic Age who, in his eyes, represented *real* Germany, eternal Germany. Maybe they have, *historically*, lived only a few millenniums before the beginning of the present Dark Age (in what the Sanskrit authors call the *Dvapara Yuga*, the third of the four great Ages) maybe, already within this present Age of Gloom itself (I mean, in the very first part of it).

That is not the point. The point is that, faithful in fact to Tradition, Adolf Hitler believed in the existence of earthly perfec-

---

[22] Kubizek, p. 99.
[23] Kubizek, p. 99.

tion as a reality both of the future and of a very, very *remote past*. The point is that, whatever might have been the epoch in which they — or their historical prototypes — actually lived, the men and women of the hallowed "world of the Sagas" *signified*, symbolised, for him, that earthly perfection, that humanity without a flaw for which he yearned with all the ardour of his heart and nearer and nearer to which one reaches to the extent one follows Time further and further upstream.

There is more. Strange as this statement may seem to the European, nay to the German reader himself, Adolf Hitler's "immeasurable love" for his people is something greater than usual patriotism. It is, no doubt, rooted in that natural feeling of blood-solidarity which binds most individuals — and certainly *all* Germans — to their countrymen. But it is, at the same time, the immediate outcome of a staggering intuitive knowledge, the expression of actual insight into the nature, meaning, and destiny of Germany as *the* privileged Nation among all those of the same blood: the most gifted, the most *conscious*, the most fit to rule, in one word, the most objectively valuable section of Aryan mankind. It is, in spite of what many may think, nay, in spite of the judgement passed upon it by such a prominent figure of the National Socialist régime as Konstantin Hierl,[24] anything but the German counterpart of the British chauvinist's attitude rendered in the well-known motto: "My country, right or wrong!"

True, Adolf Hitler himself has written in *Mein Kampf* that, had he "been French," and had France's greatness meant to him all that Germany's in fact did, he "could not and would not have acted any differently from Clemenceau."[25] But, if one is to consider him, and to try to interpret his historical career in the light of Ancient Wisdom (and subsequently, in connection with the destiny of the whole world) one is forced to say: he could not have been French — nor English, nor even Scandinavian. He could not have been anything else but German, nay, anything else but a *frontier* German, doubly aware of the tragic injustice of man-made frontiers and of the natural unity of the Reich beyond and in spite of them — and of the natural unity of the Aryan race beyond and in spite of the boundaries of the Reich. More still:

---

[24] Hierl, *Im Dienst für Deutschland*.
[25] *Mein Kampf*, p. 766.

one is bound to admit that, far from exalting Germany merely because *he* was a German, it is, on the contrary, he who *chose* to be born a German because of the predestined — God-ordained — part that Germany has played and is more and more called to play on the side of the eternal Forces of Light and Life in their struggle against the Forces of disintegration, now, as the end of this Dark Age is drawing nigh, because, *objectively* speaking, the earthly salvation of the Aryan race — the regeneration of higher mankind — can only come from and through Germany: the one Aryan Nation in which the race is still sufficiently pure to be, under given circumstances, capable of *total* regeneration, while, *at the same time*, it has, through the unbroken experience of danger, remained sufficiently awake to be *fully* awakened, and sufficiently warrior-like to carry on, to its end, the struggle against Dark Age conditions: the perennial Struggle "against Time," for integral Truth.

In other words, both the quality of her biological substance *and* the particular stamp which history has left upon her, have made Germany the one Nation capable of taking the lead of Western Aryandom (if not also of Aryandom as a whole) in the last life-and-death struggle — the struggle for the survival and rule of the best, who are the predestined founders of the *next* Golden Age, the last phase of the perennial Struggle "against Time," marking the end of the present Age of Gloom. And the inspired Man "against Time" who was, *at the beginning of that phase*, to act on behalf of the Forces of Light and Life, was bound to be a German, nay, the very embodiment of eternal Germany. And Adolf Hitler was that Man. And he knew it in the depth of his heart. He was perfectly conscious of the fact that his policy, both at home and abroad, was the only *real* German policy, and therefore the only conceivable one in the interest of Aryan mankind as a whole and — consequently — of the whole realm of Life, the only conceivable one "in the interest of the Universe," to quote the words of the Book of books. For alone regenerate Aryan man can and will save what is, in spite of all, worth saving in this doomed world, and build a new earth — open a new Time-cycle — on the basis of principles eternally true. Adolf Hitler has repeatedly said so in his speeches. And repeatedly expressed in *Mein Kampf* the same fact, namely that he was acting "in the spirit of the almighty Creator" and struggling "for the Lord's own work,"[26] i.e., for Truth upon this earth: earthly Perfection, and that his "new ideas" are "in harmony with the primeval meaning of things."[27]

What August Kubizek relates of his life in Linz and Vienna from 1904 to 1908 shows how early the future ruler had acquired a clear conception of his ultimate aim — the "ideal state" — and become aware of the *spirit* of the whole programme he was, one day, to set forth and to work out, with the help of enthusiastic millions of people, how early he knew what his policy would be (what, in fact, any policy in accordance with *truth*, i.e., with Nature, can only be): at the same time national and socialistic, nay, socialistic *because* it was to be — *is* to be — national in the full sense of the word, first in the sense of *racial*, and national in that sense because that Godhead within us which is *real* Godhead, is nothing else but the latent glory of our race in its original perfection.

To urge the German and, beyond the pale of the Reich, the Aryan in general — the youngest race of our Time-cycle, destined to the lordship of the divine Beginning of the *next* cycle — to yearn for and to strive with all his enlightened might towards that perfection on all planes, and to bring it, here and now, *collectively* as well as individually, into being (to the extent this is exceptionally possible, already during the Dark Age), to urge him to be, *now*, against the prevailing spirit of general contamination and general decay — against the current of Time — the witness and the herald of the coming Dawn, and that, on a national, or rather on a racial scale, such is and remains the actual goal of National Socialism, the Hitler faith, however astounding this may yet appear to most people, today, in Year 22[28] after the first seizure of power.[29] Important as they may have been after 1918 — or as they may be *now* after 1945 — the immediate political aims which could not and cannot be separated from the persecuted *Weltanschauung* are mere steps towards that one great positive, permanent goal.

卐 卐 卐

---

[26] *Mein Kampf*, p. 76.
[27] *Mein Kampf*, p. 440.
[28] These words were written in 1955.
[29] *Machtübernahme* — which took place on the 30th of January 1933.

As I have previously stated, Adolf Hitler was from early adolescence, and probably from childhood, conscious of the shocking disparity that exists between "real life" — life under Dark Age conditions, as it drew his attention through a thousand and one details — and his own conception of earthly perfection, a living reflection of which he sought in the world of the old Germanic Sagas (transfigured, for him, in Wagner's musical dramas) and — Kubizek tells us — in the stately blonde young maiden to whom he never spoke, but whom he idealised from a distance as the resplendent embodiment of perfect German womanhood.[30] Instances of human misery, nay — and the importance of this can never be sufficiently stressed — instances of the age-old exploitation of animals by man,[31] which another person would have deplored, but judged unavoidable, or looked upon as trifling, or not noticed at all, provided *him* with an opportunity to feel indignant and to crave for entirely new conditions of life. But it is during the years of grinding poverty and complete moral solitude, which he spent in Vienna as a young man, that the experience of the wretchedness and ugliness of this present Age imposed itself upon him for the first time in all its tragic horror. He has described it in immortal words.[32] And, more than the daily contact with material misery itself (with material misery which *he*, by the way, not merely beheld, but actually *shared*), the sight of the degrading effects of that misery upon his people and upon their young children was unbearable to him.

Two facts should, at that stage of Adolf Hitler's life, retain the attention of whoever wishes to understand him and the Movement he was to start ten years later, obviously as a political Movement for the assertion of Germany's rights, in reality, also as the moral and metaphysical basis of a new civilisation: first, the aloofness in which he lived, amidst the surrounding misery and degradation, and then, the thoroughness and *detachment* with which he studied the latter, traced its deep causes under the immediate, superficial ones, and became, through that clear knowledge, more and more aware of his own predestined role in this Age of Gloom. "One cannot 'study' the social question from

---

[30] Kubizek, pp. 76 and following.
[31] Kubizek, p. 61.
[32] *Mein Kampf*, pp. 23, 32 and following.

above," writes he, in *Mein Kampf*.[33] One has, oneself, to experience the same perpetual insecurity of life, to be acquainted with the same pangs of hunger, to dwell in the same over-crowded, dirty, noisy surroundings as the disinherited classes, in one word, to *live* the wretchedness that gnaws into them and degrades them, in order to *know* what social misery means. The future German Führer had lived it, and suffered from it, personally, day after day, for months, for years, without it ever degrading or even changing *him*. He preferred to "exist" on hunger rations, rather than sacrifice his independence or sell more than it was absolutely necessary of the precious time he needed to study both books and men and *to think*. And when he had earned a little money, he preferred to buy himself a seat in the theatre — two or three hours' holiday in the beautiful world of the old Sagas, to the accompaniment of Wagner's solemn music, away, far away from the daily dreary wretchedness that seemed to be his lot forever — rather than treat himself to a substantial meal.[34] He refused publicity — and money — rather than to allow a story which he had written to be printed by a Jew.[35] Nobody can understand him save a true artist who is, at the same time, a true revolutionary: a person of one dream and one aim, like himself. But how well every such a one — every creator and fighter of his *type*, when surely not of his magnitude, i.e., every person "against Time" — *does* understand him!

There is more. Not only did he live in uncompromising faithfulness to his ideals, inaccessible to the lure of material comfort and social advantages, but he shared none of the weaknesses of average mankind, not to mention the vices of that underworld into which fate had pushed him or, by the way, those of the so-called "better classes" of this fallen humanity. He rigorously abstained from alcohol and tobacco, and even when, occasionally, he could afford a diet other than his usual bread and milk, he ate pastry and fruits, not meat. His deeper instinct inclined him naturally towards that sort of food which people, in whose life an immemorial Tradition still plays a great part, call "pure."[36] And

---

[33] *Mein Kampf*, p. 26.
[34] Kubizek, p. 37.
[35] Kubizek, pp. 298–99.
[36] In Sanskrit: *sattwik*.

the dictates of serious reflection merely confirmed in him those of deeper, healthy instinct. Adolf Hitler was, in course of his life, to become a more and more convinced vegetarian, and though disaster robbed him of the opportunity of attempting "after the war" to give his views, gradually, the force of law, he remains, to my knowledge, the only ruler in the West who, both on hygienic *and* moral (and aesthetic) grounds, ever earnestly considered the possibility of suppressing meat eating, and of abolishing thereby the standing horror of the slaughterhouses. This is reported by Dr. Goebbels in his *Diaries*,[37] and brilliantly confirmed by numerous statements ascribed to the Führer himself in the *Table Talk*, also printed *after* 1945 by the bitterest enemies of National Socialism, certainly *not* with the intention of exalting him.

As a young man, and nay, a very attractive one, Adolf Hitler withstood the manifold temptations of the corrupt metropolis — ignored the solicitations of women, rejected with disgust those of men, and kept the sacred "flame of Life" (to use the words Kubizek quotes) pure and strong and constantly under control within himself. He did so without the slightest intention of "mortifying the flesh," without the slightest desire of "acquiring merit" for the salvation of his soul, simply because he respected that energy given to man for a higher purpose and looked upon every wanton waste of it as a sin against the Race at the same time as a profanation of the divinity of Life. The "flame of Life," felt he, was to be dedicated to the selfless service of the Race, visible Vehicle of Life eternal. It was to be used, like man's *whole* physical and moral energy, "in the spirit of the Creator," i.e., in view of the attainment of perfection on earth. The entire National Socialist teaching concerning sex and sexual relations, with its well-known stress upon absolute health and racial purity, as laid down in *Mein Kampf*,[38] has its origin and its basis in that truly religious (although anything but "other-worldly") attitude, in that standpoint of the "Man against Time" seeking, in defiance of the corruption of the Dark Age, to re-establish, here and now, the biological — i.e., fundamental — conditions of the earthly paradise, preparing the privileged, natural élite of mankind for the

---

[37] See *The Goebbels Diaries*, entry of the 26th April, 1942.
[38] *Mein Kampf*, pp. 444–46.

part it has to play in the formation of the god-like Race of the new earth, that will thrive in peace after this Dark Age has come to an end.

And all Adolf Hitler's positive measures in view of the physical and moral protection of his predestined people, natural leaders of Aryan man, after he came to power: his admirable laws for the welfare of mother and child, for the creation of ideal living conditions for workmen's families, for the education of a healthy, self-confident and self-reliant, proud and beautiful youth, and his famous "Nuremberg Laws," forwarding the growth in Germany of a pure-blooded Germanic race (forbidding sexual relations with Jews and, in fact, with non-Aryans of any description), have no other origin and no other meaning. Their aim—nay, the practical aim of National Socialism as such—was and remains not merely to improve the material lot of the German labourers (however important a part this immediate aim doubtless played in the *success* of the Hitler Movement in Germany, after the First World War); not merely to make the new state, comprising all people of Germanic blood—that "holy Reich of all Germans"[39] of which Adolf Hitler already spoke in his adolescent's conversations with August Kubizek—a strong and prosperous state, but to regenerate the German people—the most conscious among the Aryans of the West—radically, and to organise them, in all walks of life, so as to create out of them the only dam capable of withstanding and thrusting back the threatening tide of inferior humanity, whose rise is, in this as in *every* Time-cycle, the increasingly tragic sign of an advanced stage of the Dark Age; capable of thrusting it back and of carrying, beyond its defeat (and its destruction, at the very end of the Age of Gloom), the treasure of god-like life into the glory of the new Beginning.

As I said before, it is difficult to state how far Adolf Hitler could have *explicitly* given expression to this point of view. It was, nevertheless, in reality, his point of view. In particular, he was and remained all his life vividly aware of the compelling necessity of preserving, nay, of forwarding *at any cost* the racial aristocracy of mankind—the best elements of the Aryan race—if this planet is not, after an appalling period of chaos (after the

---

[39] Kubizek, p. 109; *Mein Kampf*, p. 439.

end of the present Time-cycle), "to go its way, void of human beings, through aetherial space, as it did millions of years ago."[40] Standing alone, personally untouched by Dark Age conditions at their worst, although deeply and painfully acquainted with them, he observed their effects upon the people in whom his unfailing intuition forced him to recognise, in spite of all, *the* predestined biological substance of an infinitely better mankind: the ones who *are not* yet, but who (to quote Nietzsche's words) are *"becoming,"* or at least are capable of becoming, supermen: his own German people. And, with serenity and with realism, he sought the causes of physical and moral wretchedness, the many causes: selfishness of the owning classes, indifference or cowardice of men in power, the grip of international high finance upon the national economy, the influence of Jewry upon the national body and soul, etc., etc., but under those many causes, the one cause: the rule of false values, the exaltation of untruth, which is synonymous of sickness, in all domains, rebellion against the spirit of the divine Order of Nature. *That* is what he had come to fight, so that the "reign of Righteousness" be re-established.

Adolf Hitler's second and even more shattering experience of the horror of the present Age began on the 10th of November 1918, as he stood, half-blind from the effects of poisonous gas, among his wounded comrades in a hospital hall at Pasewalk in Pomerania, and heard from the clergyman the latest news: the "November Revolution" and Germany's capitulation, the tragic end of the First World War.

More than four years before, he had joined the war with enthusiasm, as a volunteer in a Bavarian regiment, *not* in an Austrian one, clearly showing thereby that he was prepared to die anytime for the German people and "for the Reich that embodied them,"[41] though not for "the state of the Habsburgs" — that artificial state of many nationalities. For he considered the war in no way as an Austrian concern, but as a struggle of the German people (including, naturally, those of Austria) "for their exist-

---

[40] *Mein Kampf*, p. 316.
[41] *Mein Kampf*, p. 179.

ence"[42] — as a just war. And, he had done his duty thoroughly, faithfully. And although he had, for months already (especially since the general strike of 1917), been fearing — feeling — that some diabolical traitors' intrigues were being carried on to rob the German front-soldier of a victory which he well deserved, yet he had not expected such an end, and so suddenly . . .

The grief, the indignation and temporary despair that took him over as he abruptly acquired "the most horrible certitude in his life"[43] are so eloquently described in *Mein Kampf* that nothing can throw more light upon the future Führer's state of mind than an extensive quotation of his own words:

> I could not remain any longer [i.e., remain hearing the news]. While my eyes once more stared into darkness, I sought my way back to the dormitory, threw myself upon my bed, and buried my burning head under the quilts and pillows.
>
> Since the day I had stood before my mother's grave, I had not wept. When, in my youth, Destiny had been mercilessly harsh to me, I had faced it with growing defiance. When during the long years of the war, death had taken many a dear comrade and friend of mine from our ranks, it would have seemed to me nearly a sin to complain — for they had died for Germany. And when, in the days of the terrible struggle, the slowly advancing gas had taken me in its grip, and begun to gnaw into my eyes, and when the fear of becoming blind forever had made me feel, for a second, as though I would weaken, the voice of conscience had thundered to me: "Miserable wretch! You feel like weeping, while thousands are faring worse than yourself!" And I had put up with my lot in silence. But now I could not help weeping. Now I experienced how completely every personal suffering fades away before the misfortune of one's Fatherland.
>
> So, it had all been in vain! In vain all our sacrifices, and all the hardships we had endured; in vain, hunger and thirst, for months without end; in vain, the hours in which,

---

[42] *Mein Kampf*, p. 178.
[43] *Mein Kampf*, p. 222.

facing the terror of death, we had yet done our duty; and in vain, the death of two million men! Would not the graves of the hundreds of thousands who had gone forth full of faith in the Fatherland, never to return, break open and release the dumb heroes covered with mud and blood—release them as revengeful spirits among the people at home, who had treated so disdainfully the highest sacrifice which a man can offer his country? Had they died *for that*, the soldiers of August and September 1914? Had the regiments of volunteers, in the autumn of the same year, followed *for that* the elder comrades? Had those boys of 17 sunk *for that* into Flanders' earth? Was *that* the object of the sacrifice that German mothers had brought the Fatherland when, with a grieving heart, they had sent the boys to their duty, never to see them again? Had all that happened in order to enable, now, a handful of criminals to set their grip upon the Fatherland?!! . . . The more I tried, then, to think clearly about the monstrous event, the more my forehead burnt with indignation and shame. What was all the pain I felt in my eyes, compared with this wretchedness?

What followed were appalling days and still worse nights. I knew that all was lost. Only fools—fools or . . . liars and criminals—could put their hope in the enemy's mercy. During those nights, hatred grew in me, hatred against the originators of that deed.

In those days, I also became aware of my destiny. Now, I could only laugh at the thought of my own future, that had caused me such bitter worry only a short time before. Was it not ridiculous to build houses upon such foundations as this? At last it was clear to me that the very thing which I so often already had feared, without ever being able, in my heart, to believe it, had now happened.

Emperor William the Second had been the first German emperor to hold out his hand to the leaders of Marxism, in a gesture of reconciliation, without knowing that rascals have no honour. While they still held the Emperor's hand in one of theirs, their other one was already seeking for the dagger.

With Jews, no pactising policy is possible, but only that

of the hard "either—or."
I decided to become a politician.[44]

This heart-rending autobiographical account could—historically—be described as: the passage of National Socialism from the stage of an expectant or latent incarnate Idea, to that of an active one.

Surely the incarnate Idea is, if not as old as Adolf Hitler himself, at least as old as his earliest awakening to socio-political, nay, to philosophical consciousness in general. And that took place *very* early: already in Linz, if not before. Yet, then, and in Vienna, although his interest in social and political problems grew and grew with the daily experience of injustice and misery, and still in Munich, after 1912, the future ruler continued to think of himself primarily as a future architect. There may have been moments, of course, in which he thought, or at least *felt*, differently. There were such moments—one such moment at least, and a great one—already in his life in Linz, if we are to believe Kubizek's account of it.[45] But the artist's immediate goal soon reappeared. Horrible as—in Vienna, at any rate—many of them doubtless were, the experiences of daily life were not sufficiently appalling to push it out of sight altogether. Nay, *during* the war, when more and more aware of the necessity of opposing to the forces of international Socialism a *national* organisation which would be free from the weaknesses of the parliamentary system, Hitler had begun to think seriously of becoming politically active, he had merely visualised himself speaking in public "while carrying on his profession."[46] Now, his profession, nay, his art—for he still was, and could only remain, fundamentally, an artist—was out of the question. Every activity which was not to contribute directly and immediately to free Germany from the consequences and especially from the *causes* of defeat, was out of the question, and that, not merely because Adolf Hitler loved Germany above all things, but because that more-than-human intuition that classes him among the few great seers of mankind, told him that Germany's real, deeper interest was—*is*, absolute-

---

[44] *Mein Kampf*, pp. 223, 224–25.
[45] Kubizek, pp. 140 and following.
[46] *Mein Kampf*, p. 192.

ly—the real interest of Creation—the "interest of the Universe," again to quote the immortal words of the Bhagavad-Gita. (And it is not an accident—not a mere coincidence—that I, a non-German Aryan intimately connected with England, Greece, and India, should stress this fact. It is a sign, a symbol, the first expression of the homage of world-wide Aryandom to the latest Man "against Time" and to the truly chosen Nation.)

Out of the abyss of powerless despair—from that bed of suffering upon which the nameless corporal Adolf Hitler lay weeping over Germany's fate while his blinded eyes burned in their sockets, like red-hot embers, out of his appalling certitude that "all was lost," that "all had been in vain"—rose the defiant Will to freedom and Will to power of an invincible people and, beyond that, and greater than that, the perennial cosmic Will to Perfection in all its majesty, the will of the German soldier who had fought in Flanders and—identical to it, expressing itself through it—the impersonal and irresistible Will of the eternal Warrior and Seer above Time and "against Time," the Will of Him Who comes back age after age, "when all is lost," "when evil rules supreme," to re-establish on earth the reign of Righteousness.

From then onwards, the age-old Struggle for Truth—the Struggle "against Time"—was, in the West, to enter a new phase. It was to identify itself with the political struggle to free Germany from the bondage imposed upon her by the victors of 1918, no less than with the more-than-political one against the causes of physical and moral decay that were—and still are—threatening the existence of the natural aristocracy of the Aryan race. And the National Socialist German Labourers' Party—the famous N.S.D.A.P., which Adolf Hitler soon evolved out of the tiny group of idealists (seven, including himself) originally called the "Deutsche Arbeiter Partei," which he joined in 1919—was to be the one agent of the everlasting Force of Light and Life amidst the growing darkness of the Dark Age. I say: *the* one, for, contrarily to *all* other so-called movements of regeneration, religious and secular, this political *and yet infinitely more than political* Movement attacked the very root of historical decay as such: biological decay, the consequence of sin against the primary natural Commandment of blood purity, in other words (from the standpoint of original Perfection), sickness, tangible, physical *untruth, and* that moral untruth (that false conception of "man") which stands behind it.

There are, in the records of mankind, few things as beautiful as the early history of the National Socialist Movement.

The tremendous will-power, kindled through despair, out of which the latter had sprung, was, as I just said, nothing less than the divine Will to Perfection in its last (or one before last) effort to lead the best upstream against the fated current of Time and to save through them whatever is yet worth saving in this doomed Creation. The material and moral condition under which the Movement took shape — the miserable, smoky room[47] in which six unknown German workmen sat and discussed with the superman who was soon to guide them, and millions of others, to the reconquest of national greatness; these men's utter poverty, their utter insignificance in the eyes of the wide world and especially of those well-spoken of, comfortable politicians and party-leaders whom they were, within few years, to thrust into oblivion; their burning faith and, which is more, the fact that their Leader — Adolf Hitler — was in possession of cosmic truth — are highly symbolical. All life begins in darkness. All everlasting things are born in silence and away from the limelight of publicity, in faith and in truth. And whatever is not born in such a manner does not last. However noisy and widespread be its success, it will not stand the test of time and that of persecution, let alone the terrible impact of the storm in which a Time-cycle comes to its end.

The very early growth of National Socialism as an active, incarnate Idea, was like the growth of a corn seed within the snow-bound earth; it was like the slow rise of molten rock within the depth of a slumbering volcano: unnoticed and irresistible. It was the outcome of a natural Force, in fact, of the oldest and mightiest of all natural Forces: of Life's inherent instinct of self-preservation in the presence of the Powers of Death — the Force that links every Time-cycle to the following one, over almost total destruction. Started in 1919, officially founded in early 1920, it owes to that divine Force its impulse which nothing — not even

---

[47] *Mein Kampf,* pp. 240 and following.

the disaster of 1945 — was able to break.

Throughout the wide world, governments representing sheer finance interests looked with satisfaction upon their latest handiwork: the Versailles peace treaty, up till then the most infamous official document in history, intended to enslave Germany for all time. And the sheep followed their shepherds. And the parrots repeated the nonsense — and lies — which they had been taught: "This Treaty seals the victory of those who fought this war in order to put an end to all wars!" — while frenzied crowds demonstrated in the streets of the French towns howling "Germany must pay!" Never had there been so many speeches, so many sermons, so many articles and books — such a "hullabaloo" — about "peace." And never had victors yet behaved with such calculated barbarity.

In the inconspicuous little room at the back of a café in Munich, however, Adolf Hitler — the Man "against Time" — spoke to the tiny group of German workmen, to the rough men of pure blood and solid virtues, sons of the people among which he — *He*, the One Who comes back — had chosen (this time) to be born. And his words were — and his whole life was — the answer to the lies of this advanced Dark Age. They cannot have been much different from those one reads in *Mein Kampf*, although these were written five years later. He said:

> For me, as for every true National Socialist, there is only one doctrine: people and fatherland.
>
> We have to fight to secure the existence and expansion of our race and of our people, to enable them to nourish their children and to preserve the purity of their blood, to secure the freedom of our Fatherland, *so that our people may be in the position to fulfil the mission appointed to them by the Creator of the Universe.*[48]

He said:

> Whoever speaks of a mission of the German people on this earth must know that such a mission can only lie in the formation of a state which holds it to be its highest task to

---

[48] *Mein Kampf*, p. 234.

> *preserve and to promote the noblest of all elements which have, in our people, nay, in the whole of mankind, remained unspoilt.*[49]

He said:

> The German Reich should, as a state, comprise all Germans, and set itself the task not merely *to gather and preserve the most valuable original racial elements in that people, but to raise them slowly and surely to a ruling position.*[50]

He said:

> *Men do not go to ruin through lost wars, but through the loss of that power of resistance that lies in pure blood alone.*[51]

He was aware of the downfall of the whole of mankind — including Germany — in the present Age. "Unfortunately," said he, "our German people are no longer racially homogeneous."[52] And aware of the primary cause of downfall: racial mixture, the result of forgetfulness of Nature's truth. And aware of that truth, expressed in the oldest Book of Aryan Wisdom, the Bhagavad-Gita: "Out of the corruption of women proceeds the confusion of races; out of the confusion of races, the loss of memory; out of the loss of memory, the loss of understanding; and out of this, all evil."[53] He was aware of it, not because he had read the Book (it is doubtful whether he had, at least as early as 1919), but because the impersonal Wisdom of the most ancient Aryans lived in him; because he was He Who has spoken in the Book — the One Who comes back. And he knew that the Wisdom which he preached as the key to earthly salvation "corresponds entirely to the original meaning of things,"[54] and that the way he preached — return to that primeval, cosmic Wisdom in individual *and* in collective life, in thought and in deed — was — is — the only way through

---

[49] *Mein Kampf*, p. 439.
[50] *Mein Kampf*, p. 439.
[51] *Mein Kampf*, p. 324.
[52] *Mein Kampf*, pp. 436–37.
[53] The Bhagavad-Gita, I, verse 41 and following.
[54] *Mein Kampf*, p. 440.

which the chosen few can survive the last impact of the forces of disintegration and become the founders of the new Age of Truth. And that those chosen few are the best elements of the youngest great Race of our Time-cycle: the Aryan. He knew that too. And while he stressed in his speeches the necessity of freeing Germany, at once, from the immediate consequences of the Versailles Treaty—inflation, unemployment, growing misery—his ultimate aim remained to raise her to that organised power which, in the light of traditional Wisdom, can only be termed as a "state against Time"—nay, *the* "state against Time," enabling the best to carry both their privileged biological substance *and* their unmarred Golden Age ideal through and beyond the last storms of this Dark Age.

He spoke with the compelling eloquence of faith, knowing that he was right—that the endless future of the Universe (not merely of Germany and Europe) would glaringly prove how right he was. He spoke with the wild eloquence of emergency, knowing also that the struggle he was about to start had to take place then or never, that there was not an hour to waste.

And the sombre faces of the hungry, embittered men who had fought and suffered, and yet lost, gazed at him with that unconditional admiration and confidence that is the essence of worship—the faces of the six, and, soon, of many more, of hundreds, in ever broader meeting-halls, always too small to contain them, of hundreds of thousands under the open sky.

"Men do not go to ruin through lost wars . . ." The magic words—these, and others, meaning the same—rang throughout defeated Germany. And the hundreds of thousands no longer felt defeated. They now knew they had been betrayed. And they roared against the traitors and against the Dark Powers behind them—the Dark Powers that they (the German people) would one day crush. They felt strong; they felt young—invincible and immortal. They felt what the best among them really were—had been, from the beginning of Aryan history, appointed to become—the masters of an unheard-of future, the proud founders of a new world. (Only they did not—yet—know through what a terrible *Via dolorosa* they actually were to fulfil that staggering destiny.) They gathered, more and more numerous, around the Man whose inspired speech quickened in them the highest possibilities of joyous heroism—and made them see old forgotten truths in a glaring new light, whose magic radiance filled them with self-assurance: whose love for them was limitless and gratuitous, like the love of a God. They beheld in him the Leader, the Avenger, the Saviour—the living embodiment of their unvanquished collective Self, which indeed he was. And they followed him blindly. Their love carried him to power, their love, and their hatred for those whom he rightly pointed out to them as the promoters of the humiliation of 1918 and of all the subsequent misery: the Jews, and the servants of Jewry, agents of the Dark Forces by nature or by choice, Germany's—and the world's—*real* enemies.

Their real enemies and their only enemies. Adolf Hitler has pointed out no others. (And *that* is precisely the reason why the whole world—this doomed Dark Age world, stricken with madness, which exalts its foes and kills its friends—has risen against him like one man.) The fact is too important not to deserve a thorough explanation.

Nothing is more unfair to National Socialism than the all-too-easy description of its inherent "anti-Semitism" as "a means intended to turn the German people's attention away from their actual exploiters" (meaning: the German capitalists), or, as a modern expression of the age-old "envy" of the *goyim*—of any *goyim*—at the sight of the Jews' undeniable success in business. The first assumption, brought forth *ad nauseam* by the Communists and their sympathisers—reveals either a complete absence of good faith or a complete misunderstanding of the Jewish question as such and therefore of all serious, vital "anti-Semitism." The latter may well be applied to Armenian "anti-Semitism" (or to that of any commercially clever Levantines, whose trickery the Jews alone are able to outdo). It has nothing whatsoever in common with the profound, *biological*, and therefore irreducible hostility which opposes National Socialists and Jews.

No doubt, that hostility first burst out in a popular uproar in answer to all the tangible harm wrought by Jews against the German people during a few decades (and many a German whose family Jews had reduced to misery at the time of the inflation, after the First World War, welcomed the boisterous anti-Semitism of the young Movement for personal no less than for national reasons); no doubt, the first thing that made Adolf Hitler himself a definitive enemy of the Jews was his knowledge of the anti-German part played by the latter, both politically and socially, in Austria and in Germany, already before 1914, in particular, his knowledge of the Jewish spirit and Jewish leadership of Marxism, and his awareness of the presence of Jews in the press, in the theatre, etc., behind all propaganda directly or indirectly aiming at the destruction of every healthy national instinct among people of German blood. In other words, National Socialist anti-Semitism is — first — the racial self-defence of the Aryan, a vigorous reaction against the mischief the Jews *did* (and are, by the way, since 1945, again doing) in an Aryan land.

But there is more — and much more — to be said. What the Jews did and do (and cannot but do) is a consequence of what they *are* — and of what they remain even when they turn their backs on Jewish tradition (or pretend to do so) and become Christians, Theosophists, Buddhists, or just "rationalists," or Communists. And they are, fundamentally, irreducibly — already in the invisible Realm of which this world of shapes and colours and sounds is but a projection — the polar opposite of the natural Aryan élite; the dark counterpart of the youngest Children of the Sun. As racially conscious as they, if not — alas! — often more so, as tightly bound as they to one another through the most compelling solidarity, through *total* solidarity (in practical — financial and political — no less than religious or so-called religious affairs) such as one can, in history, if at all, seldom come across, nay, as devoted as they to a merciless collective purpose. Only theirs is *not* the legitimate consciousness of true superiority and the blood-solidarity of Nature's best ones; nay, it is not the healthy racial pride and patriotism of a real people *in their place* within the scheme of Life. Nor is their collective purpose by any means, like that of Adolf Hitler's followers, "in harmony with the original meaning of things." On the contrary! For the Jews are, in the first place, *not a race* in the true sense of the word — let alone "God's chosen one." They are neither a homogeneous variety of Semites nor a brotherhood of kindred Semitic types bearing to one another such a relation as that which binds together Aryans of "Nordic," "Dinaric," and other types within the German nation. One needs but to look at them, in order to be convinced of this, nay, to look at them in the country where they have been gathering for the last 30 or 40 years from all the ghettos of the world in the name of their common past and common nationhood: Palestine. One meets there, apart from the "classical" Jew, Jews of all physical types, including the Slav, including the "Nordic" — rare, no doubt, yet present and not necessarily marred by the well-known visible signs of Jewish descent. And some of the members of the strange pseudo-ethnical, pseudo-religious world-community — such as, for instance, the so-called "black Jews" of Cochin, on the Malabar Coast — have no Jewish blood, in fact, no Semitic blood at all in their veins,[55] which does not prevent them from feeling themselves "Jews."

The Jewish world community is — has been, more and more, for centuries already — not a Semitic nation but a raceless brotherhood gathered around a Semitic nucleus, a raceless brotherhood, however, as racially-*conscious* as any people can be, increasingly numerous cosmopolitan elements who put the usual characteristics of the raceless — faithlessness, unscrupulousness, disregard of order, soul-poisoning scepticism — to the service of the racial idea that they have partly inherited, partly adopted from their full-blooded brothers in faith and brothers in interests, *and* Semites — a very definite, inferior section of the broad Semitic race — in whom masterfulness in subtlety and intrigue outweighs by far all warrior-like qualities.

And its collective aim, pursued throughout history with relentless consistency, is nothing less than the prosperity and power of the Jew, everywhere in the world, at the expense of *all* non-Jews. The consciousness of being (more or less) "children of Abraham" and the common "Law" under which (nominally at least) its members live, may well keep the community together. Yet they are but means to an end. And the end — the common collective purpose: actual Jewish rule — is what really matters.

It is an unholy purpose, the fulfilment of which would imply the dissolution of *all* races and of all genuine nationalities, of all

---

[55] Those so-called "black Jews" are just low caste Indians whose forefathers have once accepted the Jewish *faith*. To this day, they marry among themselves only.

natural communities, i.e., of all those that have a solid racial background (first the dissolution of the most gifted and most conscious one, of the most fit to rule—the Aryan—and then, gradually, of all others, *including, ultimately, the Semitic nucleus of the Jewish community itself*) and the ever-tightening grip of a soulless money power—the power of the raceless, gifted with destructive intelligence—over increasingly bastardised and numberless masses of *Menschenmaterial*, possessing neither thought nor will of their own, nor the innocence and nobility of real animals. It is the purpose of the Forces of darkness, whose influence grows, whose free play becomes more and more free and shameless, and whose rule asserts itself as a more and more obvious reality, as history runs its fated downward course. It is the purpose of Time itself, as Destroyer of all creation, as Leveller and Denier. And it is the purpose of the community, "in Time" *par excellence*, of the community who, like the privileged Aryan élite gathered around Adolf Hitler, talks passionately of its "mission" and calls itself "chosen" — and rightly so, but who omits to state that, contrarily to the pure-blooded disciples of the Man "against Time," it has been chosen not by "God," not by the everlasting Forces of Light and Life, to serve Life's constructive goal, but by the Powers of Death, to bring about, through ever-increasing unfaithfulness to the original divine life pattern, i.e., through increasing *untruth*, the end of this Time-cycle. The end, *without* a new beginning—for that is the intention, the *tendency* of the Death-forces. While the purpose of the National Socialist Movement—its real, deep purpose, far beyond all "politics" — was *and remains* the glorious new Beginning—the new victory of uncreated Light over the Dark Powers, the new victory of Life in its original earthly perfection, of Order, in its true meaning, *in spite* of the temporary, unavoidable reign of Chaos, the Golden Age of the *next* Time-cycle.

In one word, the sharp hostility between National Socialists and Jews means infinitely more than that which the detractors of the Hitler faith so lightly take it to be. It reveals not the usual tension between any two rival "racialisms," but the unique opposition between the two poles of thinking Life at the very end of the present Dark Age. That is the hidden but real reason why it is absolute—and why its tangible expressions have been, and will, at the first opportunity, again be, so deadly.

Adolf Hitler knew it. The wisest among his true disciples knew it, and know it. The all-powerful leaders of world Jewry knew it, and know it.

卐 卐 卐

The National Socialist struggle against international Jewry took, in broad daylight, the form of a tremendous holy war against Marxism—the latest large-scale Movement "*in* Time"—and, in a much subtler and indirect manner, yet with equal deadly determination, that of a relentless action against all spiritual or pseudo-spiritual, open or secret organisations equally "in Time," the influence of which is, in fact, no less than that of Marxism, directed against any attempt at an Aryan regeneration "*against* Time." It took place and will, one day, be resumed—for no "de-Nazification" policy can hinder the play of the invisible Forces—with the necessary Dark Age methods.

War against Marxism seemed and still seems to be—and no doubt *is*, in the practical field—the first task of National Socialism, only because Marxism represents, today, the most immediate menace; because it is the most *successful* brand of the old, very old Jewish mass-poison for the *goyim's* consumption, intended to bring about the decay of all races, the end of all true nationalisms, and the limitless increase of a Jew-ridden humanity of poorer and poorer quality in a duller and duller—uglier and uglier—world, in one word, the consummation of the downfall of Life upon this planet. Which does not mean to say that other brands of the same, the effects of which are less obvious, less rapid, are not, in the long run, just as dangerous, if not even more so.

The greatness of the National Socialist Movement in this respect, lies less in the fact that it has, more vigorously (and efficiently) than any other party—or church—fought against the "Communist danger," than in that it has pointed out the right reason why the latter is "a danger"—*the* danger—and fought it *for that reason alone*.

Considered from the point of view of cosmic Wisdom, Communism, or rather Marxism, is not a danger because it threatens the owning classes of this earth with dispossession and the subsequent unpleasant compulsion of daily labour, and aims at the total abolition of the capitalistic economy. *That* — the main cause of all the "hullabaloo" against the Communists *outside* National Socialist circles — is a detail, and a minor one at that. The world has nothing to lose through the disappearance of capitalists and of the rotten system they represent. On the contrary! And, although private ownership, inasmuch as it be the product of personal *work*, and *not* of speculation, is recognised in the National Socialist Party Programme as "a legitimate right of the individual,"[56] I would go so far as to say that, even so, it would not be an irreparable catastrophe, were *that* also to be wiped away in the storm of radical economic changes.

Marxism is also not a danger because its true adherents — people who live thoroughly "in Time" — have little leisure for Christian and other metaphysics and, in particular, little curiosity about what might happen to them after they will be dead. Nay, it is no danger because Karl Marx's basic teaching concerning history — his famous "historical materialism" — attempts to explain all evolution in Time without the help of the hypothesis of "God" and of the human "soul." *That* — the main cause of the uproar against "Communist atheism" among Christians and other spiritually-minded people, and the main excuse set forth by the Catholic church to justify its ban on the "materialistic" doctrine — is also a detail. And the idea of God, as the overwhelming majority of anti-Communists uphold it, is vague, anyhow, vague, and of no practical use whatsoever. The danger of Marxism lies, as Adolf Hitler has pointed out in *Mein Kampf*[57] and in numberless speeches, solely — absolutely — in the fact that its conception of man as a mere product of his economic surroundings and of destiny as a play of purely economic forces, implies the denial of the importance of race and personality — the denial of the natural hierarchy of races and of the irreducible differences in kind and *in value* between one race and the other, no less than that of the natural inequality of individuals, even within the same race. In other words, it lies in the fact that Marx-

---

[56] See the Twenty-Five Points in Gottfried Feder, *Das Programm der N.S.D.A.P. und seiner weltanschaulichen Grundgedanken* [The Programme of the N.S.D.A.P. and its Fundamental Worldview] (Munich: Zentralverlag der N.S.D.A.P., 1939), p. 35.

[57] *Mein Kampf*, pp. 420 and following.

ism is *man*-centred—not *life*-centred—and equalitarian; in contradiction with the spirit of Nature, not in harmony with it, false, from the standpoint of cosmic wisdom, like historical Christianity (the source of those moral and spiritual values in the name of which the capitalistic democracies are, or rather pretend to be, anti-communistic) and like all Jewish teachings for Aryan use, but not more so. It lies in the fact that, among all such teachings ancient and modern, Marxism is in addition to that, by far the most popular and the most militant. As I said: for the time being, at least, the most successful.

Adolf Hitler has rightly stressed that the definitive victory of such an Ideology would mean the end of life upon this planet—which is precisely the aim of the more-than-human Forces of disintegration that stand behind world Jewry. The tragedy, however, is that it would *not* mean such a rapid and dignified end as one might imagine. It would mean, *first*, a general and irredeemable bastardisation of the whole human species and an unbelievable increase of the number of human beings—"producers"—at the expense of the rest of life—increase, till the last beautiful wild animals are killed off and the last patch of forest is cut down, to make place for more worthless two-legged mammals—and *then*, when all the possibilities of nourishment which the earth can provide even with the assistance of perfected agricultural technique, are exhausted, war for food;[58] bitter, savage war to the finish (also with the assistance of perfected technique) until the doomed species has blown itself to pieces. It would mean, in other words, "the reign of quantity"[59] in all its horror, and then—in the absence of any biological élite capable of starting a new Time-cycle—a full stop, on this planet at least, the final victory of that death-tendency which is, from the beginning, inherent in every manifestation within Time. And it is *that* which Adolf Hitler—the Man "against Time"—has striven to avoid, through his struggle against Communism, i.e., against

---

[58] Hans Grimm has very accurately pointed this out in his beautiful book *Warum? Woher? aber Wohin?*.

[59] A reference to René Guénon's *Le Règne de la Quantité et les Signes des Temps* (Paris: Éditions Traditionnelles, 1945); in English: *The Reign of Quantity and the Signs of the Times*, trans. Lord Northbourne (London: Luzac and Co., 1953)—Ed.

applied Marxism.

The non-Communist world—nay, the *anti*-Communist world—has understood neither the nature of the growing menace nor the real meaning of the National Socialist Struggle. Moreover, most of those who, in and outside Germany, before or during the Second World War, have answered Adolf Hitler's call to arms against the Communist danger, and most of those who, today, realise how right he was, seem to have seen and to see in his struggle hardly anything more than the "defence of the West."[60] But it is not "the West" alone that was, and is, threatened in its biological substance, and consequently in its further evolution, by the latest man-centred, equalitarian *Weltanschauung* of Jewish origin incorporated into the latest powerful world-organisation—one could say: the latest church—under Jewish leadership. It is the entire Aryan race: the man who, in Cape Town, Sydney, or Ottawa, has, up till now, kept his Germanic blood pure, no less than the "European" of Germanic blood, no less than those Aryan minorities of Asia that the racially conscious European is too often tempted to forget or to underestimate: the Persian, to the extent he has, especially throughout the last 1,500 years of the most stormy history, withstood the curse of blood-mixture; the Indian Brahmin and Kshatriya, whom the caste system has, up till now, kept aloof and protected; in particular the Brahmin of Kashmir, outwardly at least, one of the finest types of Aryan humanity. It is, nay, all pure or relatively pure races of the world that are menaced, including the non-Aryan, *including the Semitic nucleus of the Jewish people themselves*—and no one knows that better than those racially-conscious Jews, once holders of highly responsible positions within the Communist Party, who have been, during the last few years, charged with "Zionism," i.e., Jewish nationalism, before Communist courts and sentenced to long terms of hard labour, if not to death.[61] (Adolf Hitler has written: "After the death of his victim, the vampire himself dies, sooner or later."[62] The poison of man-

---

[60] Perhaps a reference to Maurice Bardèche's journal *Défense de l'Occident* [Defense of the West], founded in 1952—Ed.

[61] See the charges against the eleven Jews in the Prague Trial (1952) and against Anna Pauker, former Commissar in Rumania.

[62] *Mein Kampf*, p. 358.

centred, equalitarian internationalism, intended to bring about the ruin of all races—especially of the Aryan—for the benefit of the Jew, is ultimately bound to work *also* against its originators. For the Death-forces are not selective. They spare nobody—not even their agents.) The fact is that, at the root of that disregard for personality and especially for race, which characterises Marxism, lies the conceited belief in "man" as the measure of all things, in "man" as "the master of Nature" (not merely a part of it, a living species among others), and the illusion that anything endowed with a more or less human shape is of unquestionable value and must be allowed to live, nay, kept alive at any price, the sickly superstition of "man"—that "Jewish lie" which Adolf Hitler so brilliantly exposed in the eleventh chapter of *Mein Kampf*—as opposed to the true, aristocratic Religion of Life.

But the lie is, as I have said, no monopoly of the Marxists, no consequence of Karl Marx's particular conception of man as the product of his economic environment. It is the common basis of *all man-centred, equalitarian philosophies old and new*, Jewish *and* non-Jewish,[63] and especially of the Jewish philosophies of international scope, which all draw an arbitrary line between "men" and the rest of living creatures, thus denying the oneness of the realm of Life and the universality of its iron laws. It is, in particular, the moral basis of historical Christianity.

It matters little what hypothesis or what dogmas be set forth in order to make it sound like truth. The important fact remains that the Jewish lie—snare of the Dark Age—is accepted as truth by the anti-Communist forces of the West outside the National Socialist Movement, primarily by the Christian churches (the "bourgeois" political parties just do not count). The fact remains that these forces share with the Marxists themselves, be it under a different form, the superstition of "man," the origin of the attitude that leads to decay. And that is why none of them was, or is, anti-Communist in the true sense of the word. Not only did they and do they not fight Marxism on account of the *real* danger it represents, but every one of them would, ultimately, represent the self-same danger as it, were they today as militant and full of

---

[63] "Man is greater than everything; there is nothing above him" is a saying attributed to one of the famous Bengali "Vaishnavas" of the 14th century.

faith as they once were. They are, at the most, the rivals of conquering Marxism — or would like to be. While in non-Christian countries, the Christian missionaries are precisely *the* people who, through the alarming increase of a half-educated, bastardised population, seething with discontent (the immediate result of their equalitarian preaching coupled with medical aid) prepare the way for Communism with miraculous efficiency — extending to the whole world (be it in the manner they are the last ones to *desire*) the mischief which the Dark Forces have once wrought in the Near East and in Europe, through Christianity itself.

In other words, the National Socialist struggle against Marxism is merely the most obvious aspect of the general — infinitely more than political — deadly struggle of the bold new faith in Light and Life against every form of untruth — every doctrine setting up "man" against Nature, every cult of imperfection, in this last part of the Dark Age. It is not to be separated from the struggle against the Christian churches, against Freemasonry, and all such international and anti-national so-called "spiritual" bodies as unduly distort and exploit teachings originally "above Time," in order to forward the aims of the Death-forces.

Only the latter struggle had to be more subtle, for practical reasons easy to understand.

卐 卐 卐

It is written in *Mein Kampf*:

Poison can only be overcome through counter-poison, and only a shallow bourgeois mind can consider the middle line as the way to Paradise.[64]

A philosophy filled with infernal intolerance will only be broken through a clear and absolutely true new idea animated with the same spirit and defended with the sane tremendous will-power.

One may, today, well regret that, in the Ancient World, which was much freer than ours, the first moral terror appeared with the coming of Christianity; one cannot, however, put in doubt the fact that the world has

---

[64] *Mein Kampf*, p. 371.

been, since then, dominated and oppressed through tyranny, and that tyranny can only he broken through tyranny, and terror through terror. Then only can new conditions—constructive ones—be created.

Political parties are inclined to compromise; creeds, never. Political parties take contradictors into account; creeds proclaim their own infallibility.[65]

That which gave Marxism its success was the perfect collaboration of political will and militant brutality. That which prevented national Germany from moulding German evolution was the absence of a decisive collaboration of brutal force and of the political will of a man of genius.[66]

The conviction that one has the right to use even the most brutal weapons always goes hand in hand with fanatical faith in the necessity of the victory of a revolutionary new order upon this earth.

A movement that is not fighting for such high aims and ideals, will therefore never resort to the most extreme means (or weapons).[67]

These and other such sentences (there are many more in what one could call the Book of the new Aryan faith) define with amazing exactitude the National Socialist Movement as an upheaval "against Time," and point out the fundamental difference between Adolf Hitler and all such great historical figures as I have, in these pages, described as men "above Time" and men "in Time"—"Sun" men, and "Lightning" men. They glaringly show how foolish it is to compare the Founder of National Socialism with Napoleon—as so many have done—or to accept the well-meant but no less erroneous—though by far less popular—description which a few of his English followers have boldly given of him as a "political Christ."[68]

Napoleon is but the pocket edition of Genghis Khan. Yet—

---

[65] *Mein Kampf*, p. 507.
[66] *Mein Kampf*, p. 596.
[67] *Mein Kampf*, p. 597.
[68] The expression was used by Molly Stamford, an English woman detained during the war under the 18B act.

considered from the cosmic standpoint—he is a man of the same *sort* as he: a warlord and an organiser who put his genius to the service of his family and of nothing more, *not*, by any means, because he saw, or thought he could see, in it, the vehicle of some great impersonal Idea, but simply because it was his. In other words: a man altogether *"in* Time." Men *"in* Time" either have no ideology at all and do not pretend to have any, or they pretend to serve a faith "above Time" or "against Time" and exploit the latter for their own ends (like all the false Christians who fought for themselves in God's name, *and* all the false National Socialists for whom the struggle under the Swastika Flag was only a means to work *themselves* into power) or else—like the sincere Marxists—they have an Ideology which is, itself, an Ideology "in Time," an Ideology which is in contradiction with the divine finality of Creation, and therefore expresses the will of the Death-forces.

Christ (be he a man *and* a myth, or only a myth, it makes no difference) is, like the Buddha, a figure typically "above Time." His one resort to violence (against the merchants in the temple) is either a personal inconsistency of the historical Jesus or—more likely—a concession of the Gospel writer to popular hatred of the money-maker and money-lender. Original Christianity—in striking opposition to *historical* Christianity—finds its expression in Christ's words to Pilate: "My Kingdom *is not of this earth."* It is, like all mystical doctrines of escape, meant for those who turn their backs to "the world," i.e., to all actual and possible manifestation within Time, and seek pure Timelessness, and who, therefore, automatically forsake violence, which is inseparable from Time. (Even Akhnaton—one of the very few men "above Time" who are *not* men of escape, and, to my knowledge, the only one who undertook the unbelievable task of establishing—or trying to establish—a *state* "above Time"—did away with violence, as we have seen, to the extent he *could*.)

Adolf Hitler is a typical Man "against Time"—like Rama, like Lord Krishna, the most widely-remembered Aryan heroes who fought and ruled in India already before, or at the dawn of, this Dark Age, and, nearer to us, like the very noblest Figure of the Arab world, the Prophet Mohammed. As I said in the beginning of this book, all real great men "against Time" are, ultimately, *also* "above Time," inasmuch as any ideal of integral Perfection is necessarily timeless. In other words, that towards which the great men "against Time" strive—Adolf Hitler like the others—is "God," Perfection beyond Time as the Archetype and Principle of that perfect, tangible life-order which they seek to bring—to bring *back*, or rather to hasten back—into the world. But they thoroughly know that no changes upon this earth, and especially no changes in the direction of primeval Perfection in and, which is more, at the end of this Dark Age, can be brought about without violence. They know—infallibly—that the more the Forces of disintegration and death are successful, i.e., the more the Dark Age is advanced, the more violence is indispensable in order to break the current of decay, at least in order to stand in the way of the rush of Time, as a witness (and an active precursor) of the coming glorious Dawn of the next Time-cycle. *And they accept that physical necessity*. Contrarily even to those men "above Time" who, such as Akhnaton of Egypt, dream of an earthly "Kingdom of God," they are prepared to make use of violence—of "utmost brutality," to quote Adolf Hitler's own words—to the extent it is to forward the sacred purpose: "the destruction of evil-doers and the establishment on earth of the reign of Righteousness," of which it is spoken in the Bhagavad-Gita, the foundation of *the* socio-political order which is *"in harmony with the original meaning of things"* —true to the eternal cosmic Order—as again Adolf Hitler has, with, crystal-clear insight, understood and proclaimed.

The very fact of historical existence—existence within Time—sets a dilemma before all those who already strive towards Perfection; they must either turn their backs to this world of strife *altogether*, and seek the timeless inner Kingdom of Peace, which is not of this earth; *or*, if that which they want be an *earthly* paradise, seek *it*, by all means, against the current of Time, against the formidable and ever-increasing pressure of the Death-forces throughout any Time-cycle and, especially near the end of one, but then, far from renouncing violence, fight the Forces of disintegration with the self-same ruthless weapons as *they* use, with violence; with the impact of *quantity*, and, if necessary—if expedient—even with lies, with the weapons of the Dark Age, the only ones which can and will match theirs.

For centuries, perhaps for millenniums—perhaps ever since the day Lord Krishna proclaimed upon the Kurukshetra battlefield the Gospel of detached Violence, the creed of every hero "against Time"—no man has understood that dilemma so clearly, and faced it with such boldness and such consistency as Adolf Hitler. And unless one also understands it, unless one at least realises that it is a *dilemma*—i.e., that *one cannot go both ways* and that, after one has chosen, one is to tread the path to its end—one will behold neither the evolution of National Socialism (before 1933, between 1933 and 1945, *and after* 1945) nor the history of the Second World War, which is narrowly connected with it, nor the subsequent history of our times, in the proper light. And any judgement one might then pass will be false from the cosmic—and *a fortiori* from the historical—point of view.

Adolf Hitler chose to use the Dark Age weapons because—contrarily to that other uncompromising champion of Truth, Akhnaton of Egypt, who lived 3,300 years *before him*—he fully realised that there is, in this world, no peaceful escape from the grip of the Dark Forces. He realised it as he *experienced* that his German people, and, along with them, the whole Aryan race—the youngest creative race of our Time-cycle and the only creative race for centuries, the best—were threatened in their existence by the agents of the Death-powers; cornered, and that their definitive downfall and disappearance would mean the definitive downfall of higher organised Life upon this planet, with no hope of resurrection. That experience did not *begin* on the day Adolf Hitler was told that the First World War was lost for Germany. It had been familiar to him for years. But the news of the loss of the war and then of the infamous Treaties of Versailles and Saint-Germain imposed upon Germany by her victors, and the sight of the following misery, gave it further depth, further acuteness, and a further tremendous hold on him. A growing sense of emergency, a feverish haste—not unlike that which one can trace in the building of the capital of King Akhnaton's ideal state—drove him forwards, defining his whole policy in its positive and negative aspects, at home and abroad, to the end.

His Gospel of Germanic pride and glorious healthy earthly life—"freedom and bread"—coupled with the hard blows of the early Storm Troopers' fists that kept order in his public meetings and, when necessary, fought his battles in the streets, broke down whatever opposition stood in his way to power. There was, in that blending of mystical insight, elemental logic, and well-organised brutality — of truth and youth — that characterises National Socialism, a grandeur that appealed to the masses *and* to the very best of the best people: to those exceptionally intelligent *and* reliable men who have retained the raw vitality of the masses within their psychological make-up. Temporary setbacks[69] only kindled the bitter determination of both. And the struggle started in 1919 was a staggering triumph. On the 30th of January, 1933, Adolf Hitler was acclaimed as Chancellor of the German Reich. A few months later, the *Reichstag* was to vote him "unlimited powers," so that he might, without hindrance, remould the whole state and direct Germany's foreign policy according to his programme — which he consistently did *to the extent it could be done* in spite of the undermining activities of a well-hidden and — alas! — extremely efficient pack of traitors in Germany itself, and in defiance of the increasing hostility of the whole world, i.e., against the pressure of the coalesced forces of this Dark Age.

It is an error to believe that "after a time" the National Socialist state "should have" — *could* have, in the first place — avoided evolving into a "police state," i.e., a state permanently dominated by the consciousness of emergency. In other words, it is an error to believe that, in 1933 — or 1934 — the struggle was "over" and conditions of emergency a thing of the past. From the moment Adolf Hitler acquired a free hand to remould the German Reich according to his ideals, the National Socialist struggle merely entered a new phase. It was no longer the struggle for power. But it still was the Struggle for Truth, for cosmic Truth applied to social problems and to politics in our advanced Dark Age, i.e., the Struggle for Truth, with unavoidable Dark Age methods. And for that very reason — because it is *the* state "against Time" *par excellence* — the National Socialist state could (and can, were it again to take shape during this Dark Age) only be a state resting upon an iron coercive and military organisation, a state in which every free citizen feels himself a soldier — a voluntary soldier, glad to submit to integral (inner and outer) discipline, for the advent and defence of Adolf Hitler's ideal

---

[69] Such as the failure of the *Putsch* of the 9th of November 1923.

Reich (the Kingdom of Truth "against Time")—and in which every enemy of the new Order lives under the constant threat of denunciation and arrest, hard labour in a concentration camp, or death, what a well-known hater of the Hitler faith has tried to slander under the name of an "S.S. state."[70] (The word is, in reality, the greatest compliment paid to the glorious revolutionary state "against Time.")

"A revolution," says Konstantin Hierl, one of the men to whom the National Socialist régime owes the most, in the practical field, "can only be a transitory state of affairs [*ein Übergangszustand*]." And he adds: "Also the absolute system of government connected with the National Socialist revolution should have been only a transition, and could not be the first aim of a German revolution."[71]

It is true that revolutions in the usual sense of the word—such as the French Revolution or the Russian Revolution, which are but passages from given conditions "in Time" to different conditions, also "in Time," steps along the downward path of history—can only be "transitory states of affairs." But it is, from the cosmic standpoint, an error—an understandable error, maybe, yet a fundamental one—to consider the National Socialist upheaval as a mere "German Revolution" of the same type as those. Being an upheaval "against Time," the National Socialist Revolution was—and, as long as its guiding Idea lives in the consciousness of a militant minority, remains—a transition, no doubt, but a transition between advanced Dark Age conditions and coming Golden Age conditions, yet hardly dreamable. And therefore *only with the end of the Dark Age*—with the end of every influence of the Forces of disintegration and, subsequently, the end of all opposition to the *truth* it stands for—can and will "the absolute system of government" connected with it cease to have its justification, and the National Socialist emergency state "against Time" give place to a normal form (which will then be a Golden Age form) of collective life: a form devised for a *few*—

---

[70] This is the title of one of Eugen Kogon's books against the Third Reich. [Eugen Kogon, *Der SS Staat. Das System der deutschen Konzentrationslager* (The SS State: The System of German Concentration Camps) (Munich: Karl Albert, 1946)—Ed.]

[71] Hierl, *Im Dienst für Deutschland*, pp. 121-22.

very few — god-like men and women, of the best blood, uncontested masters of a beautiful regenerate earth more than broad enough to contain them and their descendants for many generations, and to feed them, without them needing to kill or harm or exploit any living creature, the glorious fulfilment of those very ideals of perfect *health* and more-than-human strength and beauty that the heroic Third German Reich has striven to impose yesterday, against the current of time, with Dark Age weapons.

That is the proper meaning of Adolf Hitler's own comments upon the "humane pacifist Idea" according to which every human life is supposed to have such an enormous "value." "The humane pacifist idea is, in fact, perhaps quite good, once the highest type of human being has already conquered and subdued so much of the surface of the world as to make himself the sole lord of this earth," writes he, in *Mein Kampf*.[72] "The idea can, in that case, cause no harm, inasmuch as its application" (meaning: its application in its present-day form) "will be rare, and finally impossible" — "impossible" precisely because, *then*, there will (for very many millenniums at least) no longer exist any politically dangerous or racially inferior elements, capable of corrupting the best and of marring the harmony between actual life and its divine pattern. But *now* "the highest type of human being" — the best of the best among Nature's chosen race — are far from being the "sole masters of this earth." *Now*, we are still in the Dark Age — sinking into it more and more. And therefore comes the logical conclusion of the inspired Man, Founder of the Dark Age state "against Time": "*Also erst Kampf, und dann vielleicht Pazifismus*" — "So, first struggle, and then, perhaps, pacifism."[73]

All but a very few people have thoroughly misunderstood — and millions have most unjustly condemned — the coercive methods of the Third Reich and its drastic steps intended to protect Western Aryandom against the Jewish danger (and against the influence of any man-centred, international *Weltanschauung*, all of which are, in the West, Jewish products). They have misunderstood them precisely because they have refused to acknowledge the infinitely more than political significance of

---

[72] *Mein Kampf*, p. 315.
[73] *Mein Kampf*, pp. 315–16.

National Socialism, and to see, in it, what I have called an upheaval "against Time." And they have condemned them because, as I have stated in the beginning of this book, evolution in Time goes hand in hand not with a decrease in violence (on the contrary!) but with *a steady decrease in honesty regarding violence, and in understanding concerning the right use of it*. They have condemned *them* while tolerating (and, more often than not, defending) all manner of horrors, among others vivisection, that most degrading of all crimes against Life. They have — unknowingly, perhaps, but in fact — condemned them, because the drastic coercive and preventive steps taken by the National Socialist state against the actual or potential agents of the Dark Forces had, inasmuch as they were taken in the Führer's spirit, their full justification in the light of cosmic Truth, which our Dark Age denies; because one had resorted to them *not* in order to try to find out means of patching up a sickly humanity or of prolonging the life and enjoyment of the vicious, but in order to make possible, here and now, a new world of the strong in which vice and disease would be unknown; because one had resorted to them *not* "for the sake of suffering mankind" — of mankind in its present-day, contemptible state — but "in the interest of the Universe" in the sense these words are used in the Bhagavad-Gita.

Nay, inasmuch as the men who were trusted to carry out those steps did so selflessly and without passion, simply because they knew it was their duty as Aryan fighters for the Cause of Truth, they acted exactly as the Blessed One has urged warriors to act. And one can safely say that, despite all individual cases of unfaithfulness to the spirit of detached Violence (cases with which one is bound to reckon, at such an advanced stage of the Age of Gloom as the one in which we are living) no *state* in history has, as a whole, embodied the moral outlook of the Bhagavad-Gita, as the Third German Reich has done.

That was enough for typical Dark Age people — people whose man-centred moral outlook is the exact opposite of that expressed both in the oldest Book of Aryan wisdom *and* in Adolf Hitler's words and deeds and regulations — to feel personally threatened through the mere existence of such an organised power "against Time," and to hate it.

And that hatred is, as we shall see, the real cause of the Second World War.

⚡ ⚡ ⚡

Adolf Hitler's whole constructive policy — all he did to give manual as well as intellectual work the dignity of happy, dedicated service, and to make every labourer's life a healthy, self-respecting, and *interesting* one; all he did for the welfare of mothers and children; all he did for the cultivation of bodily efficiency and qualities of character in boys and girls, from the age of six onwards, in the different sections of the beautifully organised pan-Germanic Youth Associations — the famous Hitler Youth and the B.D.M.[74] — and then, at the age of 16, in the squads of the Labour Service[75] for six months (or more) and in further bodies preparing them for the privilege of becoming worthy citizens of the proud new Reich; all he did, on one hand through the admirable Nuremberg Laws (1935) and, on the other, through the most active encouragement of early marriages and of joyfully consented racial selection, to raise sexual relations from the shameful status of "an amusement" or of a drudgery or of a "business," back to that of the dispassionate duty of the healthy and pure-blooded towards their race, in honour, innocence, and joy; all that, I say, nay, the whole structure of the National Socialist state — its very existence — had one aim and one alone: to breed, out of the best Germans, a nation of supermen in the Nietzschean sense of the word, a nation of "heroes like unto the gods," to repeat the words of Homer.

And, as I said before, the Führer pursued that aim *not* just because the Germans were his people, but because his more-than-political, nay, more-than-human insight pointed them out to him as the only people sufficiently pure-blooded and, at the same time, sufficiently militant to be the saviours of the Aryan race, here and now, in its present-day emergency, and to become the instruments of its regeneration and survival, beyond the stormy end of our Time-cycle.

The well-known National Socialist policy of German expansion towards the East is the logical consequence of Adolf Hitler's efforts to raise not only the biological *quality* of his people

---

[74] *Bund Deutscher Mädel*
[75] *Arbeitsdienst*, or rather *Reichsarbeitsdienst* (R.A.D.)

(through racial selection) but also their birth-rate, while doing all he could to avoid coming in conflict with England, i.e., while refusing to claim, for Germany, colonies *overseas*. It was as clear and consistent as could possibly be: if every healthy and pure-blooded German was to have as many children as he or she could — the more the better — (and *that* was what the National Socialist state was urging them to do), then surely that yearly increase in population was to live *somewhere* and somehow. And if emigration overseas was to be discouraged (in order to avoid all economic rivalry with England, in those days in which there still existed a British Empire), then the growing millions had to find another outlet, for Germany was anyhow, and already before Adolf Hitler came to power, too small for the population she had. The new outlet was to be "the East" — the rich cornlands of the Ukraine, and further still: Russia's unlimited expanses.

This policy has been misunderstood, even in strongly anti-Communist circles, and criticised, often nearly as bitterly as the bold stand of the National Socialist state against the Jewish danger. Adolf Hitler has been described — already *before* the war — as a "war-monger," and the wholehearted response of the German people to his appeal for "more babies" as an "output of cannon-fodder" . . . all because nobody outside a National Socialist minority understood the meaning of that appeal or of the far-sighted *Ostpolitik*.

In order fully to understand both, one has — again — to consider National Socialism from the standpoint of cosmic evolution and to recognise, in it, *the* great Movement "against Time" at the very end of the last Age of our Time-cycle. One has to realise that, throughout a Time-cycle, but especially as one nears the end of one, the *number* of human beings increases all over the world, while their quality decreases no less alarmingly. Any Time-cycle could be briefly and picturesquely described as man's passage from the Garden of Eden into a huge international slum. The passage is imperceptible; it takes myriads of years. And yet, one gets an idea of it if one looks back far enough into the past. It takes place at the expense of the noblest forms of non-human life, while the altogether inferior forms keep pace with fallen man.[76] And it goes hand in hand with a more and more conceited—and blasphemous—self-assertion of man in opposition to Nature, an increasingly vicious will of man to defy the divine finality of Creation: the intended survival of the healthiest specimens of every species: men *and* other creatures—in order to overrun the earth with his own brood of poorer and poorer quality.

That sinful will, coupled, as time goes on, with positive hatred for the eternal, natural Order, has found its latest main expression in the system of false values which stands, at an interval of 2,000 years, behind both the Christian and the Communist revolution—the system according to which "man" is everything, and man's "happiness" the end of all desirable activity—*and* in an increasing effort not to stop the silly application of "science" to the prolongation or preservation of superfluous lives—oh, no!—but, on the contrary, to encourage it, and then to organise the every day more enormous *Menschenmaterial* for the benefit of the Forces of disintegration. These, i.e., their agents, tend admittedly to do away with the vast international slum which the world has become, but . . . only in order to drill the slum-dwellers—ultimately—into factory robots with one ideal: work, work, work; "production," ever more production; and cheap enjoyment—ever more enjoyment—*quantity*, and *ever more quantity* . . . till more and more millions of bastardised world-citizens have completely killed Nature for "man's" sake; till there are no more deserts, no more forests, no more inviolate mountain fastnesses, no more broad landscapes free from human habitations and from the sound of wireless dance music; no more jungles—for the dullest of human beings is, in the eyes of the Communist as in those of the Christian, and of all believers in man-centred ideologies, worth more than the noblest royal Bengal tiger or than the most gorgeous banyan tree.

In the eyes of the believers in *quality*, however (in the eyes of those who deplore that broadening disparity between actual life

---

[76] A few centuries before the Christian era—from a cosmic standpoint, yesterday—lions were still plentiful in the woods and deserts of the classical East. They have all been killed off. While bugs and lice are as numerous and flourishing in the Near East now as in Antiquity.

and its divine pattern, which characterises evolution in Time), any Bengal tiger, nay, any healthy cat—any healthy tree, any perfect sample of manifested Life—is worth far more than an ugly, degenerate human bastard. Only man *in his perfection*— superior man "like unto the Gods," not the patched-up weakling that this conceited Age exalts—is to be looked upon as "the highest creature," "God's image," etc. . . . National Socialism— and *that* is the root of its conflict with Communism, no less than with Christianity as the latter has come down to us—strives to bring back that conception of man into living reality, and to prepare the reappearing of such a human type, through the preservation and strengthening of the best in our fallen Age, *not* at the cost of the other healthy and beautiful creatures of this earth but, no doubt—and without a qualm of remorse—at the expense of those masses of racially inferior humanity which the Dark Forces are now organising, with the help of the Jews, their permanent agents, under the sign of the Hammer and Sickle. For those organised masses are, as Hans Grimm has clearly seen—alas, *after* the disaster of 1945—tomorrow's threat to the very existence of higher mankind (*not* "Asia's" threat to "Europe"—by any means!—but the threat of raceless numbers to the pure-blooded Aryan of Europe *and* Asia, America and South Africa, and Australia, and to the pure-blooded and noble non-Aryan, also of the whole world).

That is, I repeat—one can never stress the point enough—the deep opposition between National Socialism and Marxism, nay, between National Socialism and *all* man-centred, equalitarian creeds, of which Marxism is merely the latest in date and the most consistent. It is the opposition between the Golden Age ideal of quality at all levels of existence, and the Dark Age dream of organised human quantity, submerging all life, until it itself finally sinks into chaos and death.

But we *are*, now, in the Dark Age—and, which is more, near the end of it. This is a fact which nothing can alter. And just as "tyranny can only be broken through greater tyranny, and terror through terror,"[77] *so can quantity only be crushed through quantity*. And so can the impact of well-organised, raceless masses, devoted to a false idea, only be held back and overcome through the

---

[77] *Mein Kampf*, p. 507.

stronger impact of still better organised, disciplined millions of the best Aryan blood, inspired with a fanatical faith in eternal cosmic Truth (or, at least, in as much of it as they may need to know, in order to kindle their fighting efficiency to its maximum).

The truth which Adolf Hitler gave his people, so that they might become and remain the bulwark of Aryandom against the impact of a bastardised world drilled in Marxism (the latest Jewish revolutionary creed "*in* Time"), can be condensed in a few simple sentences: "We Germans are the only possible leaders of Western Aryandom. That is our 'God-ordained' — Nature-ordained — mission. We are, therefore, valuable — *irreplaceable*. Therefore we must live, live and thrive, become numerous, at the same time as we breed an élite. Numerous at any cost (in this Age, in fact, pure-blooded quantity is the raw material out of which, here and there, quality emerges; great men are often born in large families). Therefore: become a pure-blooded quantity, produce as many healthy Aryan babies as possible! But we are a nation without space. And we need space for the many babies, space in order to live and fulfil our mission. We don't want to become England's enemies. The English are, like we, of Nordic blood (or mostly so). People of the same best blood should collaborate in view of the same lofty aim: the rule of the best of their common best blood. It is the original intention of Nature, the spirit of the eternal Order, against which we do not wish to sin. England can be (we hope) converted to this standpoint. But Russia has become the citadel of Marxism — that hated Jewish snare. It is, apart from that, a broad, rich land; it can provide plenty of space for us, and all possibilities of our growing into a huge people. Huge, *and* of exceptional quality, therefore invincible; the lords of this earth along with our Nordic brothers, the English. Therefore: expansion towards the East — *Ostpolitik!*"

It was not cosmic Truth *in its entirety*, as Adolf Hitler himself intuitively felt it. But it was a part of it. And a part of it — an aspect of it — free from any admixture with untruth, free from any concessions to the moral superstitions of this Age. It could have provided a sufficient basis for the *beginning* of a first Western and then — gradually — world-wide pan-Aryan collaboration (including that of the Aryan elements of Russia herself, and of

Asia) against the forces of disintegration and their agents, i.e., "against Time," if *only* England had not betrayed her own blood and deliberately started the Second World War.

The fact that all Adolf Hitler's efforts to avoid the war — or to end it speedily and victoriously, at least honourably — remained fruitless, proves by no means his inefficiency as a statesman or as a strategist. It only proves that the forces of disintegration — the coalesced forces of our Dark Age, embodied in all-powerful international Jewry — were, in spite of his insight, in spite of his genius, too strong for him, that it needed a still harder "Man against Time" than he, in order to break them, in other words, that he is not *the last* Man "against Time."

He knew it himself, from the early days of the struggle. And nothing shows more clearly how aware he was of his own place and significance in the history of our Time-cycle, than the words he addressed Hans Grimm in 1928, in the course of a conversation that lasted an hour and a quarter:

> I know that some Man capable of giving our problems a final solution must appear. I have sought such a man. I could nowhere discover him. And that is why I have set myself *to do the preparatory work* [die Vorarbeit], *only the most urgent preparatory work, for I know that I am myself not, the one*. And I know also what is missing in me [to be the one]. But the other One still remains aloof, and nobody comes forward, and there is no more time to be lost.[78]

Or, to speak the language of most ancient Tradition, the One-Who-comes-back, age after age, "whenever justice is crushed" — the One Who *had* actually come back in him, to reassert eternal cosmic Truth in our times, through the most heroic and most misunderstood of all political and more-than-political struggles — would have to come back at least once more during the present Time-cycle. For this Dark Age was not to come to its end in Adolf Hitler's lifetime.

Emsdetten in Westphalia (Germany), 4 May 1955

---

[78] Grimm, *Warum? Woher? aber Wohin?*, p. 14.

7. He Spoke with the Wild Eloquence of Emergency (p. 243)

Chapter 14

THE WORLD AGAINST ITS SAVIOUR

Nobody wanted peace more than Adolf Hitler. Nobody *needed* peace more than he. He needed it in order to consolidate and to extend his great work, in order to allow the understandable but nevertheless somewhat alarming differences in outlook between the old German ruling classes and ruling bodies—the nobility and the wealthy upper middle class, the "intelligentsia," the churches, but especially the General Staff, of Prussian tradition (entirely or nearly entirely recruited among the old, landowning nobility)—on one hand, and the *Reichsleiters* and *Gauleiters* and, in general, the leading men of the New Order, on the other, slowly to die out, and a synthesis of the best of all German national forces to take place under the Sign of the Swastika; he needed it to secure the undisturbed growth of a healthy and uncompromising new generation of men and women—fighters and mothers—born and brought up in the glorious National Socialist atmosphere and devoted, without any reservations whatsoever, to his ideals; to enable himself to continue carrying out his admirable social programme and—without them hardly becoming conscious of the change—gradually inducing the German people to accept the ethical and, one should add, in the deeper sense of the word, the *religious* revolution that National Socialism represents in this country: the return to racial, i.e., natural, values and, in general, to that life-centred wisdom which the new doctrine implies, after one-and-a-half thousand years of man-centred, equalitarian, anti-natural, and anti-national Judeo-Christian superstition. He needed peace in order to bring, slowly but irresistibly, into existence, under the leadership of the regenerate German Reich, the Greater Reich comprising all people of Germanic blood and ultimately all people of Aryan blood, in and outside Europe, and to remould the whole world according to the principle of the God-ordained hierarchy of races and of the rule of the best.

And nobody strove for peace as hard and as consistently as he—admittedly not on account of any humanitarian prejudices, but for the sound, practical reasons that I have just mentioned: for the sake of the success of his life's work or, in other words, in the interest of the Greater German Reich, in the interest of the Aryan Cause, i.e., in the interest of the Universe.

But the everlasting forces of disintegration and death—those which I have described as forces "in Time," and which were (and are, since 1945, more fatally than ever) leading all races to their doom—mightily stood in the way of the Man "against Time" and of his dream of Aryan regeneration. And their agents—the Jews, as a body, and the conscious or unconscious, willing or unwilling servants of international Jewry: Freemasons of high *and* low grades, members and sympathisers of the most varied pseudo-spiritual societies in the service of Jewish interests or Jewish ideals (or both), believers in the most varied man-centred, equalitarian creeds of whatever origin, afflicted with a sincere but false conception of history, and all manner of people prepared to sacrifice any possibility of general regeneration to the maintenance of personal or collective advantages of a material or *moral* nature—*needed war, in order to nip the National Socialist revolution in the bud,* in order to break its impulse *before* it had time to bring about the inner and definitive transformation of Germany, and before it spread to other countries of Aryan blood; the sooner, the better. They needed war, if they were not, themselves, to be compelled to abdicate all influence, and culturally—and *spiritually*—no less than politically, to cease to exist. And they did everything they could to start a war *in spite of Adolf Hitler's efforts to avoid it,* and everything they could to prolong it, once it had started. And they succeeded, and they won the war, not because of any fault of his, but simply because the world had not—and *has* not, yet—reached the end of the present Dark Age, because, as I have said before, Adolf Hitler is not *the last* Man "against Time," and because it is a fact—nay, an unavoidable consequence of the laws of historical development—that all Men "against Time" fail, save the very last one: the one whom the Sanskrit Scriptures call "Kalki."

In other words, seen from that higher standpoint from which all "politics" appear as consequences, never as causes, the 1939–1945 World War is, in the midst of the gigantic struggle of polar opposites, without beginning or end, which constitutes cosmic history, a tragic local instance of the fated victory of the satanic Forces—i.e., of the Forces of *untruth*—near the end of an Age of Gloom.

卐 卐 卐

"Ribbentrop, bring me the English alliance!"[1] Sincerer words than these—the last Adolf Hitler addressed to the man whom he was sending to London, as Germany's ambassador, in 1936, to sound once more all the possibilities that could lead to an understanding with England—were never uttered in the history of diplomatic relations.

Adolf Hitler had indeed been striving for "an understanding with England" nay, an "English alliance," from the beginning of his public life. Already as early as 1924 he had, in his immortal book, *Mein Kampf*, clearly laid down the main lines of this new policy ("new," at least after the First World War). And, which is more, however justified it doubtless was, from a strictly political point of view, this policy had—like everything the Führer did—a definitely more-than-political meaning and more-than-political scope, and was even more justified from the point of view of Nature, i.e., of living truth. It rested upon the solid biological fact of common blood. And although it was, admittedly, something quite *different* from Adolf Hitler's continental policy—although there was, there, for instance, no question of people of the same blood coming under "the same state"—yet it could have been formulated in sentences impressively parallel to those which proclaim, on the first page of *Mein Kampf*, the legitimacy of Austria's incorporation into the German Reich; I mean: the inspired Leader would certainly have maintained that, "even if, economically, it were a matter of indifference, nay, even if it were positively a disadvantage,"[2] still one should, in Germany, seek England's alliance, for "people of similar blood" should stand together.

---

[1] Joachim von Ribbentrop, *Zwischen London und Moskau: Erinnerungen und letzte Aufzeichnungen. Aus dem Nachlass herausgegeben von Annelies von Ribbentrop* [Between London and Moscow: Recollections and Last Notes. Edited from His Papers by Annelies von Ribbentrop] (Leoni am Starnberger See: Druffel-Verlag, 1954), p. 93.

[2] *Mein Kampf*, p. 1.

It was—again in perfect consistency with the tenets and general character of National Socialism—a thoroughly revolutionary policy. Revolutionary not merely because it was a break with the recent past and—apparently—a return to an older political tradition, but because it was the outcome of an *attitude* in complete contradiction with that of *all* European politicians for the last 1,500 years at least, and a return to the spirit and corresponding customs of a long-forgotten age, the sanity of which other-worldly superstitions, on one hand, and all-too-worldly business considerations, on the other, had not yet destroyed, and in which common blood was, as a matter of course—as Nature intended it to be—the soundest thinkable basis of friendship and constructive collaboration; in other words, because it was a break with that *untruth*—that rebellion of man against Nature—which is the distinctive (and increasingly visible) trait of our Dark Age.

The system of political alliances that had prevailed up till then, and that yet prevailed, was indeed—like practically all human institutions of this Age—stamped with the sign of untruth. Common dogmatic faith (in the first millennium of the Christian era and somewhat later) and then, more and more, common (or supposed common) material interests, had been, *irrespective of blood*, and, more often than not, in flagrant opposition to any idea of natural blood-solidarity, the main bond between allied powers. Charlemagne and his warriors had fought, with the blessing of the Catholic Church—the oldest international (and anti-national) power in Europe—against the Lombards, against the Saxons, people of Germanic stock like themselves, which was bad enough. And 700 years later, Francis the First, King of France—an Aryan king, at any rate—had, for the sake of dynastic greed, allied himself with the Turks against the German Reich, which was even worse, if worse could be. And in later history, calculations of mere material profit had played an ever greater part in the determination of the attitude of governments towards one another and in that of nations' "friends" and "foes," without the mentioned profit being, in fact, anybody's but that of a few international—Jewish, or raceless—big businessmen—which meant the complete separation of "politics" from national life in the true sense of the word. The typical Dark

Age mentality[3] behind that unhealthy state of affairs had been, already at the close of the 19th century, that of an influential British minority, championing, in the name of a misled and preeminently commercial nationalism, the most extreme anti-German policy. It can hardly ever have found a clearer and more cynical expression than in Sir Philip Chalmers Mitchell's essay "A Biological View of our Foreign Policy, by a Biologist," published in the 1st of February issue of the London *Saturday Review*, in 1896, and recently quoted *in extenso* by Hans Grimm.[4] There, not only are England's commercial interests stressed as though they were everything; not only is Germany — the prosperous and therefore dangerous business rival — pointed out as England's main enemy in spite of undeniable biological similitude, but *that biological similitude*, that community of blood and the community of nature, which is the consequence of it, that similitude in permanent, deeper qualities, is precisely *the* fact alleged to make war between England and Germany unavoidable, nay, to cause that war to be a war to the finish;[5] it is the fact which urges Sir Philip Chalmers Mitchell, professor of biology — and, later on (from 1916 to 1919) member of the British General Staff — to paraphrase, applying them to England's sister-nation, the famous pitiless words which the Roman Cato once used to repeat, at every opportunity, against Carthage, Rome's *Semitic* rival, and to say: "*Delenda est Germania*" — "Germany must be destroyed."

It is difficult to ascertain whether Adolf Hitler knew or not of the existence of that strangely enlightening piece of English literature. Possibly he did; the essay had been, already at the time of its publication, handed over to German diplomatic and military circles, in which, apart from a few exceptional men, such as Admiral Tirpitz, nobody had — unfortunately — then *or afterwards*, taken it seriously. Possibly, he did not. But even so,

---

[3] "When society reaches a stage in which property confers rank; in which wealth becomes the only source of virtue . . . then we are in the *Kali Yuga* or Dark Age" (Vishnu Purana).

[4] In both his *Die Erzbischofsschrift. Antwort eines Deutschen* (Göttingen: Plesse, 1950) [in English: *Answer of a German: An Open Letter to the Archbishop of Canterbury*, trans. Lyton Hudson (Dublin: Euphorion Books, 1952) — Ed.] and in *Warum? Woher? aber Wohin?*

[5] See the text of the essay.

he was perfectly aware of the widespread attitude which it *now* so unmistakably expresses, of that superstitious hostility to Germany, rooted in the fear of being commercially "outdone," which is, with minor circumstantial differences, Eyre Crowe's attitude and, nearer to us, Sir Robert Vansittart's, Duff Cooper's, Eden's, and Winston Churchill's.

He was aware of it, and yet, from the beginning of his public life, and over and over again—nay, as we shall see, even *during* the war—he held out his hand to England in a gesture of friendship—in a spirit of total, unconditional, thoroughly sincere reconciliation, without a shade of bitterness, let alone of revengefulness. He did all he possibly could, not to "placate" the mistress of the Seven Seas, whose might he neither feared not hated, but to win her confidence and collaboration, in absolute good faith; to break that superstitious dread of a powerful Germany, which clever or, sometimes, irresponsible agents of the Dark Forces had been breathing into her people for over 40 years at least, and to awaken in them the slumbering consciousness of the brotherhood of blood, deeper, truer, stronger than any commercial or narrowly political realities—everlasting, while profit and power are time-bound.

Governments and churches, inasmuch as they do not actually embody and adequately express a people's collective soul, are also time-bound. Maybe, England was living under a political régime entirely different from—nay, the very opposite of—that which Adolf Hitler had given Germany. But that was a secondary matter. Germany herself had lived under a different régime up till 1933. And quite possibly, even a real "people's régime" in England—in an English National Socialist state, if ever one had happened to come into existence—would have been, in many ways, profoundly different from the German National Socialist régime. Maybe, deep-rooted moral and religious prejudices (blind allegiance to time-honoured institutions and ideas) would, for years—or for centuries—prevent the English from accepting some of the hard and simple biological truths upon which genuine National Socialism is based, and from sharing wholeheartedly that heathen scale of values which is, strictly speaking, inseparable from it. Yet even *that* was, from the standpoint of permanent, *natural* reality, i.e., from the standpoint of the *Seer*, a secondary matter. That did not alter the fact that, considered with her dominions overseas, England was, before the Second World War — in spite of obvious weakness, mistakes, and crimes; in spite of her having, hardly 40 years earlier, waged the most disgraceful war upon the Boers in South Africa; in spite of her having, through her missionaries and her schools, introduced the microbe of democracy (and, unwillingly, that of Communism) into such a land as India — the great ruling Aryan power. Her Empire was, as a historical reality, one of the grand material achievements of the Nordic race — unthinkable, apart from the qualities of character of the best men among those who had built it up, and among those who were running it: daring, perseverance, sense of responsibility and sense of honour, organising genius, coupled with selfless idealism: Nordic qualities.

Adolf Hitler repeatedly proclaimed his determination to respect the integrity of the British Empire. He repeatedly declared that the German National Socialist state was to look upon every manner of pre-1914 colonial policy, and every form of aggressive commercial competition with England, as a thing of the past. And he fully meant what he said. He meant it because he saw, no doubt, in that "alliance with England" which he so eagerly urged J. von Ribbentrop to "bring him back," a guarantee of peaceful development for Germany and of further unhindered evolution and expansion for National Socialism — Germany's highest interest, immediately *and* in the long run. He meant it *also* because the friendly collaboration of the two leading nations of Nordic blood appeared to him, from a more-than-political standpoint, as the unmistakable dictate of sanity, as the course in harmony with the meaning of life (which should also be the meaning of "politics," if the latter are to cease being mere business intrigues), and the policy which was, therefore, immediately and in the long run, in the interest of superior mankind in the biological sense of the word, and consequently, "in the interest of the Universe," again to quote the old hallowed words of the Bhagavad-Gita. He held out his hand to England both as a wise, far-sighted statesman *and* as a "Man against Time."

But England's leading men — and a number of men in high office *in Germany* — were not only short-sighted politicians but active agents of the everlasting Dark Forces. Adolf Hitler's efforts were systematically neutralised through their stubborn, combined hostility and through that of the unseen Powers of disintegration and death behind them.

Had J. von Ribbentrop succeeded in bringing about that Anglo-German alliance which Adolf Hitler so eagerly wanted, there would have been no Second World War. And the unseen Powers of disintegration would have had to devise some other means of thrusting this present Creation a footstep nearer its doom. The formation in Germany of an eminently efficient National Socialist *ruling* élite would have secured the stability of the régime and, which is more, the *definitive* acceptance of the new scale of values and new conception of life "in harmony with the primeval meaning of things," first among Adolf Hitler's people and then, also — gradually — among all people of Aryan blood; in other words, it would have brought about a general rising of the Indo-European race (and, through the latter's influence, of all the noble races) against the fatal, downward pressure of Time. The success of such a rising would have meant the end of this Dark Age and, under the divine Swastika, Sign of the Sun, Sign of Life in its pristine glory, "a new heaven and a new earth." But, as I said before, this is precisely what the Death-forces were bound to try to hinder. They tried with diabolical masterfulness, knowing that it was perhaps their last chance of large-scale success on earth within the present Time-cycle.

J. von Ribbentrop's experience with England's ruling men was a steady series of disappointments. The Permanent Secretary of State, Sir (later Lord) Robert Vansittart, whom he had hoped to convince of the advantages of a close Anglo-German collaboration, proved adamant in his anti-German attitude — all the more baffling that he did not even attempt to justify it through some sort of logic.[6] "In Vansittart," the German Ambassador was to write, shortly before his martyr's death in Nuremberg, ten years later:

> I felt I had before me a man with an absolutely fixed opinion, the man of the Foreign Office, who not only supported the thesis of "balance of power" but also embodied Sir Eyre Crowe's principle: "Whatever may happen, never

---

[6] Ribbentrop, p. 96.

pactise with Germany!" I had the definite impression that this man would not even once try to bring our two countries nearer to each other. Every word was simply lost on him.[7]

Winston Churchill, although admittedly more outspoken, was no less irreducibly opposed to any Anglo-German alliance. The very thought of a powerful Germany filled him with bitterness, nay, with hatred. And he was determined to do all he possibly could to keep that nightmare of his from becoming a permanent reality. "If Germany grows too strong, she shall again be beaten down," declared he bluntly, in the course of a several hours' conversation with J. von Ribbentrop, in 1937. And he added, as the Ambassador reminded him that Germany had friends: "Oh, we are pretty good at getting them around in the end,"[8] thus foretelling that which was—alas!—actually to take place a few years later. Himself one of the cleverest and most efficient agents of the Forces of disintegration at the end of this Age of Gloom, he understood both the mentality of the professional politicians and that of the dull, conceited, inconsistent, and gullible average man: the ultimate human factors behind "public opinion" and world-politics under a democratic order.

The hopes that one might have been prompted to draw from King Edward the Eighth's friendly attitude to Germany were abruptly brushed aside through the King's well-known abdication in 1937. "With this abdication," states the former German Ambassador, in the memoirs I already mentioned, "the cause of the Anglo-German alliance had lost a possibility."[9] And the remaining possibilities were not to materialise. They rested upon the influence which a minority of racially-conscious, unprejudiced, and far-sighted Englishmen, in no way connected with open or secret Jewish or pro-Jewish world-organisations—men such as Sir Oswald Mosley and some of the most enlightened members of the London Anglo-German Fellowship—could exert in government circles, and upon the public. And that influence was practically negligible. In British government circles, Adolf

---

[7] Ribbentrop, p. 97.
[8] Ribbentrop, p. 97.
[9] Ribbentrop, p. 104.

Hitler's healthy new Germany was—wrongly, no doubt, but all-too-actually—looked upon with mistrust, as a growing menace. And the very admiration that so many thousands of English people could not help feeling for the inspired ruler's social achievements, was—with the help of the press—steadily giving way to resentment at the idea of the leading position to which Germany had risen, under him, economically and politically, within but three or four years' time *and without war*. The increasing prosperity and power of the sister nation were surely the most eloquent tribute to the proud faith in "blood and soil" that now filled the hearts and lives of her people. In England, one wanted peace, of course. Who did not, after a world war such as that of 1914-1918? And it was—or should have been—quite clear that an Anglo-German alliance would have meant lasting peace. Yet, one dimly felt that such a peace could only help Germany to become stronger and stronger, and National Socialism to win prestige within *and beyond* the frontiers of the Reich. Now Britons had been taught for centuries that every country which rose to prominence upon the European mainland was "a threat to England." This was not merely the opinion of the Foreign Office; it had grown into a widespread British superstition, harder to uproot than any "opinion." Germany was, therefore (and whether this were or *not* in the interest of peace), not to be allowed to become "too strong."

It was easy—again with the help of the almighty press—to bring the average Englishman to believe, on that point, the same as Mr. (later Sir) Winston Churchill. All the more easy that new Germany was inconceivable apart from her National Socialist creed, and that the average Englishman was from several sides, at first, discretely, and then, quite boldly, being told that the creed had a "dangerous" more-than-political bearing nay, a decidedly anti-Christian one (which no doubt was true, although in a far deeper sense than that stressed in the newspaper articles and propaganda pamphlets).[10] The organisations which financed the latter were, *in fact*, keener on harming Germany than on saving "Christian civilisation"—let alone the essence of origi-

---

[10] Among these one should remember the booklets published by "The Friends of Europe" and quoting extracts of National Socialist writers.

nal Christianity (the other-worldly teaching "above Time") which was by no means threatened. But the pious arguments were clever—the more illogical, the cleverer, well-calculated to impress the non-thinking masses and the false-thinking half-learned. They bore fruit. In addition to that, the more and more "uncompromising attitude"[11] which Adolf Hitler himself was beginning to take with regard to the Christian churches—i.e., his very definite attempt to prevent any interference of the churches in state affairs—was bound to give grist to the anti-Nazi propaganda mills. It led to the greatest tension between the National Socialist state and the Vatican "and to the mobilisation of all the energies of the churches against us, *in Protestant lands also*," writes J. von Ribbentrop, "a most significant and disadvantageous development from the standpoint of foreign policy."[12]

It thus became clearer and clearer that the "English alliance" which Adolf Hitler had so earnestly striven for was a psychological impossibility. Not merely the most influential men in the British Foreign Office but "the atmosphere" in the whole country was against it. A few weeks before his promotion from the position of Ambassador in London to that of Foreign Minister of the German Reich, i.e., already at the close of 1937,[13] J. von Ribbentrop sent Adolf Hitler a detailed report[14] at the end of which the following sentences are, among others, to be found: "I do not believe any longer in the possibility of an understanding with England. England does not want any mighty Germany in her neighbourhood . . ."; "Here one strongly believes in the efficiency of National Socialism" (i.e., one believes it will give Germany more and more power).

> Edward VIII was compelled to abdicate because one was not sure whether he would lend a hand to a policy of hostility towards Germany. Chamberlain has now appointed Vansittart, our most important and toughest opponent, to such a position as enables him to take a leading part in the diplomatic play against Germany. However much one

---

[11] Ribbentrop, p. 127.
[12] Ribbentrop, p. 127.
[13] He was appointed *Reichsaussenminister* on the 4th of February 1938.
[14] Deutsche Botschaft, London, A. 5522.

might, in the meantime, for tactical reasons, try to come to an understanding with us, *every single day in the future in which our political considerations should fail to be fundamentally determined by the thought of England as our most dangerous opponent would be a gain for our enemies.*[15]

There was indeed nothing else to do but to face the fact that Adolf Hitler's great dream of Aryan world-leadership on the basis of a solid, peaceful collaboration of the two main European nations of Germanic stock, was *not* — and was, for a very long time at least, not likely to become — England's dream. It was, no doubt, a pity, a greater pity even than the few racially-conscious Englishmen probably realised at the time. But it was a fact. England's ruling classes were completely in the grip of international Jewry, which cunningly used, in its own interest, both their business-like fear of a powerful Germany and their moral objection (or so-called such one) against the National Socialist view of life, in particular against National Socialist anti-Semitism. And the British people, robbed through the whole modern conditioning apparatus of their natural capacity of doubt, analysis, and free choice, believed what they were told and reacted to world events as their unseen masters — the Jews — expected them to. One day, perhaps, they would wake up — when it would be too late. (And Adolf Hitler, the Man "against Time," first a seer and then a politician, never left off feeling sure that such a day would come.) In the meantime, however, their masters saw to it that the sight of Germany's grand awakening did not raise them out of their comfortable apathy — at least, not quickly enough for them to discover the tricks that were being played upon them and to refuse to follow their wicked shepherds on the path of fratricidal war.

Unable to break Jewish influence in England, Adolf Hitler strengthened his bonds with the two nations with which Germany was in ideological agreement: Japan and Fascist Italy, who both had — the former in November 1936, the latter a year later — signed with him the Anti-Comintern Pact, which England had steadily refused to sign.[16]

---

[15] Quoted in Ribbentrop, pp. 122-23.
[16] Ribbentrop, p. 112.

Yet, again because he was first a Seer and then a politician; because he felt real, eternal England, in spite of all, behind the judaised England of today, and the essence of hallowed Aryandom behind eternal England, he never abandoned the old dream of friendship, and never gave up watching for a "change of heart" on the British side.

The germs of the Second World War lay in the Versailles Treaty. And, not merely in a complete revision of that shameful piece of work, but in the definitive suppression of the spirit which had produced it—i.e., in the abolition of that old, morbid fear and gratuitous hatred of a strong Germany in the hearts of most Europeans—lay the only possibility of a lasting peace. In fact, the infamous Treaty was never revised and the political map of Europe never given back the outlines of sanity on the basis of that "right of people to dispose of themselves" which the victors of 1918 had so often and so loudly proclaimed. And instead of being suppressed, or at least left to die out, fear and hatred were systematically and most cunningly cultivated in England, in France, in the smaller European countries that had fought on the Allied side during the First World War, in those that had remained neutral, in the United States of America—of all lands, the one which had the least reason to feel "menaced" by a Greater German Reich beyond the Atlantic Ocean—and, strange as this may seem, in a number of *non*-European countries such as India, whose people had nothing whatsoever to do with the frontier problems of Central and Eastern Europe, and did not (apart from one or two resplendent individual exceptions) possess the slightest idea of European history,[17] countries which, moreover, Germany had never harmed, while England had . . . and how!

Under the influence of those agents of the Dark Forces who had prepared the yet greatest crime in diplomatic history and

---

[17] To be fair, one should point out that many of the "Americans" — sons of European emigrants—*and Western Europeans* who helped in the concoction of the Versailles Treaty, knew no more about the history and geography of Central Europe than any Indian coolie is likely to know.

who were now supervising its consummation, the people of the whole world outside the "fascist countries" were systematically made to forget or kept from learning the fact that "Austrians" — representatives of the small German nucleus that had, for ages, held together and ruled the many and varied national groups comprised within the "Kingdom of Austria and Hungary" — were and always had been Germans; and that their Parliament had, immediately after the splitting up of the Austro-Hungarian state at the end of the First World War (*long before* Adolf Hitler had come to power, nay, before his Party had taken shape) *unanimously* voted the fusion of Austria with Germany. They were made to forget or kept from learning the fact that there had never existed and could never exist any such creatures as "Czechoslovaks" and that "Czechoslovakia" was an entirely artificial state,[18] set up, at the Allies' command, in 1919, out of Czechs, *and* out of Slovaks, Ruthenians, Carpatho-Ukrainians, etc., all unwilling to come together under Czech rule, *and of over three million most unwilling Germans*, torn away from their fatherland thanks to the Versailles Treaty, and more resentful of Czech domination than all the other components of the ridiculous state rolled into one; and the fact that the *only* reason for the concoction of such a state — against biology, against history, against geography, against economics, against Nature — lay in its appointed action as a permanent thorn in the flesh of the already mutilated German Reich. They were purposely kept in ignorance of the daily provocations of the Czechs in German Sudetenland and wherever Germans lived within the new state; kept in ignorance, also, of the oppression the Czechs exerted upon the other, non-Czech elements of "Czechoslovakia": Slovaks, Ruthenians, Carpatho-Ukrainians, etc. The people of the world were systematically kept in ignorance of the fact that the "new Poland" that the victors of 1918 had brought back into existence after over 150 years, far from being homogeneously Polish, comprised important German and Russian minorities; of the fact that the "corridor" linking the bulk of it to the Baltic Sea — and separating East Prussia from the rest of Germany — was German territory, the inhabitants of which were submitted to continual vexations on the part of the Poles, and that Danzig was a German town.

---

[18] "A historical lie," to quote Hans Krebs' words.

They were made to forget—or kept from learning—that the Saarland, and the territory on the Memel were parts of Germany; that the Rhineland—occupied by the French since 1923—was also a part of Germany. And every effort which Adolf Hitler made to break *without war* the belt of hostile states and hostile armed forces that the victors of 1918 had tightened around the German Reich; every effort he made to win for Germany *without war* a status of "equal treatment"—*Gleichberechtigung*—among the leading nations of the West—the re-annexion of the Saar, after a plebiscite in which 99 percent of the inhabitants had voted for Germany, in 1935, the peaceful reoccupation of Rhineland in 1936, the re-incorporation of Austria (in March 1938) and, a few months later, of Sudetenland into the Reich, not to speak of Germany's earlier withdrawal from the League of Nations and her decision in favour of conscription after *all* Adolf Hitler's honest proposals of a *general* disarmament had been turned down, was presented to them *everywhere*—be it in the London newspapers, in those of New York, or in those of Calcutta—as the outcome of a revival of "German militarism" and as the evidence of a "menace to civilisation."

As already stated, far from accepting the friendly hand that Adolf Hitler stretched out to her, England became more and more unbending in her resolution not to treat with Germany, happen what might, i.e., more and more fatally launched in the direction Sir (later Lord) Robert Vansittart and Mr. (later Sir) Winston Churchill etc., were striving to give her foreign policy. Nay, there are serious grounds to believe that the vexations that the German population in Sudetenland and in the Polish "corridor" suffered on the part of Czechs and Poles, were, more often than not, encouraged, when not actually provoked, by secret agents of the British "Intelligence Service." In other words, England was not only doing all she could to create such conditions as were the most likely to lead to war, but also, seeing to it, beforehand, that she could, *one day*—again as in 1918—throw the blame for it upon Germany; as a matter of fact, this time upon *Nazi* Germany. Her most important European satellite—France—and the world-power of which she was herself (quicker than she expected) to become a satellite—the USA—helped her efficiently in this dirty game.

Still, war would—perhaps—not have become unavoidable,

had it not been for a well-organised set of *German* traitors in high position—von Weizsäcker and Kordt, both holders of leading posts in the German Foreign Office; General Beck and General Halder, both in turn Chiefs of the German General Staff; *Oberstleutnant* H. Boehm-Tettelbach and other first-rank officers of the German Army; Wilhelm Canaris, head of the German Military Intelligence, and a number of others, some of whose names were to become widely known overnight, in connection with the attempt on Adolf Hitler's life, on the 20th of July 1944; and also a few militant Christians, priests and laymen, all-too-conscious of the fact that a definitive victory of National Socialism could mean nothing less than the end of Christianity and of "Christian civilisation," and determined to prevent such a happening at any price, even at the cost of Germany's destruction; men to whose feelings Bonhoeffer was, during the war, to give expression, in a very clear sentence: "Better a devastated Germany than a National Socialist one!"

Such elements were far more important than one is generally inclined to believe. Post-war political literature—and, to begin with, in various detailed "memoirs," the surviving traitors' own description of their past doings—goes to prove that the whole machinery of the National Socialist state was simply honeycombed with them. And the fellows were active *long before* the war, in fact, from the very day Adolf Hitler rose to power. And they were in constant secret touch with Germany's bitterest enemies in diplomatic circles abroad.

They did all they possibly could to encourage the foreign and especially the English politicians in their stubborn and shortsighted will to hinder at all costs any further materialization of Adolf Hitler's territorial programme—in their determination to "stop Hitler," as they used to say, as the six million Germans of Austria had, after those of Saarland, greeted with unprecedented enthusiasm their integration into the common motherland. They kept the men of the British Foreign Office regularly informed about Adolf Hitler's plans[19] and gave them, at the same time, the false impression that the National Socialist régime expressed by no means the German people's actual choice, and that it would

---

[19] See Ernst Ulrich von Weizsäcker, *Erinnerungen* [Recollections] (Munich: List, 1950).

be most easily overthrown at the outbreak of war. And whenever tension arose between Great Britain and Germany, they sent secret envoys to London, with precise instructions to prompt the British government "not to give in." Thus were, for instance, Ewald von Kleist-Schmenzin, in August 1938, and *Oberstleutnant* Hans Boehm-Tettelbach, a fortnight later, dispatched, the former on behalf of General Beck, the latter on behalf of General Halder (General Beck's successor as Chief of the German General Staff) in order to come in touch "with the men the most closely connected with the Foreign Office" and "to request the British government to oppose a categorical 'no' to all Hitler's further claims,"[20] in particular, "to cause England to remain adamant in the Sudeten question."[21] It is now known that Ewald von Kleist-Schmenzin paid visits to several notoriously anti-German leading British politicians—in particular to Sir Robert Vansittart and to Winston Churchill—between the 17th and the 24th of August, and that he brought back a "private" letter of Winston Churchill to Wilhelm Canaris, one of the most powerful German traitors, already mentioned.[22] It is now known that the German Secretary of State, von Weizsäcker—who himself boasts of his "constant activity" consisting of "obstruction with regard to foreign policy," in the memoirs he was to write twelve years later—also did his very best, in early September 1938, to impress upon the British government (through Carl Burckhardt, High Commissioner of the League of Nations for Danzig, who at once sent on the message to Sir G. Warner, British envoy in Bern, who in his turn telegraphed to the British Foreign Office) the necessity of sending to Germany not Chamberlain, but "some energetic military man, who can shout and bang his walking-stick upon the table, when he must"[23]—i.e., a man who, instead of signing with Adolf

---

[20] Hans Boehm-Tettelbach declares so himself. See the *Rheinische Post* of 10 July 1948.
[21] Ribbentrop, p. 141.
[22] See Ian Colvin's *Master Spy: The Incredible Story of Wilhelm Canaris, who, while Hitler's Chief of Intelligence, was a Secret Agent of the British* (New York: McGraw-Hill, 1952).
[23] See Heinz Holldack, *Was Wirklich Geschah: Die diplomatischen Hintergrunde der deutschen Kriegspolitik* [What Really Happened: The Diplomatic Background of German War Policy] (Munich: Nymphen-

Hitler the well-known Munich Agreement, would have broken off the negotiations and, apparently, caused war: the common aim of all the enemies of the National Socialist New Order.

This much — which is just a sample out of the enormous (and ever-increasing) amount of evidence today available — goes to show that, if, in fact, such a supple person as Mr. Chamberlain was twice sent from London to meet Adolf Hitler, and given power to sign the Munich Agreement, securing peace (at least for another year), it was certainly not the fault of the German anti-Nazis. The reason *why* the British Cabinet sent Chamberlain — and not the "energetic military man" whom Herr von Weizsäcker would have preferred — and the reason *why* Chamberlain finally acknowledged the integration of Sudetenland into the German Reich, is the very same one which had, two months earlier — i.e., *before* the last intrigues of the German traitors with a view to provoke war — caused the dispatch of Lord Runciman to Prague, as a possible mediator between the Czechs and the German Sudeten Party, to the satisfaction of both (and of the German Reich), namely: the necessity for England to gain time — "once more to do something for peace" — because she was not yet ready for war,[24] or, more exactly, because the leaders of international Jewry *behind* the British politicians had not yet completed their preparations for a world war. Which did not mean that the British government was not bent on war, sooner or later; war to "stop Hitler" because he had made Germany — the dreaded commercial rival — free and powerful, *and* war to "stop Hitler" because he had put Germany's power to the service of such more-than-political truth as this advanced Dark Age hates the most.

Adolf Hitler was happy to interpret the Munich Agreement as the first decisive step towards that broader, lasting Anglo-German collaboration which he so sincerely desired. Was it not emphatically stated in the "Common Declaration" which both he and the English Premier had signed on the 30th of September, as an additional document stressing the meaning and importance of the Agreement?

---

burger Verlag, 1949), p. 95.
[24] Ribbentrop, p. 140.

> We look upon the Agreement signed yesterday evening and the (earlier) Anglo-German Fleet Agreement as symbols of the desire of both our people *never again to wage war upon each other*. We are determined to handle also other questions which interest our countries by way of negotiation and to brush aside eventual causes of divergences in opinion, so that we might contribute to secure peace in Europe.[25]

The German traitors were less pleased with the result of the Munich Conference. Their hopes of "putting Hitler aside" had to be given up—for how long? They did not know.[26] But they continued their shadowy intrigues, in Germany and in every foreign land the policy of which they could directly or indirectly influence, relentlessly trying to provoke or strengthen every manner of hatred against the Man to whom their lips had sworn allegiance, and against the régime they outwardly professed to serve. As for England, her attitude towards new Germany—the state against Time—grew, in spite of all Adolf Hitler's honest and earnest efforts, less and less friendly, not to say more and more hostile. Only three days after the solemn Declaration just quoted, Chamberlain announced in the House of Commons the decision of the government of Great Britain to arm at any cost. Then, "on the 7th of December 1938, the Munich Agreement was, through the *veto* of the British State Secretary for Colonies—doubtless not without the approval of his government—denied all validity in connection with the question of colonies and mandate territories, and the 'way of negotiation' between England and Germany closed with regard to the same." ... "At the same time," writes J. von Ribbentrop in his memoirs:

> the British government started a policy of still closer collaboration with France, and the United States of America were clearly invited to join in a coalition against Germany.

---

[25] Ribbentrop, p. 310.
[26] Erich Kordt, *Wahn und Wirklichkeit: Die Aussenpolitik des Dritten Reiches* [Dream and Reality: The Foreign Policy of the Third Reich] (Stuttgart: Union Deutsche Verlagsgesellschaft, 1947), pp. 128 and following.

The aim of this new policy consisted quite openly in an encirclement of Germany. War psychosis was cultivated in England *already before* the integration of the remnant of Czechoslovakia into the Reich. The European political horizon was systematically swept in search of possibilities of anti-German alliances. What Churchill had prophesied to me [von Ribbentrop] in 1937 was now happening. Germany had, according to British opinion, become too strong and was again to be beaten down.[27]

The German traitors in high office have, I repeat, no small responsibility in this tragic development. I am personally convinced that, without the knowledge of their activity, England would not have declared war on Germany in 1939 and that "the people would have remained satisfied with a solution of the Corridor question imposed through violence."[28] In other words, war between Germany and Poland would not have extended into war between England and Germany.

But I am also convinced that war between England (with her European satellite: France) and Germany, could have (and would have) been localised and ended in 1940, after the victorious campaign in France, had it not been for an enemy immeasurably more powerful than all the frustrated German officers (and intellectuals) and short-sighted, old-style British politicians and businessmen rolled in one, namely: the leader of the anti-Nazi forces (openly or secretly) *all over the world, the* enemy: the Jew.

That one — and whoever, in any part of the world, allowed himself to be, directly or indirectly, influenced by him — is responsible for the fact that the war between England and Germany did not — could not — end in 1940 with the honourable peace which Adolf Hitler generously offered the sister-nation, which he did not hate, but that it spread further and further, becoming the Second World War.

---

[27] Ribbentrop, pp. 146–47.
[28] Friedrich Lenz, *Der ekle Wurm der deutschen Zwietracht: Politische Probleme rund um den 20 Juli 1944* [The Loathsome Worm of German Discord: Political Problems Around July 20, 1944] (1952), p. 100.

The World Against Its Saviour 289

卐 卐 卐

There was (originally), be it in Adolf Hitler's own mind, be it in that of any of his disciples who had a say in the interpretation and application of his teaching, not the slightest intention of persecuting the Jews. There may, of course, have been, on the part of rank and file National Socialist fighters, *individual* cases of violence against specimens of that particularly obnoxious and thoroughly unwanted variety of foreigners—sporadic instances of long-repressed (and quite understandable) national hatred or less laudable personal revenge, neither encouraged by the leaders of the young Movement nor justified in the light of the National Socialist *Weltanschauung*. There was no systematic molestation of Jews—not to speak of planned extermination of them. Such drastic steps as mass "liquidations"—or mass sterilisations—were not foreseen.

All what Adolf Hitler had done was to point out international Jewry—international Jewish finance, surely, yet *not international Jewish finance alone, but the Jews (and half-Jews) themselves, and the Jewish spirit*—as the sinister force at the back of Germany's betrayal during the First World War, of her defeat in 1918 and subsequent humiliation and misery, and as the soul of the whole Versailles policy—which was indeed, historically speaking, absolutely true. And all he wanted was to rid Germany (and, if possible, Europe) of the Jewish pestilence—under *all* its forms and in all domains: politically and economically, no doubt, but also biologically and spiritually. (He acknowledged, in fact, from the beginning—and that, because he was infinitely more than "a politician"—that biological separation from the Jews and freedom from their influence in the moral and spiritual domain, meant *automatically* political and economical riddance of them also.)

In Point Four of the famous Twenty-Five Points—the unshakable basis of the National Socialist Party Programme—he did away with that old and all-too-widespread lie which consists in calling a Jew, who speaks the language of a foreign people in whose midst he was born and brought up, a man of that people. And he boldly proclaimed that, on account of his blood, *no Jew*—whatever be his capabilities or achievements, and however long his family be settled in Germany—can be a German citizen. He thus laid—for the first time in the West since the decline of the Greco-Roman world (i.e., since a non-Aryan could, if he liked, become a Roman citizen), and since Theodoric the Great's healthy Gothic kingdom—the foundations of a natural and rational state, of a state according to the dictates of Life.

In that long, dull process of decay which is (with a short, very short halt under that exceptional Germanic king) the history of the West from the day Roman citizenship lost its meaning and value, this *was* a revolution—and what a one! But it was *not* an act of hostility towards the Jews. It was a healthy and enlightened reaction against the folly of every "naturalisation," to the extent the latter is an insult to biology, a proclamation of the eternal truth of blood against the long-accepted but nevertheless shocking lie embodied in all such man-made regulations as defy it. In other words, it was an act "against Time," against the ever-increasing untruth of our Age of Gloom. (The fact that Jews, and neither Negroes nor Hottentots nor Papuans are mentioned in Point Four is simply due to the presence of the former as the *only* non-Aryan community living in Germany and playing a part in German life.)

Already in the days of the struggle for power, every National Socialist fighter called upon the German people not to buy from Jewish shops, not to believe the newspapers financed by Jews, etc., in one word, to free themselves by every possible means from the Jewish bondage, be it through individual initiative, *without* the help of laws that did not exist. One must admit that this was natural in a campaign led in the name of national freedom—natural, and neither new nor unique. Yet the reaction to it was, all over the world (and not only in Communist circles), a louder and louder outcry against National Socialist "anti-Semitism."

Curiously enough, in far-away India, Mahatma Gandhi, the prophet of "non-violence"—a man in many ways in glaring contrast to Adolf Hitler, but still, like him, a man "against Time"—was also, from 1919 onwards, urging his disciples to "boycott British goods" no less than "Western"—i.e., Christian-capitalistic—education and customs; to spin their own cotton, to weave their own clothes, and return to the simple life of older days; to free themselves from both the economic dependence and the moral corruption resulting from the foreign yoke. Nobody blamed him for it. Many in England itself—and some among the most prominent Englishmen in India, whose job it was to hinder his action—could not help admiring him. The only criticism he attracted to himself (mostly from Marxists or sympathisers of Marxism) was that of being an enemy of "progress" and an utopian, whose passive resistance was not the proper answer to "colonial oppression." But nobody blamed him for seeking to rid his people of foreign rule—nobody, not even the English themselves.

Jewish rule in Germany (and in Europe at large) was, however—and is, once more, since 1945—far worse than British rule in India or, by the way, than any obvious and brutal foreign rule in any conquered land. It was—and is—invisible and anonymous, *not felt* by the masses (who have neither leisure nor inclination to seek out subtle evils and their hidden causes) or even by most of the so-called thinking people, and thereby all the more dangerous; all the more soul-killing. (In fact, England's real crime against India was not so much her unheard-of exploitation of the land's resources as the introduction—or strengthening—of that silly exaltation of "man" in opposition to Nature, which is, as I said before, the essence of the Jewish spirit compared to the Aryan, and which was to pave the way for later Marxist influence.) Still, Mahatma Gandhi's struggle was looked upon with sympathy or at least with indifference, Adolf Hitler's with increasing uneasiness, mistrust, and soon positive hostility. Point Four of the Party Programme, and all Adolf Hitler's bold—and so accurate!—statements about the nefarious part played in world history by the Jews, were quoted (half the time without their context) and hammered upon as ominous signs of a regression into "barbarism." And, *although no harm had yet been done to them*, a number of Jews residing in Germany left the country of their own accord, their hearts filled with hatred for that new, *free* Aryan world which they felt growing all around them and in spite of them, for that new world which they would soon no longer be able to corrupt and to exploit at will. And they carried their hatred wherever they went and started, by every means within their reach—every means which hatred can devise and which money can secure—a world-wide campaign against National Socialism—already *then*, *before* Adolf Hitler's rise to power. Any true National Socialist who, at the time, happened to be living outside Germany *anywhere in the wide world* where there exist such things as newspapers, magazines, books, cinemas, and public lectures (wireless sets were not yet so popular as they soon became) remembers this fact all too well.[29] Other people — 99 percent of whom were to be, in some way or another, influenced by Jewish propaganda — may not necessarily *remember* it — a circumstance which only goes to prove how subtle and clever the latter was.

Every racially-conscious Jew — and every Jew of the world (whether pure-blooded or not) is racially-conscious — experienced the news of Adolf Hitler's *legal and perfectly democratic* victory in the last Reichstag elections of the Weimar Republic, and his no less legal and democratic appointment as Chancellor of the German Reich on the 30th of January 1933, as a personal insult from the whole German Nation (the overwhelming majority of which obviously stood behind the National Socialist Leader) and as a defeat of the Jewish people: their first glaring defeat for many centuries, and an eloquent warning to them. Everyone was decided to do his best to unsettle that now settled fact of Aryan rule in Germany (for Adolf Hitler's rise to power meant, first and foremost, *that*) and to destroy at any cost any possibility of German rule in Europe (which would have meant the end of the long, unseen Jewish domination of the West, nay, of the Jew's secret influence in the world). Hans Grimm has, in a recent book, quoted the words which a "prominent English-speaking Jew in Australia" addressed "a well-known German admiral" on the 31st of January, 1933, i.e., the very day after the "Seizure of power": "You have heard that President Hindenburg has, in accordance with the results of the Reichstag elections, made the National Socialist Hitler *Reichskanzler*. Well, I give you my word in this connection, and think of me later on: *we Jews will do everything to wipe this fact out of existence!*"[30]

And an organisation was actually founded under the name of

---

[29] I myself spent those years before the *Machtübernahme* partly in France, partly in Greece, partly in South India — and remember the atmosphere (and a few incidents in support of what I have here written) most vividly.

[30] Grimm, *Warum? Woher? aber Wohin?*, p. 187.

"International Jewish Economic Federation to Combat the Hitlerite oppression of Jews," and, in July, 1933, in Amsterdam, Samuel Untermeyer was elected president of it. Samuel Untermeyer's speech in New York, less than a month later, is the first official declaration of war on Adolf Hitler's new Germany. And, in perfect keeping with the character and purpose of his people—the very brood of the "Father of lies"[31]—and with the spirit of this Dark Age in which all natural values are reversed, the Jew calls this war, which is to be conducted relentlessly, "to the finish" against the young state "against Time," a "holy war" . . . "for the sake of humanity." And he mentions the "millions of non-Jewish friends" whose collaboration he knew all too well his people could expect. And he forgets to mention the real and only motives of his campaign: hatred and fear of any genuine Aryan awakening—the only motives, indeed, for all the other ones (which he stresses), namely the desire to prevent "starving and extermination" of Jews, and to "bang the last nail into the coffin where bigotry and fanaticism are to disappear" were spurious ones. As Hans Grimm—who never was a follower of Adolf Hitler—clearly points out, "not a single responsible word had been uttered in Germany about starving, killing, or exterminating [Jews] *till after* 1938, and not a single action had been taken in that direction."[32] And the National Socialist attitude to Jewry before or after 1938 had—and has—anyhow, nothing to do with "bigotry" or "fanaticism."

In 1938—i.e., *before* the war with Poland—the newly-founded state of Israel officially declared war on Germany, again on behalf of all the Jews of the world. This second act of open hostility was, like the first, presented as an answer to Adolf Hitler's supposed "persecution of the Jews," which had not yet begun. It aimed in reality at impressing once more upon the minds of the Jews far and wide (through the enormous prestige of the state of Israel, symbol of their unity and centre of their hopes) that National Socialist Germany, the proud citadel of awakening Aryandom, remained their enemy number one; their enemy, whatever she did or did not do, simply because she was the stronghold of those forces which were, are, and always will be the

---

[31] The Gospel according to Saint John, 20, verse 44.
[32] Grimm, *Warum? Woher? aber Wohin?*, pp. 187–88.

polar opposite of their collective self. It also aimed at impressing upon the minds of those "millions of non-Jewish friends" of the Jews (whose obedience Samuel Untermeyer had so rightly surmised) that the first cry of the people of Israel—"God's own people," according to the sacred book of all Christians—out of Palestine—the "Holy Land"—after 2,000 years of silence, was a curse against "the Nazis," both "godless" and "inhuman." (And such a cry could only be a cry of justice; or at least the "millions of non-Jewish friends"—Christians, lovers of "man," haters of all revolutions in the domain of fundamental *values*—were expected to believe it was.)

In fact, a lot had been done for the Jewish cause since the first Jews of Germany—far-sighted people who (also) could afford to travel—had judged that things were, there, likely to become, one day, too hot for them, and gone abroad, *with their whole fortunes*, before 1933. A lot had been done, thanks to the undue yet almost magical effect of certain empty and yet extremely popular words such as "mankind," "freedom," "democracy," etc.; thanks to the fathomless gullibility of most people who can read; and thanks to the masterful suppleness with which the Jews took advantage of both these negative traits of this end period of our Dark Age. "Humanity" and "freedom of the individual" and "respect of the human person" were, in the West, at once linked with Christianity and with the "cultural tradition of Europe," dear to all (or supposed to be).

As I said, the Jews were not—yet—in the Third Reich, the object of any particularly drastic measures. They just were no longer legally looked upon as "Germans." They were no longer allowed to teach in schools and universities, or to finance newspapers for German readers; to be actors, lawyers, professional musicians, writers, etc., for the German public—i.e., to influence that which Germans were expected to call art or literature, to consider as "good" or "bad" or as morally right or wrong. In one word, it was, now, since the establishment of National Socialist rule, forbidden to them to poke their noses into the actual life of the country in which they lived but which never had been and never could be theirs. It was also, since September, 1935—since the proclamation of the admirable Nuremberg Laws for the preservation of racial purity—forbidden to them to marry Germans or, by the way, to have, be it outside the bond of marriage, sexual relations with them. (Under National Socialist rule, abortion was, in the case of a pure-blooded Aryan child, looked upon as murder and severely punished, while the yet unborn product of a shameful union was—and rightly so—to be destroyed. And a German who, *before* the Nuremberg Laws, had taken a Jewess to wife, was either to divorce her or to have her sterilised.) But, as Hans Grimm says, "these regulations had nothing to do with a malignant anti-Semitism."[33] They applied, in fact, not only to Jews, but to all people of non-Aryan race, as the systematic sterilisation of the half-German half-Negro children, shameful traces of the occupation of Germany by African mercenaries after the First World War, goes to prove. And the Jews should have been the last people on earth to criticise the new laws, they who, contrarily to so many better races, have remained faithful to their tribal God, Jehovah, who—like all tribal gods of all lands and of all times—is said to hold blood-mixture in abomination,[34] they who were, themselves, in 1953, to forbid by law, in the state of Israel, marriages between Jews and non-Jews.[35]

And yet . . . the wise "Nuremberg Laws" were, whenever possible, presented in the whole world as an attempt to "curtail the freedom of the individual"—as an "insult to the human person," etc.; the dismissal of Jewish or half-Jewish government clerks and government officials, journalists, actors, theatre-managers, judges, doctors, professors, etc.—especially that of Albert Einstein, whose "Relativity Theory," "explained" to lay people in thousands of cheap booklets, was said to be the marvel of our times—as acts of wild racial hatred, which they were *not*. A couple of German songs, admittedly anti-Jewish, but by no means *more* bloodthirsty than certain Greek songs I know against the Turks or against the Bulgarians (or Turkish songs against the Greeks) or than the well-known French national anthem "La Marseillaise," or any war-songs of this planet, were translated into number of languages and repeatedly quoted as "proofs" of the "murderous spirit" of National Socialism. Even the suppression of "kosher" slaughterhouses—that standing

---

[33] Grimm, *Warum? Woher? aber Wohin?*, p. 188.

[34] See the Old Testament, Ezra, chapter 9.

[35] The actual Jews of Cochin on the Malabar Coast do not marry their coreligionists of local blood, the so-called "black Jews."

Jewish horror — was often criticised as an "attack against religious freedom" — criticised, nay, by many of those who looked upon the suppression of the old Indian *Sati* rite by the British as a laudable step. Societies composed *not* of Jews, but of well-meaning Aryans under the double misguiding influence of their contemporary Jew-ridden press and of centuries of a man-centred religion, rooted in Judaism, sprang up here and there, with the definite purpose of saving the world's soul from Adolf Hitler's grip — in fact, of preventing Adolf Hitler from saving Aryan man, body and soul, in all countries, from the ever-tightening grip of international Jewry. One of these societies — the "Friends of Europe" — published in booklet form, in or about 1935, a series of extracts of the works of National Socialist writers, with comments showing that Adolf Hitler's *Weltanschauung* is a denial of the fundamental scale of values which Europe has accepted along with the Christian faith (which indeed it is). The Jews and their "millions of non-Jewish friends" did not, however, lay stress upon this fact in order to save Christian love (which, being "above Time," cannot be threatened) or historical Christianity (which has played its part, and is dying out, anyhow — or gradually merging into its natural and logical earthly successor: Marxism) but merely with a view to hindering by any means the healthy (if tardy) reaction of the better West against the Forces of decay — the ruling Forces of the Dark Age and originators both of the old and of the new form of the everlasting Jewish lie.

In the East, the Jews had to be more subtle. Christianity is, there, less popular, and there are countries such as India in which a life-centred scale of values is (theoretically at least) the fundamental one — nay (in India's own instance) where a deep-seated belief in the natural hierarchy of races and in the God-ordained superiority of the Aryan is the belief of millenniums, backed by the unshakable metaphysical dogma of endless rebirth.

I think it is not superfluous to say, here, a few words about what was destined, in my humble estimation, to have a decisive bearing upon the turn events were to take in subsequent years, namely, about the part played in India by the Jews and their friends during the years before the Second World War.

Most of those Jews from Germany who, in Bombay, as a rule *after* 1933, but still—strange as this may seem—*with all their possessions*, poured out of the first-class cabins of the great liners, had little knowledge of the history and religions of Asia in general or of India in particular, and little desire to bother to acquaint themselves with either. The mysterious subcontinent of many races, upon which they had landed, then under British rule, looked anyhow too miserable and powerless to be worth winning over as an ally in Untermeyer's "holy war" against the Third German Reich. Its half-starving millions could not possibly have an opinion about anything outside their own daily struggle for life, least of all about distant nations' problems. And allowing that they could have, that opinion did not count, for they were poor. But there were rich and influential Europeans, and a few rich Indians, too, in whose hands lay the economy of the dumb subcontinent. The Europeans, mostly Englishmen (or Scotchmen) were white, wore European clothes, lived in fine houses, had clubs of their own into which Indians were not admitted, played golf—or bridge—and read newspapers in their spare time. The Jews from Germany were also white (more or less) and were dressed in European clothes and could afford to live in fine houses. And, curiously enough, those proud English merchants and Civil Service officials, who kept aloof from the Indians—who looked upon them as "coloured people" even when they happened to be of Aryan blood and no darker than many an Italian—were not unwilling to welcome as "Europeans," despite the obviously non-Aryan features most of them had, rich men and women of fair or tolerably fair complexion, who had been "German citizens" till 1933. The cotton and jute bosses, members of clubs "for Europeans only," and the officials themselves, had little interest in racial characteristics deeper and more significant than "white" or "coloured." The spirit of the great Aryan revolution that was taking place in Europe against all undue acts of "naturalisation" was totally foreign to them. Had they not already welcomed rich English-speaking Armenian residents of India—"British subjects"—as fit to enter that exclusive society—that tropical Europe—which they formed? And not only Armenians, but also rich English-speaking Jews, some of whom belonged to that titled nobility of money which is, in Great Britain, slowly displacing the old nobility of warrior-like merit![36] (Well, Queen Victoria had set the example in granting such favour to Disraeli, hadn't she?) Then why not also welcome those "persecuted" Jews, who had come—first class!—all the way from Germany, to tell them that Adolf Hitler's repeated expressions of admiration for the British Empire as an achievement of the Nordic genius, and his regard for England, and his desire to live in peace with her, nay, to have her as his most trusted ally, were all *Quatsch*[37]—a mere trick to gain time and that his aim was "world domination" at England's expense? The cotton and jute bosses—simple souls, with a very poor historical background, despite all their show of pride and power—believed the Jewish bankers and nightclub owners who spoke of "England's interest" in the same tone as Winston Churchill and Sir Robert Vansittart, and who interrupted the boredom of tropical Europe with juicy descriptions of "Nazi tyranny." They never bothered to find out whether the descriptions were true to fact or not. In tropical Europe, one is lazy . . . outside business hours, too lazy to think, let alone to criticise . . .

Soon the newcomers—every month more numerous—got in touch with other rich Jews, residents of India, who knew more than they did about the country, and started planning with them the best contribution they could bring the "holy war." And articles expressing doubts about Adolf Hitler's sincerity in his dealings with England; articles accusing him of "aggression" every time some German land, which had been put under foreign administration by the Versailles Treaty, gladly *and peacefully* returned to the Reich; articles presenting him more and more openly as *the* enemy, appeared in the Calcutta *Statesman* and other papers in the English language for British and Anglo-Indian readers.

But that is not all. The islands of tropical Europe in Bombay, Calcutta, Madras, never were India. On the contrary, there was a permanent tension between India and they who embodied foreign rule and (which was much worse) a way of life shocking,

---

[36] Example: *Sir* David Ezra, resident of Calcutta; and *Lord* Reading, at one time Viceroy of India.
[37] Nonsense—Ed.

from the standpoint of a Hindu, in many of its aspects. In case of war between England and the Third Reich—and nobody knew better than the Jews that war would one day break out: they were themselves preparing it—India would (should, logically) stand against England, that is to say on Germany's side. The problem for the Jews was to have English (and Anglo-Indian— tropical European) opinion on their side, without, for all that, setting India herself automatically against them. (There *were* Jews who knew better than to underestimate the weight the Hindu millions could throw into the scale of fate.)

It would have remained an unsolvable problem, had it not been for two facts: first, India's own age-old reaction against Aryan influence—probably as old as Aryan conquest itself, and certainly detectable in all those ancient and modern Indian religions and teachings of "non-violence," which either reject the caste system altogether or rob it of all racial significance; and, in addition to that, among the official and non-official representatives of the Third Reich in India, a regrettable lack of insight into (and perhaps even an underestimation of) the *other*— the Aryan—side of Indian Tradition and the astounding possibilities that lay within it.

What I have just called "India's own reaction against Aryan influence" is nothing else but that deep-rooted reluctance to any struggle "against Time," which seems to underlie an enormous amount of Indian experience (and culture) throughout history. It is anything but aggressively, or even positively, *anti*-Aryan—so little so, that some of the most perfect masters in whose lives, religious teachings, or literary works it has found expression, were Aryans by blood: men of the warrior-like, princely caste—Kshatriyas—such as the Buddha or Mahavira, or Brahmins, such as Chaitanya, or, in our times, the outstanding poet Rabindranath Tagore. It is just the attitude of men who live or aspire to live "above Time" either because this is the last resort of whoever carries logical thinking to its end *after having lost faith in this earth*, or because it is the spontaneous attitude of peace-loving and life-loving dreamers, or because it represents, for some sections of humanity—as I believe it does for the extraordinarily sensitive and intuitive Dravidian race, whose masses have always exalted the saints and poets of non-violence, if not also of renunciation—the sole natural alternative to purely sensual life "in Time." But it is—and has always been, for the two-and-a-half or three last millenniums at least—by far the most popular in India, whatever may be the proper explanation for it from the standpoint of ethnology or psychology, or both. And it certainly is quite a different thing from that bold philosophy of action considered as "better than inaction," and of serene but resolute acceptance of violence as a necessity of this earthly life in our Age, which appears to be the most substantial gift of the young Aryan race to the already old subcontinent, in Antiquity, and which is, no doubt, the *other side* of India's classical Tradition.

This remarkable duality in India's outlook on life and this tendency of the older mystical and moral attitude, congenial to the enormous non-Aryan substratum of the Indian population, to gain more and more prominence at the expense of the other, has been masterfully exploited by the agents of the Dark Forces in the course of centuries. The Jew's subtle action in certain influential Indian circles—in particular, in Indian Congress circles—before and during the war, is merely the latest phase of that exploitation.

Much the same thing has happened, in practice, to the otherworldly Indian philosophies and religions of non-violence as, in the West, to the *original* Christian faith, that spiritual path for people who strive to live, like their Master, "above Time": they have become, in this world of the Dark Age, an excuse for disregarding the Nature-ordained separation of races, for neglecting the duty of keeping one's blood pure, and, in addition to that—and far *more* so than Christianity in Europe—for taking up an hypocritical attitude to violence. Buddhists and, later on (in Bengal at least) Vaishnavas, started despising not merely the letter but also the spirit of the caste system, in the name of universal love. And this old propensity gained new tempo already in the first half of the 19th century among the so-called "educated" Hindus, i.e., among certain Hindus who had undergone "Western," or, to be more accurate, Judeo-Christian, influence, and in particular (more often than one cares to believe) the influence of World Freemasonry. This most dangerous secret organisation of our Dark Age, controlled by Jews ever since the day Jews were admitted into it, was (as it still is) entirely devoted to the promotion of the one aim of international Jewry: the permanent and peaceful—economic and cultural—domination of the Jew over a world robbed of all racial pride no less than of all desire to fight. It would be of great interest to note how many of the prominent leaders of the Brahmo-Samaj and other such bodies of "reformed" Hindus, were, for the last hundred years and more, directly or indirectly connected with Freemasonry, or with the Rosicrucian Order, or any such other "spiritual" society of similar type, under philosophical (and financial) Jewish leadership.

In the second half of the same century, the Theosophical Society, an international body having (ultimately) the same secret aims and the same leadership as Freemasonry (to which an enormous proportion of its members are also affiliated), was founded upon the double basis of an arbitrary, syncretic doctrine, *partly* of Indian origin, and presented as "occult," and . . . of the belief in the equal rights of "all men" regardless of race—the old Jewish lie for non-Jews. It has to this day its headquarters in India—in Adyar, near Madras—and stands for a close collaboration between so-called "enlightened" Hindus and no less "enlightened" Westerners—Westerners supposed to understand "India's message," but who, in reality, interpret the Hindu Scriptures in the way the most suitable to the Society's secret aims, and who (whenever they can) have a say in Indian politics.[38] Like the Hindu "reformed" bodies, products of Judeo-Christian influence upon India's *intelligentsia*, it has done whatever it could to deny the importance of the idea of race in Hindu Tradition, to combat the interpretation of the word "Aryan" in the racial sense, wherever it is to be found in Hindu Writ, and to rob the teaching of Detached Violence—the Teaching of the Bhagavad-Gita—of its true scope; to give this sacred Book—against the spirit of India's greatest hero both "above" and "against Time," Lord Krishna—such a "strictly symbolical" meaning as cannot justify that raw, material violence which the fighters "against Time" (be they also "above Time," as all such *great* fighters necessarily are) need to display, today, near the end of the Age of Gloom. Well did the orthodox *and* really enlightened, racially-conscious, and God-conscious Brahmin, Lokomanya Tilak, whose whole work bears witness to the unity of Eastern and

---

[38] Annie Besant, for years President of the Theosophical Society, was elected President of the Indian National Congress for 1917.

Western Aryandom and to the power of Aryan genius, liken Dr. Annie Besant to the legendary female demon Putna, whose poisoned milk was intended to kill Krishna, the predestined Warrior and Teacher of Detached Violence, when He was still a child.

The Theosophical Society itself may well have played but a secondary part in India (despite the public prayers its President, Dr. Arundale, was to offer there for the victory of the anti-Nazi forces, during the Second World War). But the spirit embodied in it and in the other so-called "spiritual" organisations which claim to do away with the God-ordained inequality both of men and of human races no less than with the law of violent Action (now, in this Dark Age), in other words, the spirit of all groups which deny or reject the perennial struggle "against Time," has corrupted to a great extent the conscious strata of the country. It has taught thousands of Hindus to lie to themselves and to the world, and to accept only such forms of the Struggle "against Time" as use moral violence as a weapon (calling it "non-violence," as Mahatma Gandhi did—in fact, had to, for the sake of his success in contemporary India) and to hate any frank acknowledgement of the necessity of material violence in the service of the Cause of Life no less than any frank acknowledgement of the life-bound and life-ordained inequality of races and inequality of birthrights—including the so-called "right" of "all men" to live.

In the end, no doubt, the divine Child—the growing Forces of Light and Life, will, like in the Hindu legend, kill the poisonous demoness of untruth. But in the meantime, the poison has gone very far. It has, slowly but steadily set *beforehand* thousands of "educated Hindus" against any living—contemporary—Incarnation of Him Who comes, back, over and over again, to fight the forces of decay and death and to "establish on earth the reign of Righteousness," through openly accepted Dark Age methods—the only expedient ones in the times in which we live. It has prepared them to swallow the clever moral and cultural Jewish propaganda of the years before 1939 and all the lies of the following moral and political campaign against National Socialism and the Third German Reich, to this day. It has enabled the Jews to win over to their cause, before, during, and after the war, thought-forces and will-forces which would, otherwise, have worked in support of the Aryan awakening in the West, or at least remained neutral.

The Jews from Germany who, already before the war, were beginning to gain credit amidst certain groups of Hindus, were not the same ones as those who met the rich Europeans — and pro-British Armenians, and Jewish residents of India, all termed "British" — in clubs and at bridge parties. They had less money. Some (so, at least, they said) even had no money at all, and begged the kind-hearted Hindus to help them to get work, if possible in their own line. They had "lost everything" — lost, at any rate, their former right to carry on their job as doctors, lawyers, actors, professors, or journalists in the once so tolerant "land of thinkers and poets" which had, through the victory of National Socialism, suddenly become a vast soldiers' camp where nothing was to be heard save the regular stamping of jack-boots and the awe-inspiring repercussion of war-songs, where there surely was no longer any place for their refined intellectuality or their sensitive care for "mankind." They were "persecuted" — or said they were — even more so than the other Jews. And, in contrast to these, most of them were "learned," if not erudite — or pretended to be — had, at least some summary knowledge of Indian philosophy and Indian customs, of which they drew the utmost advantage. They were to be found in places in which one was the most likely to come in touch with "educated" or, which is more, influential Hindus: Hindus, on one hand broad-minded enough to welcome the friendship (and admiration) of Indianised foreigners, on the other sufficiently Tradition-bound to be regarded, by a few people or by many, as true champions of Hinduism: places such as Adyar, Shantiniketan, or Sabarmati (and later, Sevagram) Gandhi's abode. Some of them visited the three and stayed there for a fairly long time, establishing further connections for themselves or for their friends. (One — Margaret Spiegel, alias Amala Bhen — spent two years at Gandhi's feet, clumsily spinning cotton yarn, thoroughly learning Gujarati, and telling people every time she could what a flat denial of the Mahatma's doctrine Adolf Hitler's new Germany was, and then — in 1935 — came to Shantiniketan to infuse further hatred of National Socialism into the students whose "German teacher" she was, and ended up as a professor at Elphinston College in Bombay.) Others would just secure themselves comfortably-settled Hindu husbands or — in the case they were men — became "holy men": Buddhist monks, Vaishnava devotees, harmless and solitary Theosophists committed to the "Hindu way of life," aspiring after nothing but "spirituality." Jewish females who lacked sex-appeal also turned holy, or charitable — or both. They offered their loving zeal (and technical efficiency, whenever they had any) to Hindu organisations connected with social relief, and became popular as friends of the poor, comforters of the sick, foster-mothers and teachers of orphans — angels of pity! The orphans belonging to the most far-apart castes would naturally be brought up to eat and work and play together, against the custom of orthodox Hindus, but in accordance with the views of "reformed" Hindu leaders. And it was secretly hoped that some of them — as many as possible — would one day also marry against the time-honoured custom and the old aspiration towards blood-purity thanks to which there are, 6,000 years after the Aryan settlements of Vedic days, still Aryans in India. The bitterest enemies of the modern Aryan faith would undo what the Vedic Aryans had done; destroy, to the extent they could, the stamp of Aryan rule in Asia.

Thus, in the distant Indian sub-continent — which should, logically, have been a bastion of the Aryan forces *against* the machinations of both — the less rich Jews played as important a part as their apparently more influential racial brothers. Silently — humbly, one could say — but relentlessly, they were contributing to the formation of that bastardised world in which the consciousness of the "dignity of man" is expected to replace former racial pride; they were dragging whatever they could of India's better substance into that world. And they were making themselves popular among the Hindus — at least among certain Hindus — because they helped them (or seemed to help them) and because they flattered them. And when, from 1933 and especially from 1935 onwards — thanks to the Jewish press and literature and to the efforts of Mr. Untermeyer's "millions of non-Jewish friends" — (Freemasons and such) — it became, from one end of the earthly sphere to the other, more and more obvious that Adolf Hitler was "persecuting the Jews," many Hindus *among those who had a say in India's affairs* were at once prepared to look upon him if not — yet — as "a monster," at any rate as a dangerous tyrant. Jews! — such good and kind people as "Amala Bhen," Gandhi's devoted disciple, whose photo at the side of the prophet of non-violence every newspaper-reader had seen; or as Miss Gomparst, the efficient social worker of the Bengal Relief Association, who was (and, as far as I know, still is) running a children's home and a dispensary amidst the slums of North Calcutta; or as that fair-complexioned monk, Govinda, who wrote learned articles about Buddhist metaphysics and could be seen walking through the lawns of Shantiniketan in yellow robes, under an impressive Burmese parasol! . . . or as those sympathetic sari-wearing "*memsahibs*" who gave Hindu names to their half-Indian half-Hebrew children, and had taken to Indian ways to such an extent that some of them had even become tolerable members of "joint families"![39] Really, how could he!—how dare he! Maybe the British themselves were also tyrants (and which national-minded Indian looked upon them as anything else?). But surely they were right when calling the world—louder and louder—to "stop Hitler."

Of course, not all Hindus were taken in by the Jews' clever adaptability to Indian ways, by their real or supposed interest in "Indian philosophy," and by their comments upon new Germany. Millions, unable to read, and completely indifferent to the outside world, were never even aware of the anti-Nazi campaign of hatred. Some saw through it and despised it. One at least—a worthy Brahmin little known to the public at large, yet one of the finest characters of modern Aryavarta, Sri Asit Krishna Mukherji—fought against it "with tooth and claw" from the start, through the fortnightly magazine *The New Mercury*, which he published in Calcutta from 1935 to 1937 (in collaboration with the German Consulate), and was, later on—throughout *and after* the war, *to this day*—to prove his unfailing loyalty to the Aryan cause. Others, simple folk lacking such political consciousness, and often illiterate, yet *felt* that the inspired Western ruler whom so many *sahebs* seemed to hate was the one ruler in the world who professed *and lived* the doctrine of Detached Action preached in the Bhagavad-Gita. And they admired him. They related that he had come to replace the Bible by that most hal-

---

[39] A "joint family" is, in India, a family in which several brothers all live together—under the same roof—with their parents, wives, and children.

lowed Book of Aryan Wisdom, among the Aryans of the West.[40] But they were powerless, the lot of them. Powerless, while isolated, disconnected from the revolutionary forces of Life at work in the West. The support given to *The New Mercury* represented practically the only tangible attempt ever made by the authorities of the Third Reich to collaborate *on the ideological plane* with the racially-conscious Aryan minority of India. And I do not know a single European National Socialist, besides myself, who made it a point to beat the Jews on their own ground and to try to win over India—*including* non-Aryan India—to the Pan-Aryan cause, preaching the modern philosophy of the Swastika—the unity of Life, *within diversity*; the divine hierarchy of races; the ideal of blood-purity and the selfless struggle for the creation of a higher mankind; Adolf Hitler's wisdom *and that* of the ancient Aryan Conquerors of Aryavarta—in Indian dress, in Indian languages, and from the standpoint of Indian Tradition; presenting his or her effort as the will to free *India* from the influence of the anti-racialist doctrines of equality: misrepresented Christianity and Islam, and Marxism (all three, in fact, more or less deeply rooted in Jewish thought).

The international, ubiquitous Jew did not restrict his far-sighted propaganda to the Hindus. He carried it on among Mohammedans also—despite the old hostility between Hindus and Mohammedans (which was no concern of his) and, which is more, despite the permanent tension between Arabs and Jews in and around Palestine ever since the famous Balfour Declaration, and the natural sympathy of every follower of the Prophet for

---

[40] The young servant's name was Khudiram. For a fuller telling of this story, see Savitri Devi, "Hitlerism and Hindudom," in the online Savitri Devi Archive: http://www.savitridevi.org/hindudom.html. The essay was originally published as "Hitlerism and the Hindu World," *The National Socialist*, no. 2 (Fall 1980), pp. 18–20. Cf. *Gold in the Furnace: Experiences in Post-War Germany*, 3rd ed., ed. R. G. Fowler (Atlanta: The Savitri Devi Archive, 2006), pp. 5 and 278; *Defiance: The Prison Memoirs of Savitri Devi*, ed. R. G. Fowler (Atlanta: The Savitri Devi Archive, 2008), pp. 202–203 and 337; and *And Time Rolls On: The Savitri Devi Interviews*, ed. R. G. Fowler (Atlanta: The Savitri Devi Archive, 2005), p. 123.—Ed.

the Arabs. He carried it on—in a different way, and with increasing help from his friends the Marxists—among the Chinese and Annamites and other people of the yellow race, among Filipinos and Malays, and "educated" Negroes and half-Negroes. He carried it on everywhere, and always concentrated his efforts upon the proper men, i.e., upon those who were, at the same time, sufficiently gullible to take for granted whatever they were told about the Third German Reich and its "racial hatred," and sufficiently influential for others to hold whatever opinion *they* might express, for the right one. The slogan of "humanity" and of the "rights of man"—the old slogan of the French Revolution— acted as a spell. With its help, the Jew overcame all difficulties, rousing, out of light-hearted indifference, feelings of aggressive indignation which verged more and more on crusaders' zeal. The little one did to counteract his game (when one did anything at all) remained without a lasting effect.

The visit of a few prominent members of the National Socialist Party, headed by the leader of the Hitler Youth, Baldur von Schirach himself, to Damascus, in 1937, was (to mention that one instance) but a partial success. It disturbed for a few days the peace of mind of the French High Commissioner in Syria, who was no Nazi, and who tolerated the honourable guests more than he welcomed them. And it was the occasion of valuable personal contact with several Arab personalities, some of whom were to help Germany during and, maybe, also after the war; none of whom was, however, powerful enough to throw the weight of the whole Moslem world on Adolf Hitler's side—a difficult task from the standpoint of Islam, admittedly, for how can, after all, believers in even a warrior-like faith which *any man* can join, wholeheartedly stand for Aryan racialism (or for *any* racialism, by the way?). The utmost which the sincerest anti-Jewish Arab—including the Grand Mufti of Jerusalem—could do, was to be Germany's *political* ally against the Jews. And he was, thereby—in spite of the difference of race—perhaps a step nearer German National Socialism than even the well-known Indian nationalist Subhas Chandra Bose or any of Adolf Hitler's other political allies against *England* ever were to be.[41] But those

---

[41] An agreement between Adolf Hitler and England against Russia, at the eleventh hour, would have sufficed to detach from his alli-

thousands of well-meaning but ill-informed Hindus, Mohammedans, Chinese, Indo-Chinese, Malays, literate Central Asian steppe-dwellers, and "educated" Africans, who were impressed by the cheap anti-colonialism, preached to them in the name of the "rights of man" by the international Jew and his friends (especially the Marxists) and who, on the ground of clever misquotations from and misinterpretations of *Mein Kampf*, held National Socialism to be a new form of "abominable imperialism," were—unfortunately—more solidly bound to the sinister anti-Nazi forces than any of the non-Aryan (nay, than many of the Aryan) friends of new Germany were bound to the forces of Light and Life. And, I repeat, nothing or practically nothing was done, to my knowledge, on the part of the official representatives of the Third Reich, or through the private initiative of full-fledged European followers of Adolf Hitler (with one individual exception)[42] to win over those millions of dull, perhaps, but nevertheless existing, and therefore—in the Invisible realm—to some extent effective human centres of psychic energy and willpower. (*Now*, in the one or two European papers that stand for the real interests of Aryandom, and in the catacomb gatherings of the German National Socialists of 1955—the genuine ones, who stood the test of defeat—it is for the first time openly proclaimed that colonialism in its old accepted form is incompatible with a true "ethnic" —*völkisch*—attitude to life and to politics. *Then*—20 years ago, and more—I was myself, in India, as far as I know, the only European National Socialist who stressed that truth, and pointed out, in Adolf Hitler's *ideological* pact with Japan,[43] the first step towards the collaboration of the racially-conscious aristocracy of Aryandom *and that of the noblest non-Aryan races* in the new world that was taking shape under the sign of the Swastika.)

Among the nations of the yellow race, Japan, protected by her immemorial Shinto philosophy—the East Asiatic equivalent of the National Socialist cult of Blood and Soil—and by Tōyama's[44]

---

ance those Indians who were merely anti-British without being Aryan-conscious.

[42] Savitri Devi's husband, Dr. Asit Krishna Mukherji—Ed.

[43] The Anti-Comintern Pact, signed in 1936.

[44] Possibly a reference to Tōyama Mitsuru (1855–1944), a Right-

silent but far-sighted and far-reaching activity, was, in fact, the only one to escape the infection of anti-Nazi propaganda more or less entirely. Japan remains, however, a non-Aryan nation. Her ideological sympathy for that Aryan way of life which a Japanese was, in 1941, so accurately to characterise as "Western Shintoism," did not bind her to Germany in the manner England *could have felt herself bound*, had she only been able to shake herself free from the influence of Sir Eyre Crowe, Sir Robert Vansittart, and Winston Churchill, etc., *and* from that of those hundreds of rich Jews from Germany who positively "invaded" London and all the large British towns from 1933 to 1939. Japan went her own way — even though she had, on the 25th of November, 1936, signed the Anti-Comintern Pact; even though she was, later on — on the 27th of September, 1940 — to sign an actual Treaty of friendship with Adolf Hitler. Precious as it was, her alliance stood merely as a "second best" after the long-desired "English alliance" had — thanks to the atmosphere created in England and practically all over the world by the Jews and their friends — revealed itself as a psychological impossibility.

Germany's other partner, Fascist Italy, was unreliable, as further history was so tragically to prove. And the Dark Forces "in Time" — the self-same ones as are embodied in international Jewry — were there, in spite of Fascism, tremendously active through the Catholic Church: that twin-sister of Freemasonry (shocking as these words may sound to pious Catholics, and contrary as they may be to all *public* statements, both of the Catholic leaders and of the Masters of the Lodges, concerning the separation of the two organisations, nay, their mutual hostility). The one powerful man in Rome with whose unfailing collaboration Adolf Hitler could reckon absolutely — Mussolini, his personal friend — was not Fascist Italy, and was, *in fact*, less powerful than he looked. And Fascism itself was not National Socialism, contrarily to what so many haters of both seem to think. It was a political — and economic — system, not a more-than-political creed,

---

wing Japanese political figure, who in 1881 founded *Genyosha*, a nationalist secret society that promoted Japanese imperial expansion and used terrorism and assassination as tools. In 1901, his followers founded a successor organization, the Black Dragon Society (*Kokuryūkai*), which pursued the same aims. — Ed.

and it inspired a Movement of practical and immediate—of *time-bound*—significance, not one of cosmic scope. It did not lay stress upon the all-important idea of race and the ideal of racial purity as National Socialism does.

In other words, notwithstanding the Anti-Comintern Pact and her further bond with Italy and Japan, National Socialist Germany was practically alone, alone at least in the invisible realm of quality and purpose—of aspiration and will-power and meaning, in that realm of "energy" in which material happenings are mysteriously but mathematically—unavoidably— determined; the only Aryan power as conscious of its natural mission as the leading agents of the Dark Forces—the Jews— were (and are) of theirs; the only Aryan state "against Time." More so: the Führer and, I would not say "the men of his entourage" (for there were, among these, persons of different shades of National Socialist orthodoxy and also of different degrees of loyalty), but "his true disciples" (whether they were to be found in his immediate entourage or elsewhere) were alone: *a minority in Germany itself*, despite Adolf Hitler's immense popularity, and, in the world at large, an unbelievably small number of dedicated revolutionaries, at arms against both the obvious *and the deeper* characteristics of this end-period of the Dark Age.

The Jews had, on the other hand—thanks to the untruth into which the West and the East have been sinking for centuries; thanks to that silly superstition of "man" which has everywhere replaced healthy reverence of the Divine as manifested within all life but especially within the "hero like unto the Gods"—the whole world more or less on their side; "passively" on their side, when not "actively." The Christian churches *and* anti-clerical Freemasonry, the Communists *and* all those who still stand for bourgeois Capitalism, the gullible pacifists *and* the cleverest of all war-mongers, all internationalists and all anti-German (or anti-European) short-sighted nationalists were gradually to coalesce with them, in the name of "humanity," against the more-than-human Wisdom embodied in the revolutionary state "against Time."

This astounding success of the Dark Forces was due— partly—no doubt, to the suppleness of their agents who, like Paul of Tarsus—one of the most remarkable of them in world history—acted "as Greeks with the Greeks and as Jews with the

Jews." (One should give the devil his due and admit that he — the Lord of the sinister Powers — is a businessman of genius, and that his children take after him!) The main and deeper cause of their victory lies however in the fact that, in this last period of the Dark Age, this world *belongs* more and more irredeemably to the forces of deceit; in the fact that this is *their time* par excellence — to which the *last* Man "against Time" (Whom the Hindus call "Kalki") can alone put an end — and their domain, slowly conquered through lies and trickery in the course of millenniums; *their domain,* which Kalki alone can win back to the Powers of Light and Life; and that Adolf Hitler was not "Kalki" — not "the" one, the *last* one. He knew it, being, however, the one-before-the-last Embodiment of Him Who comes back. And he admitted it in his own way, as early at least as 1928, in that significant conversation of his with Hans Grimm, which I have already mentioned.

In November 1938, i.e., after the Munich Agreement, and before the developments that were to lead to the Second World War, Oswald Pirow, then Defence Minister of the South African Union, paid a visit, on behalf of General Smuts, both to Chamberlain and to Adolf Hitler. He was to mediate in order to bring about a lasting understanding between England and Germany. In the report which he published, in 1951, about his undertaking, under the title "Was the Second World War Unavoidable?," one reads these most enlightening sentences:

> Already through my first conversation with Chamberlain it became clear to me why the two governments did not understand each other. It was not lack of good will on the part of Chamberlain: the latter had made his whole future political career dependent upon an understanding with Germany, and he was ready to make great concessions to that end. *But, between Chamberlain's good will and positive reality, stood, as firm as a rock, the Jewish question.* The British Prime Minister had to reckon with a party — his own Conservative Party — and especially with a public that worldwide Jewish propaganda had influenced to the utmost. Unless this agitation could be cooled down, concessions to

Germany were unthinkable for Chamberlain. . . . The factors which stood against Chamberlain's peace policy were: *the world-wide propaganda of the Jews, bitter beyond all measure*, the political selfishness of Churchill and of his followers, the half-Communist tendencies of the Labour Party, and the war-mongery of the British chauvinists, encouraged by German traitors. In November 1938, this remarkable coalition had not yet succeeded in shattering Chamberlain's political position, as it was to later on. But it had convinced the British public that Adolf Hitler was the greatest persecutor of man of all times, and that any pactising with him could only lead to further humiliation.[45]

And, I repeat — for this can never be, nowadays, sufficiently stressed — up till then, *the Jews in the Third Reich had not been persecuted*. Eugen Kogon himself — that fanatical hater of National Socialism if there ever was one, admits, in the virulent book — *The S.S. State* — which he published in 1946 against the Hitler régime, that up to November 1938 there had only been "individual instances" of molestation of Jews within new Germany. And, which is more, Adolf Hitler had no intention whatsoever of "persecuting" — let alone of "exterminating" — the nefarious foreigners whom he knew to be the agents of Germany's defeat in 1918 and the deadliest enemies of her people and of Aryan mankind as a whole. He had — unfortunately! — allowed thousands of them to leave the country *with all their property*. And he was prepared to arrange for them *all* to go, taking with them that much of their money as could suddenly be withdrawn from Germany without tragic consequences for the German economy.[46] He was not unaware of the mischief they could work against Germany, once abroad. The world-wide propaganda which those of them who had already emigrated were financing was too obvious for him not to have known of it. But he was generous. And he believed in the loyalty of his own people, whom he loved. And he

---

[45] Oswald Pirow, "Was the Second World War Unavoidable?" (quoted by Grimm, in *Warum? Woher? aber Wohin?*, p. 192).

[46] Jewish property in Germany was estimated at one thousand million [one billion (short scale)] pounds.

trusted the strength of that splendid German youth that was growing under his eyes, full of faith in him and in his eternal ideals; full of the will to live as a dedicated élite in the service of the latter, and ready to die, if necessary, so that new Germany might live. He knew that, *provided* they stood like one man behind him, and stuck to his principles, the German people had nothing to fear from the outer world. He did not know how many influential traitors of German blood were already in the service of the Dark Forces—against him, and against their own people—nor how far Jewish influence was at work, secretly, subtly (and all the more efficiently) through the occult bodies that he had forbidden (Freemasonry and all societies affiliated to it) *and* through the Christian churches, in Germany herself. His constructive plans—in the biological, social, economic, and cultural, not to mention also religious spheres—which could indeed only lead to the invincibility of the German Reich, *needed time* to be carried out. The eternal truths he preached (after one-and-a-half thousand years of false doctrine) *needed time* to become once more, first among the Germans, and then among all people of Nordic blood, undisputed, self-evident articles of popular faith. ... The Dark Forces were determined anyhow not to leave Adolf Hitler time—or peace. Working from all sides, they did their best to make a permanent understanding between England and Germany impossible, in particular, to prevent all further personal contact between Adolf Hitler and Neville Chamberlain: the one development which, according to Oswald Pirow, *might have*, still at the eleventh hour, changed the whole atmosphere (and that, too, provided Chamberlain managed to remain in power). It looked, for a time, as though they would, in spite of all, *not* succeed. Then, suddenly, an apparently unexpected—in fact, cleverly prepared—incident came to their rescue: an attaché of the German Legation in Paris, von Rath, was, on the 7th of November, 1938, for no accountable reason at all, murdered by a Jew.[47]

This was not the first act of provocation on the part of the sworn enemies of the Third Reich as the leading power of regen-

---

[47] Ernst vom Rath (1909–1938), who worked at the German Embassy in Paris, was the victim of Jewish assassin Herschel Grynszpan. — Ed.

erate Aryandom. Some time before, Gustloff, *Landesleiter* of the N.S.D.A.P. in Switzerland, had also fallen the victim of a Jewish murderer.[48] And there were the daily insults of the Jewish press of the whole world, against all that the Germans held sacred. And there was Untermeyer's formal declaration of war—on mendacious grounds—already in August, 1933.[49] This was but "the last straw" which "broke the camel's back." Up till then, the many and varied—louder and louder—expressions of Jewish hostility to Germany had, save for a few bloodcurdling articles (and eloquent caricatures) in *Der Stürmer*, remained without an answer. *This* provocation roused, throughout the Third Reich, an uproar of indignation, taking advantage of which some of the most impulsive among the leaders of the National Socialist fighting formations organised, in the night of the 8th to the 9th of November, under the direction of no less a man than Dr. Goebbels, what is known as the "*Kristallnacht*": breaking up of Jewish shops, burning down of synagogues, with all the rough handling of individual Jews that one can imagine; from evening to dawn, all over Germany, a proper orgy of Jew-baiting. The next day, the Führer burst out in righteous indignation at the news of this useless and anything but detached violence, the repercussion of which he could well foresee. I have already quoted the words he addressed Dr. Goebbels: "You people have thrust back National Socialism and spoilt my work for many years, if not for good, through this nonsense!"[50]

His unmitigated disapproval of the pogrom did not, however, hinder or lessen the explosion of hatred which the news of it provoked in the whole world. It was surely not the first time in history that the murder of a man—in fact, of two men—in high position, at the hands of a foreigner, had become the occasion of tough reprisals against the murderer's compatriots.[51] Up till

---

[48] Wilhelm Gustloff (1895–1936), the leader of the Swiss National Socialist Party, was assassinated by the Jew David Frankfurter.—Ed.

[49] This took place in March, 1933. See M. Raphael Johnson, "The Jewish Declaration of War on Germany: The Economic Boycott of 1933," *The Barnes Review*, January–February, 2001.—Ed.

[50] Quoted in Grimm, *Warum? Woher? aber Wohin?*, p. 184.

[51] For example, the scenes of violence that took place in Lyons against Italians, after an Italian, Caserio, had murdered Carnot, Pres-

then, unconcerned nations had generally kept aloof from such affairs. But this time, the murderer's compatriots were Jews. And in this Jew-ridden world of the end of the Dark Age, whatever is done to Jews is the whole world's business. Not only did *the Jews* literally "foam with rage" (to quote O. Pirow's words), but the newspaper-reading population of the most varied lands reacted as though the most horrible event within 10,000 years had just taken place under their eyes. In England and in the USA "public opinion" — so important, in democracies! — flared up in an anti-Nazi outcry and thundered against all collaboration with the Third German Reich — that exponent of "barbarism" in the midst of our "civilised" century! The British Ambassador in Berlin was called back "to report about the happenings." Chamberlain's position was shattered, the days of his political career numbered. Oswald Pirow's official mission to Berlin as a mediator was now out of the question. And the *unofficial* journey which he undertook there — in agreement with Chamberlain, in spite of all — was beforehand stamped with the sign of failure. By the time Oswald Pirow came back to London to tell the British Premier of Adolf Hitler's unaltered good will and readiness to treat with England, "Chamberlain's position had become so difficult that he dared not take the initiative of approaching Hitler."[52] The two men, whose collaboration could, according to Oswald Pirow, "have saved Europe" were never to see each other again. On the other hand, the American ambassador in Berlin was recalled on the 13th of November, 1938, and diplomatic relations between the USA and Germany suspended. The Second World War — for which, as we shall see, the USA bear the responsibility at least as much as England herself, if not even more — was now unavoidable. Maybe, it was not yet clear which local conflict would become the occasion and *the pretext* of it. But it was already certain that nothing could prevent it.

---

ident of the French Republic, in 1905.
[52] Oswald Pirow, "Was the Second World War Unavoidable?"

8. Adolf Hitler during the Second World War

An exceptionally prominent Freemason,[53] Franklin Roosevelt, had been inaugurated[54] President of the USA in January 1933, i.e., at the time of Adolf Hitler's rise to power. With him, the hidden agents of world Jewry — and, behind them, the everlasting Dark Forces "in Time" — the self-same ones that were already building up, in Russia and beyond Russia, Marxist Eurasia — took over the government of the United States of America.

Knowing this, it is interesting to follow from the start the signs of increasing hostility which the USA showed National Socialist Germany: at first, mere acts of unfriendliness — full support of the French standpoint against the German, in every disarmament conference; and the dispatch of a notorious hater of Germany, William Dodd, to Berlin as American Ambassador — then, on the 5th of April 1937, Roosevelt's well-known "quarantine" speech in Chicago against the "aggressive" authoritarian states: Japan, Italy, Germany, but not Soviet Russia; then, in early 1938, his plea for intensified armament (to "defend the world" against an eventual "return to barbarism," as the American newspapers stressed); then, the break of diplomatic relations which I have mentioned, and the feverish activity of both the American Ambassadors in London and in Paris in order to bring about war between England (with France at her side) and the Third Reich — war at any cost, war before National Socialism (cosmic Wisdom applied to modern political and more-than-political problems) had time to make the Third Reich invulnerable.

"In the USA powerful forces had been at work for a long time, urging the country to wage war on Germany," writes J. von Ribbentrop in his memoirs.[55] And he shows, as plainly and clearly as can be, from official documents seized by the Germans in Warsaw and in Paris — in particular, from the reports full of "very enlightening details" dispatched by the Polish Ambassador in Washington, Count Jerzy Potocki, to his government — that, as early as spring 1939, President Roosevelt had already, to

---

[53] He had reached the "32nd degree" of initiation — the very highest which any man who is not of Jewish blood can reach in that world brotherhood.

[54] Replacing "elected" — Ed.

[55] Ribbentrop, p. 165.

a great extent, completed his preparations in view of America's participation in a coming war against Germany"[56] and that he had decided "not to take part in the war from the start but *to bring it to an end, after England and France would have begun it.*"[57] William C. Bullitt, the US Ambassador in Paris and his London colleague, Joe Kennedy, were instructed to exert pressure upon both governments (the French and the British) and to insist that they "put an end to every policy of compromise with the totalitarian states and do not enter with them into any discussion aiming at territorial changes."[58] They were, in addition, to give "the moral assurance that the USA had forsaken their isolation policy and were ready, in case of war, to stand actively on the side of England and France, putting all their money and raw materials at their disposal."[59]

In the light of these and other no less eloquent and authoritative documents, one is — irrespective of whatever attitude one might personally have towards National Socialism — compelled to see in the European developments of the fated year 1939, the product of an actual world-conspiracy against National Socialist Germany. Every talk about "Hitler's policy of aggression" is either a shameless, blatant lie or . . . silly women's babble. Adolf Hitler remained, in his dealings with the outer world, after his rise to power — before *and during* the war, as he had, during his struggle against the rotten Weimar Republic, "within legality unto the bitter end." And his policy was one of active and sympathetic protection of *all real national communities*, i.e., of all ethnic communities, not one aiming at their destruction. And such leaders of non-German minority groups as were sufficiently wise to understand that the Versailles Treaty was, through its scorn of ethnography, history, and geography — its scorn of Nature itself — an insult to *their own* people's dignity at the same time as a crime against Germany, readily beheld in the greatest

---

[56] Ribbentrop, pp. 165–66.

[57] Report of the 16 January 1939 (from Count Jerzy Potocki). Report 1-F-10, February 1939 (from Lukasiewicz, Polish Ambassador in Paris).

[58] Report 3/SZ tjn 4 of 16 January 1939 (Count Jerzy Potocki).

[59] Same report 3/SZ tjn 4, of 16 January 1939, dispatched from the Polish Embassy in Washington.

of all Germans the supporter of every genuine, healthy nationalism. President Tiso appealed to him, in March 1939, to protect the new Slovakian state which had, on the 6th of October, 1938, proclaimed its independence from the Czechs. And a month earlier Professor Tuka, another Slovakian leader, had vehemently implored his help against the government of Prague: "I lay my people's fate into your hands, my Führer! My people await from you their complete liberation"[60] (from Czech rule). And, which is more, placed before *the fact* that the artificial Czechoslovakian state was breaking up *from within* (though the sheer unwillingness of its elements to pull together), Hácha, its President, and Chvalkovský, its foreign Minister, and the whole Czech government, which Hácha had consulted, were in agreement with Adolf Hitler's decision to declare "Bohemia and Moravia" a "Protectorate of the Reich" and to send German troops to occupy the land. "Not a word of protest was raised on behalf of the Czechs, and Hácha gave instructions that the German Army should be received with friendliness."[61]

The only protest came, on the 18th of March, from Paris and from London—three days after Chamberlain had clearly declared before the House of Commons that the happenings were in no way a violation of the Munich Agreement, and that Great Britain could anyhow not deem herself bound to defend the existence of a state which had broken to pieces *from within*. The British and French ambassadors were called back from Berlin "to report upon the situation." And in the USA and in all countries vehement newspaper articles and radio comments stressed once more the necessity of "stopping Hitler" in the interest of the "free world." The sincere indignation of millions of people of all races was systematically roused and directed against the Third German Reich, bringing the world another step nearer the war which the Dark Forces were preparing.

The long tension between Germany and Poland—another consequence of the nonsensical situation created by the Versailles Treaty—was, ultimately, to lead to war. It could have come to an end through an honourable agreement. And Adolf Hitler had done everything within his power so that it might.

---

[60] Ribbentrop, p. 148.
[61] Ribbentrop, p. 150.

The proposals he had made to Poland, through the Polish Ambassador Lipski, in view of an honest treaty of good neighbourhood, were not merely reasonable but generous. Admittedly, he had insisted that Danzig—that old German town—should be recognised as part and parcel of the German Reich. But he was, on the other hand, prepared to give up all claims upon the "corridor" linking Poland to the sea through German territory, provided an extra-territorial *Autobahn*, and an extra-territorial railway of several lines, running through it, would assure the undisturbed connection of East Prussia with the rest of the Reich. And he offered the Poles an extra-territorial road and railway of their own, as well as a free port, in the Danzig region.[62] The one fact that stood in the way of further negotiations between him and the Polish government (despite the failure of J. von Ribbentrop's mission to Warsaw in January 1939) was England's sudden "guarantee" of the integrity of the Polish frontiers as they had been fixed by the Versailles Treaty. From a report sent by Raczynski, the Polish Ambassador in London, to his government, on the 29th of March 1939, and found in Warsaw by the Germans during the Poland campaign in the autumn of the same year, it is clear that England's promise of help in case of "attack" on Poland (i.e., England's promise to declare war on Germany—and to start a world war—if Germany were to occupy Danzig) "was given him, orally at any rate, as early as the 24th of March." On the 26th of March—two days later—Lipski, the Polish Ambassador in Berlin, handed over to J. von Ribbentrop a "Memorandum" in which he rejected in the name of his government all the suggestions Germany had made concerning Danzig and the "corridor." "Any further attempt to bring the German plans to materialisation, and especially any further attempt to incorporate Danzig into the Reich, means war with Poland" declared he.[63] On the 6th of April, the Polish foreign Minister Beck signed in London, with England and France, a "tem-

---

[62] Ribbentrop, pp. 155–56. Adolf Hitler's *final* proposals were that a plebiscite should take place in the "Corridor," and that the state that the population would not choose to belong to—be it Poland *or* Germany—would receive in compensation an extra-territorial *Autobahn* and a railway through the contested area.

[63] Ribbentrop, p. 162.

porary agreement" which was soon to be replaced by the permanent Pact which everyone remembers.

That Pact, directed against Germany alone and not against any other possible "aggressor" of Poland, was England's moral excuse—and the German occupation of Danzig, the *occasion* England chose—for declaring the Second World War. In reality, however, as so many documents published after the war abundantly prove, England's "guarantee of the integrity of Poland's frontiers" had been dictated to her (as Poland's own stubbornness in the Danzig question, to Poland) by the pack of Jews and of slaves of Jewry which had been ruling the USA ever since Roosevelt's election to the presidency.[64] It had no meaning and no purpose other than that of being the best thinkable pretext for a Second World War against Germany. The real cause of the Second World War was and remains the hatred of the Jews and of their "millions of non-Jewish friends" and willing or unwilling tools—the hatred of every simpleton who had been impressed by the Jewish lies—for the Man and for the state "against Time" who embodied the true Aryan spirit, and were the forerunners of a world-wide Aryan awakening.

卐 卐 卐

The only thing Adolf Hitler could do in order to avoid the complete encircling of Germany was, indeed—in spite of the profound differences that had, from the beginning, opposed National Socialism and Marxism—to turn to Russia. He had no choice.

Had it not been for England's nonsensical attitude towards him and his people—nay, for the actual madness which she had succeeded in breathing into political life, under the constant pressure of Roosevelt's agents—it may be that he "would have fought Russia without any later conflict with England,"[65] as Joe Kennedy, the American Ambassador in London, himself seems to have believed. It *may be*, I say, for the young Reich needed

---

[64] See Professor Charles Callan Tansill's *Back Door to War: The Roosevelt Foreign Policy, 1933–1941* (Chicago: Regnery, 1952). Also James Forrestal, *The Forrestal Diaries*, ed. Walter Millis (New York: The Viking Press, 1951), p. 121.

[65] *The Forrestal Diaries*, p. 121. Quoted in Ribbentrop, p. 168.

space for its growing population; and also because there was no possible co-existence of true National Socialism and of its sharp and ruthless contrary, true Marxism, *forever*.

As things stood, the Führer was compelled to accept that co-existence for the time being, so that he might try to hold back in 1939 that which was fated to take shape in 1941, namely: the formidable coalition of capitalism and Marxism (or rather, of the Jew-ridden Western plutocracies and of the also Jew-ridden Soviet state) against Germany, the fortress of National Socialism and the hope of awakening Aryandom. One may deplore the fact that he could not accept it or, at any rate, that it did not last for a longer span of time: *no external force could have shattered the mighty bloc formed by Germany, Soviet Russia, and Japan.* Such a bloc, economically self-supporting, would have been invincible, had it not been bound to fall to pieces, sooner or later, from within, being the outcome of an unnatural alliance. It is a tragedy that its dislocation could not be postponed at least till after a definitive victorious end of the war with England (and then, probably, with the USA). The fact that Stalin and Molotov were not Jews; nay, the fact that they were—perhaps—more *Russian* (and pan-Slavist, in the old sense of the word) than Marxist, made the signature of the Russo-German Pact of the 23rd of August 1939 possible. The fact that Jewish influence was as powerful (even if not always *as obvious*) in Russia as in England or in the USA and that it exerted itself within Stalin's most immediate entourage, lies behind Russia's stubborn attitude with regard to territorial questions from the start, and explains her breaking of the Pact and all the marks of growing hostility that were to bring the Führer to declare war on his ally within less than two years. The Pact was, politically speaking, a wise act. It meant the realistic recognition of common interests despite widely diverging faiths. It had to be broken if the enemies of National Socialism were to win the war. And the Jew ultimately exploited Russia's old pan-Slavist tendency against the Third German Reich—apart from any *Weltanschauung*—as cleverly as he had used British and French and Norwegian and Dutch misconceived and misguided patriotism against the same.

But in the meantime, as long as the unnatural but politically masterful alliance lasted, Adolf Hitler had only one enemy to fight, namely the Western brand of anti-Nazism embodied in

Jew-ridden England . . . for the unpleasant Polish affair was brilliantly settled within three weeks, and France brought to her knees within about six months.

This chapter is not a history of the Second World War, but merely a humble attempt at detecting and pointing out, in the light of *cosmic* evolution, the unseen but all-important — the real — factors behind the succession of events. Many of the facts themselves, purposely suppressed by the Allies at the time of the Nuremberg Trial, have, since then, been mentioned by soldiers and diplomats — Germans *and* others — in serious technical memoirs without a shadow of passion. All go to support the thesis I have already put forth, namely, the one that, far from being Adolf Hitler's "crime" or even in any way the result of his policy, the Second World War is the outcome of a world-conspiracy of the Forces *"in* Time," i.e., of the Dark Forces, against him and his Golden Age ideals; against his consistent effort to "establish on earth the reign of righteousness" with the methods of this Age of Gloom, i.e., to build a state, and, through that state, a world-order *"against* Time."

It is now proved that Adolf Hitler's last desperate efforts to avoid war with Poland — his last and generous proposals, sent forth from all German wireless stations on the 31st of August 1939 at 9:15 p.m., and known as the "Sixteen Points" — were made useless through a British declaration to the Warsaw government, that England considered any further visit of the Polish Foreign Minister, Beck, to Berlin — i.e., any further negotiations with Adolf Hitler — as "undesirable."[66] It is now proved that Great Britain alone stood in the way of Mussolini's attempt to secure peace, be it at the eleventh hour, through an international conference, on the basis of a general revision of the Versailles Treaty, that primary source of the whole political tension.[67] It is now proved that Germany's occupation of Denmark on the 9th of April 1940, and that of Norway, were but temporary and *necessary* military measures forestalling and hindering the *previously planned* occupation of the same by British troops, and that,

---

[66] Ribbentrop, p. 200.
[67] Ribbentrop, p. 201.

moreover, both Norway and Denmark had, *before the 9th of April*, given up their neutrality through the conclusion of secret agreements with England.[68] It is proved that the so-called German "attack" on Holland and Belgium was no "attack" at all, but a sheer act of self-defence, considering that the two states had already resorted to "steps of a military nature" aimed at forwarding aid to England and France, which were at war with Germany. It is now proved that not a single military decision in the name of the Third Reich — not the German intervention in Greece, on the 27th of March 1941, to prevent a renewal of the Allied tactics of 1915–1916; not even the "attack" on Russia, on the 22nd of June 1941 — was taken in a spirit of "aggression," but that *all* were motivated (and justified) by previous and easily traceable marks of gratuitous hostility on the part of Germany's alleged "victims."

"God knows I have striven for peace!" declared the Führer before the German *Reichstag*, in that memorable speech of the 4th of May 1941, in which he left no doubts about the reasons that had compelled him to order the occupation of Greece:

> God knows I have striven for peace! But when a Master Halifax sarcastically states that everyone agrees that I have, and boasts of the fact that we were forced into war as of *a special triumph of British statesmanship*, I can, in answer to such wickedness, do nothing else but protect the interests of the Reich by all means which are, thank God, at our disposal![69]

Whatever may be the comments of propaganda in the service of the Dark Forces, dispassionate history — nay, the merciless logic of life itself, which underlies that endless net of causes and consequences which history describes — will one day confirm these words of the one-before-the-last divine Man "against Time." The everlasting Powers — the Shining Ones, Who worked through him, *and* the very Powers of Darkness and Death, the Powers "*in* Time," whom he fought, knew that he was right; knew that the interest of his young Reich was and remains the interest of higher Creation. But, as I said before, practically the

---

[68] Ribbentrop, p. 213.
[69] Adolf Hitler's Reichstag speech, 4 May 1941.

whole world was coaxed into believing him to be a deceiver and a tyrant. And not merely the sheepish average man, who does not think, and who takes all he reads in his morning paper for Gospel truth, but many an otherwise remarkable person, who should have known better, was taken in by the accusation of "wanton aggression" brought against Germany and the broader (and vaguer) accusation of "inhumanity" brought against the proud new Creed of the Swastika. Such an outstanding man as Gandhi — a rare blending of business-like shrewdness and saintly aspirations — declared at the outbreak of the war that his sympathy lay with England and France "from a purely humanitarian standpoint." And in the resolution which the All-India Congress Committee passed at Wardha, on the 8th of August 1942, insisting upon the withdrawal of British rule from India, it was stated that "*a free India would assure success in the struggle against Nazism, Fascism, and Imperialism*," and that "free India" (whose provisional government was immediately to be formed, in case of non-compliance with the withdrawal demand) would "be an ally of the United Nations." Buttressed by Gandhi's moral authority, such declarations as these determined the attitude of millions of men towards Adolf Hitler and National Socialism. They wrought incalculable mischief.

The wonder is not that, less than five years after Adolf Hitler's splendid *Leibstandarte* — glorious foreshadowing of the Golden Age mankind of his dreams — had marched along the Avenue des Champs-Élysées in conquered Paris, National Socialist Germany was forced to capitulate "unconditionally." The wonder is that, facing practically alone the frenzied hatred of the whole earthly sphere, she resisted its assaults as long as she did. The wonder is that, in spite of the enemy's open fury and secret machinations; in spite of the impact of the Red Army (as fanatically convinced of *its* "truth" as every German soldier of his); in spite of the traitors on the front and at home (*all* of them, from the anti-Nazi diplomats and generals and princes of the Church — the men of the 20th of July, and Dibellius, and von Galen, Archbishop of Münster, and the sinister theologian Bonhoeffer and all the leading Freemasons — down to the humblest simple squeamish old woman who was horrified at her grandson's harshness towards the "poor Jews"); in spite of the two gigantic hostile power blocs — the Communist world *and* the Capitalist world—closing in, tighter upon her, every day, National Socialist Germany did not capitulate *earlier*. The wonder is that her armies marched as far as they did into so many conquered lands; and that they and the German people kept their faith in Adolf Hitler till the end and—to a great extent—despite ten years of systematic "re-education," *after* the end, to this very day.

Not only had Adolf Hitler done all he possibly could to avoid war, but he did everything he possibly could to stop it. Again and again—first, in October 1939, immediately after the victorious end of the Polish campaign; then, on the 22nd of June 1940, immediately after the truce with defeated France—he held out his hand to England; not the hand of a supplicant, still less that of a man afraid, but that of a far-sighted and generous victor whose whole life was centred around a creative idea, whose programme was a constructive programme, and who had no quarrel with the misled blood-brothers of his own people, nay, who saw in them, despite their hatred of his name, his future friends and collaborators.

And nearly a month before his second peace offer to England, the Führer had already given the Nordic sister-nation a tangible sign of his generosity—nay, of his friendship, in spite of all, in the midst of the bitterest struggle—and such an extraordinary one that history writers have not hesitated to characterise it as "a wonder." The Allied armies—the British Expeditionary Corps and a remnant of the French troops—were fleeing towards Dunkirk as fast as they possibly could before the German advance; fleeing from the Germans towards the sea. And the German Commander in Chief, General von Brauchitsch had, on the 23rd of May, given the order to press them in from all sides and take the lot of them prisoners before they had time to embark. It was, from the military point of view—*and* from the normal political point of view; from the point of view of immediate success—the thing to do. But Adolf Hitler appeared unexpectedly at General von Rundstedt's Headquarters in Charleville and cancelled the order of attack on Dunkirk. The German armoured divisions—the "A" *Heeresgruppe*, as well as the "D" *Heeresgruppe*, which was, under General von Bock, pressing towards Dunkirk from the East—where to slow down their speed and leave ten kilometres between their foremost ranks and the fleeing enemy. These counter-orders, "that held back the German advance for two days, and gave the British time to bring home safe and sound the most valuable section of their army,"[70] are utterly incomprehensible unless one boldly admits that they were dictated by considerations which exceed by far the domain of "politics" no less than that of strategy; considerations not of a statesman but of a seer.

The generals did not know what to think, but they obeyed: orders were orders.

To anyone who, in the name of a pan-Aryan view of things (or merely in the name of "Europe's" interest) stood—and stands—without reservations, on the side of National Socialist Germany, the tragedy of the situation was—and remains, retrospectively—maddening. The capture or destruction of the whole British Expeditionary Corps at Dunkirk, and the immediate invasion of Great Britain—by parachuted troops, if a proper landing was, on account of the British fleet, impossible—could have, one feels, put an end to the war: crushed rotten, Jew-ridden, West European democracy before the USA had time to save it, and united all Europe under the strong hand of the greatest European of all ages. And that new unity in the spirit of National Socialism would have made Europe the bulwark of higher mankind, not "against Asia," but against the Dark Forces "in Time" embodied in the latest and lowest form of the old superstition of the "value of every man": Marxism; against the Dark Forces which are, with the help of the Marxist doctrine, threatening Europe *and* Asia and the whole world. And the Führer himself destroyed that possibility with one word.

That is, at least, the spontaneous (and superficial) view of the average racially-conscious Aryan, Adolf Hitler's German or foreign disciple. But that was not Adolf Hitler's own view. The Führer's more-than-political and more than strategic intuition

---

[70] Kleist, *Auch Du warst dabei. Ein Buch des Ärgernisses und der Hoffnung* [You Were There Too: A Book of Scandal and Hope] (Heidelberg: Vowinckel, 1952), p. 278 (quoted by Grimm, *Warum? Woher? aber Wohin?*, pp. 364–65).

reached "far beyond any quickly concluded, timely peace."[71] It grasped—whether he was himself in a position to *exteriorise* that vision of things or not—the only *real* earthly peace that ever was and ever can be: the peace of the coming Golden Age, of the far-gone latest one, and of *all* successive Golden Ages; the peace of this earth whenever the visible world-order is in full harmony with "the original meaning of things,"[72] i.e., with the invisible and eternal cosmic Order, as it is, in fact, at every great new Beginning and at no other time. *That* peace excludes such bitterness as is bound to arise as the consequence of the humiliation of a great people. Adolf Hitler did, therefore, all he could to spare England the humiliation of total defeat. The baffling orders he gave on that fatal 23rd of May 1940—the date Germany "began to lose the war"[73]—and the astoundingly generous peace proposals he laid a month later before the English, have no other significance.

Rudolf Hess' much misunderstood, lonely heroic flight to Scotland as a desperate, self-appointed peace-maker, on the 10th of May 1941, has also no other significance. It was, on Hess' part, neither the rash action of a man half-insane (as it *had to be* described, officially, for the sake of convenience, and as Rudolf Hess himself wished it to be described, in case of failure) and still less an attempt at rebellion against the Führer's policy; an effort to end the war *against his will*. Quite the contrary! Rudolf Hess undertook his long-planned flight, doubtless *without* Adolf Hitler's knowledge, as all the details of the event (and especially Hess' own last letter to the Führer), clearly show. But he was guided from the start by the unfailing certitude that his was *the* supreme chance—if any—to bring about, in the teeth of the most adverse circumstances, that which the Führer had, in vain, always wanted, and always striven for: lasting peace with England—the sister-nation, in spite of all the insults of her Jew-ridden government and press; the great Aryan power, in spite of her betrayal of the Aryan Cause—constructive collaboration with England, first step towards the constructive collaboration of all peoples of the best Nordic blood.

---

[71] Grimm, *Warum? Woher? aber Wohin?*, p. 367.
[72] *Mein Kampf*, p. 440.
[73] Grimm, *Warum? Woher? aber Wohin?*, p. 367.

Rudolf Hess failed — in the realm of visible facts, at least — as Adolf Hitler himself was destined to fail, and for the very same basic reason: namely because he is, like he, one of those uncompromising idealists *and* men of action whose intuition of permanent earthly realities exceeds and overshadows the vision even of the most compelling emergency; one of those men, "against Time" — both "Sun" and "Lightning" — who have in their make-up too little "lightning" in proportion to their enormous amount of "sun." (In fact, of all the Führer's paladins, none — not even Hermann Göring; not even Goebbels, who was so passionately devoted to him — seems to be so deeply *like him* as Rudolf Hess.)

England's answer to Adolf Hitler's repeated peace proposals was, after a categorical "no," an intensification of her war effort, and a hardening of her war methods.[74] England's answer to Rudolf Hess' supreme appeal to her sense of responsibility before the dead, before the living, and before the yet unborn was . . . a cell in the Tower of London (and, later on, in Nuremberg, and finally in Spandau, to this day) for the daring self-appointed messenger of peace. England's answer to all the understanding and friendliness that National Socialist Germany had showed her from the very beginning, her answer to Adolf Hitler's sincere profession of faith in Anglo-German collaboration; her answer to his unheard-of generosity at Dunkirk was . . . war to the finish: hundreds and thousands of bombers — one wave after the other, in tight formations — pouring night after night (and often in the daytime) streams of fire and brimstone over the German towns, and on the other hand — unlimited, *enthusiastic* aid to Soviet Russia, no sooner had Adolf Hitler declared war on her. England's answer to the German Führer's repeated plea for honest pan-European anti-Bolshevistic solidarity rooted in the consciousness of common Aryan blood (or of a high proportion of it at least) resounded in Churchill's jubilation at the news of the "second front," thanks to which the German forces were now divided. Churchill — the anti-Communist, but still wilder anti-Nazi — declared: "The cause of Soviet Russia is now the cause of every Englishman." England's answer was, in August 1941, the Atlan-

---

[74] It is now proved that England began her mass bombing of civilian populations on the 11th of May 1940; see on that point J. M. Spaight's book *Bombing Vindicated* (London, Geoffrey Bles, 1944).

tic Charter—an open alliance with the main tool of Jewry in the USA, President Roosevelt, who (although the USA were not *yet* at war with Germany) now ordered actual firing at every German ship the Americans met on the high seas. England's answer was two years later the Yalta and then the Potsdam Agreements between Churchill, Roosevelt, and Stalin: the sinister coalition of the Western plutocracies and of the Marxist Empire—of *all* the forces "*in* Time"—against National Socialist Germany; the coldblooded planning of Germany's dismemberment and enslavement forever; and the relentless advance of the crusaders of hatred from the East and from the West, until their two hosts of hundreds of thousands, in one of which there were Englishmen, had met and merged into each other over the martyred Land. England's answer was, through British accusers along with others, the shameful distortion of history in the Nuremberg Trial, the condemnation of the peace-maker Rudolf Hess for "crimes against peace," and the prolongation of the whole propaganda of infamy against both the National Socialist doctrine and the German Nation, to this day.

Maybe, the Jew-ridden United States of America have, under the Freemason Franklin Roosevelt, played an even greater part than that of England in the preparation, conduct, and gruesome conclusion of the Second World War. But England is the nation to which Adolf Hitler had, over and over again, the most sincerely, the most appealingly held out his hand, in the name of the natural brotherhood of Nordic blood, in the name of the peaceful regeneration of the West. Her crime against him, against his people, against herself and the whole Aryan race, is therefore greater than that of any other of the Allies of 1945. *And nothing — absolutely nothing — can ever make good for it.*

It is, as I said before, a tragedy that the unnatural but, for the sake of immediate expediency, brilliantly conceived alliance of Germany, Soviet Russia, and Japan did not endure at least till the war with England—and, if necessary, with the USA—was brought to a victorious end. But, whatever many people (and, more specially, the sympathisers of Communism) may think, it is *not* through Adolf Hitler's fault that it did not. Russia—not

Germany—first broke the Pact of August 1939. She broke it in her haste to expand westwards and southwards, towards the Baltic coast and towards the Balkans and the Mediterranean (the Adriatic and the Aegean Seas); in other words, in the resumption of her old tendency to pan-Slavism, be it at the expense even of non-Slav populations. Or perhaps would it be more accurate to state that the coalesced forces of world Jewry, nearly as powerfully represented in Soviet Russia as in the USA, *used* that old Russian tendency (as they had used England's short-sighted chauvinism and commercial jealousy) in order to reach their own end: the encirclement and destruction of National Socialist Germany—which was Adolf Hitler's personal opinion.[75]

The occupation of the Baltic states[76] and their final incorporation into the Soviet Union on the 3rd, 5th, and 6th of August 1940, contrarily to Stalin's agreement with J. von Ribbentrop "not to change the inner structure" of such lands as he would take into his "sphere of interests"; the Russian occupation of the whole of Bessarabia—including North Bukovina, with its mainly German population—and then, the exorbitant conditions which Molotov put (during his visit to Berlin in November 1940) on Russia's proposed adhesion to the Axis[77] and, last but not least, the support which Stalin gave Simovitch and the other members of the anti-German conspiracy who, in March 1941, seized power in Yugoslavia, and soon declared war on Germany, all contributed to renew and, gradually, to increase to the breaking point the tension which the Pact signed on the 23rd of August 1939 had temporarily suppressed between the Third Reich and the leaders of the Marxist Empire. The last interference, immediately following the signature in Vienna of the treaty which was to make Yugoslavia a member of the Axis, was particularly resented by the Führer as an act of hostility.[78] It certainly was, both in fact and in spirit, a flagrant violation of the Pact of 1939.

---

[75] Ribbentrop, p. 242.

[76] Lithuania—including the part of it designated, in the Pact, as in the German "sphere of interests"—in June 1940, and, soon afterwards, Lettonia [a.k.a. Latvia—Ed.] and Estonia.

[77] See Chester Wilmot's book *The Struggle for Europe* (London: Collins, 1952).

[78] Ribbentrop, p. 225.

It is, however, Adolf Hitler's refusal to accept Molotov's conditions in November 1940, which made that unfriendly Communist interference possible, by cancelling all hopes of closer collaboration with Soviet Russia. The truth is that such collaboration could only have lasted as long as political (and more specially, strategic) necessities were sufficiently compelling to overshadow the profound opposition between the two régimes, nay, between the two faiths, of new Russia and new Germany: Marxism, and its contrary, National Socialism. It could hardly have been expected to endure more than a short time *after* a victorious conclusion of the war with the Western slaves of world Jewry. The problem was, at most, how to make it endure *till then*. And the only practical way, to make it endure was to give in—for the time, at least—on all the line; to accept the Russian Ambassador's conditions without even discussing them.

Exorbitant as they were, those conditions—withdrawal of all German troops from Finland; conclusion of an additional pact between Russia and Bulgaria (i.e., gradual absorption of Bulgaria into the Marxist Empire); strategic bases on the Bosphorus and Dardanelles to be granted to Russia; recognition of a Soviet sphere of influence South of the Caucasus; and Japan's renunciation of her privileges in North Sakhalin—may well seem *today*, to many an average observer, be he himself a sincere National Socialist, ridiculously mild in comparison with the terrible consequences of the disaster of 1945. Apparently—one is, retrospectively, tempted to think—was it not worthwhile accepting even such conditions, rather than running the risk of opening a second front, and what a gigantic one?

The right answer—the only answer—to that question, is: "From a purely political (or military) standpoint—from the standpoint of *immediate* necessity, regardless of further consequences—yes; it was, no doubt; from the more-than-political standpoint of the selfless seer—i.e., 'in the interest of the universe,' to use the language of the immemorial Book of Aryan Wisdom, the Bhagavad-Gita, the spirit of which is, in our times, embodied in genuine National Socialism—no, and a thousand times no."

It is notable that, by choosing war with Russia instead of a Russian alliance at the expense of Finland and Bulgaria and all the countries menaced by the undue expansion of the Marxist

Empire (ultimately, at the expense of the whole world) Adolf Hitler acted, as he had already in several important circumstances, against the suggestions of his entourage, and not merely of most of his generals, but also of his Foreign Minister, J. von Ribbentrop, who had signed the Pact of August 1939. "During these months" (preceding the declaration of war on Russia) says the latter, in his Memoirs:

> I missed no opportunity of trying to bring about a definitive Germano-Russian alliance, in spite of all. I believe I would have reached that goal, whatever might have been the difficulties, *had it not been for the opposition of the two philosophies*, opposition on account of which no foreign policy could be carried out. First from an ideological point of view, and then because of Russia's attitude, because of her military preparations coupled with her demands, *the vision of an enormous danger imposed itself upon Adolf Hitler's mind*. In addition to that, the news of Anglo-Russian conversations, of Sir Stafford Cripps' visit and of his negotiations with the Kremlin government, acted upon, him in a disquieting manner.[79]

In other words, the Führer took the terrible risk of a second front rather than become—and make the German people, in whose name he was conducting the war—responsible for such an expansion of Soviet influence as, *even after a complete German victory in the West*, would automatically have placed half the world under the control of the mighty citadel of Marxism. He acted in full consciousness of Germany's natural mission as bulwark both of the Aryan race and of the eternal Aryan values, rooted in the race, against every possible threat of the Forces of disintegration, be it from the East or from the West. Such a threat was, in June 1941, admittedly more apparent in the West than in the East; Russia was preparing herself for war, but England was *at war* with the Third German Reich. Nay, it was becoming more and more obvious that the USA would soon join the struggle on England's side. And the Führer *knew* in what danger Germany would be, when America *and* Russia would "simultaneously

---

[79] Ribbentrop, p. 237.

throw in against her the whole bulk of their power."[80] Yet, he knew also that a Russian alliance, sealed through his acceptance of the co-existence of a National Socialist Germany — be it of a National Socialist Europe — and of a tremendous Marxist Empire stretching from the Aegean Sea to the Bering Straits, would be, *in the long run*, no guarantee against the absorption of Aryan man into that ugly, raceless, and characterless sub-humanity typical of the end of this Dark Age. He knew it precisely because, being himself infinitely more than a politician, he thoroughly understood the more-than-political meaning of the war which was imposed upon him: *not* the usual clash between rival ambitions of a similar nature, but a world-wide coalition of all the forces that I have called "*in* Time" against the one modern state "*against* Time": the National Socialist state. He knew that Marxism — and *not* the diluted (and, moreover, obsolete) forms of Jewish poison for Aryan consumption known as Christianity and Western democracy — is *the* final man-centred faith in the service of the Dark Forces; *the* doctrine destined to urge mankind to take its last step along the old way leading from primeval Perfection to the fated depth of degeneracy, and ultimately to death. Surely there could be — and can be — no *definitive* co-existence of a powerful National Socialist Order either with a Marxist Order *or with a Capitalistic one of the Western type*. But, of the two, the Marxist Order, being, according to the hard logic of increasing decay, the vigorous young successor of the other, is the most dangerous. To strengthen Russia's position as the conquering Marxist power, in order to buy her temporary alliance against the West, could have seemed, to a statesman (were he of genius), who would have been a statesman and nothing more — let us say, to a German counterpart of Winston Churchill — merely an unpleasant political necessity within a clever diplomatic game. To Adolf Hitler, the Seer, the Man "against Time" — the One-Who-comes-back in His modern garb — it appeared as the very betrayal of Germany's mission, nay, as the very denial of Germany herself. For no spectacular victory over England and the USA would have spared new Germany, real Germany — Germany, the fortress of the National Socialist faith; the one modern Nation "against Time" — the assaults of a Marxist Em-

---

[80] Ribbentrop, p. 239.

pire bent on ideological and political expansion, which the possession of key positions in Europe and Asia would have rendered formidable. A German counterpart of Winston Churchill would doubtless have been hypnotised by the immediate interest of the Reich (or what appeared as such) and have lost sight of the Reich's significance. The Man "against Time" knew that the two were not to be separated. He knew that, precious as it surely was in the practical field, the Russian alliance was not to be bought at the cost of the possibility of crushing Marxism in the future; for the regeneration of Aryan man implies the defeat of the agents of the Dark Forces on *all* fronts, and the end of *all* forms of the age-old Jewish lie.

And, accepting the responsibility and risks of the double struggle, he took the tragic decision of declaring war on the expanding Soviet Union, on the 22nd of June 1941. He hoped, no doubt, to reduce it to submission within a few months, after which he would have been free to continue to fight the slaves of world Jewry in the West, with endless resources at his disposal. He was, however, aware of the gravity of his decision. "If ever we be compelled to break through the door in the East, we do not know what power lies behind it," had he told J. von Ribbentrop.[81] And yet, he gave the word to "break through" — for it was the only thing he could do, in keeping with the unbending, more-than-political, nay, more-than-human logic of his personality, of his mission, and of Germany's; in keeping with the cosmic logic "against Time," which had determined the growth and success of National Socialism, and which was now provoking this fatal turn in history.

The Russian campaign presented undeniable natural difficulties. One had, among other things, to reckon with the terrible conditions created by the Russian climate — the bitter winter that had protected Russia against all invaders (save the Mongols). And the inexhaustible man-power which the Soviet Union could afford, regardless of losses, to throw into the battle — that fanaticised Red Army composed of all the races of North and Central Asia (and of Russia herself) under very efficient Russian com-

---

[81] Ribbentrop, p. 240.

mand—was doubtless a tremendous force. A force, also, those hundreds of thousands of partisans who, full of the same unwavering faith in the Marxist ideology, or simply in "Mother Russia," led a relentless guerrilla war against the German occupation troops.

Yet, during the particularly severe winter of 1941-1942, the German Army victoriously stood the test of unheard-of hardships; exceedingly low temperatures—35 and 40 degrees under the freezing point—coupled with unusually primitive indoor conditions of life in *isbas* full of vermin. And although it was, on account of hostile weather, prevented from capturing Moscow, it reached, in the course of 1942, such a remote front line as no European invaders pushing Eastwards on that latitude had yet attained. The Swastika Flag fluttered above the everlasting snows of the Caucasus, at the top of Mount Elbruz, and on both sides of the Volga, and on the shores of the Caspian Sea. And the activity of the Russian partisans had yet anything but developed into a menace. A normal evolution of the campaign would doubtless have reduced it to nought and secured Germany a complete victory over the Marxist Empire and a lasting control of the limitless Eastern expanses, source of no end of raw material for the growing industry of the Greater Reich.

On the other hand, Japan—who, through her well-known attack on Pearl Harbor had stepped into the war on the 7th of December 1941—had conquered the Isles of the Pacific and all South-East Asia: Indo-China, Malaya, with Britain's great Eastern stronghold, Singapore, and Burma, up to and even past the border of Assam and Bengal. And for a time the hope that the two advancing armies, bearers of the two banners of the Sun, would meet and greet each other upon Indian soil, and that Adolf Hitler would soon receive in old Indraprastha, the seat of legendary Aryan Kings—now imperial Delhi—the solemn allegiance of the whole Aryan world (Europe and Aryan Asia) while leaving his Japanese allies to organise the Far East, that unbelievable hope, I say, that superb dream of glory, did not seem unjustified. No amount of desperate efficiency on the part of the fanatical, disciplined, but insufficiently equipped Red Army—and surely no number of ill-inspired Indian Congressmen's resolutions condemning in one breath "Nazism, Fascism, and Imperialism," and no "free India's willingness to become the ally of the United Nations"[82]—could have, apparently, stood in the way of its materialisation.

In fact, however, the splendid hope was a short-lived one. Instead of a rapid and definitive victory over the Marxist Empire—a victory which would have allowed Germany to concentrate her whole war-effort upon the Western front—came, in January 1943, the disaster of Stalingrad, where the Sixth Army and many thousands of auxiliary troops (22 divisions in all) were trapped and cut to pieces, despite acts of superhuman heroism. And then, after this tragic turning point in the evolution of the war in Russia, a series of setbacks: the immobilisation of the German forces before Leningrad, the stemming of the German offensive in the Caucasus, and the recapture of Kursk, Belgorod, Rostov, Kharkov, Krasgorod, and Pavlograd, one after the other by the Russians, in the course of February 1943.

With the sincerity and detachment that characterise him, Adolf Hitler could not help seeing in that desperate and successful reaction of the toughest of all Germany's enemies a further glaring proof of "what a single man can mean to a whole nation." Any people, declared he to his Foreign Minister, J. von Ribbentrop, "would have broken down after such defeats as the German Army had inflicted upon the Russians in 1941–1942. The present Russian victories are the work of an iron personality, that of Stalin himself, whose unbending will and courage have called his people to a renewed resistance." . . . "Stalin" said he, was "the great opponent" he had, "both ideologically and in the military realm." And he added, with the natural chivalrousness of a real warrior, that, were that irreducible opponent ever to fall into his hands, he "would respect him, and assign to him as a residence the most beautiful castle in Germany."[83] (One cannot help comparing that treatment reserved to Stalin in the case of a National Socialist victory, with the one that the coalesced leaders of democracy and of Marxism—the crusaders of world Jewry—were actually to inflict upon the members of the German government after the war, not to mention the no less atrocious manner in which they *would have* handled Adolf Hitler

---

[82] See the resolution of the All-India Congress Committee of August 1942.
[83] Ribbentrop, 263.

himself, had they succeeded in capturing him. Nowhere, perhaps, does the contrast between the inspired Man "against Time" and the mean, short-sighted men "in Time" of the end of this Dark Age, appear more clearly.)

There is truth—and *a lot* of truth—in the Führer's generous homage to Stalin's greatness as a determining factor in the evolution of the Second World War. That greatness does not, however, suffice to account for the fatal change of fortune of which the tragedy of Stalingrad is but one of the first signs. Nor can, I repeat, Russia's inexhaustible man-power coupled with harsh climatic conditions account for it. The complete and cynical explanation of it has been given on several occasions, and, among others, on that of the American "Independence Day," the 4th of July, 1950, by Mr. (since then, Sir) Winston Churchill himself: *"Alone America and England have prevented Hitler from pushing Stalin behind the Urals."* [84]

In other words, no amount of man-power organised in a spirit of desperate resistance could have kept the German Army from conquering Russia (and pursuing its triumphant march through Central Asia and Afghanistan to and beyond the easternmost limits of Alexander's empire) had it not been for America's and England's direct and indirect help to the Communists; had it not been for the fantastic quantity of arms, ammunition, and equipment that the USA sent over, in order to make the Russian (and other) partisans increasingly dangerous, and the Red Army irresistible; had it not been for an ever closer and more effective collaboration of the two sinister tools of world Jewry in the West—Roosevelt and Churchill—*and of their misled people* with the Marxist Empire, in the political, strategic, *and psychological* realm: the intensified bombing of the German civilian population by British and American planes, and the intensified anti-German propaganda financed by England and the USA (and more specially by the Jews of those countries) in all lands occupied by the German Army *and in others also*, all over the world, calling the whole world to take part in the "Crusade" against National Socialism; the British landing in Libya; the Allied landing in Sicily and, a year later, in Normandy; and the

---

[84] Churchill's speech, the 4th of July, 1950. It is quoted by Grimm in *Warum? Woher? aber Wohin?*, p. 385.

stubborn refusal of the Western democracies to put an end to the war until Germany had surrendered "unconditionally"; in one sentence, had it not been for the readiness with which England and the USA — and practically the whole earth, under the influence of their tremendous propaganda — accepted (and acted up to) the statement broadcast by Winston Churchill at the news of Adolf Hitler's declaration of war on Russia (and all the more impressive that the British Prime Minister was universally known to be an *anti-Communist*): "The cause of Soviet Russia is now the cause of every Englishman, nay, that of the entire freedom-loving world."

The historical landmarks in the development of the combined "crusade" against National Socialist Germany — the hypocritical Atlantic Charter, as early as mid-August 1941; and then, the well-known successive agreements of Casablanca, in January 1943, of Teheran, in November of the same year, of Yalta, in February 1945, and finally Potsdam, in August 1945, destined to tighten the grip of the Death-forces upon the world from pole to pole — are all immediate and logical consequences of the spirit of that sentence. And so are the no less historical horrors that were to take place on German soil and elsewhere *after* the two victorious waves of destruction — the Red Army, and Eisenhower's "crusaders to Europe" (and their British and French, and Belgian and Polish and Czech satellites) — had met and mingled upon the smoking ruins of the proud Third Reich: in Dresden, overcrowded with refugees, the murder of half a million men, women, and children under Anglo-American bombs, on that dismal night of the 13th of February 1945; the lamentable exodus of 18 million Germans — also men, women, and children — from the eastern provinces torn away from the Reich to be given to the Poles, the Russians, or the Czechs, with the full approval of Soviet Russia's Western allies; the atrocities of the Red Army and of the soldiers of the capitalistic democracies of the West in Germany, and of the anti-German partisans in all countries of Europe; the arrest, torture, and murder (or long imprisonment) of thousands of National Socialists, from the martyrs of Nuremberg to the humblest of Adolf Hitler's followers, for having done their duty thoroughly and faithfully; and, until 1948, the criminal attempt to kill Germany's industry and to starve her people or force them to emigrate; and, until this very day — in *fact*, if no longer in name—that sinister farce known as "de-Nazification" and "re-education" of the German people: the systematic attempt to crush the pride, nay, to kill the soul, of the finest nation of the West.

Soon after the Japanese attack on Pearl Harbor, which had prompted Germany's declaration of war on the USA, i.e., more than a year before the war was to enter its critical and decisive phase, J. von Ribbentrop told Adolf Hitler "We still have one year's time to cut Russia off the supplies she receives from America through Murmansk and through the Persian Gulf, while Japan must take Vladivostok. *If that cannot be done*, and if American armaments and Russian man-power succeed in coming together, then the war will enter a stage in which it will be very difficult for us to win it."[85] And the Führer had "taken this remark in silence and made no comments."[86] He made no comments because there were none to make. J. von Ribbentrop had spoken the truth—a tragic truth, indeed. And Adolf Hitler knew it. And he knew also that nothing could alter it.

J. von Ribbentrop had seen and described the situation from a political and strategic point of view. Adolf Hitler saw it, or rather felt it, intuitively, as the result of the interaction of forces infinitely more than political. It is foolish to believe that he could have avoided the difficulties the diplomat was pointing out to him, by not declaring war on the USA. The USA had declared war upon him and upon National Socialist Germany, *in fact*, if not officially, as early as 1937,[87] and had increasingly and openly been helping England's war effort since 1939. They actually *were* England's allies—and Russia's—*before* Adolf Hitler's formal declaration of war came as an answer to that alliance and as an act of solidarity with Japan. There was nothing which the German Führer could do, save to face the great event of our epoch with all his—and all his people's—determination, and to fight to the bitter end a war in which Germany's existence was at stake. By "the great event of our epoch" I mean the coalition of the Dark Forces of the whole world—of those forces which I have called forces "in Time" —against the one living reminder of all the glo-

---

[85] Ribbentrop, p. 260.
[86] Ribbentrop, p. 260.
[87] Ribbentrop, p. 164.

rious great Beginnings of the past, and the one living herald of the coming one: the state "against Time" at the very end of this Age of Gloom.

And Adolf Hitler, the Seer, the Man "against Time" — the creator, nay, the soul of that extraordinary state — knew that this coalition, of which the Jews were, no doubt, the earthly instigators, but *nothing more* than the mere instigators, was and remains *a cosmic fact*; a sign of the times. And that is precisely why he faced it as he did: refusing to the end all compromise with Soviet Russia, in spite of J. von Ribbentrop's repeated suggestions,[88] and all compromise with the Western agents of world Jewry, in spite of the repeated suggestions of other important men of the National Socialist Party and, which is more, of his generals; and treating with more and more mercilessness — through the *Reichsführer S.S.* Heinrich Himmler, to whom he gave increased powers — *all* actual or potential enemies of the New Order, and, among these (apart from the German traitors that one was lucky enough to detect) the two main varieties of moral slaves of Jewry — the Christians and the Communists — and especially the Jews themselves. "As the war followed its course," states J. von Ribbentrop, "the Führer became more and more anchored in his view of it as the result of an international Jewish conspiracy against Germany."[89] I would say more: not only did Adolf Hitler see in the Jews as a nation the secret instigators of this as well as of the last World War, but (and his writings and his whole career go to prove it) he thoroughly understood their real, deeper meaning in world history; their cosmic meaning as hereditary embodiment of the darkest forces "in Time," foremost agents of that more and more rapid corruption and downfall of the naturally higher races, so impressive as the end of the present Time-cycle draws nigh.

And that is why he knew — and proclaimed at every opportunity, from the start — that the struggle he was conducting in Germany's name was, for the German people and for *Aryan humanity at large*, a life and death struggle.

---

[88] Ribbentrop, pp. 236–39.
[89] Ribbentrop, p. 211.

It proved materially impossible to prevent, within a year, American supplies from reaching Russia. And far from capturing Vladivostok, Japan did not even declare war on Germany's most irreducible opponent (with whom she had, on the 13th of April 1941, sealed a non-aggression pact). Japan, as I said in the beginning of this study, went her own way—the way *she* deemed the most likely to secure her domination over East and South-East Asia and to solve her own "living space" problem—without realising that her active contribution to Russia's defeat, in coordination with Germany's new war effort, would have brought her, in the long run, nearer to her goal than all her spectacular victories in the South Seas, Malaya, and Burma. As for Italy—whose partnership had been for Germany, from the start, more of a liability than of an advantage—less than six weeks after Mussolini's fall from power she hastened to betray her great ally in her "most critical hour,"[90] as she had in the First World War. The formation of a new—separate—Fascist government in North Italy (after Mussolini's dramatic rescue from captivity, by Skorzeny) was of no practical avail. By the end of 1943, National Socialist Germany was alone—pressed between the two coalesced halves of a world in rebellion against the eternal Idea that she had more or less consciously embodied throughout history, and that she now proclaimed, louder and more defiantly than ever, through Adolf Hitler's voice; alone to fight not on "two" but on a thousand fronts: against regular armies and against partisans in Russia, in Greece, in Italy, in Africa, in France, in Belgium, in Holland, in Norway—everywhere—and, at home, against increasingly destructive British and American bombers and increasingly active and arrogant German traitors, anti-Nazis of all descriptions; alone to stand against the thought-power and will-power and power of hatred of millions and millions of men, women, and children of all nationalities and of all races; of a whole Dark Age humanity, bent upon its own degeneracy and doom; marked with the sign of perdition and, for that very reason, blind and mad: exalting its enemies and holding its true saviours in abomination. And it is difficult to say which one of

---

[90] Mussolini fell from power in July 1943; Italy capitulated and entered the war on the side of the United Nations (under the Badoglio government) on the 8th of September 1943.

the hostile factors—the "crusaders" from the East and from the West; the German traitors at home *and on all fronts*; the relentless streams of fire which men of Anglo-Saxon blood poured night after night upon the helpless German civilians, killing *over three million* of them; or the silly, but sincere (and therefore efficacious) indignation of millions of apparently powerless people of all lands, as they repeatedly heard on the wireless about the "Nazi monsters"—played the crucial part in the disaster of 1945.

To the extent the happenings of the invisible realm determine those of the visible, one can safely state that untiring hatred is, from the cosmic point of view, as efficient as power of arms. The victorious Allies—or rather the Jews, who animated the whole show—were, at the Nuremberg Trial, after the war, to put forth the principle of "collective responsibility" and (strange as this may sound from someone who has exposed the famous Trial as one of the greatest infamies of history) they were, in *that* connection, again from the cosmic point of view, rigorously right. Anyone whose heart and will have carried Adolf Hitler to power, whose voice has hailed him as Founder and Leader of a new world, was and remains morally responsible for all that has been, is, or ever will be done in his name and in his spirit. I am the first one to accept this fact. And I accept it joyfully, with pride, as far as I am personally concerned. On the other hand, the principle of collective responsibility cannot be restricted to any particular group of people to the exclusion of other groups. It holds good for *all* those who admit a bond of solidarity with brothers in faith—or be it brothers in hatred—and, in particular, for all anti-Nazis, whether they be ill-informed or not, intelligent or not, capable or not of judging in full liberty. A child of ten who sat before his parents' wireless in Calcutta or Shanghai, and was glad to hear the news of the Allied landing in Normandy— the 6th of June 1944—is responsible for the world-disaster of 1945. A child of ten who, in Sydney or Melbourne or San Francisco, added his voice to the chorus of hatred against the accused of Nuremberg, is responsible for the death (or long imprisonment) of those men, and bears his share of the infamy of the historic Trial. As I said before, the Second World War is nothing less than a monstrous crime *for which practically the whole world is collectively responsible*—a collective crime of the whole world against its Saviour, Adolf Hitler, against National Socialist Germany, against Aryan man and the possibilities that lie within him. It is the crime of the whole world which has completely yielded to the law of Time, i.e., the law of decay and death, against the last—or one before the last—grand scale expression of the age-old counter-tendency "against Time," which the natural aristocracy of blood and character—the élite of the Aryan race—has been embodying, more and more consciously, for centuries already.

Among the millions who bear the guilt for it, the German anti-Nazis—from those high officers who, on the 20th of July 1944, attempted Adolf Hitler's life, to the most unimportant and inactive opponents of the National Socialist régime—occupy a special place, or rather, have a special significance. Being Germans—the Führer's own countrymen, whom he so loved—they represent more than any others the waste of natural Aryan virtues in the service of untruth; the grip of the Dark Age even upon the finest race of this earth; the defiling of the Aryan mind through false teachings of "humanity" and principles in contradiction with the laws and purpose of Life. And one should add that, along with them, and to a hardly lesser degree, *all* anti-Nazis of Nordic stock—Norwegians, Danes, Dutchmen, or Britishers (or Americans of Nordic origin, such as the sinister "Crusader to Europe," Dwight Eisenhower, himself)—represent the same. For National Socialist Germany was not fighting the war imposed upon her for herself alone, but for the whole of higher mankind; for the reassertion of the eternal natural values and of the natural human hierarchy, i.e., for the rule of truly higher mankind upon this earth (irrespective of "nationality" in the narrow sense of the word).

Speaking of the future Europe of his dreams and of the splendid Aryan élite that was to lead it, Adolf Hitler said that it "mattered little" whether a member of that élite were "an Austrian or a Norwegian."[91] All that counted in his eyes was that the ruling aristocracy be, physically, morally, and culturally, a real Aryan one. The same idea, namely that National Socialist Germany was but the first step towards a regenerate National Socialist Europe, is most clearly expressed in the last known text

---

[91] Adolf Hitler's *Tischgespräche* [Table Talk], published after the war.

dictated by the Man "against Time": his "Political Testament."[92] And one may add that a National Socialist Europe is, logically, but a first step towards a racially-conscious and legitimately proud Pan-Aryandom, organised according to Adolf Hitler's principles—accepting him as its everlasting Leader—and occupying in the world the place Nature has assigned it.

As I wrote in another book,[93] every person of Aryan blood—be he or she a thoroughbred European or a high-caste Indian—who fought Germany during the Second World War, and thus hindered the materialisation of that glorious programme, is, hardly less than the German anti-Nazis themselves, a traitor to his or her own—to *our common*—race.

Others have described—or tried to describe—far better than I (who was not on the spot) ever could do, the last days of the Third German Reich: the irresistible advance of the two frantic invading armies (and of their respective auxiliaries) into the heart of the land, in which *years* of unheard-of bombardment had left nothing but ruins; the terror of the last and fiercest air raids that disorganised everything, while streams and streams of refugees kept pouring westwards (realising that they had, in spite of all, less to fear from the Americans—enemies of National Socialism with *no* faith to put in its place—than from the Russians, who were fighting in full awareness of their allegiance to the contrary faith); the horror of the last desperate battles, intended to immobilise for a while an enemy that one now knew to be the winner; and the moral breakdown—the frightening, blank hopelessness, the bitter feeling of having been mocked and cheated—of millions in whose hearts faith in National Socialism had been inseparable from the certitude of Germany's invincibility: the "moral ruins," even more tragic and more lasting than the material ones. Others have described or tried to describe the horror of the last days of Berlin under the relentless fire of the Russian guns—Berlin, which, seen from above,

---

[92] Published by L. Battersby.
[93] In *Pilgrimage* (Calcutta: Savitri Devi Mukherji, 1958), written in 1953–1954, Introduction.

"looked like the crater of an immense volcano."[94]

In the midst of the capital ablaze, stood the broad and yet untouched gardens of the Chancellery of the Reich. There, surrounded by a few of his faithful ones, in his "bunker," underground, Adolf Hitler, the Man "against Time," lived the apparent end of all his life's work and of all his dreams, and the beginning of his people's long martyrdom. More or less accurate reports have reached the outer world about his last known gestures and words. I have just mentioned the publication of his "Political Testament." But nobody has described in all its more-than-human grandeur the last real *inner* phase — the tragic failure, and yet (considered from a standpoint exceeding by far that of the politician) the culmination — of his dedicated life.

Throughout the war and before the war, for two-and-a-half decades, Adolf Hitler had conducted Germany's struggle (and that of Aryan man) — the modern aspect of the perennial Struggle for the triumph of Light and Life — against the coalesced forces of the whole world. And he had not lost faith in victory, not even when everything seemed to turn against him and his people: not even after Stalingrad; not even after the Allied landing in Normandy; not even after the Russians and Americans and their satellites had marched into Germany from the East and from the West, and were advancing, every day deeper into the heart of the torn and blasted land, in spite of desperate resistance and useless counterattacks. "He lived in a dream"[95] a French author has written, in a heart-rending book. And that is true, in a way — partly because deliberate traitors purposely kept him ill-informed about the actual situation on every front, in every occupied country, and in practically every essential service at home (as it clearly appears, from various most outspoken war memoirs), and partly because he was himself more of a Seer than of a politician. He knew he was deceived and betrayed — "See how they lie to me, and for how long already!" declared he, in 1944, to the *Luftwaffe* hero, Hans-Ulrich Rudel, after a talk in which the latter had given him the right picture of a war sector

---

[94] These are the words of the well-known German airwoman, Hanna Reitsch, who *saw* it.

[95] Georges Blond, *L'Agonie de l'Allemagne, 1944–1945* [The Agony of Germany, 1944–1945] (Paris: Fayard, 1952).

where he had himself fought. But he did not know till very late—*too* late—to what extent one betrayed him. (He admitted it himself in his last speech.) The confidence he put in any German who *seemed* entirely devoted to the National Socialist Idea was complete. And traitors took advantage of it.

He also "lived in a dream" in the manner every great Seer has done, from the beginning of the ages. Aware as he was of the absolute truth of his doctrine, and of the absolute genuineness of his mission and of that of his people, and knowing, as he did, that truth is bound to conquer in the long run, he was tempted to underestimate the power of the Death-forces that are, in accordance with the law of evolution in Time, to drag the world to its doom *before* the new Golden Age (and, with it, a new Time-cycle) can dawn. The clear vision of eternal, infinitely more-than-political, earthly reality (of earthly reality "in harmony with the primeval meaning of things") towards which he strove throughout his career, had made him, for years, blind to the terrible signs of impending disaster. The certitude that the German Reich, as he had wanted it and founded it anew and organised it at the end of this Dark Age, was the first step towards the glorious earthly Reich of re-conquered Perfection—the regenerate Aryandom of the awaited Golden Age—and that the advent of that Kingdom of gods on earth was as mathematically positive a fact as sunrise after every night, made him, for years, at least, forget that the Third German Reich—the state "against Time," his own creation—had to disappear before it could rise again, transfigured into a Golden Age state.

He had, no doubt, in the course of the war, become more and more conscious of the enormity of the forces set against him, both abroad *and* at home; more and more aware of widespread, lurking treason; and especially more and more convinced of the sinister part played by world Jewry in the conduct of events.[96] From 1942 onwards, he had, nay—with Heinrich Himmler's ever closer collaboration—faced and tackled the Jewish question—at last!—with some amount of that ruthlessness with which it should have been tackled years before. *But it was too late.* That tardy mercilessness—that delayed awakening of the righteous "lightning" side of his nature, in him who, as I said in the begin-

---

[96] Ribbentrop, p. 273.

ning of this book, had, in his make-up, more "sun" than "lightning" — could no longer save the Reich. The mass-liquidation of about 750,000 Jews[97] from Germany and other European countries in the gas chambers of Auschwitz and of a couple of other concentration camps did not prevent the influential Jews, living in safety in the USA, in England, in Russia, in India, in Palestine — anywhere in the wide world — from directing the fury of all mankind, including that of the Aryan nations, against new Germany. (And after the war, when the fate of the few executed Jews — who were — unfortunately! — by the way, not necessarily the most dangerous ones — became known in foreign lands, the figure of 750,000 became overnight 6,500,000 and even 8,000,000, in older to give the victorious Allies, "crusaders of humanity," an excuse for torturing and killing as many of Adolf Hitler's followers as they could. While thousands of the most nefarious Jews had, thanks to the Führer's astounding generosity, already left Germany before the war.)

Similarly, the severity with which were handled such conspirers against the National Socialist régime as were detected near the end of the war — the men of the 20th of July, for instance — did not prevent others from continuing, undetected, their treacherous activities. Nor could it undo all the mischief wrought, from the beginning of the régime, by those men in high position who were secretly bent upon its destruction at any cost, even at that of the destruction of Germany herself, along with it. Harsh, exemplary repression of such elements also came too late. More so: Adolf Hitler's mistrust of all classes of his own people, save of the honest, simple-hearted workmen, faithful to him to this day,[98] came too late. And that, I repeat, because, contrarily to the Prophet Mohammed, contrarily to Lord Krishna, and to all Men "against Time" — both "Sun" and "Lightning" — who died victorious, our Führer had, in his personal make-up, too much sunshine in proportion to his "lightning" power.

---

[97] This figure was given to me by an S.S. officer. The Jewish publication *Shem* — written *for Jewish readers* – states, however, about half that number only.

[98] That mistrust of all but the working classes is often expressed in the Führer's *Tischgespräche* — conversations of his published after the war.

The World Against Its Saviour

And now, the end had come. Adolf Hitler no longer "lived in a dream." He knew that the supreme counter-offensive—the Ardennes offensive—had failed to stem the advance of the Western Allies. He knew that the Russians had, on the other hand, broken through and crossed the Oder River and that they were massing around Berlin. In a desperate effort to hope against all hope, he kept on mentioning General Wenck's army—which in fact no longer existed—and waiting for it to appear and free the capital of the Reich. But he knew within his heart that General Wenck would not come; that the war was finished—and lost. And he could well imagine the atrocious ordeal that his people were now to experience at the hands of the agents of the Dark Forces—their enemies and his.

The Russian guns kept on firing without cease. And Berlin continued to burn. It had been burning for days. It had become a down-right inferno.

In the depth of his "bunker" under the yet untouched gardens of the Chancellery—Adolf Hitler could hear the thunder of the explosions and feel the death-convulsions of his capital, through the torn and battered earth. And he knew it was the end

Within the "bunker," a few faithful ones—Eva Braun, who had never thrust herself into the limelight of the Great Days, but who loved him, and was now his wedded wife; Dr. Goebbels, with his family; General Krebs, Admiral Voss, Martin Bormann, and some others—were waiting with him to kill themselves at the appearing of the Russians. At the entrance of the gardens and of the "bunker"—on the margin of that roaring and flaming hell that was rolling nearer and nearer, as irresistible as an ocean of lava—S.S. men kept watch, ready to die. There they remained, with as much impassibility, as much dutiful detachment as those Roman guards of old who, in 79 A.D. had stood at the gates of Pompeii—there where their officers had ordered them to stay—under the showers of burning ash from the suddenly erupting volcano; within sight of the streams of molten rock, till the end; till they had lost consciousness and sunk to the ground under their armour, while the advancing lava rolled over them. But the stream that was to roll over the bodies of these last defenders of the Third German Reich and to submerge half (and, soon, perhaps, *all*) Europe, was the inexhaustible Red Army; the most formidable human instrument in the service of the levelling forces. Of the heroic state "against Time" — Adolf Hitler's creation — no trace would be visible after its passage. And those very men of Nordic blood, traitors to their race, those "crusaders to Europe" who were, now, welcoming and helping its advance, would be, one day — soon — wiped away before it.

Unaware of that atmosphere of cosmic disaster (for such it was) which has been compared to that of a living "Twilight of the Gods," the six Goebbels children — Helga, twelve years old; Hilde, eleven; Helmut, nine; Holde, seven; Hedda, five; and Heide, three — as prettily dressed as in peace time, thanks to their heroic mother, played hide and seek in the corridors of the last unconquered fortress of National Socialist Germany. Sometimes, the Führer, or those of the S.S. men who were not on duty, would play with them, or tell them stories. A day or two before the end, the famous airwoman, Hanna Reitsch, piloted General von Greim to the "bunker" and stayed there a few hours with him. Magda Goebbels told her, among other things: "They believe in the Führer and in the Third Reich; when these cease to exist, there will be no place in the world for my six children." And she added: "Provided Heaven gives me enough courage to kill them!" The admirable woman actually did kill them. And she and Dr. Goebbels killed themselves afterwards.

According to the writing that has been published as his "Political Testament" and to the statements of several people who were present in the "bunker" *nearly* to the end, Adolf Hitler and his wife, Eva, did the same. According to other, equally plausible assumptions, they left the "bunker" in time — *not* in order to save themselves, but in order to continue the struggle, one day — and the Founder of the National Socialist faith still breathes somewhere upon this earth, several years after the destruction of his life's work, ready to inspire the new rising of his trusted ones to power and to preside over the new triumph of the Swastika, that nothing can hold back. There is no actual *proof* this way or that, but only — as years pass without bringing any sign of his being alive, an increasingly strong *probability* that the Führer did not survive Germany's total sacrifice.

This may be, no doubt, a depressing fact for his disciples, nay, a heart-rending fact for such ones among them who never had the honour and the joy of seeing him. From the cosmic point of view, it matters little; for Adolf Hitler's significance remains just the same whether he be, in the flesh, visible or invisible, alive or dead. Alive or dead he remains the hero who, in our atrocious epoch — very near the end of the Dark Age of the present Time-cycle — stood alone, at the head of his privileged people, against the fiercer and fiercer downward current of Time; against the whole world that had become (as in every successive Dark Age) the domain of the forces of disintegration and death, exalting and obeying their agents while hating every genuine Messenger of Life. Alive or dead, he has sacrificed himself for his people; and his sacrifice (and that of his people for the entire Aryan race) is just as complete in either case — nay, if he be alive, his life must have been all these years, many times worse than death. Alive or dead he *is* He Who comes back "age after age, when justice is crushed, when evil triumphs, to establish upon earth the Reign of Righteousness";[99] the Man "against Time" Who, again and again in the course of history, *and every time with the methods of the age in which He appears*, fights for that ideal of integral perfection — of absolute *health* — that no Age save a Golden Age — an "Age of Truth" — can live on a world-wide scale, in all its glory. Alive or dead, he is eternal, *and will come back, for he is He*: the One Who spoke for all times through the most ancient known discourse of Aryan Wisdom, the Bhagavad-Gita.

In the "bunker" within the gardens of the Chancellery — last material bastion of National Socialism amidst Berlin ablaze — he dictated his "Political Testament." It is difficult to say whether the wording we possess of it is the right one or not. If, as some say, the Führer survived the disaster, the mere mention of his "voluntary death" within the document would be enough to make it inaccurate. But, whatever be the wording, nay, whatever be the debated facts themselves, *the spirit* of Adolf Hitler's last known message and the serenity one breathes in it — the calm, unshakable certitude, even at the darkest hour, that truth will conquer in the end, in spite of all — are genuine. The glorious vision of a "united and National Socialist Europe," the formation of which represents "the work of centuries to come," is genuine.

---

[99] The Bhagavad-Gita, IV, verses 7 and 8.

The consciousness and pride of Germany's historic mission, in particular, of the mission of that splendid German youth who bore Adolf Hitler's name, as forerunner, inspirer, leader, and organiser of a regenerate Aryan humanity within *and beyond* the geographic boundaries of the Reich, are genuine. Genuine, and not new; for the Reich-Idea, in a more-than-political sense, had always held *the* main place in Adolf Hitler's life.

In August Kubizek's biography of him as a young man, there is a passage too significant for me not to quote it nearly *in extenso*. It is the description of a walk to the Freienberg (a hill overlooking Linz) in the middle of the night, just after the future Führer and his friend had attended together, at the Opera, a performance of Richard Wagner's *Rienzi*. "We were alone," writes Kubizek:

> The town had sunk below us into the fog. As though he were moved by an invisible force, Adolf Hitler climbed to the top of the Freienberg. I now realised that we no longer stood in solitude and darkness, for above us shone the stars.
>
> Adolf stood before me. He took both my hands in his and held them tight — a gesture that he had never yet made. I could feel from the pressure of his hands how moved he was. His eyes sparkled feverishly. The words did not pour from his lips with their usual easiness, but burst forth harsh and passionate. I noticed in his voice even more than in the way in which he held my hands, how the episode he had lived (the performance of *Rienzi* at the Opera) had shattered him to the depth.
>
> Gradually, he began to speak more freely. The words came with more speed. Never before *and also never since* have I heard Adolf Hitler speak like he did then, as we stood alone under the stars as though we had been the only two creatures on earth.
>
> It is impossible for me to repeat the words my friend uttered in that hour.
>
> Something quite remarkable, which I had not noticed before, even when he spoke to me with vehemence, struck me at that moment: *it was as though another Self spoke through him*; another Self, from the presence of which he

was as moved as I was. In no way could one have said of him (as it sometimes happens, in the case of brilliant speakers) that he was intoxicated with his own words. *On the contrary!* I had the feeling that he experienced with amazement, I would say, that he was himself *possessed* by, that which burst out of him with elemental power. I do not allow myself a comment on that observation. But it was a state of ecstasy, a state of complete trance in which, without mentioning it or the instance involved in it, he projected his experience of the *Rienzi* performance into a glorious vision upon another plane, congenial to himself. More so: the impression he had received from that performance was merely the external impulse that had prompted him to speak. Like a flood breaks through a dam which has burst, so rushed the words from his mouth. *In sublime, irresistible images, he unfolded before me his own future and that of our people.*

Till then I had been convinced that my friend wanted to become an artist, a painter, or an architect. In that hour there was no question of such a thing. He was concerned with something higher, which I could not yet understand. . . . *He now spoke of a mission that he was one day to receive from our people, in order to guide them out of slavery, to the heights of freedom.* . . . Many years were to pass before I could realise what that starry hour, separated from all earthly things, had meant to my friend.[100]

It is shattering to recall, in the light of the "Political Testament," that extraordinary episode from the time Adolf Hitler was a young man of 17. The serenity of the Führer's last known message, dictated under the fire of the Russian guns, becomes all the more impressive. It is the serenity of that bright starry night that had surrounded him and penetrated him as he had, 40 years before, taken full consciousness of his mission for the first time. Then, the grandeur of his destiny had overwhelmed him. And the mysterious greater Self that had revealed it to him had appeared to him as "another Self," not his own. Now he knew the

---

[100] Kubizek, pp. 140–41.

two were the same. Now, the destiny was accomplished. The Way of glory and sorrow had come to its end. In a few hours — perhaps in a few minutes — the enemy would be there, and the last symbolical bastion of National Socialist Germany — the "bunker" in the gardens of the *Reichskanzlei* — submerged.

And yet . . . Calmer now, amidst the thunder of explosions and the noise of crumbling buildings — the flames and ruins of the Second World War — than *then*, at the top of the Freienberg, under the stars; freed from the temporary wild despair that had seized him at the news of the Russian advance West of the Oder River, Adolf Hitler beheld the future. And that future — his own, and that of National Socialism, and that of Germany, who had now become, forever, the fortress of the new Faith — was nothing less than eternity; the eternity of Truth, more unshakable (and more soothing) in its majesty even than that of the Milky Way.

The Russians could come, and their "gallant Allies" from the West could meet them and rejoice with them upon the ashes of the Third Reich (as Winston Churchill and his daughter Sarah, who were actually to be seen, a few days later, giggling with Russian officers before the skeleton of the *Reichstag*); Berlin could be wiped out — or "Bolshevised" — and Germany, cut in two or in four, could, for years and years, suffer such an ordeal as no nation in history had yet suffered. In spite of all, National Socialism, the modern expression of cosmic Truth applied to sociopolitical and cultural problems, would endure and conquer. "The heroism of our soldiers, who have kept towards me feelings of unfailing comradeship, is a guarantee that a National Socialist Germany and a united National Socialist Europe will, one day, take birth," wrote Adolf Hitler in his "Political Testament." "May my faithful ones keep in mind that it is the job of the coming centuries to establish a National Socialist Europe, and may they place collective interest always above their own! . . . May they — Germans *and non-Germans* (all the forces of National Socialist Europe) — *remain racially conscious, and resist without weakness the poison which is about* to corrupt and kill all nations: the spirit of international Jewry."[101]

The tragic state "against Time" which he had set up as the one possible dam against the everlasting forces of decay, and

---

[101] Adolf Hitler's "Political Testament."

which now lay in the dust, would one day rise again on a pan-European (or even a pan-Aryan) scale, in all the vigour and splendour of regained youth. It would rise under the leadership of the One Who is to put an end to this Dark Age; of the One-Who-comes-back, under His last aspect—*equally* "Sun" and "Lightning," whereas Adolf Hitler, more "Sun" than "Lightning," is but His one-before-the-last Incarnation. It would rise again as the Golden Age theocracy to come—a theocracy *from within*, the earthly kingdom of Aryan gods in flesh and blood.

And the atrocious end? The agony of the proud Third German Reich? It was but the beginning of the *Via dolorosa* leading to the great New Beginning. All the horror of the present and of the immediate future would pass. The hell in which the German people were to live, for years, would pass. National Socialism would rise again *because it is true to cosmic Reality*, and because *that which is true does not pass*. Germany's *Via dolorosa* was, indeed, the Way to coming glory. *It had to be taken*, if the privileged Nation was to fulfil her mission absolutely, i.e., if she was to be the Nation that died for the sake of the highest human *race*, which she embodied, and that would rise again to take the lead of those surviving Aryans who are—at last!—to understand her message of life and to carry it with them into the splendour of the dawning Golden Age.

Oh, now—now under the ceaseless fire and thunder of the Russian artillery; now, on the brink of disaster—how the Man "against Time" clearly understood this!

Above him and above the smoke of the Russian cannons and of the burning city, above the noise of explosions, millions and millions of miles away, the stars—those same stars that had shed their light over the adolescent's first prophetic ecstasy, 40 years before—sparkled in all their glory, in the limitless void. And the Man "against Time," who could not see them, knew that his National Socialist wisdom, founded upon the very laws of Life; his Wisdom that this doomed world had cursed and rejected, was, and would remain, in spite of all, as unassailable and everlasting as their everlasting Dance.

9. The Man Against Time

Chapter 15

GODS ON EARTH

Today—ten years after the disaster of 1945—when half the world is shivering and shaking before that which it calls the "Communist danger," nothing seems more out of date than the old alliance of the capitalistic states with Soviet Russia (and the Communist forces of all countries) against National Socialist Germany. People who never had anything to do with National Socialism—sincere Catholics who are, at the same time, sincere French patriots, such as Professor Maurice Bardèche—expose the stupidity of the anti-German policy of the Western democracies, which led to the war, and the iniquity and folly of the Nuremberg Trial—that glorification of treason—and the folly of a "de-Nazification" effort which, if successful, can only throw Germany into the arms of Soviet Russia. Nay, such a notorious anti-Nazi as Sir Winston Churchill admitted publicly, only a couple of years after the end of the war, that the Western Allies had "killed the wrong pig," meaning—in glaring contradiction with his own former words and actions—that it would have been more reasonable for the enemies of Communism to help National Socialist Germany to crush Russia, instead of helping Russia to crush National Socialist Germany and then to "Bolshevise" half of Europe and then three-quarters of Asia. The sinister world-wide coalition without which Adolf Hitler would, no doubt, have won this war, appears more and more as a bad bargain in which the leading diplomats of Soviet Russia—and Stalin (that old fox!) at the head of them all—"did" their gullible partners of the capitalistic camp with masterful skill. And the Anglo-Saxon politicians who prepared the Agreements of Teheran and of Yalta and of Potsdam, and those who signed them, and those who welcomed them, and the millions of newspaper-reading sheep who, under the anti-Nazi intoxication of the time (and the subsequent atmosphere of "war crimes" trials and of "de-Nazification") found them wonderful, now feel small and bitter at the idea of having been "done"—nay, so thoroughly "done"!—and are taking to hate Soviet Russia, the fortress of conquering Communism, as violently—and as unintelligently—as they ever hated National Socialist Germany.

Many a *political* sympathiser of National Socialism in and outside Germany beholds this fact with unconcealed satisfaction and says: "The wheel is turning—so much the better!" *But this is not true*; not true, at least, in the sense it is meant. It is not true, because it is contrary to the laws of evolution in Time—to the laws of Life—that a world, or even half a world, should halt on its way to perdition and try to go back, against the current of history. The wheel of history is turning. It never stopped doing so. But it is not turning towards the general acceptance, still less towards the broad-scale glorification of National Socialism, the typical Wisdom *"against* Time." On the contrary! It is turning as it has been ever since the fall of man, i.e., ever since the end of the far-gone latest Golden Age, in the direction[1] of the stream of Time: towards untruth, towards chaos, towards degeneracy and death—further and further *away from* the Wisdom of salvation embodied, age after age, in all true Men "against Time" and nowadays in Adolf Hitler and his disciples. It cannot turn otherwise, as long as the *last* Man "against Time"—the victorious Destroyer-and-Creator, equally "Sun" and "Lightning," Who will put an end to this humanity and to this Age of Gloom and open the coming Time-cycle—has not manifested Himself.

What gives so many people the illusion that the growing anti-Communism of a large section of post-war mankind is necessarily linked (or susceptible of becoming, one day, linked) with a change in the world's attitude to National Socialism, is a blissful ignorance of the true nature of the latter *Weltanschauung*. It is, in particular, the error which consists in taking it for a purely political doctrine, while it is, in reality, infinitely more than that; the ignorance of its character "against Time," i.e., of its cosmic significance and place. It is, also, the ignorance of the true nature of the world-wide anti-Nazi coalition that caused the Second World War and finally broke the power of the Third German Reich. That fatal coalition of hatred against the Hitler faith is also something more-than-political. It is, as I have tried to show in

---

[1] Replacing "sense." Savitri uses the English "sense" to mean "direction," as if it were equivalent to the French *"sens,"* which means both "meaning" and "direction." —Ed.

the preceding chapter, the logical alliance of all the agents of the Dark Forces against the one doctrine "against Time" and the one state "against Time" in our epoch. The Dark Forces are just as alive, just as active, now, after the war—after *their* victory—as during or before the war; nay, more so, as every day brings us nearer the unavoidable "end of the world." The fact that their various agents have started quarrelling among themselves does not mean that they have ceased being what they always were, namely, agents of disintegration and death—still less that any of them has suddenly become an agent of regeneration. They are, now—all of them—becoming blind to their deep similitude and are exaggerating their differences and forgetting their common origin and their common purpose *only because the one obstacle that stood in their way*—the National Socialist state, with that unassailable Wisdom "against Time" that underlay all its institutions—is no longer there. *Were it, before their doom, to rise again, again they would automatically coalesce against it.*

The alliance of the capitalistic world with the citadel of Marxism may now appear, *politically*, as a bad bargain for the "Christian West." In fact—from the standpoint of cosmic truth—it was and remains a most natural and reasonable bond: that of all those who believe the old Jewish lie against those who boldly and boisterously expose it, that of all those who share the superstition of the value of the two-legged mammal as such, against those who proclaim, in defiance of the spirit of this and of all fallen Ages, against the tendency of history—"against Time"— the merciless Doctrine of human selection and of Detached Violence, leading to the kingdom of living gods on earth. More so: it was, *ideologically*, on the part of Russia's former "gallant allies," a step dictated by an unfailing instinct of self-preservation. They, whose philosophy of life rests upon the old and obsolete form of the man-made and man-centred creed—upon the Christian *values*, whether or not, also upon the Christian metaphysics—ran, for the protection of their very *raison d'être*, for the defence of all that they were accustomed to love, to those who uphold the selfsame creed of man in its new, young, materialistic form, feeling quite rightly that they alone could help them, if the creed and all it meant to them—the love of *man*, the cult of *man*, pity for *man, as he is*, with all his weaknesses, and the artificial barrier between him and the rest of Creation—were to survive. They ran to them spontaneously, as old men run to young and strong ones for protection against other young and strong ones of a different world.

Now that they have to pay the price for Russia's help—the price for the survival of their precious "human values," which Russia alone (Russia who, deeply speaking, *shares them*) could save for a time—and that they find it too high, they see, in it, the "Communist danger." They forget who their once only possible ally against that danger was, and what he signified. They forget that the price they would have had to pay *him* (in the long run) for being freed forever from the "menace of Asia" mobilised under Russia's leadership, was nothing short of a definitive, irrevocable renunciation of that man-centred scale of values, which is dearer to them than anything else. For Communism is the natural product of evolution of capitalistic democracy, while National Socialism is the flat negation of it—a revolt against its spirit. The Marxist values—centred around the love of *all men* irrespective of race (of all men as potential "workers")—*are* the Christian values within a technically advanced world in which the notion of an "immortal soul" is rapidly losing all appeal. The National Socialist values are the negation of these as well as of all man-centred ones.

The Western Allies of 1945 believe National Socialism is dead. That is why they feel safe to quarrel with Soviet Russia and to speak of a "Communist danger." The youngest expression of *their own values* "in Time" frightens them, because there no longer is, now, a powerful state "against Time," bearer of the eternal life-centred values and denial of theirs, to remind them, through its sheer existence, of that which surely is, from their point of view, *the* greatest danger of all, namely, of the unavoidable advent of the *last* Man "against Time" and of the dawn of a new Time-cycle.

In his remarkable book *Warum? Woher? aber Wohin?*, Hans Grimm, who never was a National Socialist, but who understands, better than many a German who once called himself one, the nature and grandeur of Adolf Hitler's mission, writes, among other things:

And had he [i.e., the Führer] been able to say, in full awareness, from the beginning: "We are, in consequence of human fertility, from which a false 'humanitarianism' has taken away the restrictive interference of Nature, faced with a smothering of Europe under a flood of invading masses from the East. We Germans are the first to be threatened. We can and must raise a dam against that mass-inundation. In order to be in a position to do so, we must again, physically and morally, take root in ourselves and in our race, and put an end to nonsensical quarrels for power among our own people; then, we must be given living space according to our number and abilities, as others have, or we must conquer that living space there where no valuable creation risks to be spoilt. And this must now become our accepted moral goal, for indiscriminate breeding coupled with mass-levelling means accelerated sinking into decay. But the Creator has made man healthy in body, spirit, and soul, and wishes him to remain so, and every glance at Nature all around us — at Nature uncorrected by man, in which alone the healthy and fit to live are allowed to survive — confirms this point of view." . . . Had he dared to say *that* after the successful seizure of power . . . *would not the whole world have, then, defended itself even quicker than it actually did against him and against his institutions and against us?*[2]

In these words lies the secret of the apparently strange coalition which started the Second World War, which persecuted National Socialism as long as it could after Germany's defeat, and which is, in spite of all protestations of "anti-Communism" on the part of the Western democracies, still persecuting it, preventing, at least, its free expression. Through the sinister alliance of the Western plutocracies and of the Marxist Empire — the alliance of Christianity as it has come down to us (and also of humanitarian Free Thought) *and* Communism — against National Socialist Germany, the fallen world of this advanced Dark Age was, indeed, just "defending itself"; defending the erroneous principles which have been, more and more completely, for

---

[2] Grimm, *Warum? Woher? aber Wohin?*, pp. 155–56.

centuries, governing its thoughts, its feelings, and its life; the erroneous—anti-natural—values which its conscience has gradually evolved or accepted since the far-gone day decay began to set in, and which it has more and more cunningly glorified, as decay increased and spread; defending its very existence as a Dark Age world "in Time."

I have tried, in two former chapters,[3] to explain what this means, insisting upon the fact that the state of present-day humanity (including that of the noblest races) is the natural and unavoidable result of millenniums and millenniums of ever-increasing aloofness from the primeval divine pattern of the Universe, in other words, from primeval life in Truth. I have also tried to show the part played by that extraordinary nation, the Jews, in our advanced Age of Gloom, which can, historically, be considered as *their* particular reign.

At the beginning of our Time-cycle (as it is shown in the myth of the Garden of Eden, which the Christians borrowed from the Jews, and the latter from immemorial non-Jewish sources) man—Golden Age man, in all his pristine health and beauty—was a perfect part of a perfect Creation, in harmony with himself and with it; with every living being, which he at first respected. "Sin"—the cause of degeneracy—consisted not in man's rebellion against a man-loving "God" distinct from the Universe and "Maker" of it in the manner an artisan is the maker of a pot or of a watch, but in rebellion against that divine living Nature of which man was and remains a part and nothing but a part. It consisted in man's implicit claim to dominate and even to "change" Nature for his own ends and, as time passed and as "civilisation" spread, in his increasing contempt for the silent daily example given him by less evolved (but also less corrupt) living species, still faithful to the spirit and purpose of Creation; in his deliberate transgression of the laws of Life for the sake of pleasure, temporary convenience, or mere superstition. In other words, it consisted—and consists—in the sacrifice of the divine whole to the part, and of the future to the present,[4] of the Universe to "man" and of every human race to the individual, and

---

[3] In chapter 1 and in chapter 14.

[4] M. Edmond Goblot, the French logician, used to define all sin as "a sacrifice of the future to the present."

of the individual's own immortality in his race and of his proper mission in the universal scheme, to a passing whim or a tiny, selfish "happy life."

It is noticeable that in this Dark Age—the only one, the *historical* evolution of which we can somewhat follow—religion itself has become, everywhere (in practice at least, when not also dogmatically) more and more man-centred and more and more individualistic.

The Bhagavad-Gita, definitely *life*-centred—the Gospel of detached action "in the interest of all creation" (and not only of "man")—expresses, whatever be the epoch in which it was *written* in its present form, the Wisdom both "above Time" and "against Time" of the Ages *preceding* ours. (The *epos* in which it is inserted is significantly placed by Tradition *before* our Age of Gloom.) The great religions of escape that took birth in Ancient India—Buddhism, Jainism—are, no doubt, life-centred. But they are religions of escape, doctrines of integral pessimism with no bearing, in fact, upon this earth. In *practice*, their devotees, in or outside India, and even their ascetics, have little to do with that truly universal and active love which prompted the Blessed Buddha, in one of his many marvellous lives (so the *Jatakas* relate) to give up his own body to feed a hungry tigress; little to do, nay, with the moral attitude behind that legend. One only has to see, in Buddhist countries, the general indifference to all creatures' suffering, for which the passers-by are not directly responsible, and the indifference of most Jains or so-called such to the misery of animals other than cows, to be convinced of it. In addition to that, they reject not only the traditional form but the very spirit of the caste system: the idea of the natural hierarchy of human races. They reject it in perfect keeping with the logic of their attitude of escape from life. The result of this is, however—as I have tried to show in another book[5]—the lowering of the biological quality of the whole bulk of them who are *not* committed to an actually monastic life. And this levelling provides, in its turn, the ground for the development of a man-centred philosophy in *practice*, be it against the logic of the original faiths.

But it is in Christianity and Islam, the great international

---

[5] See *Gold in the Furnace*, pp. 147–51.

equalitarian religions rooted in Jewish thought, that the man-centred tendency, characteristic of our fallen world (and more especially of the advanced Dark Age) appears in all its strength. There, far from being an attribute of the faithful, in contradiction with the philosophy that they are expected to profess, it is buttressed by that which is, perhaps, *the* fundamental dogma of these religions (so fundamental that, save in exceptional cases, it survives as a moral postulate in the hearts of those who have rejected all "articles of faith" once connected with it) namely: the dogma of "human dignity," i.e., the unquestioned belief in "man," irrespective of race or personal worth, as *the* creature set apart from all creatures; God's darling, infinitely valuable. It is, in fact, this dogma — expression *par excellence* of the general human tendency "in Time" — that secured these religions their immense success in the Near East and in the West (where they spread) and in the further East and in the whole world, where their moral influence is undeniable, even there where they met and still meet the most fanatical opposition.

One may not — and, it would seem, one *should* not — think that the two prophets, whom the religions exalt as their respective founders, implicitly adhered to that already old dogma, denying the unity of Life. I have said in this book (and elsewhere) that I personally look upon Jesus Christ, whose race is uncertain, to say the least, and whose teaching, anything but Jewish, as a man "above Time," and upon the Prophet Mohammed (who, contrarily to him, dreamed of a new Order of justice *on earth*, and used violence to establish it) as a man "against Time." No really great Leaders of that type can share with fallen humanity a belief contradicting the harmonious indivisibility of Creation. It is, however, not Jesus Christ but Paul of Tarsus who gave Christianity its impulse as a conquering religion, and Christendom its historical character as a community "in Time," exploiting (in disfiguring it, and *adapting* it to Dark Age conditions) a doctrine originally "above Time," intended for small groups of unworldly devotees, never for the questionable "faithful" of a church numbering millions. As for the great warlike Man "against Time," Mohammed, founder of a theocracy *in this world* which he was to establish by frankly using the methods of this world and, which is more, of this Dark Age (and not by pretending to scorn them while using them nevertheless, as the Christian churches did), I have already said of him: he was endowed with more "Lightning" power than "Sun" — the very reason for which he was, in our Age of Gloom, able to triumph during his own lifetime. The enormous concessions he made to the weaknesses and superstitions of the Dark Age — in particular to that dogma of the "dignity of every human being" and to the corollary conception of a community of *faith*, destined to spread over the whole earth, destroying or absorbing all the former communities of blood — were weapons in his hand; weapons without which he never would have overcome his rival Christianity in North Africa as well as in West Asia and laid the basis of Islamic civilisation.

One may not, also, trace that now so broadly accepted dogma necessarily to a Jewish *origin*. Religious books that have no connection whatsoever with Judaism — the Popol-Vuh, of the Maya-Quiches of Central America, for instance — lay stress upon it with no less insistence, and even more childish candour perhaps, than the Bible does. Chandidas and certain other exponents of 14th- and 15th-century Bengali Vaishnavism, have implicitly — and sometimes explicitly — adhered to it.[6] And if the spirit expressed in it be precisely that which provoked, in the mist of an unreachable past, the fall of Golden Age mankind (as one should believe, in accordance with the logic of evolution in Time), then it is much older than the Jews themselves. *But it is certain that it has become one of the most obvious postulates of Jewish thought, from the very dawning of the latter onwards*, and that it has asserted itself more and more with the development of philosophical speculation among the Jews and with the evident (or subtle) growth of the influence of Jewish thought in the advanced Dark Age. Man is, *irrespective of race and personal worth*, according to Jewish tradition, "made in God's own image," while other creatures, however perfect they be as samples of their kind, and however noble, are not. And the Kabbalah defines man — also irrespective of race and of personal worth or capability — as "the creature who, in his turn, creates," in double opposition to God — the Non-Created Who creates — and to the whole non-human living world, "creatures who do not create." And from the time outwardly Hellenised Jews, settled in cosmopolitan, Greek-speaking Alexandria, started systematically

---

[6] See p. 248, note 63.

"blending" Greek ideas with their own "esoteric" doctrines— i.e., from the 4th century B.C.—to the present day, the whole development of thought and religion could, in the West at least, I repeat, be defined as centred around an increasingly tyrannical belief in the so-called "dignity of man" as opposed to all other living creatures.

That belief is as much the *outcome* of the fatal mixture of races which characterises fallen humanity in general and especially Dark Age humanity, as it is, on the other hand, the promoter of ever deeper physical and moral degeneracy, through further mixtures—further sinning against the blood of the superior races, in the name of an erroneous conception of life. And in the eyes of whoever studies history in the light of cosmic Truth, the 4th century Before Christ—the beginning of the "Hellenistic period" in the annals of the Near East, which are inseparable from those of imperial Rome and of the "Christian West"—should be considered as the beginning of the last part of the present Dark Age, of which we are, now, nearing the end. Accelerated decay had, no doubt, already set in amid the Greek world (as elsewhere) *before* the foundation of Alexandria. It had set in, and was spreading—a sinister sign of the times. But the confusion that started in 323 B.C.—after Alexander's sudden death—gave it a new impulse (much against the spirit and intentions of the Conqueror).

The latter had, better than any of his most broad-minded contemporaries, understood the necessity of transcending that strictly Hellenic—be it *pan*-Hellenic—patriotism, that sharp distinction between Greek and non-Greek expressed in the words: "*Pas me Hellen Barbaros.*"[7] Yet, far from setting the example of such internationalism as many modern ideologists would doubtless like to attribute to him, he drew a very definite line between one sort of "non-Greeks" and the others. He encouraged his pure-blooded Macedonians to marry *Persian* women—Aryans like themselves who merely spoke a different language and had different customs—but, significantly enough, not women of other races. And both his own foreign wives were of Aryan blood. In other words, whether he acted in this connection in full, clear consciousness, or through some vague intuition—an intuition of

---

[7] "If not Greek then barbarian" —Ed.

genius, however vague it might have been — he seems to have been, in our advanced Dark Age, one of the first great forerunners of *true* racialism as opposed to narrow state-patriotism, a practical champion of the idea that racial similitude should help to break down artificial barriers between people, being, moreover, as it is, *the only reality* in the name of which the suppression of such long-accepted accepted barriers is justified. One should not make him responsible for the shocking blood-mixtures that took place all over the Near East at a yet unheard-of rate, *after him*. They were fateful — as I said: signs of the times. And consequences of a rapidly spreading man-centred attitude to life, for the generalisation of which the Greek-speaking Jews of all the important trade and culture centres of the Hellenic world, especially of Alexandria, bear the heaviest responsibility.

Outspoken racialists with regard to their own people, but active promoters of anti-racial internationalism in the midst of other nations, it is they, the everlasting "ferments of disintegration," chosen agents of the Death-forces in our advanced Dark Age, who prepared, through multifarious "esoteric" adaptations of Hebrew ideas to Greek philosophy (and, at the same time, through intensified intimacy with women of all races in all the seaports of the Mediterranean) the double conditions for the development of a great international, man-centred, anti-racial, and anti-natural religion, intended, in the course of centuries, to deliver the West — and, through the growth of Western influence, the world: teeming bastardised masses, and an *intelligentsia* entirely won over to a man-centred philosophy — into their hands. Whether to their own knowledge or not — certainly to the knowledge and under the pressure of those invisible Powers of Darkness who rule the visible world more and more absolutely as one millennium succeeds the other in the Age of Gloom — they made possible the career of such a man as Philo the Jew, also called Philo the Platonist,[8] who paved the way which the Fathers of the church and, after them, so many Christian writers were to tread. Their intellectual internationalism, rooted in that idea of the "dignity of man" which is so perfectly expressed in the Jewish Kabbalah, drew the thinking Greeks of Alexandria and of the Near East further away from the example, the

---

[8] Philo taught in Alexandria in the first part of the 1st century A.D.

dreams, the spirit of the fair-haired young warlord from the North to whom Greece, in her collective pride, had rendered divine honours. And they slowly replaced their more and more obsolete state-patriotism not by the consciousness and pride of a broader brotherhood of similar blood comprising Hellenes and Persians (and, ultimately, all Aryans) but by the superstition of "man" in general—"man" as distinct from and opposed to both created Nature and Godhead. And thus their descendants were, less than 300 years after the death of the Macedonian hero, willing to accept the new wording of the old Jewish lie—Paul's message: "God hath made *all nations out of one blood*"[9]—at least, willing to hear it with the smiling equanimity of indifference, while their children or grandchildren would accept it wholeheartedly.

The old lie of the fallen ages—the superstition of "man," older in fact than the Jews—corrupted the blood and killed the spirit not merely of the Hellenes but of many other Aryan nations, from the Romans onwards. It is the curse of the modern world.

Christianity is also not the only expression it assumed in order to spread far and wide, taking advantage of most men's damnable conceit and insurmountable cowardice: of their mania of wanting to feel personally important in some way or another—in someone's eyes—and of wanting to "hang on" to something, when faced with the mystery of death. Several Eastern religions of "salvation," in particular the new forms of the very ancient cults of Cybele and of Mithra, centred like Christianity, around the "infinite value of the individual human soul" irrespective of the body it animates, had, along with the young religion of crucified Jesus, a following in the Roman Empire. But none possessed that conquering fanaticism which the latter owed to the tradition of the "jealous God" of the Jews. None proclaimed itself, like it, not *a* way among others but *the* only way to salvation. None was, like it, prepared to use any Dark Age methods in order to raise itself, in the Empire and beyond, to the status of the only faith. In other words, none had, like it, already become, or was, at the first given opportunity, susceptible of becoming, to the same extent as it, a formidable organisation "*in* Time." And that is precisely why Constantine, that perspicacious politician, gave the Christians his imperial protection:

---

[9] Acts of the Apostles 17:26.

salvation-seekers as well-adapted as they to the conditions of success in this world were the most likely to give the Empire, *quickly*, at least some sort of unity of faith—better than no unity at all. And that is also why so many kings and warlords of the best blood—personally, the last men one could have expected to adhere either to the unworldly, peace-loving creed "above Time" which Christianity originally was, or to the equalitarian, unnatural religion which Paul had made of it—sought the friendship of the church, asked to be baptised, and, what is more, forced the new, foreign faith upon the healthy nations of Northern Europe, who first did not want it, but who took to it all the same, and sooner or later got used to it, for they too had to go the way of decay, in accordance with the law of evolution in Time and the will of the dark Powers, rulers of our Age.

The surest moral factor of decay is, indeed, none other than that old superstition of "man"—that sickly love of fallen man as he *is*, as we see him all around us, that sickly longing to "save" even the ugliest specimen of humanity at any cost, in one word, that sickly belief in the "dignity of *all* men," which the Jews possibly did not invent, but which they proclaimed louder and louder and exalted more and more systematically before the whole world, in all international thought-currents or religions which they have started or helped to start, or influenced, in particular in Christianity as it has come down to us. This is so true that the mentioned superstition (for it is one) seems to be the strongest and most uneradicable element—the really living element—of the official religion of the West. No typically Christian dogma, no article of faith in the theological sense of the word, has, like it, in public consciousness, stood the test of centuries; none has, nay, like it, with time, in so-called Christian lands *and* elsewhere—*all over the world*—become accepted as self-evident truth by votaries of the most varied religions and by men who profess no religion at all. It has been spared—nay, strengthened—by every successive storm which shook the prestige of dogmatic Christianity itself. It was never questioned, let alone rejected, by the boldest "rationalists" whose very profession of thought was doubt and impartial investigation. (On the contrary, some of them, such as Descartes, made it the basis of their whole philosophy.) It was and is likewise exalted by haters of the Catholic Church such as the theists of the French Revolution, and by detractors of all other-worldly faiths such as our 20th-century Communists. In one word, it is—and more and more thoroughly and more and more consciously so—the common faith of practically all men of the advanced Dark Age: of those who profess some creed originally "above Time" *and* of those whose philosophy is unmistakably and openly "in Time" (for all creeds originally "above Time"—or even *"against Time"*—have, whenever successful, given birth in this Age to churches and civilisations decidedly "in Time," churches and civilisations settled upon compromises with the Dark Forces).

Alone three classes of individuals are free from it: a minority of people *"in* Time," consciously self-centred, of the type of those money-makers and power-seekers who would sacrifice anybody and anything—the whole world—to their personal ends; a minority of contemplative thinkers and saints "above Time," of the type of those who have realised the unity of their deeper being with all *life*; and finally, a minority of fighters "against Time" devoted to an unbendingly life-centred ideal.

The people of the first of these groups hide their cynical self-centredness under a noisy lip-adherence to the dogma of the "dignity of all men." They are, nay—while busy causing, directly or indirectly, in view of their goal, the suffering and death of any number of human beings—the strongest supporters of that precious dogma, the promoters of an increasingly widespread belief in it. Who would ever dream of attacking *them* in defence of it? Contemplative saints and thinkers are, whatever may be the truth that they have realised, too far above the world—too inactive—to be looked upon as dangerous. They know one has to wait for the coming Golden Age in order to see eternal Truth once more integrally reflected in the institutions of this world. And they do not mind waiting. But the militant minority "against Time," *who not only in thought but in action*, here and now, denies the very basis of all man-centred creeds in the name of a truer, life-centred wisdom, automatically rouses against itself and its ideals the coalesced fury of all the forces of disintegration. The Dark Age world ceases (for a time) being divided against itself, in order to wage upon it—from the cosmic point of view, its real enemy—a war without compromise, without the hope of an "honourable peace," a proper war of extermination. Such was the nature and the purpose of the coalition of Communists and anti-Communists, Jews and Christians, Freemasons and Catholics, men of all races and all creeds, against National Socialist Germany: the state "against Time" *par excellence*.

The noisy "anti-Communism" of a great number of notorious anti-Nazis, from President Eisenhower and Sir Winston Churchill downwards, should not today impress us. Considered from the standpoint of immediate, practical interests, it may well be genuine. Considered from the standpoint of permanent—of absolute—reality, it is skin-deep.

In the eyes of short-sighted politicians—and *all* politicians who are nothing more than politicians are necessarily short-sighted—the distribution of the forces in presence has entirely changed since the world-wide anti-Nazi coalition, the last works of which were the Yalta and Potsdam Agreements and the Nuremberg Trial and the "de-Nazification" imposed upon Germany, began to break in two, i.e., since 1948 or so. Since then—so they imagine—National Socialism is out of the picture. And the anti-Communists (thousands of "former National Socialists" and millions of definite anti-Nazis of all countries) form more or less one bloc—the so-called "free world"—under American leadership, against the Communists of Europe, Asia, and Africa (and America)—the other bloc—under Russian leadership. It looks as though it were so. And since the "free world" is more or less willing to absorb the "former Nazis," it must be that the latter— the anti-Communists of always—have more affinity with it than with the Communists. The simple logic of all those who, but yesterday, had become the allies of Communism in the name of the "rights of man," would, it appears, point to such a conclusion.

But the conclusion is false, and the logic too simple, and those who profess it, ignorant of the great historical fact of our epoch: the growth of a militant minority "against Time," at war with the whole Dark Age world and its ideals—at war, in particular, with the old superstition which proclaims the "dignity of all human beings."

The short-sighted politicians overlook the fact that neither international agreements, nor law-courts, nor interdictions, nor measures of "re-education" can kill thought-currents which have their roots in cosmic reality; the fact that National

Socialism—or, to be more precise, Hitlerism—continues to exist after the disaster of 1945; more so: that the disaster of 1945—the unavoidable defeat of the National Socialist *state*—has purified the National Socialist community; separated, in it, the good corn from the weeds; tried it, like fire tries a mixture of pure gold and base metal, and isolated the pure gold. They overlook the fact that there are no such creatures as *"former* Nazis," even if there be—alas!—plenty of former members of the N.S.D.A.P., nay, plenty of people formerly in high position in the National Socialist state, who never were National Socialists at all. Such people were, in the days they acclaimed Adolf Hitler, either unaware of what they were doing, or consciously playing a double game for the benefit of the anti-Nazi forces: either simpletons or traitors. Adolf Hitler's full-fledged followers, who knew from the start what they stood for and what they wanted, have neither denied their principles nor accepted compromises. And if some of them seem to have done so—outwardly—it is only in order that they might deliberately work themselves into the governing machinery of *both* halves of the hostile world, and bring about its collapse at the first opportunity. They may—those real ones, more supple but no less genuine than their silent brothers in faith—appear to have affinities with the "free world" in a renewed and, this time, shockingly insincere "struggle against Communism," or, under different circumstances—when it suits the one sacred purpose—they may seem to have affinities with the disciplined Communists of East Germany, in a no less insincere "struggle against the Money-power." In reality, they are that which they always were, that which their genuine brothers in faith have stubbornly and openly remained, that which all true followers of Adolf Hitler are: bearers of the perennial faith of Light and Life in its present-day form, enthusiastic agents of the perennial cosmic forces "against Time." They reject within their hearts, as uncompromisingly as they always did, the Jewish-sponsored dogma of the "dignity of man." Both Communists and anti-Communists of the present brand would flatly refuse to have anything to do with them, if only they could read into their souls and know them as they are. And were they, with or without the material help of any section of the hostile Dark Age world, again to rise to power, again Communists and "anti-Communists" would forget their non-essential antagonism, and coalesce against them and against the reborn National Socialist state, exactly as they did during the Second World War. Again the whole world, stamped with the every day more glaring characteristics of the advanced Dark Age, would "defend itself" — defend its tired, sickly, increasingly bastardised, ugly humanity, and the deep-rooted prejudices without which the latter could not survive — against the defiant detractors of every weakness and of every sickness, the haters of all forms of decay. Again it would rise in an unanimous "crusade" to crush the men who love *not* "man" as he is, but the proud human aristocracy in the making, *as it one day will be*, once it will have stood the test of the Dark Age, the men who are ready, here and now, and without a need of pity or sadness, to sacrifice present-day man to that race of living gods, which the youngest and boldest of the races of this earth — the Aryan — is to *become*, through the ceaseless struggle of its natural élite against the current of Time. Again it would react as it did only a few years ago, for it would again more or less dimly realise that the actual forces facing each other on the material plane are (and always have been, and always will be) the same: the forces "in Time" and the forces "against Time." (They will be the same till the definitive triumph of the latter, and the end of the Dark Age.)

As I said before, all historical movements originally "against Time," which are successful — which *look*, at least, as though they were "lasting still," after centuries of expansion — owe their success to some ideological compromise with the forces of decay, i.e., to some inner corruption, some irredeemable deviation from their inspiration and purpose, some unfaithfulness to their nature "against Time." In other words, they have sunk to the level of movements "in Time," or given birth to churches and civilisations "in Time" — denied themselves — in order to endure nominally.

National Socialism refused every compromise with the spirit of the faiths "in Time." That is the reason why it did not — could not — triumph, materially, *now*. That is, however, the reason why it shall triumph, materially, one day — upon the ruins of all faiths "in Time" and of all man-centred civilisations.

Its crime, in the eyes of the short-sighted foreign statesmen, was that it had made Germany self-sufficient and powerful and that it would have, within a generation or two, made her invincible. And the jealous politicians coalesced against it in order to hinder that extraordinary achievement. In the estimation of the Dark Forces of this Age, that stood behind them and behind the war-lords of the United Nations, and used them as a murderer uses his knife, and in the eyes of all its enemies, be they foreigners or Germans, who knew what they were doing, the crime of National Socialism was that it rejects the superstition of the "dignity of man" in favour of the everlasting, life-centred Wisdom "against Time" and, what is more, that it claims to remould the Aryan world in accordance with that Wisdom; that it proclaims the rights (and duties) of the strong and beautiful—of the healthy, pure-blooded élite—in the place of the rights of "man" indiscriminately, and that it did all it could to rule "against Time," in the spirit of that proud faith of the best; in one word, that it raises what I call "the S.S. outlook on life" (I can find no more eloquent expression to characterise it) in the place of the Judeo-Christian (and Communist) love of "man."

It certainly is no mere coincidence that, of all the organisations closely connected with the defence of the National Socialist state, the S.S. is precisely the one which has been (and still is) the most bitterly hated by the enemies of the Hitler faith: first and foremost by the Jews, whose aversion to it is well-nigh pathological; then by the Communists and by the Catholics, and finally by the non-descript "decent people" of all degrees of mediocrity—even by such narrow-minded nationalists of countries other than Germany as should normally (given the personal career of some of them)[10] be the last ones to censure *any* supporters of ruthlessness in warfare *or* in coercion. The most bitterly hated and the most widely slandered; and the most relentlessly and the most savagely persecuted, no sooner persecution became materially possible; the one body, hundreds of thousands of members of which have died a martyr's death in the anti-Nazi extermination camps of practically all countries of Europe—and of their colonies—and of the Soviet Union, or in the cellars and torture chambers of the Allied prisons, after the war; thousands

---

[10] For example that of the French *"résistant"* Jacques Soustelle, as Governor of Algiers, in 1956.

of members of which are still in chains for so-called "war crimes," in Siberia, no doubt, but elsewhere also—in Holland, in France, in Greece—even ten years after Germany's unconditional surrender; *all* members of which were collectively stamped by the judges of the international Tribunal of Nuremberg as "belonging to a criminal organisation," and *are*, still today, after all these years, more or less everywhere (save in Germany itself) looked upon as such by the broad, uncritical masses, who have lived (or have been told about) the Second World War.

It is no mere coincidence. And by no means also, a fact which the so-called "crimes against humanity," rightly or mistakenly or wilfully wrongly ascribed to numbers of S.S. men by the Nuremberg judges, would suffice to account for. No armies, ancient or modern—and those of the united *anti*-Nazi front, less than any—and no police organisations are innocent of so-called "crimes against humanity": acts of violence which obvious military necessities (or state necessities) cannot entirely justify. The history of the whole world is eloquent enough—and that of all great colonial powers of the past and of the present, particularly eloquent—in that respect.

But why mention colonial powers and the multifarious horrors connected with the repression of resistance movements in tropical lands—or with the conquest of those very lands—by greedy crusaders of man-loving creeds? Were not Eisenhower's gallant "crusaders to Europe" themselves lashingly censured, and that by non-Nazis and even by *anti*-Nazis—by Maurice Bardèche, a sincere Christian; by Freda Utley, a Communist, or at least the wife of one—for their disgusting behaviour in Germany in and after 1945? And has not the American judge Van Roden, who was sent to investigate into the atrocities perpetrated by his compatriots upon Germans (in fact, upon S.S. men) in connection with the all-too-notorious "Malmédy case," clearly declared in 1948 that, were one seriously desirous of detecting and chastising "war criminals," one should send home the "whole American Occupation forces" so that they be legally and impartially tried?

It is true that the victors of 1945 never had the slightest desire of being "impartial," let alone "just." Apparently what they had decided to punish were German "war criminals" only—not their own. But even that is not rigorously accurate. At least, that does not *suffice* to explain *why* they drew such a definite line between German soldiers of the Wehrmacht and German soldiers of the Waffen S.S. and no line at all between the latter and the members of the elder organisation known as "Allgemeine S.S.": the only one out of which were recruited the Security Service, the Secret State Police (commonly known as the Gestapo),[11] and the staff of the concentration camps, i.e., all men entrusted with the *inner* defence of the National Socialist state. It does not suffice to explain why the German (and, during the war, *also non-German*) regiments labelled as *Schutzstaffeln*—S.S.—be they police or field units, were, as a whole, and without discrimination, branded as units of a "criminal organisation," while their fellow formations of the Wehrmacht—the Kriegsmarine, Luftwaffe, etc.—were not; why the victorious Allies and, along with them, the post-war press and radio, literature, and cinema industry—all the forces of the anti-Nazi world—went out of their way to persecute, humiliate, or revile every S.S. man, whatever he might have done or not have done, while they persecuted mostly *individual* officers and men out of the Wehrmacht and other German fighting forces, and presented their occasional so-called "war crimes" as individual cases of unjustified violence. It does not suffice to explain that reputation of cold-blooded barbarity which the whole S.S.—the Waffen S.S. no less than the "Allgemeine"—has acquired during and after the war, and the horror attached to its name to this day among the gullible masses of practically all countries, with the natural exception of Germany (and of Austria, which is, whatever one may say, a part of Germany), of Spain, and probably of Japan, where, I expect, no amount of democratic nonsense can kill men's inborn admiration for *any* faithful soldiers.

The truth is that what roused—and still rouses—the hatred and fury of the "common man" in nearly all lands—and the very understandable fears of the intelligent leading anti-Nazis, especially of the topmost Jews, actual rulers of the present-day world—was (and is) not so much the German so-called "war crimes" themselves as the particular conception of life, the particular scale of values of some of those men who are alleged to have committed them or ordered them. For that which nearly

---

[11] Geheime Staatspolizei

the whole world of this advanced Dark Age stood up to combat and to crush, with a more or less clearly expressible but nevertheless most definite sense of *self-defence*, was not, in reality "violence," not "crime" — not even "crimes against humanity," in the material meaning of the word — but National Socialism, or, more precisely, Hitlerism: the latest expression of the perennial cosmic Wisdom "against Time"; Hitlerism, the creed of the healthy, strong, and beautiful, in their place at the head of a creation of which "man" is but a part; the creed of triumphant Life — of Nature — as opposed to the commonly accepted creed of "man." And that which distinguished the whole S.S. — the "Allgemeine" *and the other* — from the rest of the German forces, and justified, in the eyes of the world of our Age (from the Nuremberg judges and the leading Jews behind them, down to the most irresponsible specimen of two-legged mammal whom anti-Nazi propaganda could possibly reach) that name of "criminal organisation" indiscriminately applied to it, remains the sole fact that it was, or, at least was intended to be, *the* National Socialist body *par excellence*; *the* physical and moral élite of awakening Aryandom; the living, *conscious* kernel out of which and around which the yet unborn race of gods on earth — regenerate Aryandom — was to take shape and soul.

In other words, the S.S. as a whole had, in new Germany, the meaning which new Germany herself had among the people of the broad Aryan family: that of being the innermost and uppermost stronghold of the wisdom "against Time"; the ferment of regeneration, determined to overcome millenniums of decay. Is it a wonder that the very agents of the forces of decay treated it as they did — and as they do?

卐 卐 卐

A few quotations out of Georges Blond's book *L'Agonie de l'Allemagne* will help to buttress what I have just said. The French author may have held Pétain's policy of collaboration with Germany for the right one, in France's interest, but he never was and never pretended to be a devotee of the Hitler faith. His words are therefore neither those of an enemy nor those of an admirer but those of a reporter whose sole desire is to give an accurate picture of what was.

"S.S. men," says he — and although he speaks only of the

Waffen S.S. this applies also to the "Allgemeine" — "had to measure at least one metre eighty (nearly six feet) and to undergo an extremely severe physical and medical examination. They were not to have a single tooth which had once needed the attention of a dentist."[12] It strikes me as a remarkable coincidence that this same condition (of not having even a single decaying tooth) was, among others, imposed, in ancient Greece, upon those who wished to become priests of Apollo, the god of Light. I must also add that, apart from revealing, at the medical test, a more than average sharpness of sight and hearing, S.S. men were all to be possible givers of blood. The letter indicating his particular blood-group — A, B, or O — was tattooed under the right arm of every one of them, to make things easier in emergency cases. It is needless to stress that all S.S. men had to be of irreproachable Aryan blood. The genealogy of each and every one of them was studied with utmost care — generations back[13] — before his admission.

The ideal of physical cleanliness and of absolute health — the natural basis of more-than-physical purity — was exalted among them to the supreme degree; exalted in their training as a conscious élite and in their daily life within the barracks and outside:

> The rooms in which they lived and all objects which they used had to be washed and scrubbed, polished and shined every day. S.S. men were entitled to have uniforms and equipment of the very best quality, but the obligations imposed upon them with regard to presentation and cleanliness were unbelievable. At the time of the daily inspection the soldier was expected to look as though he had come "fresh out of a box." . . . As a result of the most severe inspection of all — the one that took place before the weekly day's leave — one man out of three was sent back on account of some trifling omission.[14]

An S.S. man who caught a venereal disease was punished.

---

[12] Blond, p. 103.
[13] Back to 1600 A.D. at least.
[14] Blond, p. 104.

The punishments consisted in supplementary military exercises (*Aufmarsch*: standing, lying, marching, running, crawling, with full equipment, for an hour), in imprisonment, or expulsion from the S.S. community.[15]

And, side by side with a deadly, machine-like efficiency, carried, through intensive drill, to the limits of perfection, were cultivated — carried, they too, to their highest degree — among S.S. men, those exceptional qualities of character, the outcome of which is personal value and *also* efficiency: a complete mastery over one's nerves; serene indifference to one's individual fate; absolute detachment within utmost thoroughness and utmost skill. In other words, being already *the* physical and racial élite, the S.S. was expected to be, at the same time, a perfect organisation and a perfect aristocracy of character and deeper intelligence; an unfailing instrument of war (or of coercion) and a brotherhood of real supermen; *the* all-around conscious élite of our Age: heroes "against Time" accepting all the conditions of their extraordinary mission; accepting the mechanising tyranny of drill — twelve hours a day of the most exacting military exercises[16] — not with "resignation" but with understanding and with joy, knowing it was a means to invincibility, at any rate a means to the most terrible efficiency in the fulfilment of duty; and loving duty — *their* duty; their action for the triumph of truth on earth; their struggle "in the interest of the Universe" — above all.

The military exercises were carried out under the actual conditions of modern war, with all the dangers that this implies. "Danger of accidents bred vigilance, and was an element of the S.S. education."[17] The young future officers were put to even harder tests than the soldiers.

One of these tests, intended to develop self-control, was the following: the young officer, standing in the position of "attention," held a grenade in his right hand. On com-

---

[15] Blond, p. 104.

[16] In the second degree training of the Waffen S.S., after the young recruits' oath. See Blond, p. 106.

[17] Blond, p. 105.

mand, he was to unscrew it, to hit upon the fire-lever, and then . . . to place the grenade upon his helmet and while remaining in the position of "attention" — erect and immobile and perfectly calm — "to wait for the explosion."[18]

A Hindu would probably think: a beautiful exercise in the training of Western *"Karma Yogis."* And he would be right.

All this however — the fact of being a physical and, what is more, a racial élite, no less than a deadly efficient instrument of action (a merciless police-force and, in the case of the Waffen S.S., the toughest of all tough troops of the German Army) — would hardly have been enough to raise the S.S. above the best German military bodies of all times; to place it in a different class of warriors; and to bring down upon it, indiscriminately, the hatred of the Dark Age world. But let me once more quote Georges Blond:

> Three times a week the S.S. recruits had a course in political education: lectures about the Führer's person and about his life; about the National Socialist doctrine and the history of the Party; but before all about the racialist Teaching. The two basic books were Walther Darré's *Die Rasse*[19] and Rosenberg's *Der Mythus des 20. Jahrhunderts.*[20]
>
> On the form he had filled out requesting his admission, the future S.S. man had nearly always written, opposite the word "religion," the answer: *Gottgläubig* — believer in God. It was not the thing to do to write down "atheist," or "Lutheran"; still less "Catholic." *Gottgläubig.* That "belief in God" did not [religiously, or rather, dogmatically speaking][21] imply much. The important point was to be convinced, or ready to let one's self be convinced, *of the necessity and of the excellence of the advent of a "blood aristocracy" that was to rule alone over the rest of mankind.* The superi-

---

[18] Blond, p. 106.

[19] Probably Richard Walther Darré, *Das Bauerntum als Lebensquell der Nordischen Rasse* [*The Peasantry as the Life-Source of the Nordic Race*] (Munich: Lehmann, 1929). — Ed.

[20] Alfred Rosenberg, *Der Mythus des 20. Jahrhunderts* [*The Myth of the Twentieth-Century*] (Munich: Hoheneichen, 1930). — Ed.

[21] Savitri Devi's insertion — Ed.

or blood was the Aryan, and more particularly the Germanic or Nordic. The Latin people were held to be not very interesting, the Jews were looked upon as mud and vermin. *Christianity was a religion soaked in Judaism, and even an undertaking carried on under Jewish inspiration, with a view to revile man by inculcating him a feeling of sinfulness.*

It is an error to believe that cruelty was systematically cultivated. Friendliness and kindness towards children and towards animals were recommended to S.S. men. But the tree of blood aristocracy and of the deified state could not bear fruits of meekness and humanity. Pride always carries within it the seed of cruelty.[22]

Through this reportage of a non-Nazi — and nobody save a non-Nazi, nay, nobody save a definite opponent of the Hitler faith in its essence (i.e., an opponent of it not necessarily on the political but certainly on the philosophical plane) could write such a sentence as the last one, which I purposely quoted — one can, to some extent, understand the historical significance of the S.S. and account for the world-wide hatred of which that organised, warlike Aryan aristocracy has been, and still is, the object.

At the root of both, there is that explicit and uncompromising repudiation not merely of "Christianity," but of that which I have called "the values common to Christianity and to all man-centred faiths"; to all faiths "in Time," be they otherworldly or of this world; the repudiation of the values which appeal to bastardised masses (and all the more so that these are more bastardised); there is the haughty rejection of that dogma of the super-excellence of "man," outcome of immeasurable human conceit and, more and more, for the last two-and-a-half thousand years or so, of Jewish sophistry. *That,* and that alone, is what this Dark Age world could not and cannot and never will be able to forgive the S.S.; *that,* and not its so-called "war crimes" and "crimes against humanity" (the "decent people" and their leaders commit or encourage or tolerate far worse horrors); *that,* and not its terrible efficiency, nor its purity of blood as a fact, nor even its German pride and thirst of expansion.

The famous Teutonic Knights of the Middle Ages were pure-

---

[22] Blond, pp. 102–103.

blooded Germans and merciless warriors, conquerors of new lands for a German Reich that was already pushing eastwards with all its young strength. They were the sword that prepared the way for the German settlers' plough—*exactly what the S.S. would have been*, had the Russian campaign ended victoriously, i.e., had the anti-Communist Western Allies left Russia to her fate. Yet *they* were not "war criminals" or "criminals against humanity," whatever violence they might have exerted. For they fought and conquered in the name of Christianity, with the blessing of the Catholic Church—it was the only way to carry on a successful German *Ostpolitik* in the 12th, 13th, or 14th century. And had the toughest among the modern German forces—the S.S.—done the same, or that which can be, today, regarded as the equivalent of the same, namely, had it fought and conquered with the self-same violence, the self-same ruthlessness, nay, the self-same national fanaticism, but in the name of the "rights of man" against the "Bolshevik danger" considered as a menace to "man's dignity" and to "individual freedom," never would it have been collectively branded as a "criminal organisation" by an international law court—never; not even if Germany had finally lost the war. (In that case it is, in the first place, probable that Germany would have won. For the world-wide coalition of Communists and anti-Communists against her would not have taken shape.)

But there is more: whatever people may say, now that powerful material interests have torn asunder the Yalta front, I doubt whether the toughest and most fanatical units of the Red Army—whose fanaticism can match that of the S.S. and whose brutality has, already in this war, by far beaten it—be, even after a conflict between the so-called "free world" and the Soviet Union ending with the latter's unconditional surrender, collectively stamped as groups of a "criminal organisation." I doubt it because, however much the so-called "free world" may profess to hate Communism, Communism does not profess to attack that deep-seated superstition of "man" which is the implicit faith of the Dark Age. On the contrary! That very superstition lies at the root of Marxism even more so than at the root of historical Christianity or of humanitarian atheism, of which Marxism is but the logical prolongation in a world increasingly dominated by "technique." The only way to carry on any successful national *Ostpolitik* (or *Westpolitik*) in our Dark Age, is to carry it on under the mantle of some form or other of that international superstition.

National Socialist Germany carried on the struggle for her existence against that superstition; *against* the accumulated moral prejudices of Dark Age mankind; I repeat: "against Time." She fought for her existence, being herself the citadel of the Hitler faith. And the S.S. — indiscriminately, whether Waffen S.S. or "Allgemeine" — was and remains the great dedicated Knightly Order of the Hitler faith. For no other reason has the Dark Age world persecuted it with such elemental hatred.

After all that has been written before, during, and after the war concerning the alleged "ungodliness" of National Socialism, it is striking to read in Georges Blond's reportage that the word a young man would generally write down in, answer to "religion," in the form he had to fill in view of his admission into the S.S., was *not* "atheist" but "believer in God." It is striking to read that "it was not the thing to do" to write down "atheist" — "atheist" *or*, by the way, "Lutheran" and still less "Catholic"; in other words: "atheist" *or* "Christian." And yet, therein lies, perhaps, a hint at the fundamental difference between the National Socialist *Weltanschauung*, or, rather, the National Socialist attitude to life, and that of all anti-Nazis. For the "atheism" with which one is here concerned — that "atheism" which is "not the philosophy to profess" for a man expected to set the example of National Socialist orthodoxy — has nothing to do with the wisdom of the various "atheistic" schools of thought of Ancient India. It is just usual modern European "atheism": the hasty — uncritical — denial of, or at least, the complete absence of interest in, "all that one cannot see," on the part of men who have rejected the personal God of the Christian churches *while remaining as faithful as ever to the Christian values*, i.e., to what I have called the superstition of "man."

Is not "man" as a whole the most evolved of all visible creatures upon this planet? True, the enormous differences in beauty, in nobility, in intelligence, which distinguish human races from one another are so obvious, they too — so *visible* — that one should hardly need any definite metaphysics in order to acknowledge them, and to regard not "man" but alone superior man—man of the superior races—as the masterpiece of Life's patient artistry as we *see* it. Yet, 99 times out of 100, people who style themselves as "materialists"—as "atheists," believers in "hard facts"—are, in that respect, as blind as those who postulate the existence of some invisible, transcendent, yet personal and man-loving "God." Their "atheism" has all the ethical characteristics of historical Christianity. It is intimately interwoven with the self-same moral prejudices as it in favour of "all men," irrespective of personal and racial differences; with the self-same ferocious partiality in favour of "man" in general, as opposed to other living creatures. Like it—and like all man-centred faiths of whatever metaphysical tenets and whatever origin—it places the most idiotic or perverse, and ugly, human weakling of any race infinitely above the most perfect specimen of non-human Creation: above a splendid healthy lion or tiger; above a beautiful healthy tree. Or, to speak more accurately, the average European "atheist" or "materialist," sub-consciously soaked in Judeo-Christian morals, *loves* any repulsive human weakling (or human devil) *more* than he does the most majestic dumb animals of the earth; more than he does the most loveable and beautiful cat or dog or horse, and all the trees of all the forests. Like the average Christian, he believes that Nature is there for man to exploit to his utmost advantage. And the most abominable forms of that ever-intensified exploitation—vivisection; circuses; the fur industry, etc.—do not trouble his moral conscience; at least have never yet troubled it enough for him to cause their suppression. "Man" is, in his eyes, whatever be his objective value as a living creature, his individual and racial place in the general scheme of life, the one creature (or, at any rate, by far the first creature) to be loved and helped and saved. However contemptible he be, individually or racially, from a cosmic standpoint, he is, in his estimation, *always worth saving*—be it at the cost of any amount of suffering, disfiguration, or destruction of the rest of living creatures; always worth saving just because he happens to be "a man."

To those few full-fledged believers in Adolf Hitler who have well understood and wholeheartedly accepted the basic principles of his Teaching with all their logical implications, *nothing is as repugnant as that moral and metaphysical attitude.* All brands of Christianity imply it. That is the reason why none of them was, on the part of whoever accepted to become a model of National Socialist orthodoxy, "the thing to write down" in answer to the question: "religion?" Atheism—I repeat: *not* the abstract atheism of certain schools of Aryan thought in Ancient India, but average present-day Western atheism: that of the Communist associations of the "Godless" in Russia; that of 99 percent of those Europeans who have stepped out of every Christian church without realising in the least the absurdity of all man-centred ethics—is, *in fact*, closely connected with it, although it may, philosophically speaking, imply nothing of the kind. That is why the orthodox National Socialist, or he who sincerely wished to open his heart to the influence of National Socialist orthodoxy, could be no "atheist."

He could—and can—be no follower of any man-centred faith, for all these are faiths "in Time," faiths of decadence, faiths expressing in a more or less naïve, more or less sophisticated form, that unchanged blasphemous conceit of man as such—that rebellion of man against the Cosmic Order—through which decay started, millenniums ago. He was—and is—to be a "believer in God"; not in the personal, transcendent and all-too-human "God" of the Christians (and of many "Theists"); not in a "God" made in the image of any man or men—least of all in the image of the Jews—but in that *immanent* Creative Force which manifests Itself in all Life's masterpieces at all levels of its endless effort; in *perfect* man *and* in every perfect specimen of non-human creation; in other words, he was to be a believer in the reintegration of man into the cosmic Scheme, according to the original divine pattern of the latter, which implies the natural racial hierarchy of human beings and their individual inequality, *not* their indiscriminate "dignity" and "equal rights." For his "belief in God," which, in Georges Blond's eyes, "did not imply much," implied at least *that*—or the readiness to accept *that* as unquestionable truth. Georges Blond immediately says so himself, strangely disconnecting this admission from his former statement. Let me repeat my quotation of his words: "The important thing was to be convinced or ready to let one's self be convinced *of the necessity and of the excellence of the advent of a 'blood aristocracy' that was to rule alone over the rest of mankind.* The superior blood was the Aryan, and more particularly the Germanic or Nordic, etc. . . ."[23]

It is a fact that this conception of a naturally hierarchised world, with a natural—God-ordained, *not* arbitrarily man-chosen—blood-aristocracy, in its place at the head of it, is incompatible with any faith that exalts "man" *en bloc, man* as an alleged privileged species (regardless of the tremendous differences between one human race and another, nay, between one human individual and another) at the expense of all the rest of the living. It is a fact that it is incompatible with all faiths and all philosophies, the scale of values of which rests upon the dogma of the "dignity of man": upon the idea of the infinite price of the "human soul" (to the exclusion of all other living souls) and of the "rights" of man, whoever he be; incompatible with all faiths and all philosophies which proclaim, among other things, that "all men" have the "right to live" and that they are "all" worth saving.

According to that proud and ruthless wisdom—both essentially aesthetic *and* warrior-like—which was and remains that of the S.S., the supreme blood aristocracy of mankind (the militant élite of the Aryan race) has not to "save" its inferiors, but to continue perfecting itself, according to Nature's purpose; it has not to "love all men" and to sacrifice the rest of the beautiful realm of Life to "man's" ends, but to love perfection—*health, in all its glory*—*both in its own members and in the lovely healthy representatives of all natural species* (including those of the noblest non-Aryan human races) and to sacrifice, always and everywhere, the sickly and the deficient to the healthy, the weak to the strong, the imperfect to the perfect; it has to be the privileged Legion that prepares "against Time"—regardless of the general tendency of the present-day world to forward decay—the godlike Perfection of the coming Golden Age; the chosen minority which, already now, at the darkest period of the Dark Age, foreshadows, through its own very existence, something of the unthinkable Golden Age beauty, just as the first streak of light at the Eastern horizon foreshadows, in the yet lasting night, the splendour of the coming Sunrise. It has to be the vanguard of those whom a mathematically just Destiny, rooted in their inher-

---

[23] Blond, p. 102.

ited virtues, will prompt to cross the "bridge" which Nietzsche mentions—the bridge between animalhood and supermanhood—while men of lesser dynamism and lesser detachment will fall from it into the primeval Pit. It has to possess the mercilessness of the Nietzschean warrior—not that of the fool, who does not know *why* he kills; nor that of the passionate, who thinks he knows why, but makes a mistake, and deplores his own violence when it is over, but that of the wise, conscious of the necessity of his violence in the interest not of fallen "man" but of "the Universe" (again to use a word from the Bhagavad-Gita); the mercilessness of the wise, in the interest of the perfection that he represents and prepares; of the wise who *knows* himself to be in the service of the forces of Life, and who regrets nothing. It has to possess, also, the kindness of the Nietzschean warrior, which is a sign of understanding and of serenity, and a tribute to the divinity of Life. Georges Blond cannot help mentioning the fact (although he may not give it its full significance) when he actually writes that "friendliness and kindness towards children and animals were recommended to S.S. men."[24]

They were not recommended, in fact, to S.S. men alone, but to each and every National Socialist. They are in absolute keeping with the whole philosophy of the Swastika, which is a typically life-centred one. They are in keeping with those simple and beautiful commandments contained in that which the Nuremberg judges have condemned as Alfred Rosenberg's "Nazi Catechism": "Thou shalt be brave. Thou shalt never do anything mean. *Thou shalt contemplate and love God in all living creatures, animals and plants.* Thou shalt keep thy blood pure . . ."[25] (Nothing is more cowardly and more *mean* than indifference to the suffering of dumb creatures, let alone than cruelty towards them.) The most one can say is that S.S. men, being *the* élite of the National Socialist forces, were to set the example of a definitely life-centred scale of values, with all that it implies.

People who have, on the contrary, a scale of values rooted in what I have called the "superstition of man"—i.e., more or less

---

[24] Blond, p. 103.
[25] Quoted by Maurice Bardèche in *Nuremberg II ou les faux-monnayeurs* [*Nuremberg II or The Counterfeiters*] (Paris: Les Sept Couleurs, 1950), p. 88.

all people of this Dark Age—are puzzled at the thought of that "kindness towards children" so strongly stressed by National Socialist ethics and, one should add, so thoroughly practised by the Führer himself. "And what about the Jewish children, who were no better treated than their elders by Himmler's men?," they retort, "And what about the deficient children of all races, who were 'liquidated' as useless consumers of valuable energy? Or about those babies who were not even deficient—and *not* Jewish—and who were, nevertheless, under the supervision of National Socialist doctors, 'painlessly put to sleep' because it was, amidst the atrocious conditions that prevailed in Germany at the end of the war, no longer possible to feed them?"[26] The world's reaction to the National Socialist and in particular to the S.S. attitude towards animals is quite different, but perhaps even more characteristic of this Dark Age mankind—even more instructive. It has been dearly expressed by all those who, having heard that vivisection had been declared illegal in the Third Reich, at the Führer's orders, find it "queer" that, in the same state "against Time," concentration camps were tolerated as a necessity. It has been clearly expressed by Count Robert d'Harcourt in his preface to the French translation of Adolf Hitler's *Tischgespräche*, published in 1952: "Humanity towards animals, bestiality towards human beings—we have seen that mystery of coexistence. . . . At Dachau, at Buchenwald, the torturers who used to push their victims into the gas chambers . . . were those same men who would nurse a wounded dog's paw with all a hospital sister's tender care."[27] In the first case: bewilderment and indignation. In the second case: also bewilderment, but an indignation of a still baser nature; an indignation rooted in the bitterness of wounded conceit; in the jealousy of the two-legged mammal who cannot bear the thought of anybody treating a four-legged creature better than him or at least better than certain specimens of his kind. In both cases, on the part of the alleged defenders of "liberty," a complete lack of understanding for any scale of values which is the denial of their own; in both

---

[26] See Frau Schmidt's case in my book *Defiance*, pp. 220-32.

[27] Translated under the title: Adolf Hitler, *Libres propos sur la guerre et la paix recueillis sur l'ordre de Martin Bormann*, trans. François Genoud, ed. Robert d'Harcourt (Paris: Flammarion, 1952), p. xxiii.

cases, on the part of the average man, soaked in his man-centred superstition—for millenniums accustomed to regard his increasingly decaying brood as the centre of all things—hatred; wild hatred for that iron Legion of men "against Time" who love cosmic Perfection, *not* "man"; or, at the most, man *and all creatures, to the extent they reflect and announce cosmic Perfection.*

What a votary of the actual S.S. faith could answer—what, in fact, no National Socialist *dares* to answer, precisely because he more or less dimly feels, in this controversy of *values*, the real cause of the world-wide coalition against all he loves and reveres—is the following:

> Of course we do not, as you people, love *all* children just because they are "man's" young ones! We are, thanks to our natural privilege of superior blood, destined to build, patiently and stubbornly, *collective* supermanhood. "Man"—fallen man; sickly or bastardised man, promised to perdition, i.e., lost to this earth—does not interest us. We love, no doubt, the beautiful, healthy, pure-blooded children of our own young and beautiful Aryan race: those who can and will grow into supermen—who will, at least, beget and bear supermen, in the course of time. We love the healthy, pure-blooded children of other noble races: they are beautiful at their own level and according to their own pattern; beautiful, when healthy; and we hope to make them, sooner or later, our allies in the struggle we are carrying on. But Jewish brats—and that, in war time, of all things; when the food problem was becoming acute for our own people? And when the British and Americans were pouring streams of fire upon us, to please their Jewish masters? No, my friends! Anyhow, a two-year-old Jew is a Jew. And in 20 years' time, he will be 22, and will work against us and against our purpose. It is *his "raison d'être"* to be our opponent, in the natural play of forces. Why on earth should we spare him in the bud? Because "God made him"? "God" made all sorts of parasites: fleas and bugs and lice and what not. Do *you* spare those? Or their eggs? The Jains—or some Jains—I am told, do. They are as logical and uncompromising as we, but serve a different ideal: an ideal entirely "above Time," which leads

their ascetics straight to pious suicide through wilful starvation. But we, whose kingdom is of *this* earth, again, why should we spare whatever stands in our way? A human parasite—or possible parasite—is far more dangerous than a six-legged one; a human "ferment of decomposition," far more dangerous than any mildew.

Of course, he is "human." That may be a reason for you people to confer upon him that "right to live" which you so flatly deny to thousands of harmless dumb animals that you sacrifice every day to "man." It is no reason for us to do the same. We are free—always have been; always shall be *free*—from the superstition of "man." I say: superstition, for your idea of "man" is false; contrary to the dictate of Nature that made man a creature to "be overcome" or to perish through decay; false, and dangerous, for it paralyses the healthy impulse of men who, otherwise, *could* follow us along the harsh and bloody road to collective supermanhood.

As for deficient children—or, by the way, deficient grownups—well! We are in the world to help Nature suppress all that is deficient; all that is irredeemably deficient, that goes without saying; and also all that *could*, perhaps, be "saved"—patched up—with a lot of patience and care, but that is not worth saving. You people believe "all men" to be "worth saving," worth patching up. *We don't*. We believe that the time, money, and energy that one now wastes on prolonging most sickly lives would be far better employed in promoting the creation of such social conditions as would favour the birth of healthy people only. Let the incurable weaklings be put out of the way from the start, like among the Spartans, like among our own Nordic forefathers, Vikings and others! Place to the healthy! Place to the strong—to the plants that grow, victoriously amidst wind and storm, not in the artificial, even heat of greenhouses!

Those children that we painlessly "put to sleep" because we could no longer feed them, after your bombs had smashed our transport services to atoms, were a different problem. We find it bitterly ironical that "humanitarians"—and nay, such ones as took an active part in the savage world-wide "crusade" against us—should reproach us with such acts of mercy. Is not a painless death a thousand times better than death through starvation—since anyhow death was to be the unavoidable solution? What were we to do, according to your "superior" moral code? To watch the children's agony for days and days, while you continued setting our supplies on fire and shelling our railway stations—and the children's homes? It is strange, to say the least, that such tender-hearted people as you did not think of the "poor kids" before, and refrain, for their sake, from bombing our land. Surely the kids would now still be alive, had we not been faced with the most tragic hunger dilemma.

And now, let us speak of the alleged "contradiction" between what you call our "humanity towards animals and bestiality towards human beings." It seems a contradiction *to you*, because you judge us with your scale of values. But *we* have not your scale of values. We have not your silly infatuation for "man"—for man is anything but a homogeneous species of which one can talk in one breath. We do not systematically love each and every two-legged mammal more than the most noble four-legged ones. On the contrary! We love, nay, we respect a perfect specimen of animal life—a beautiful horse, dog or cat, or a wild beast in all its majesty—infinitely more than a personally deficient or racially contemptible man; a so-called "thinking creature" who does not think, or whose thoughts are mean, or dangerous; especially if, in addition to that, the creature stands in our way in the political field, as our alleged "victims" all did, more or less. We do not worship "man" as he is—man in rebellion against Nature and against our Nature-inspired wisdom—nor do we bow down before any man-loving, whimsical personal "God," conceived in the image of the meanest of men; before a "God" who "saves" man alone, among all living beings (and that, all the more joyfully that the darling creature is more sinful!). We worship that impersonal, pitiless Godhead which abides in *all* beings to the extent they are healthy and beautiful—perfect; that Godhead, which is more alive and infinitely nearer to us in the magnificent four-legged aristocrats (in a velvety black panther, a royal Bengal tiger), in the noble birds, nay in the noble trees, than in most men of the present-day degenerate world, including many conceited "intellectuals" of sickly constitution and questionable Aryan descent. The royal tiger or lion, the eagle, the unbending oak tree, are our equals, in a way; our equals, or rather our counterparts, on a different plane — as the perfect Japanese warrior or the pure-blooded, chivalrous Arab aristocrat, are our human counterparts outside the Aryan race. The decaying masses of *Menschenmaterial*[28] of various degrees of bastardisation, which we are out to use (whenever they can be used) or gradually to eliminate (whenever they prove useless) are neither our equals nor our counterparts in any way.

In addition to this, don't forget an important point: animals of whatever description can never stand in our way in the struggle for the triumph of National Socialism. People — including God knows how many millions of misled or criminal men of Aryan blood — *can*; and did, and do, and will again, at the next opportunity. You don't expect us to handle such ones (when we are in power, and manage to lay hands on them) as gently as we do our faithful parade horses and police dogs, do you? Once more: we are worshippers of hierarchised Life; fighters for the rule of the Best, in the interest, not of "man," but *of the whole scheme of Life*. Our goal is not to "save man." (Let man perish, if he cannot either become a god on earth, or integrate himself into our world, ruled by gods on earth!) Our goal is to build up, consciously, against the stream of millenniums and millenniums of decay, that earthly order of Truth in which perfect man will again be the kind and wise king of a world where there will be no place for sickness; to build it up, or, at least to prepare its next, irresistible return.

You all, who persecute us in the name of "humanity," put this into your pipes, and smoke it!

Such an answer would make the philosophical position of

---

[28] Human material — Ed.

Hitlerism absolutely clear. It would, however, only make *it*—and Germany, the privileged Land of its birth—more unpopular than ever in this broad Dark Age world.

It is here the place to recall a great German and a great Aryan, whose name has become, after 1945, in the hearts of most non-German (and, I may say, also of a considerable number of German) people, thanks to world-wide Jewish propaganda, the symbol of every abomination: the *Reichsführer* S.S., Heinrich Himmler. I have said: of all National Socialist organisations, the S.S. is the one the anti-Nazis of most varied shades hate the most. Now, of all S.S. men, Heinrich Himmler—"head of Germany's whole Police forces, and later on, Home Minister; *Reichskommissar* for the 'Consolidation of German Nationhood,' Chief of the Reserve Army, Chief of the Prisoner of War Department, and, for a short time (at the very end of the war), Commander of a section of the Army"[29]—is the one the whole world detests the most.

I say: the whole world, and not merely "the anti-Nazis," this time, for I know quite a number of sincere National Socialists who anything but revere the *Reichsführer's* memory, and that, apart from any personal reasons which they might have to dislike him. They esteem he was "too hard"; in Georges Blond's words, too "indifferent to human realities." More than one former concentration camp warder (or wardress) has told me so—after having suffered for years in the Allied jails, for having carried out his orders. People who feel that it is high time to do something to attract attention upon whatever can recommend Adolf Hitler and the Third Reich to the admiration of an increasingly "anti-Communist" West, try, more often than not, in that laudable intention, to shift all the widely spoken of "horrors" of the National Socialist régime onto Himmler's account. Had it not been for that "ice-cold fanatic," never would the Hitler Movement, originally so sound and beautiful, have "deviated"; never would Germany have become a "police state"; and never would the world have been faced with such atrocities as were, in 1945, discovered to have taken place in the German concentration

---

[29] Paul Hausser, *Die Waffen S.S. im Einsatz* (Göttingen: Plesse, 1953).

camps. So they say. One would think it were Himmler's fault if the world's stubborn and stupid millions believed Roosevelt's — and Untermeyer's — propaganda instead of Adolf Hitler's repeated warnings, and prepared — *before* 1945 — Soviet Russia's victory!

Maybe it is not particularly "diplomatic" to render justice to the head of the Gestapo, and to point out that his much misunderstood ruthlessness takes on all its meaning in the light of the fact that he — he more than any other, apart from the Führer himself — acted "against Time." Perhaps it is also not particularly "diplomatic" to remind people that Adolf Hitler had granted him his favour from the beginning, and, precisely — as Georges Blond rightly states — "less because he found him remarkably efficient than *because* he recognised in him the perfect National Socialist believer";[30] and that he never withdrew from the *Reichsführer* S.S. that absolute confidence which he had put in him — never, at least, till the very last week of the war; till the 29th of April, 1945, when the translation of a BBC Home Service message, relating Himmler's attempt to negotiate, without his orders, some sort of an armistice with the Western Allies, was suddenly handed over to him. *Now* — now, when the Western world, the "free" world, the world of the "decent people," should systematically be led to forget the Gestapo and the German concentration camps, and the wild elemental "anti-Semitism" (or rather anti-Judaism) which is inseparable from the history of National Socialism, and made to remember only Adolf Hitler's struggle "for Europe" — perhaps it is, I say, not exactly a National Socialist's duty to go and stress that, although he surely did not know (*could* not know) every step which Heinrich Himmler (or his subordinates) took, in connection with individual cases, the Führer was, and remained to the end, in complete agreement with him *with regard to the spirit and general lines of his coercive activity*; that, in fact, when he did, finally, withdraw his favour from him,[31] it was not for having been "too hard," but, on the contrary, not hard enough — not uncompromising enough — in a different, yet parallel line of action, namely in the last phase

---

[30] Blond, p. 182.

[31] To the extent the document published as Adolf Hitler's "Political Testament" is genuine.

of that desperate struggle "against Time," which the two men had carried on together for so many years.

I should myself feel that way, and would not mention the *Reichsführer* S.S. at all, were I writing a political pamphlet, intended to be read today, and thrown into the fire tomorrow, after having served its one purpose of contributing to bring my German comrades back to power. I entirely agree that, for the time being, the memory of many of those who have rendered the greatest services to the National Socialist cause — if necessary, even that of such a man as Heinrich Himmler — should be sacrificed to the demands of the cleverest possible policy, in the immediate interest of the Cause. But this book is not a political pamphlet. And to hide this particular historical truth concerning Heinrich Himmler, would not serve the interest of Hitlerism *in the long run*. The frank acknowledgement of it leads anyhow to a better *philosophical* understanding of the great new faith "against Time" (and also of the world-wide coalition against it). This truth must, sooner or later, be expressed. For it is nothing less than the consequence of a fundamental datum, which explains it (and even explains the abrupt end of Himmler's close and long collaboration with the Führer), and which is the following: Heinrich Himmler was what I shall call, for the sake of convenience of speech, the Führer's "lightning" counterpart: a man "against Time," he too, despite the enormous distance that separates him, the well-meaning disciple, from Adolf Hitler, *the* Man "against Time"; an idealist he too, as so many held him to be in the early years of the Movement and as some (who understand their National Socialist faith better than others) still dare to consider him today, and *not* that unscrupulous and faithless fellow, devoured with lust for personal power, that a pernicious propaganda has tried to make out of him. (One has no grounds whatsoever to believe such propaganda.) But an idealist with hardly any of the "Sun" qualities that the Führer so eminently possessed, and with all the "Lightning" characteristics — all the traits of a man destined to act successfully "in Time" — which he partly lacked; a man "against Time" by far "more 'Lighting' than 'Sun,'" in glaring contrast to Adolf Hitler.

He was not — and never pretended to be — a Master. He lacked that tremendous intuition which gave Adolf Hitler such an insight into cosmic realities. He lacked that *aesthetic* type of intelligence which distinguishes all creators and most prophets. He lacked that particular type of sensitiveness which draws unfailingly the right line between the *spirit* and the *letter* of a true doctrine; and also that particular suppleness which allows one to avoid hasty generalisations. But he was an admirable disciple — one of the best ones Adolf Hitler had; a man of faith, who not only adhered to the National Socialist doctrine, as millions did, on account of the political horizons it opened (because it was the only creed that could save Germany), but who accepted it in its essence, and that, because it struck him as being true: capable of saving Germany, surely; but, apart from that, true absolutely, eternally, independently of its success or failure on the material plane; a man who accepted its basic idea of a natural racial hierarchy and of the eminent superiority of Aryan blood, its scale of moral values, entirely rooted in that idea, and its flat denial of the old Jewish-sponsored superstition of "man." And a man of works, who, once he had embraced that creed (which he did wholeheartedly, and *very early* — when one had all to lose and nothing to gain by proclaiming one's allegiance to it) was to forward it with all the fanaticism of an 11th-century Crusader; to defend it with all the ruthlessness, the method, the cold-blooded, meticulous thoroughness of a 16th-century Grand Inquisitor. He applied, with detached exactitude and with an iron hand, the principle expressed by Adolf Hitler in *Mein Kampf* — the principle steadily applied, in the course of history, by such men "against Time" or "in Time" who have succeeded in uprooting an old faith and in forcing a new one upon dynamic nations; the rule of every struggle "in Time" and *a fortiori* "against Time" — "Poison can only be overcome through counter-poison" . . . "Tyranny can only be broken through tyranny, and terror through greater terror."[32] Few famous men of the Third Reich — apart of course from the Führer himself and also from Dr. Goebbels — were as thoroughly convinced as he of this practical necessity. Few — apart from the same (and from Julius Streicher) — were, as vividly as he, aware of the sinister historical role of the Jews, nay, of the fact that they have been, directly or indirectly, for centuries, and remain, *the* ferment of disintegration — *the* natural agents of the Forces of death — in the midst of all Aryan na-

---

[32] *Mein Kampf*, p. 507.

tions.

The only pity is that Heinrich Himmler was not given immediately—on the 31st of January 1933—the full powers that he was but gradually to acquire (and to enjoy, practically without control, but years later—during the war). In that case, many dangerous Jewish "intellectuals" who, through written and spoken word, stirred the whole world against National Socialist Germany, would quietly have been packed off to Auschwitz without a return-ticket (or disposed of in some still less spectacular but equally safe manner) instead of being allowed to take the boat (or the aeroplane) that carried them to London, to New York, to Bombay, and where not. In that case, no rich Jews would have been able to leave Germany. They would have worked hard—dug canals, built roads, cut stones for the rest of their lives—under the vigilant supervision of S.S. men, instead of financing anti-Nazi newspaper articles, and books, and lectures, and movements, all over the world. And not only the Jews, but also many a German enemy of the régime would have been denied the opportunity of becoming, in later years, the hidden accomplice of Great Britain, the U.S.A., and Soviet Russia, in their struggle to crush the new Aryan order in the making. That beautiful New Order would have had, thanks to Himmler's methods applied in time to its defence, a *chance to live*.

These methods—and the spirit behind them—are, as regards their application to war, defined in the *Reichsführer's* well-known, and most vehemently criticised, Posen speech of 1943:

> ... What happens to a Russian or to a Czech does not interest me in the least. ... That hostile nations be prosperous or that they starve to death interests me only in connection with that number of their citizens which we need as slaves. Otherwise, it does not interest me. That 10,000 Russian women may die of exhaustion in digging an anti-tank ditch interest me only to the extent that the ditch is completed for Germany. ... When someone comes and tells me: "I cannot have that ditch dug by women and children; it would kill them, and therefore be inhuman," I reply: "It is *you* who is the murderer of your German race! For if the ditch be not dug in time, German soldiers will

perish; and these are sons of German mothers: men of your own blood. . . .

This speech has given, after the war, any amount of grist to the anti-Nazi propaganda mill. One has deliberately forgotten that it is a war speech, delivered at one of the most critical moments of a life and death struggle. One has also, deliberately forgotten that the very equivalent of what Himmler here openly *says* has been practised over and over and over again, in the course of all wars and all revolutions of history, without it hardly ever having been as bluntly *worded*. No fighter is indeed interested in what might happen to his enemies: all he wishes is to defeat them. And as for women and children, one is compelled to use them as slave-labour when none other is available and when the work to be done is *urgent*. Nor can one afford to measure each and every person's task to his or her strength, when the work has to be ready within a definite and very short delay. To pretend one can is nonsense. Not a single one of those "humanitarians" whom the Posen speech fills — so they say! — with indignation, would sit and watch the enemy's tanks roll over his own people, instead of having an anti-tank ditch dug in a *timely* manner across their way by *whoever it be*, including women and children if no male labour be at hand. Again, as I noticed in one of the first chapters of this book: it is not violence, but honesty about violence, which rapidly decreases at the end of the Dark Age; not ruthlessness, but the frank and straightforward admission of the necessity of ruthlessness in any revolutionary struggle, nay, in any struggle whatsoever, if one wishes to be *lastingly* victorious; the admission that "to overcome poison through counter-poison" — in the present case, to overcome Marxism through National Socialism, its *only* antidote — implies, in war, exactly *that* which Himmler here mentions, and, in the domain of coercive activity, concentration camps and gas chambers (or their equivalent).

The reason why Heinrich Himmler is so widely and so bitterly hated is not really that he *acted* with the ruthlessness that one knows — that self-same ruthlessness, I repeat, which has characterised the historically decisive action of *all* great fighters "in Time" or "against Time": of those European rulers who once forced Christianity upon their subjects or upon the people they conquered; of the early warriors of Islam; of the Mongols in all their campaigns; of the agents of the Holy Inquisition who defended the Roman church against heresy; of those early Shoguns of the Tokugawa Dynasty who defended Japan against Christianity; of the men of the French Revolution; and finally of the European colonialists who, willingly or without meaning to (ironical as this may sound in the case of some of them!), helped to spread the Judeo-Christian infection—and its unexpected, but logical consequence: the later Marxist infection—all over the world. It is not that he *did* this or that (or, rather, caused it to be done). It is that he admitted, nay, proclaimed, in such blunt and brutal words, the necessity of his action. It is, more especially, that his action was accomplished neither in support of any already existing man-centred creed (whether Christianity, "humanitarian" democracy, or Marxism) nor in the name of any new one, but for the triumph of Germany viewed as the citadel of an unbendingly *life-centred* faith "against Time"; for the glory of that cosmic (and not merely human) faith; for the preparation of the advent and rule of Aryan supermen: gods on earth.

The advanced Dark Age world hates supermen, and is increasingly *anti*-Aryan. It loves "man"—average man; the more mediocre the better!—"man" as "God's" alleged darling (and the actual darling of all philosophies rooted in, or mixed up with, Jewish thought); it loves "poor, suffering humanity": the incurably sick; the cripple; the degenerate; and the vicious weaklings of all races, to whom it would gladly sacrifice all the healthy beasts of the earth. It believes in "human solidarity." And any defiant denial of the latter, such as is contained in the Posen speech, "shocks" it profoundly. (What shocks *me* profoundly is that, among all those who feel "indignant" at the "monstrosity" of the Posen speech, hardly any—*if* any at all—have ever been kept awake, be it for half a night, at the thought of the sufferings of the countless innocent sentient creatures tortured in the vivisection chambers of the whole world in order to gratify man's criminal curiosity, or to help him "save"—or prolong—the lives of people who are not worth saving, or, at any rate, to help him commercialise his diabolic ability as long as possible, at those patients' expense. This does not urge *me* to "love humanity.")

But there is more: the advanced Dark Age world, whose unifying faith is, more and more, the superstition of "man," felt, and still feels (be it dimly) that, had Heinrich Himmler enjoyed from the beginning of the National Socialist régime the full powers he had in 1943; or, rather, had Adolf Hitler, who actually was "more 'Sun' than 'Lightning,'" possessed, along with his godlike vision, and dynamism and power of synthesis — along with all the virtues and potencies and knowledge of a great creator "against Time," who is, as I once stated, *necessarily* a Man "above Time" *also* — Heinrich Himmler's cold-blooded, abstract, exact, and indiscriminate — mechanical — destructiveness, untiringly directed against anything and anybody that stood in the way of National Socialism; had he possessed Himmler's policeman's estrangement from "human realities," his contempt for all manner of shades and distinctions between Jews and half-Jews (or quarter-Jews) on the one hand, as well as between "more or less" dangerous anti-Nazis of Aryan blood, on the other, the glorious Swastika faith would have triumphed. And a glorious new Aryan humanity, an aristocracy of gods on earth, would have risen, pushing aside (and leaving to die out naturally) or eliminating the bastardised millions we know only too well. And it would have governed the earth in justice and in truth — according to the scale of eternal natural values, which has nothing in common with Christian-democratic, Social-democratic, or Marxist morals.

But then, Adolf Hitler would not have been Adolf Hitler the One-before-the-last and most tragic of all that series of men "against Time" that stretches from the beginning of the far gone legendary "Silver Age"[33] to the end of the one in which we are living. He would have been, in our Time-cycle, *the last* Embodiment of Him Who comes back, age after age "to establish on earth the reign of righteousness"; the last, and fully successful One, Whom Sanskrit Tradition names *Kalki*. For He alone will possess, mathematically balanced, and all to the supreme degree, the virtues which seem incompatible. He alone will be not merely "both 'Sun' and 'Lightning,'" but *equally* "Sun" and "Lightning."

Considered in the light of cosmic truth, the hatred of this advanced Dark Age world for Heinrich Himmler is but an unconscious expression of its fear of the invincible divine Destroyer —

---

[33] The *Treta Yuga* of Sanskrit Scriptures; the age immediately after the "Age of Truth."

Kalki—Who is to come. The East and West—Marxists and anti-Marxists or so-called such—vaguely felt (and feel) that, had it been but for a little more "Lightning" power—a little more "cold-blooded inhumanity" such as Himmler possessed—Adolf Hitler *would have been He, and have put an end to this Time-cycle.*

This is so true that, of all anti-Nazis the most justifiably such—the most *naturally* such—the most conscious, the most purposeful, and those who, by far, understand the best the more-than-political nature of National Socialism, namely, the Jews, seem to have been aware of it. In December 1942, after noisy demonstrations in the streets of Jerusalem and after a day of fasting, they gathered at the famous Wailing Wall and there "invoked the Old Testament Jewish curse"[34] against Adolf Hitler and three of his closest collaborators. Which ones? Not Rudolf Hess, the chivalrous idealist; the man who had risked his life and lost his freedom in order to try to stop a fratricidal war. Hess was too deeply *like* the Führer; he possessed, like he, more "Sun" than "Lightning" in his psychological make-up, and therefore was not to be feared; moreover, he was, for a year-and-a-half already, a prisoner in the Tower of London. Not Julius Streicher either, although few were as demonstratively "anti-Jewish" as he. For the Jews are practical people—at least when they act systematically, as a nation. They do not object to people being anti-Jewish; they merely object to their being dangerous (from the Jewish point of view). And Streicher was precisely too demonstrative and too impulsive to be dangerous. Even the stories he published in *Der Stürmer* were too crudely related to be the last word in anti-Jewish propaganda. (The Jewish horrors presented as a matter of course, by Jews themselves, in the Old Testament, beat them anyhow!) No; the three great Germans that the Rabbis of Jerusalem took the trouble to curse, through immemorial performances of black magic, along with the Prophet and Leader of awakening Aryandom, were Dr. Goebbels, Hermann Göring, and Heinrich Himmler:[35] all idealists;

---

[34] See *The Goebbels Diaries: 1942–1943*, p. 250—Entry of 18 December 1942.

[35] See the same.

men "against Time," in the service of the same ideal as himself, but men possessing, to an even greater degree than he, the qualities or advantages which secure success "in Time": ruthlessness, coupled with suppleness; a convenient and adaptable eloquence that can lie convincingly, whenever it is in the interest of the Cause; or that extraordinary personal charm—the manners, the many-sided intellect, and princely extravagance—which made Göring's contact with foreign plutocrats so easy and so helpful;[36] or Heinrich Himmler's unhesitating mercilessness wherever the defence of the new German Reich, centre and citadel of a new, regenerate Aryandom, was concerned. Men who were, precisely, *not like* the Führer, but whose capacities completed his and forwarded his creation, in which they all believed; men who often could, better than he, defeat the Dark Forces with their own weapons, be it with the diplomat's friendly smile and irresistible words of deceit, be it with the policeman's irresistible pressure upon alleged plotters until they break down and give away the names of other plotters and the details of the plot—or die. Dangerous men, from the Jewish standpoint; men such as Adolf Hitler needed; personalities such as, could they have been harmoniously woven into his, would have made him the dreaded One Whom he merely precedes and foreshadows: the *last* Man "against Time," Destroyer of this Dark Age world.

It is not that Adolf Hitler lacked eloquence or that he could not, when he liked, be full of charm. More than anything else, his inspiring speech and the fascination he exerted upon the masses, carried him to power. And his personal charm won him many a friend. But his were the devastating eloquence and the genuine, hypnotic fascination of a Prophet, not the artful persuasiveness of a diplomat or of a "man of the world" — or of both in one. The masses—the German masses, who are genuine, primitive; fundamentally in quest of justice—and the real élite—the aristocracy of blood *and character*; the men "against Time"— followed him as a matter of course. But he was not the man to bargain with the wily leaders of this advanced Dark Age, be they of the capitalistic or of the Communist brand. He tried

---

[36] Blond, p. 290.

(how many times did he not stretch out his hand to England in a spirit of peace!) — but failed. An abyss gaped between all crafty professional diplomats and him; nay, between all men who accepted the "values" of this Age and him: an abyss which he (and they) increasingly felt to be unbridgeable, but which did not exist (or at least was not obvious) between those same people and Hermann Göring, not to mention J. von Ribbentrop and other men of the Third Reich. There were moments in which the Führer was particularly aware of this difference and of his isolation in the midst of a hostile world that had let hell loose all around him. It is in one of those moments that he is said to have declared — on the 22nd of April 1945, in presence of General Keitel and General Jodl — "If it comes to negotiating, Göring will do it much better than I."[37]

One cannot say, either, that Adolf Hitler could not be ruthless, when placed before exceptional circumstances. He proved himself to be, nay, more and more so, as the war drew nearer and nearer to its tragic end. Nothing buttresses this statement more definitely than the words he addressed all the *Gauleiters* of the Reich on the 24th of February 1945, commanding them to rouse the people to a "pitch of Teutonic fury" against the invaders from the East and from the West, so that the whole German nation might perish sword in hand, rather than surrender. "If the German people give way," said he, carrying the logic of the National Socialist doctrine to its supreme conclusions, whatever these be, "that will only show that they have not a stamina worthy of their mission, in which case they deserve destruction."[38]

It is not a sheer coincidence that these words were spoken on the 25th anniversary of the foundation of the National Socialist Party. They express the natural and logical reaction of the Man "against Time," before the material impossibility of his dream within this Dark Age. The terrible "scorched earth" policy which he forwarded in a new message, addressed to the *Gauleiters* hardly three weeks later — on the 16th of March 1945 — is an outcome of the same. In that message, the Führer commanded that all power-stations, gas-factories, all manner of manufacturing

---

[37] Quoted in Blond.
[38] Quoted in Blond.

centres, mines, railways, canals, water-supplies, clothes and food supplies etc., be totally destroyed. On the other hand, the generals received orders to turn into deserts the regions they were to defend to the death of their last soldier. They were to destroy not only the bridges, and all the works enumerated within the message to the *Gauleiters*, but even the water-tanks, the granaries full of corn, whatever is necessary to life—whatever could be useful to the enemy. Never mind if the people who would survive bombing and battles would die of hunger and thirst![39]

Those orders were never carried out. Albert Speer, Minister of Armaments and Industries, saw to it that they were not. And although he came to know of this, the Führer never had Speer arrested, nor did he insist upon the execution of his own orders. The further desperate struggle absorbed all his energy. I have quoted these messages of the 24th of February and 16th of March 1945 merely on account of the light which they shed upon his spontaneous reaction to a state of affairs that allowed no hope. A later episode is no less instructive. When informed, on the 29th of April 1945, that the Russians were advancing, through a passage of the Underground Railway under the River Spree, into the heart of Berlin, Adolf Hitler ordered that the passage be at once flooded. There were wounded soldiers in it: German soldiers who had fought and were dying for the love of him and of his dream of Aryan pride and power. General Krebs told him so. The builder of the Third German Reich, mastering his feelings, replied that it could not be helped, and maintained his order, which, this time, was carried out. The wounded Germans were drowned, along with a whole battalion of Russians[40]—sacrificed to the ruthless logic of total war even though, viewed from a practical standpoint, the sacrifice was useless; even though the war was now lost *anyhow*.

There is more: it would seem that it was precisely for not having kept, to the end, that superhuman detachment in front of "the fruits of action"—that attitude of the warrior who knows he is defeated, but yet fights and dies, sword in hand—that he finally dismissed Hermann Göring (the man who "could negotiate" better than himself; who—some hinted—was willing to negoti-

---

[39] Quoted in Blond.
[40] Episode also quoted in Blond.

ate with the Western Allies) and rejected and condemned Heinrich Himmler (who had, at the last moment, actually tried to conclude an armistice with them). He had Fegelein—Gruppenführer S.S. married to Eva Braun's own sister—shot for having, without permission, attempted to go home, and thus "to survive" the ruin of the Reich. He made apparently no distinction between Himmler, who had tried to negotiate with the Allies for Germany to live, and Fegelein, who had merely tried to spare his own life. In the last days of that titanic struggle against the coalesced forces of the whole Dark Age world, all discriminations and all proportions lost their meaning. Germany and *a* German became the same—or about the same—just as a light-year and a light-hour are the same in the agelessness of the Infinite.

Adolf Hitler condemned Himmler precisely because he, "the perfect National Socialist believer," who had followed him so far, and for so many years—already when the Party was small and illegal—who had, nay, in many circumstances, gone further than he along the way of indiscriminate ruthlessness, did not follow him to the end; could not, it would seem, like he, and like Goebbels, and like the admirable Magda Goebbels, understand the mathematical necessity of Germany's Passion in view of the earthly salvation of the Aryan race, and of the ultimate reestablishment of the divine world-Order (never mind when and *how*); could not understand, like he, the necessity of her sacrifice "in the interest of the Universe." (Albert Speer had also "not understood." He too had stood up against the Führer's determination to fight to the finish. He had prevented the execution of his "scorched earth" orders. And yet the Führer forgave him. True, Speer had joined the Party in 1933, after its rise to power, not like Himmler, ten years before, when the success of National Socialism seemed problematic. Nor was he that fanatical defender of the National Socialist *doctrine* that Himmler was. Moreover, morally tortured at the thought of having broken his oath of allegiance to Adolf Hitler, Speer came, at, his own risk, and opened his heart to him. It is difficult to say whether the Führer would have pardoned Himmler's attempt to negotiate with the hostile powers, had the Reichsführer S.S. come to him and done the same. Adolf Hitler *expected more of him* than of Speer or anybody else.)

The truth is that the Führer's ruthlessness and Heinrich

Himmler's were not of the same *quality*, or, to repeat what I have already so emphatically stressed, that Adolf Hitler was essentially one of those heroic but unfortunate Men "against Time," "more Sun than Lightning," who, as long as this Dark Age lasts, are bound to lose, while Himmler would have won, had he but possessed something of Adolf Hitler's genius. He would have sacrificed anybody and anything to the one goal, *from the beginning* — when the sacrifice would have had the greatest practical justification. He would not have cared for the losses. And he would have won. But he would not have been "Kalki" — the last one — for all that; not even with genius. He lacked "Sun" qualities to a too great extent. But then, National Socialism, like the ancient Aryan order in India — or like early Islam — would have fallen to pieces from within a few generations, thanks precisely to those compromises with the Dark Forces, which every victory "*in* Time" implies.

Adolf Hitler did not want such a victory.

The only victory he wanted was a definitive one — the definitive one; the one which only He, the *last* Man "against Time," the last Incarnation of the everlasting World-Sustainer in a human body — Kalki — can win.

And yet — for such is the law of every sincere, genuine struggle "against Time," which asserts itself more and more compellingly as time flows by, and as the Dark Age draws to its end — he was, from the start, aware of the necessity of those qualities "in Time," of those "Lightning" qualities, which all ruthless National Socialists, and especially Himmler, eminently possessed; which he possessed himself, to a very high, even if not yet sufficient, degree. He was aware of their necessity if, in his own words, "poison" was to be "overcome through counter-poison, tyranny through tyranny, and terror through greater terror." He has more than once compared the rise of the new Movement to that of the early Catholic Church, thereby recognising the solid worldly capabilities of its organisers and of his fighters — even of its spiritual fighters — as a condition *sine qua non* of its development and triumph, at once and in the long run. It may seem somewhat unexpected — not to say somewhat irrelevant, when not absurd — to mention in this connection such a thing as the immemorial symbolism of colours. Still in that most powerful church of the Dark Age, that National Socialism is out to combat and to crush, but the long worldly experience of which it was — and is, now and in the future — to meditate upon and to make use of, every ritual colour has its meaning. The Pope, Head of the faithful, is clad in white, recalling thereby the spiritual purity and lucidity of the Initiate — the Man "*above* Time," whose otherworldly truth has been distorted and exploited in historical Christianity. The scarlet, purple, and gold of the high church Dignitaries also symbolise states of advanced spirituality — the ideal towards which the church is supposed to aspire. But the church is an organisation of this earth — an organisation in Time. It is the militant hierarchy acting under the inspiration and orders of Dostoyevsky's "Grand Inquisitor" "for the greatest glory of Christ" but surely *not* according to Christ's wisdom, which is "not of this earth." And its actual fighting forces — *all* its priests and nearly all its monks and nuns, who are its strength in the day-to-day struggle against all contrary (or rival) powers and its obvious witnesses among the people — *are clad in black*, the colour of this Age; at the most (as in the case of the Dominicans) in black *and* white — the colour of this Dark Age and of Light "above Time."

It strikes me as an extremely eloquent fact that the Swastika, Symbol of Life and Health[41] and Symbol of the Sun, which Adolf Hitler chose to place at the centre of the German flag — not to say of the Pan-Aryan flag, for Germany is to remain, in the light of the Hitler faith, the head of a Pan-Aryan Movement — was *black* upon a *white* background, nay, black upon a white *disk*, amidst a further scarlet surface. And this is all the more remarkable if one assumes that the Führer took his decision intuitively, without being aware of its meaning (which I, personally, however, do not believe).

It is, also, remarkable that, although the exigencies of war imposed the inconspicuous greyish-green (*feldgrau*) uniform upon the Waffen S.S., the elder S.S. organisation — the "Allgemeine" S.S., entrusted with the inner defence of the régime — wore *black* — black, I repeat, the colour symbolising *par excellence the Dark Forces, which can be crushed only through forces of a similar nature*; the colour symbolising the harsh qualities "in Time" that the S.S. men were to put to the service of an ideal of

---

[41] *Swasti*, in Sanskrit.

Golden Age perfection.

Far from considering the black Swastika and the black raiment of the Knights of the new Faith as a "mistake from the standpoint of the Invisible" — still less as a "proof" of "black magic" — I see in them signs of an unfailing knowledge of the laws of action in Time; a knowledge at least as sound as that of the builders of the Catholic Church; a recognition of the fact that alone through qualities "*in* Time" — through those "Lightning" qualities that carry all agents of the Dark Forces to success and all great men "in Time" to greatness — can a Movement triumph here and now, in this Dark Age; especially near the end of it, *and especially a Movement against the spirit of it.*

And, I repeat — for one cannot repeat it enough — had those capabilities and tendencies symbolised in the black Swastika upon the German flag and in the black uniform of the toughest defenders of National Socialism been displayed *to their full, from the beginning,* by the Man "against Time," Adolf Hitler (and not only the qualities of ruthlessness and fanaticism; characteristic of all revolutionary movements in their youth, but also such qualities of cunning, of deceit, of shameless unscrupulousness, as alone can match and beat the cunning, deceit, and selfish unscrupulousness of this advanced Dark Age mankind); had, first of all, the Jewish question been solved *in time*, not only with all Himmler's mercilessness, but also with all the necessary diplomacy, i.e., had the Jews — and all the Jews; all the dangerous ones, especially — been disposed of quietly, without the world knowing of it or being able to *prove* it; had even the influential Jews in foreign lands somehow been lured into confidence and brought to their doom, already before the war; had, on the other hand, the question of the collaboration of certain technicians, capitalists, and high officers, whose National Socialist convictions were more than doubtful, but whose capabilities the Third Reich *needed*, been tackled in a both more ruthless and more supple manner — as similar problems were handled in Russia, by the Communists, on their coming to power — had Adolf Hitler also proved himself both more merciless and more supple in his dealings with the outer world; had he, instead of displaying, in the last days of the war, a materially useless ruthlessness towards his own people, crushed England without hesitation, without pity, without remorse, in 1940, and made the widest possible concessions to Russia at England's expense, regardless of the number of Europeans (Aryan brothers) whom he would have sacrificed to Stalin's convenience (the self-same ones whom Roosevelt and Churchill were to sacrifice two years later, but this time *against* the German Reich); in one word, had he been himself *plus* the extraordinary man "in Time" who could have deceived Stalin and crushed England and the U.S.A. (or deceived Roosevelt and Churchill, and crushed Russia, in the case that was more advantageous in the long run), it is more than probable that the National Socialist state would be lasting still.

But that was not to be, for the simple reason that I have already given—the reason which Adolf Hitler himself expressed, in his own way, to Hans Grimm, in 1928—namely that he, the Leader of the National Socialist Movement, was not "the Leader Who is to come"—i.e., the last Man "against Time"—but only the One-before-the-last; the one who was to do "the preparatory work" (*die Vorarbeit*) for the One Who will come after him.

He felt—not being, himself, that One "equally 'Sun' and 'Lightning'"—that, were he to allow the ruthless (and cunning) men around him to act from *the beginning* as they liked, the state "against Time" that he wanted to build would, very soon, in their hands (or very soon after him and them) degenerate into an ordinary state "in Time"—as the early, noble, and warlike Islamic state so quickly degenerated into the dreary, corrupt Caliphate, nay, Caliphates, of which history tells us, after the rule of saintly Ali.

Rather than such a victory—the only possible one for any great Man "against Time," save the last One—he preferred the terrible risk (and, soon, the terrible reality) of heroic defeat. And he faced defeat, fully conscious of its meaning, in the spirit of detached (apparently useless, yet, spiritually necessary) dutiful action, which is that of that other divine Man "against Time" Who spoke upon the Kurukshetra Field, thousands of years before.

His S.S. men—those of them, at least, who were worthy of the name—faced it in the same spirit. It was natural to them. We read in one of the most impartial foreign reportages written about them—in that book of Georges Blond's, already quoted—the following statement:

War, modern war, with its power of death and its essential inhumanity, was for them a pleasure. Or, if not exactly a pleasure, at least the most interesting, the only *really* interesting way of life. Most of the Waffen S.S. men *did not even raise within their minds the question of the possible issue of the war*: all that interested them was that it lasted.

And the French author adds: "Such was the result of National Socialist fanaticism coupled with drill."[42] We see, in the S.S. men's attitude to war the outcome of the glorious Aryan Wisdom of detached Action, which is both theirs and that of the Bhagavad-Gita. It reminds us of verses of the Book of books: ". . . looking to thine own duty, thou shouldst not tremble; *for there is nothing more welcome to a Kshatriya* than a righteous war";[43] "Happy the Kshatriyas who obtain such a fight, offered, unsought, as an open door to heaven";[44] ". . . Slain, thou wilt obtain heaven; victorious, thou wilt enjoy the earth, therefore, stand up, son of Kunti, resolute to fight!"[45] *"Taking as equal pleasure and pain, gain and loss, victory and defeat, gird thyself for the battle; thus, thou shalt not incur sin."*[46] It reminds us that the S.S. men — the real ones — élite of the privileged Nation out of which Adolf Hitler tried to make a Nation "against Time" — are Aryan warriors "Kshatriyas" of the West. And if "National Socialist fanaticism coupled with drill" strengthened or created in them such an attitude, we should say that "National Socialist fanaticism coupled with drill" made genuine "Karma Yogis" out of them.

Moreover, around them and beyond them, the Führer's people at large, who were to continue to live, and to fulfil in suffering their long-appointed historical mission, had the same attitude, more or less, and did the same. Every true disciple of his did — and does — the same, according to his conscience; every one, from the martyrs of Nuremberg — those who were hanged and those who, to this day, are prisoners — to the humblest faithful German; to the humblest faithful Aryan of other lands, who

---

[42] Blond, p. 106.
[43] The Bhagavad-Gita, II, verse 31.
[44] The Bhagavad-Gita, II, verse 32.
[45] The Bhagavad-Gita, II, verse 37.
[46] The Bhagavad-Gita, II, verse 38.

believes in him; every one, beginning with the three men who had the honour of being cursed, along with him, by the rabbis of Jerusalem in December 1942 — the three, two of whom had been, unfortunately, cut off from him in the fever of the last days of the war. (Dr. Goebbels died, with his wife and children, the voluntary, heroic death one knows, in the historic "bunker." Heinrich Himmler was killed — shot, and then ignominiously thrown into a cesspool, by British soldiers[47] — a few days later. And Hermann Göring took poison in the night between the 15th and the 16th of October 1946, after having gone through the whole infamous Trial on the bench of the accused, and having justified before his judges and before posterity, in a last splendid speech, Adolf Hitler and the Third German Reich, and the more-than-German and more-than-human aristocratic ideal that both embody forever.)

In the Allied jails and camps, after the war, and in the midst of the atrocious conditions under which all Germany was to live for years, the merciless purge began. The impersonal Forces of Light and Life, Whose ways are mysterious, used the Jewish torturers and Allied hangmen — and the politicians and businessmen whose interest it was to keep Germany down all these years — to sort out and separate, within the National Socialist ranks or so-called such, the good corn from the tares.

There were months and months of savage persecution, during which a host of martyrs sealed with their blood their allegiance to the Man "against Time." I shall recall one — one among thousands; the worthy comrade and mouthpiece of thousands: a young S.S. warder of the Belsen camp, whom the British and their Jewish acolytes tortured in April 1945, in the hope to get I do not know what information out of him. One evening, he was brought to the infirmary, unrecognisable: eyeless, his jaw hanging; his bones broken, his face and body one raw, bleeding mass of torn flesh. He was placed upon a bed. And a British officer told the German doctors: "See to it that he lasts till tomorrow morning; we must try once more to make him speak . . ." In the middle of the night, the young man called the nurse in charge. He could not move; hardly utter a word. She leaned over the

---

[47] Heinrich Himmler's widow has, herself, given me the confirmation of this fact.

bed. He whispered; "Heil Hitler!" and gave up the ghost. I do not know his name; but I have often thought of him—and of others—and recalled the verse of the Horst Wessel Song: "Comrades whom the Reaction and the Red Front have slain"—whom all the agents of the Dark Forces have slain—"march in spirit with us, within our ranks!"

Countless such episodes have taken place in Germany (in Schwabisch Hall[48] and elsewhere) and in all lands of Europe and in Russia. And there are the martyrs who died, and there are those who survived—who, to this day, are waiting in the prisons of Western Germany and Western Europe: in Werl, in Wittlich, in Landsberg, in Breda, in Fresnes, etc., in Spandau *and* in the camps of Russia and Siberia; working as slaves in the Ural mines, in the freezing gold-fields of Kolyma, and waiting; waiting for a liberation that never comes. There are the thousands of civilians who are not—or are no longer—in jail, but who have no place in a world in which the citadel of all hopes "against Time"—the Third German Reich—has disappeared.

Some of them—more and more every day—give way; gradually change; let themselves be absorbed into the ugly, dreary, anti-Nazi post-war world. A few resist and remain—stronger as the flood spreads and roars all around them; victorious rocks—invincible rocks—in the midst of the ever-expanding flood. They make no noise; they are not spoken of; not mentioned in any connection. They work, and they live; apparently, "like other people"; in fact, as National Socialists. They forget nothing, forgive nothing, and learn all that they can. They keep within their hearts and live up to the commandments of the new faith of Aryan pride and cosmic Truth, expressed by Alfred Rosenberg, the martyr: "Thou shalt be brave; thou shalt never do anything mean. Thou shalt love God in all living things, animals and plants. Thou shalt keep thy blood pure . . ." They gather now and then, when they can—and read Nietzsche's works, and Rosenberg's and Frenssen's, but especially Adolf Hitler's *Mein Kampf.* And they comment upon the eternal words. They remember and tell their children the message of hope—the secret

---

[48] The place in which the S.S. men involved (or alleged to be involved) in the notorious "Malmédy case" were tortured. See the report of the American judge Van Roden published in 1948.

of invincibility; the call to power—one of the last sentences of the Führer's book: "A state which, in the Age of racial contamination, devotes itself to the care of its best racial elements, is bound to become, one day, the master of the earth."[49]

They work. They wait. They live. They are, in this darkening Dark Age, the irreducible element "against Time." They gradually take full consciousness of themselves and of their meaning and of their mission, in a small number of initiates such as that one who told me, on the 28th of October, 1953: "Up till 1945, we were a Party. Since 1945, we have become the kernel of a great new faith. We have discovered who we are, and Who our Führer is."[50]

They live. They marry pure-blooded Aryans of the same faith as themselves. They have children—for the privileged Race must continue to be, and the Reich, its stronghold in the West, must reconquer its power. They bring up their children in the same Hitler faith, in spite of all difficulties. They teach them to be proud of being, they too, members of the small, pure, healthy—indestructible—community. They give them in marriage to worthy young men and women who will, with them, bring the community a generation further along its way to final power and glory.

They are, of course, mostly Germans; there is, nay, a *very* strong proportion of former S.S. men among them. But there are also a few non-Germans—so that the Führer's words be fulfilled: "In the new world that we are building, it will matter little whether a man comes from Austria or from Norway, provided he be a pure-blooded Aryan."[51] (There were, during the war, non-German S.S. divisions—including an Indian one—fighting for the Third German Reich and for the Aryan Cause.) And the non-Germans look up to Adolf Hitler's Land as to the Holy Land of the West.

The whole faithful community is already a *Pan*-Aryan community. But a Pan-Aryan community conscious of Germany's

---

[49] *Mein Kampf*, p. 782.

[50] The speaker was Heinrich Blume. See Savitri Devi, *Pilgrimage* (Calcutta: Savitri Devi Mukherji, 1958), pp. 258–70 and *And Time Rolls On*, first ed., p. 78.

[51] Adolf Hitler, *Tischgespräche*, published after the war.

place and significance in the history of the West and especially in the history of these last years; conscious of the debt of the Aryan race to the National Socialist Reich—the state "against Time." Its members are dispersed all over the earth. But the young faith "against Time," the Hitler faith—that no de-Nazification efforts can kill, for it is the modern expression of something eternal—is the link between them, wherever they be.

They live, and work in silence, remembering Adolf Hitler.

They live, and wait. Knowingly or unknowingly, they are waiting for Kalki; Kalki, the last Man "against Time"; the One Whom Adolf Hitler foresaw in 1928; the Avenger Who will give them—or their children—the world.

15th February 1956

Part V

EPILOGUE:
KALKI, THE AVENGER

10. Hari Hara

12th-century Indian sculpture found in Bihar

Chapter 16

KALKI, THE AVENGER

The last Incarnation of Him-Who-comes-back — the last Man "against Time" — has many names. Every great faith, every great culture, nay, every true (living *or* obsolete) form of a Tradition as old as the fall of man (and as the subsequent yearning for the lost earthly Paradise) has given Him one. Through the eyes of the Visionary of Patmos, the Christians, behold in Him Christ "present for the second time"[1]: no longer a meek preacher of love and forgiveness, but the irresistible Leader of the celestial "white Horsemen" destined to put an end to this sinful world and to establish "a new Heaven and a new earth," a new Time-cycle. The Mohammedan world is awaiting Him under the features of "the Mahdi," Whom Allah shall send "at the end of times," to crush all evil through the power of His sword — "after the Jews will once more have become the masters of Jerusalem" and "after the Devil will have taught men to set even the air they breathe on fire."[2] On the other hand, in nearly every country of Europe, popular Tradition has greeted the One-Who-comes-back either in the form of a departed and returning King, or as the very Soul of a mythical, hidden Army: in Germany, as Emperor Frederick Barbarossa, who shall one day come out of the cave in which he has been asleep for centuries, and save his people, and lead them to unheard-of glory; in Denmark, as Holger Danske, of the Kronborg Mountain; in Poland, as the "Sleeping Host" of folk-tales; in Hungary, as "Attila," who is, one day to re-appear at the head of "Csaba's Army" and to work divine vengeance upon the wicked and to mete out justice; while the old solar religions of Central America pictured Him as the radiant white god Quetzalcoatl, returning in glory and power — like

---

[1] "Deutera Parousia" — "Second presence" — (of Christ) is the Greek expression for the "end of the world."

[2] This tradition can be, in Islam, traced up to the 14th century. In Persia the Twelfth Imam — who disappeared mysteriously, to come back at the end of times — has been identified with the "Mahdi."

the rising Sun—from beyond the Eastern Ocean. And the millions of Hindustan have called Him from time immemorial and still call Him "Kalki," the last Incarnation of the world-sustaining Power: Vishnu, the One Who will, in the interest of Life, put an end to this "Kali Yuga" or "Age of Gloom" and open a new succession of ages. I have called Him in this book by His Hindu name, not in order to show off an erudition which I am far from possessing, but simply because I happen to know of no Tradition in which the three types of manifested existence — "above Time," "against Time," and "in Time" — which I tried in these pages to evoke and to define, have so obviously their counterpart in the basic trinitarian conception of Divinity Itself, and in which (as a consequence of this) the Man "against Time" is, in *all* His successive embodiments, but especially in His last one, more eloquently — and more logically — considered as *the* divine Man *par excellence*.

A few words will make this point clear.

The well-known Hindu Trinity — Brahma, Vishnu, Shiva, so masterfully evoked in Indian art — is anything but the blending of three inseparable "gods" into one, nay, anything but the triple aspect of one transcendent and personal God. It symbolises something by far more fundamental, namely Existence in its entirety: manifested and unmanifested, conceivable, nay visible and tangible, *and* beyond conception. For Existence — Being — is the One thing divine. And there is no Divinity outside It, and nothing outside Divinity.

Now "Brahma" is Existence *in und für sich* — in and for Itself; Being unmanifested, and thereby outside and above Time; Being, beyond the conception of the Time-bound mind, and thereby, unknowable. It is significant that "Brahma" has no temples in India — or elsewhere. One cannot render a cult to That which no time-bound consciousness can conceive. One can, at the most, through the right attitude (and also through the right ascetic practises) merge one's self into It, transcend individual consciousness, live "above Time" — in the absolute Present which admits no "before" and no "after," and which is Eternity.

"Brahma" — their own deeper Self and that of the world, experienced on the level of Eternity — is That which all men "above Time" seek to realise: *the* positive state of "peace, perfect peace," of peace, not through non-existence, but through liberation from the bondage of "before" and "after" and of all "pairs of opposites."

"Vishnu" — the World-Sustainer — is the tendency of every being to remain the same and to create (and procreate) in its own likeness, the universal Life-force as opposed to change and thereby to disaggregation and death, the Power that binds this time-bound Universe to its timeless Essence — every manifested being to the Idea of that being, in the sense Plato was one day to give the word "Idea."

All men "against Time" (all centres of action "against Time," in the cosmic sense of the word) are "embodiments of Vishnu." They are all — more or less — "Saviours of the world," forces of Life, directed against the downward current of irresistible change that is the very current of Time, forces of Life tending to bring the world back to original timeless Perfection, to that glorious projection of the Unmanifested that *begins* every Time-cycle.

"Shiva" — the "Destroyer" — is the tendency of every being to change, to *die* to its present and to all its past aspects. He is Mahakala — Time Itself, Time that drags the Universe to its unavoidable doom and — beyond that — to no less irresistible regeneration, to the Spring of a new Golden Age, and, again, slowly and steadily, to degeneracy and death, in an endless succession of Time-cycles, any one of which is an individual cycle, *parallel* to all others, no doubt, *but like unto none other before or after it*.

The truly great men "in Time" — men such as Genghis Khan, or, nearer to us, Stalin — reflect something of His terrible majesty. *The greatest men "against Time" also* — inasmuch as they all must possess (more or less) the qualities of character that are especially those of the men "in Time," the qualities in which is rooted the efficiency of organised violence. For Shiva is not only the "Destroyer"; He is the Creator — the "Good one,"[3] the "positive" One — also, to the extent all further creation is conditioned by change, and ultimately by the destruction of that which was there before. He is — as the Essence of destructive change, as Time — turned towards the future. The wild, cosmic joy of His Dance in the midst of flames, at the end of every successive Time-cycle, is both the joy of destruction *and* of new, perfect

---

[3] The word "Shiva" means the "Good One."

Creation. So much so that one cannot distinguish it from the joy of the heroes "against Time," Incarnations of Vishnu. These are all, as I said before, also men "above Time." A typical historic figure "above Time" — the Buddha — has been, in fact, classified as an "Incarnation of Vishnu" by the wise men of India, and there is indeed, in the cry of triumph attributed to him on his death bed — "Now, I shall never, never again enter a womb!" — something of the exultant intoxication of Lord Shiva's cosmic Dance. And, on the other hand, Lord Shiva Himself — Time personified — is also (strange as this may seem to the purely analytical mind) "above Time." He is the great Yogi, Whose face remains as serene as the blue sky while His feet beat the furious rhythm of the Tandava Dance, amidst the flames and smoke of a crumbling world.

In other words, Vishnu and Shiva, the World-Sustainer and the World-Destroyer, the Force "against Time" and Time Itself — Mahakala — are One and the same.[4] And they are Brahma, timeless Existence, the Essence of all that is. They are Brahma manifested, "in Time" (and, automatically, also "against Time") *and yet timeless*. Hindu art has symbolised this metaphysical truth in the figure of Hari-Hara (Vishnu and Shiva in one body) and in the famous Trimurti: three-faced Brahma-Vishnu-Shiva.

In the manifested Universe as we experience it at our scale, no living being embodies that triple and *complete* idea of Existence — the everlasting, universal Law of constant change away from, and of untiring aspiration towards and ceaseless effort back to original Perfection, *and* the ineffable inner peace of Timelessness, inseparable from It — better than the everlasting and ever-returning Man "against Time," He-Who-comes-back, age after age "to destroy evil-doers, and to establish upon earth the reign of righteousness."[5]

The man "in Time" has hardly any of the "Vishnu" or, as I have called them, "Sun" qualities.

The man "above Time" has hardly any of the "Lightning" qualities of Shiva, the Destroyer.

The man "against Time" — the exceptional Kshatriya, who

---

[4] Sri Krishna, Incarnation of *Vishnu*, says, in the Bhagavad-Gita: "*I am Time everlasting*, I, the Supporter, Whose Face turns everywhere."

[5] Bhagavad-Gita, IV, verses 7 and 8.

lives in Eternity while acting in Time according to the Aryan doctrine of Detached Violence once proclaimed upon the Kurukshetra Field—has Vishnu's faithfulness to the original divine pattern of Creation, Shiva's holy fury of destruction (in view of further Creation), and Brahma's fathomless serenity which is, I repeat, the serenity of all three: timeless peace beyond the roar of all wars in Time.

Yet *no* hero "against Time" has, in any Time-cycle, ever expressed that triple aspect of immanent Divinity with absolute adequacy, save the last one. And none was permanently successful (to the extent *anything* is permanent in Time-bound existence)—i.e., successful at least for a few myriads of years—save the last one. The life-work of every other one either gave way from within after an incredibly short span of time—securing itself, at the most, a purely nominal survival at the cost of ever greater compromises with the forces of disintegration—or was crushed from outside after a desperate struggle against those increasingly efficient forces. It is as though, throughout the countless millenniums of every successive Time-cycle, from the end of the Golden Age onwards, Divinity seeks to express Itself in a new World Order, faithful to the eternal pattern, through the agency of inspired Leaders of the greatest races of the earth, and *never can do so till the end*. Or rather, it is as though "the end" could be defined as the historical moment in which immanent Divinity, i.e., the Soul of the Universe, is again able to express Itself in a *true* World Order, through the agency of the one and only fully successful great Individual "against Time."

That last great Individual—an absolutely harmonious blending of the sharpest of all opposites, equally "Sun" and "Lightning"—is the one Whom the faithful of all religions and the bearers of practically all cultures await, the one of Whom Adolf Hitler (knowingly or unknowingly) said, in 1928: "I am not he; but while nobody comes forward to prepare the way for him, I do so,"[6] the One Whom I have called by His Hindu name, Kalki, on account of the cosmic truth that this names evokes.

卐 卐 卐

---

[6] See Hans Grimm, *Warum? Woher? aber Wohin?*, p. 14—Ed.

The world has been waiting for Him for hundreds of thousands of years. Every Man "against Time" has, knowingly or unknowingly, foreshadowed Him, and paved the way for His coming. The youngest great race of our Time-cycle on this earth—the Aryan—is awakening in order to bear Him in full consciousness and pride. And the most heroic and the most selfless of all its Leaders, Adolf Hitler, the One-before-the-last Man "against Time"—more heroic than any of the elder ones, for he fought against the downward pressure of many more centuries; more selfless than the very *last* One, for he was, contrarily to Him, to reap nothing but disaster—sacrificed himself and his people—at large in order to give Him (out of the faithful surviving few) *compagnons* at arms in the last decisive battle.

And the signs of the times proclaim that the day He—Kalki—will appear is drawing nigh.

He will appear when all but the last and toughest of the natural Aryan aristocracy—His chosen *compagnons* at arms—have definitely taken the way to the abyss. And all but the chosen few are rapidly taking that way.

A more and more glaring sign of fate is to be observed in the shocking increase of the population of the globe from year to year,[7] especially in the increase of the lower races and in the rapid bastardisation of the higher ones and the resulting accelerated fall of the whole of mankind to the level of an enormous unthinking herd.

I have, in another part of this book, already mentioned the fact as one of the main characteristics of the advancing Dark Age. In the Golden Age—symbolised, in Christian Tradition, in the much older myth of the "Garden of Eden"—extremely *few* people, *but all god-like*, lived in a lovely world, covered (wherever the climate permitted) with a luxuriant vegetation that nobody destroyed, and full of beautiful, free, and friendly animals that nobody killed or injured. However, with the appearance of what I have called the superstition of "man," expression of the

---

[7] I have mentioned in this book Hans Grimm's tragic warning. (See his book *Warum? Woher? aber Wohin?*, pp. 107–108 and 206 and following.)

oldest human selfishness and conceit—i.e., meanness—which cut him off the harmonious brotherhood of living creatures and caused his fall from the Golden Age state of existence, man ceased to be the righteous king of Creation to become, gradually, its tyrant and, more and more—as myriads of years rolled by and as he sunk into the Dark Age—its torturer. And his rebellion against the divinity of Nature led him, along with this, to despise Nature's great purpose. A short-sighted quest for indiscriminate individual enjoyment made him indifferent to the call to supermanhood. And he degraded himself ever more. Now, at the *end* of the Dark Age, the Edenic picture is completely reversed. Upon the surface of this unfortunate planet, which is losing with alarming rapidity its once so broad and thick mantle of forests, of this unfortunate planet, where whole species of proud wild creatures—the aristocracy of the animal world—have already been or are being, with no less speed, wiped away—killed off to the last—one notices an increasingly obnoxious and steadily expanding swarm of dreary (when not positively ugly), vulgar, silly, worthless two-legged mammals. And the more worthless they are, the quicker they breed. The sickly and the dull have more children than the healthy and bright, the inferior races, and the people who have no race at all, definitely more than the 100 percent Aryan, and the downright rotten—afflicted both with hereditary diseases *and* racially indefinable blood—are, more often than not, terrifyingly fertile.

And everything is done to encourage that mad increase in number and that constant loss in quality. Everything is done to keep the sickly, the crippled, the freaks of nature, the unfit to work and unfit to live, from dying. One "prolongs" as much as possible the lives of the incurable. One inflicts torture upon thousands of lovely, innocent, *healthy* animals, in the hope of discovering "new treatments," so that deficient men, whom Nature has, anyhow, condemned to death, might last a few months—or a few weeks longer, so that they be patched up, or artificially given an illusion of vitality... while remaining a burden to the healthy. And that, whoever they may be, just because they are "human beings." Hospitals and asylums—bluntly described as such, or politely christened "homes" are full of such dregs of humanity, old and young... while the healthy are (physically and morally) made unhealthy through the conditions of life imposed upon them by a false civilisation: through joyless work and overcrowded houses, lack of privacy, lack of leisure, through compulsory inoculations and cleverly advertised unnatural food, through nerve-wracking mass-music, not to speak of a soul-killing, brain-softening mass-propaganda exalting unnatural values. Hospitals and asylums are, after slaughterhouses, one of the most depressing features of the advanced "Kali Yuga" or Dark Age, the one which would automatically provoke the greatest disgust in the heart of a strong man of the beginning of this Age, not to mention one out of the preceding "Dvapara Yuga" and *a fortiori* out of a remoter Age, if such men could come back as they once were.

But why speak of hospitals and asylums? The streets are full of dregs of humanity, at least full of bastards and of sub-men. One only has to look at the faces one sees in the overcrowded buses, or in the cinemas and dancing halls and cafés in large towns, nay even in small ones, even in the *countryside*, everywhere, save in those lands in which the dominant race is relatively pure. It is a pitiful sight, a pitiful world, a world up-side-down, a world in which the average cat or dog is, *as such*, immeasurably healthier, more beautiful—more perfect—than the average man or woman and *a fortiori* than the average post-1945 state ruler, nearer to the ideal archetype of his species than most present-day human beings and *especially* than the official (*and* the hidden) leaders of the present-day "free world"—President Eisenhower (or rather, Mr. Baruch), Churchill, Mendès-France, etc. (let alone their most obedient servants Konrad Adenauer, Theodor Heuss, and Co.)—ever were to the ideal archetype of man, God's masterpiece.

If only the ugly sub-men were capable of lofty thoughts—or simply of *thought*—that would be something! But they are not. And their leaders are worse than they, not better. True, they all *speak* of "free thinking"; speak of it, and write about it. They criticise their former friends (the Communists) for "killing individual thought." Yet they are themselves the first ones to lack both freedom of judgement and individuality. They all have the same views, and the same ideal. Their views are those of the ruling press. Their ideal is to "get on in life," i.e., to make money and to "be happy," which means: to enjoy tasty food, fine clothing, lodgings provided with the latest commodities, and, in addition to that, as often as possible, a little drink, a little light music, a little sport, a little love-making. Maybe they call themselves Christians—or Hindus, or anything else. But whatever religion they might profess, their faith is skin-deep. Nothing, absolutely nothing more-than-personal—and, *a fortiori*, more-than-human—interests them. The one thing they all pray for, when they pray at all, is "peace," not the unassailable, inner peace of the Best (of which they have not the foggiest experience), but peace in the sense of absence of war, the indefinite prolongation of a *"status quo"* which allows them to think of tomorrow's little pleasure without the fear of today's deadly danger; peace, thanks to which they will, undisturbed—so they hope—be able to go on rotting in the midst of that increasing comfort which technical progress secures them; peace, thanks to which they expect to remain (or gradually to become) *happy*—in the manner pigs are happy, when they have plenty to eat and clean straw to lie upon.

Accelerated technical progress is, along with accelerated human degeneracy, an all-important feature of the advanced Dark Age.

It is—or seems to be—the "triumph of man" over Nature. And it is interpreted and exalted as such by the sub-men, all the more proud of it that they have nothing else—no real, living culture; no disinterested work or knowledge—to be proud of. It is—or seems to be—the "proof" of man's superiority over all other sentient beings, the "proof" of his superiority *en bloc, regardless of race*, for ... a Negro can drive a motorcar, can't he? And there are very clever Jewish doctors. It forwards or strengthens the age-old superstition of "man," which lies at the root of all decay. It is, or seems to be, the way to universal "happiness," the ideal of those increasing millions—and soon, milliards[8]—who have no ideal. In fact, it helps the ruling powers of the Dark Age, the skilful agents of the forces of disintegration, to keep the millions under their control. For, paradoxical as this may sound, masses who can read and write are easier to enslave than masses who cannot, and nothing is so easy to subdue and to *keep* down as masses who consider their wireless and television sets and cinema shows as indispensable necessities of life. (The modern men "against Time" know that, as well as the men

---

[8] Billions (short scale)—Ed.

"in Time." Only they do not dispose of the inexhaustible financial resources of the latter.)

Technical progress, in all fields in which it does not automatically imply cruelty towards man or beast (or plant),[9] is not a bad thing in itself. Actually, it is not it that makes the Dark Age. What *makes* the Dark Age is the fall of all but an extreme minority of men to the level of a brainless (and heartless) herd, and, at the same time, their endless increase in number. And technical progress is a curse only inasmuch as it is *the* most powerful instrument in the hands of all those who, directly or indirectly, encourage that indiscriminate increase and, consequently, forward that herd-mentality (even if they do not explicitly intend to); in the hands of the doctors who keep the weak and deficient and mongrels alive, and do nothing to prevent further such ones from being born; in the hands of the politicians "in Time" who, precisely because they all share—like the doctors—the age-old superstition of "man" and of man's individual "happiness" at any cost, are opposed to any systematic selection in view of the survival and welfare of the healthiest, let alone to systematic *racial* selection *also*, in view of the survival and rule of an all-round biological human aristocracy.

As I said above, technical progress and its wonders could just as easily be put to the service of a decidedly "life-centred" philosophy "against Time," of an aristocratic doctrine of personal and racial *quality*, such as National Socialism, if only the exponents of such a doctrine could maintain themselves in power in this advanced Age of Gloom—which they cannot.

The reason *why* they cannot is not that there exist electric trains and electric irons, radios and television sets, aeroplanes and washing machines and "electronic brains" and all manner of major and minor commodities, products of technical skill, but that the overwhelming majority of *mankind* in this Age—the more and more numerous and duller and duller herd of all races, in process of general bastardisation—is against any and every aristocratic wisdom. The reason is that the millions and millions—soon milliards—of sub-men feel themselves threatened in their dream of pig-like "happiness," nay, in their no less pig-like existence, by whoever embodies such a wisdom "against Time."

---

[9] Destruction of forests, for instance.

The reason is that the increasingly powerful agents of the death-forces, natural leaders of this Age, *use* radio, cinema, television, and all technical means that money can secure, to excite the unthinking herd against the Best, while doing everything they can, through the advertisement of more and more wonderful commodities, to keep the average man's slumbering mind away from higher things—away from every aspiration "against Time," away from every aggressive criticism of the fundamental Dark Age dogmas and, in general, away from all impersonal problems . . . until its slumber ends in the definitive sleep of death.

It is not—surely not!—technical progress as such which so deeply shocks Kalki's future *compagnons* at arms (or the fathers of such ones), those natural aristocrats of the youngest human race, whom I have described as "the Best." It is the glaring disparity between the perfection of modern technical achievements considered as "means" and the worthlessness of the ends to the service of which they are put; it is the contrast between that wonderful Aryan intelligence, which stands and shines behind practically every discovery of modern science, every invention of modern technique, and the steadily increasing degeneracy of the sub-human multitudes who enjoy the products of its creative ingenuity in daily life, as a matter of course, nay, who, through their *misuse* of them, are sinking lower and lower into that brainless and soulless "happiness"—I repeat: that pig-like "happiness" — which is the ideal of our times.

That ideal is *the* one forwarded, under one form or another, more and more unmistakably in the course of centuries, by all typical Dark Age leaders "in Time," in particular, by that most efficient of all agents of the Dark Powers during the last 2,400 (at least) and especially during the last three or four hundred years: the international Jew.

The advanced Dark Age of this present Time-cycle is the reign of the Jew—of the negative element; of the reverser of eternal values for the sake of "human" ones, and, finally, for that of his own, selfish interests; the reign of the "destroyer of culture," as Adolf Hitler so rightly pointed out; of the age-old "ferment of disintegration." It is natural that "ferments of disintegration" should become more and more active—more and more alive—as a Time-cycle nears its end.

It is—or was, for a very long time—a widespread belief among Christians that when the Jews become once more the masters of Palestine, their "promised Land," the "end of the world"—i.e., the end of the present Time-cycle—will not be far away. The Mohammedans behold, they too, in that same event, one of the tokens announcing the advent of the long-awaited "Mahdi."[10] Thanks to England's steadily pro-Jewish policy, the Jews have, in Palestine, since 1948, a state of their own. If the collective belief of many generations of men, both in the West and in the Near East, corresponds to any reality (and collective beliefs of that nature generally do, to some extent), then the great end must be drawing nigh. The existence of that strange—at the same time ultra-modern and unbelievably archaic—Israelitish state is an extra "sign of the times" or, rather, the symbol of a by far mightier and more dangerous reality, which is the *actual* "sign." And that reality is none other than the ever-tightening grip of the Jew upon the whole world.

The truth about the Jewish state in Palestine remains that which Adolf Hitler had already understood—half through his knowledge of the Zionist Movement, half through his intuition of the natural enemy of Aryan mankind as such—and expressed, fourteen years before its foundation, namely that the Jews never intended to live in their independent country (which is, anyhow, far too small to contain them all) but that they just wanted "protected headquarters—headquarters with sovereign rights, free from the interference of other states—for their world-wide international organisation of deceit, a place of refuge for rogues who have been detected, and a high-school for rogues in the making . . ."[11] In other words Palestine may well be the mystical—and practical—centre of world Jewry, but the Jewish danger has no "centre." It is everywhere, and all the more difficult to fight that most people either refuse to see it or reject as "inhuman" the only methods through which it could be neutralised.

One need not read the famous *Protocols of the Elders of Zion* or the more modern speech which Rabbi Emanuel Rabinovich de-

---

[10] See above, p. 409.
[11] *Mein Kampf*, p. 356.

livered in Budapest, on the 12th of January, 1952 before the "Emergency Council of European Rabbis,"[12] in order to be convinced of the double, world-wide effort of the Jews, on one hand, to lower the biological level of all non-Jewish races, especially of the Aryan, and, on the other, to work themselves into all key positions in the economic, political, cultural, and spiritual life of all leading nations. It is, on the contrary, the obvious reality of that double effort — the presence of the international Jew (or of organisations entirely under his control) behind all "spiritual," "cultural," or political movements or thought-currents that allow, encourage, or logically lead to the mixture of races; behind all or practically all "literary," "artistic," commercial, or "medical" concerns, the aim of which is to encourage sexual perversity and any manner of vice, to provide silly amusements or to forward the love of empty speculation, in one word, to lower the physical, intellectual, and moral level of the individual; and, along with that, the ever-increasing number (and influence) of Jews (or of men completely under Jewish control) in world finance, world industry, and world politics — it is the fact that, whoever shows that he or she is fully aware of that effort and fully prepared to fight against it, "gets nowhere"; the glaring fact that nothing indeed happens in this ugly post-1945 world without the Jews' order or permission, which strengthens, at least in *us*, the conviction that both the *Protocols of the Elders of Zion* and the recent Rabinovich speech, and the like of them, are genuine documents. As genuine as the much older Bible and Talmud that also proclaim the Jews "God's Chosen People."

There resides, perhaps, the whole meaning of the rise and temporary victory and world-wide rule of the Jews as a "sign of the times"; it is based upon a lie; it is lasting through a lie; it is the most logical feature of the advanced Dark Age, which is, more and more, the Age of Lies.

The truth is that there is no other "God" but the immanent, *impersonal* divinity of Nature — of Life, the universal Self. No tribal god is "God." Tribal gods are more or less divine, to the extent they embody and express a *more or less divine* collective soul. Yahweh, the tribal god of the Jews, is as little divine, as *negative* as they themselves — they, the typically negative human

---

[12] Published through the care of Einar Åberg, Norrviken, Sweden.

element of our Time-cycle. Through a series of lies, the Jews have been for the last 3,000 and especially for the last 2,400 years, leading an increasingly intensified campaign for the reversal of the eternal, *natural* values—i.e., an anti-truth campaign—in view of their own exaltation. They have, through the mouth of their prophets and "philosophers" proclaimed Yahweh "God of all men"; they have, then, concealed as many as they could of his nasty characteristics through a clever exploitation of the Christ myth by Paul of Tarsus and other Jews, half-Jews,[13] and judaised Greeks; they have, through the same, stressed anew the old, very old denial of the unity of the Realm of Life and proclaimed "all men" different in nature from the rest of creatures—and therefore above the general laws of Life—in order to buttress the false teaching that "one blood"[14] flows in the veins of "all nations," and to kill the idea (and the instinct) of a natural, God-ordained racial hierarchy. They have preached meekness and forgiveness and pacifism (to all, save to their own people) in order to rob the young, warlike Aryan race of its stamina, in order to kill its healthy pride. They are, now more feverishly than ever, encouraging its adolescents to make fun of "Nazi prejudices," to despise purity of blood, and to marry outside their race (if thus be the impulse of "individual love")—so that the race may disappear, encouraging them into perdition, both through the old superstition of "man" under its various modern forms, and through the whole atmosphere of subtle corruption in which the post-1945 world is literally soaking.

They must win—and they shall win—*for the time being*. Otherwise, it would not yet be the End. They must—and shall—see their dream—their immemorial dream of easy domination over a peaceable, "happy" hotchpotch of bastardised millions and ever more millions, that their long-drawn disintegrating action has rendered even more contemptible than they—at a hair's breadth from its complete materialisation. Otherwise, the measure of iniquity—the measure of *untruth*—would not be full. And it would not yet be time for "Kalki"—the Avenger—to come.

卐 卐 卐

---

[13] Timothy, the faithful follower of Paul of Tarsus, was a half-Jew.
[14] See the "Acts of the Apostles," chapter 17, verse 26.

I am not qualified to venture precise and especially *political* forecasts. This whole book has, moreover, little to do with that which people ordinarily mean by "politics." It is history, no doubt, and therefore *also* "politics," but politics considered from a cosmic angle, from which current events and the men who stand behind them appear in an unusual light.

Those who are daily and directly in touch with the social, economical, and military realities which are, already, moulding the immediate future, can say nothing about that future, *for they know nothing*. And I know even less than they do about precise events, i.e., about the details of *the road* the world is taking. But I know the road. I know it, because that knowledge is not the concern of politicians, sociologists, economists, or military experts but precisely that of people who look at history, past and present, and who *live* the history of our times, from the cosmic standpoint. There is nothing in the way of documents, very little in the way of statistics, to "prove" the soundness of what I say. Times to come will confirm it or not confirm it. All I can state now, in favour of my point, is that it tallies with all the forms of the one, unwritten Tradition which I happen to know. It is orthodox in the light of Tradition—orthodox as far as an *interpretation* can be.

Tradition has not given us the date of the last return of Him Who comes back. Nor has it given us the means of calculating it. Tradition is neither history nor astrology. Yet, according to the signs I have mentioned, the last embodiment of the Forces "against Time" in our Time-cycle—Kalki—must appear soon. He will come when all will seem irretrievably lost: when nothing will be left of the real Chosen Race—the natural Aryan aristocracy—but a silent, unnoticed, yet conscious, unwavering, and active handful of men and women of the type of those I have described at the end of the last chapter of this book. Now, everything *does* actually seem lost without hope. As Rabbi Emanuel Rabinovich declared in 1952, "the goal towards which the Jews have been striving for over 3,000 years"—namely, peaceful domination over a "happy," bastardised earth, in which the "most dangerous enemy"—the polar opposite—of Jewry, i.e., the Aryan, will (in the Rabbi's own words) be "nothing more than a memory"—"*is within hand's reach*." And the few men who are already more than men—the toughest votaries of the perennial

Faith of Light and Life in its most recent form—are waiting; waiting to recognise their own beloved Leader, Adolf Hitler, in the irresistible apocalyptic Warrior Who is to avenge him and his people—their comrades and themselves. The divine Warrior is bound to come soon.

It is impossible to say "where" He will appear. Since the fargone days of the fall of man, all those who have been awaiting Him have looked upon Him as an exponent of their particular faith and as one of their people. The Jews themselves who have the strongest grounds of all to *dread* Him—have taken over the immemorial myth announcing His advent and distorted it—*reversed it*, in the manner they reverse all truth—into the dogma of a Jewish Messiah, to suit their purpose. The Jewish and judaised founders of Christianity—Paul of Tarsus and the others—have built up around the mysterious person of Jesus (whose real origin is unknown) a whole pernicious—man-centred, anti-racialist, anti-natural—philosophy, in which they blended together, with astounding skill, Jewish Messianism and the old cosmic myth of the God Who dies and rises from the dead. They did so in order to give the Jews, the negative element *par excellence*, the appearance of a positive mission of salvation, i.e., in order to make the negative values appear as positive, and the positive ones as negative—the genuine sons of the "Father of lies," which indeed they are! For, whatever be the nation destined to bear Him, one thing is certain: Kalki will not, directly or indirectly, draw His origin from the Jewish people. None of the inspired men of action "against Time" ever did. The last One is also not to. Moreover, He will not be born among any of the older races which have had their centuries of beauty and of glory in the Ages that lie irretrievably behind us and that are now (in spite of apparent revivals—false nationalisms, bad copies of those of the Aryan nations) in definite, *wholesale* decay.

According to the laws of development in Time which are those of the logic of history, Kalki, the Avenger, the final Redeemer, can only belong to the youngest race of our Time-cycle: the Aryan. For it is the youngest and most dynamic race of *any* Time-cycle which provides "the bridge" into the following one: the chosen Vanguard who will have the enviable privilege of living in *both* Time-cycles, who will fight the last battle of the Forces of Life in the doomed world *and* experience amidst the perfection of the new-born (or, rather, regenerated) one, that glorious Golden Age state of existence—Godhead in flesh and blood—which we fail to conceive even in our loftiest dreams, today, in the Age of Gloom. Out of the youngest and most dynamic race of any Time-cycle come, if not all, at least the greatest number of its latest heroes "against Time" (i.e., those of its very last 60 or 70 centuries). It is at any rate remarkable that *all* the *human* "avatars" or earthly Incarnations of Vishnu mentioned in Hindu Tradition—five, out of the nine that belong to the past—are looked upon as "Brahmins" or "Kshatriyas," i.e., Aryans. It is within the logic of Tradition that the "tenth" and last—Kalki—should also be born as a member of the privileged race.

Will He be none other than He whom I have described as the One-before-the-last Man "against Time" — Adolf Hitler—returning with more-than-human power? There is no reason why this should not be, provided the inspired Leader still be alive, and provided the world becomes, within his lifetime, ripe for the great End (which would in no way be a wonder, at the rate decay has set in everywhere, after 1945). The terrible experience of defeat through treason, and the sight of the systematic degradation of his people through far subtler and deadlier means than the ridiculous "de-Nazification" rules and regulations, would probably be enough to rouse the Führer's "Lightning" qualities until they balance in him the "Sun" ones and make him a new man—infinitely more merciless than he was in his first career.

But even if it be not so—even if Adolf Hitler really be dead in the flesh, as an increasing number of his faithful ones believe—still one is, considering things *in their essence*, justified in saying that "Kalki" will be he, come back. For "Kalki" will be *all* Men "against Time," come back. He will be the exponent of all that for which every one of them fought in vain against the ever more powerful current of decay—the very current of history—the exponent of that eternal cosmic Order, the earthly projection of which is the "reign of righteousness" mentioned in the Bhagavad-Gita. He will be both He Who spoke to the Aryan warrior, Arjuna—and to all Aryan warriors—on the Kurukshetra Field, and He Who spoke to the German people—and to every racially-conscious individual Aryan of the world—from the *Hofbräu-Festsaal*, from the Luitpold Arena, and from the German *Reichstag*. For the two are the same One: the One Who came back, and Who will come back again.

And "Kalki" will be nearer to and more intimately connected with the latest great Man "against Time," Adolf Hitler, than with any of the many former ones. For He—the last One—is, as I said in the beginning of this study, none other than *the* One of Whom the Führer spoke when, with that unfailing cosmic intuition that raises him so high above the cleverest of Dark Age politicians, he told Hans Grimm, in 1928: "I know that Somebody must come forth and meet our situation. I have sought him. I have found him nowhere; and therefore I have taken upon myself to do the preparatory work, *only the most urgent preparatory work*. For that much I know: I am not He. And I know also what is lacking in me."[15]

He is that One. And He will, in the midst of the most hopeless circumstances, continue the old—the perennial—Struggle against the downward stream of Time—the Struggle which the disaster of 1945 has *apparently*, but only apparently, interrupted—and bring it to a victorious end for a few myriads of years, make Adolf Hitler's dream, through means that were yet unthinkable during (or before) the Second World War, a glaring reality for a few myriads of years.

The means cannot be foretold, for things will have changed, by then. Things *are* changing—and the science of war, progressing—every day. One point is, however, as a main feature of every recurring "great End," beyond doubt: "Kalki" *will act with unprecedented ruthlessness*. Contrarily to Adolf Hitler, He will spare not a single one of the enemies of the divine Cause: not a single one of its outspoken opponents but also not a single one of the lukewarm, of the opportunists, of the ideologically heretical, of the racially bastardised, of the unhealthy, of the hesitating, of the all-too-human, not a single one of those who, in body or in character or mind, bear the stamp of the fallen Ages.

As I said before, His *compagnons* at arms will be the last National Socialists; the men of iron who will have victoriously stood the test of persecution and, what is more, the test of com-

---

[15] Quoted by Hans Grimm in his last book *Warum? Woher? aber Wohin?*, p. 14.

plete isolation in the midst of a dreary, indifferent world, in which they have no place; who are facing that world and defying it through every gesture, every hint—every silence—of theirs and, more and more (in the case of the younger ones) without even the personal memory of Adolf Hitler's great days to sustain them; those I have called "gods on earth" and parents of such ones. They are the ones who will, one day, make good for all that which men "against Time" have suffered in the course of history, like they themselves, for the sake of eternal truth: the avenging Comrades whom the Five Thousand of Verden[16] called in vain within their hearts at the minute of death, upon the bank of the Aller River, red with blood; those whom the millions of 1945—the dying, the tortured, and the desperate survivors—called in vain; those whom all the vanquished fighters "against Time" called in vain, in every phase of the great cosmic Struggle without beginning, against the Forces of disintegration, co-eternal with the Forces of Life.

They are the bridge to supermanhood, of which Nietzsche has spoken, the "last Battalion" in which Adolf Hitler has put his confidence.

Kalki will lead them, through the flames of the great End, into the sunshine of the new Golden Age.

And it will all begin again: the succession of Ages, in the same unchanging order, submitted to the same unchanging Laws; the unavoidable reappearing of that decay, the seed of which is contained in any and every manifestation in Time, the Struggle "against Time," and, finally, the rush to the abyss—in spite of it—for the millionth and ten millionth time. And a new great End, and a new radiant Beginning, and a new Time-cycle—again and again and again. There *is* no definitive *End*.

We like to hope that the memory of the One-before-the-last and most heroic of all our Men "against Time"—Adolf Hitler—will survive, at least in songs and symbols, in that long Age of earthly Perfection which "Kalki," the last One, is to open. We

---

[16] The five thousand German Chiefs, beheaded on the same day in 787 A.D. by order and in the presence of Charlemagne (and of a number of dignitaries of the Christian Church).

like to hope that the Lords of the new Time-cycle, men of his own blood and faith, will render him divine honours, through rites full of meaning and full of potency, in the cool shade of the endless re-grown forests, on the beaches, or upon inviolate mountain-peaks, facing the rising Sun.

But even if it be not so, still he will, like all his divine predecessors, live, throughout the ages in the faithful consciousness of the Universe, the life-rhythm of which he symbolises. Still the long and more and more intense and finally almost desperate aspiration "against Time," which characterises every recurring Time-cycle as soon as decay has set in obviously enough to be felt, will be, every time, a new expression of that self-same yearning after manifested Perfection for the sake of which he fought and lost, a new, long-drawn cosmic outcry, proclaiming that he was right in spite of all. And still every further Golden Age to come—every successive Dawn of Creation—will be the living materialisation of his highest dream, a further hymn of glory, proclaiming, every time for myriads of years, that he—He—has once more won.

Ended in Hanover, on the Spring Equinox,
the 21st of March, 1956

INDEX

A
Abaka, 110, 118
Abdashirta, 184–86, 189
Abdikhipa, Governor of Jerusalem, 184, 185, 187, 189, 193
Abi-Milki of Tyre, 184–85
abortion, 295
Action, Detached, 305, 409, 410; disinterested, 133; men of, 25, 29, 36, 77, 82, 88, 104, 161, 329, 432; vs. Speculation, 130; violent, 302
Adyar, 301, 303
Aegean Isles, 129
Afghanistan, 86, 98, 101, 110, 119, 338
Age of Truth, 4, 6, 22–26, 46, 49, 149, 195, 243, 351, 400; see also: Golden Age, *Satya Yuga*
Age of Gloom, 47, 53, 136, 149, 160, 175, 180, 196, 202, 227–34, 261, 271, 277, 290, 301, 323, 341, 358–67, 418, 426, 433; see also: Dark Age, *Kali Yuga*
Agni, 141, 154
Ai-Yuruk, 110
Akhetaton (The City-of-the-Horizon-of-the-Disk), 136, 139, 166, 169–78, 181–82, 184, 189, 193
Akhnaton, Pharaoh, 44–47, 53–54, 122, 131, 127–208, 225, 255–57; see also: Nefer-kheperu-Ra, Ua-en-Ra
Ak-Kum (desert), 96
Albuquerque, Afonso de, 206
Alexander the Great, 64, 338, 366

All-India Congress Committee, 325, 337n82
Allah, 14, 99, 417
Altai Mountains, 78, 83, 85, 93, 110, 119
Altyn Uruk (the Golden Family), 63, 85, 88, 100–101, 107, 109, 113–17, 121, 123
Amarna style, 173, 176, 177
Amenhotep II, Pharaoh, 197n3
Amenhotep III (Amenhotep the Magnificent), Pharaoh, 132–33, 135, 165
Amenhotep IV, Pharaoh, 133, 135, 138, 140, 162, 182n51; see also: Akhnaton
America, 265; ancient, 4; Central, 3, 50, 365, 417; South, 50, 179; see also: United States of America
Amon, 129, 132, 135, 140–41, 155, 162–66, 176, 181, 182
Amor (Northern Syria), 184–89
Amur River, 62, 73
Anglo-German friendship, 276–78, 286, 329
Anglo-German Fleet Agreement, 287
Anglo-Saxons, 343, 357
animals (kindness and cruelty to), 7, 15, 17–19, 23, 29–33, 182–83, 191, 208, 231, 250, 363, 381, 384, 387–92, 412, 422–23; see also: slaughter, kosher; vegetarian question; vivisection
Anti-Comintern Pact (1936), 280, 308n43, 309–10
anti-Communism, 249–52, 263, 329, 339, 358, 361, 371–72,

382–83, 393
anti-Semitism, 244–45, 280, 290, 295, 394
Antiquity, Ancients, 3–20, 22–27, 132, 141, 161, 253, 264n76, 300
Anu (Heliopolis), 132, 139
apocalyptic warrior, 432; see also: divine warrior, eternal warrior, Kalki
Apollo/Apollon, 156, 378
Ardennes Offensive, 349
Arhats, 43, 54
Arjuna, 208
Armenians, 244, 297, 303
Artatama, King of Mitanni, 130–32
Arundale, George, 302
Aryans, 23, 125, 130–33, 143, 152–58, 200–208, 211–15, 218, 220, 226, 228–30, 234, 239, 242, 243, 245, 247–48, 250–52, 254–55, 257, 260–62, 265–66, 269–70, 272, 275–76, 280–81, 290, 292–312, 314, 321, 322, 327–36, 341, 344–52, 355, 366, 368, 373–81, 385–86, 389, 392–93, 396–413, 421–23, 427–33
Aryan blood, 131, 156, 208, 266, 269–70, 276, 297, 329, 345, 366, 378, 392, 396, 400
Aryan gods, 132, 152–53, 158, 355; see also: Gods, Sun-Gods
Aryandom/Aryavarta, 220, 229, 239, 260, 266, 293, 302, 305–306, 308, 314, 322, 345, 347, 377, 401, 402
Asoka, Emperor of India, 19, 134, 188, 190–92, 207
Assam, 336
Assyria, Assyrians, 4, 22, 64, 130, 197n3, 203
Aten, see Aton
atheism, 249, 380–85

Atlantic Charter, 339
Atmu (Tem), 139
Aton, 129, 132–33, 135–42, 144, 145, 148, 149, 151–53, 155–58, 161–73, 177–82, 193; see also: Solar Disk
Aton teaching, 137, 140, 147–48, 156–57
atrocities, 14–18, 25, 31–33, 102, 337, 339, 349, 351, 355, 375, 388, 393, 411
Attila, 417
Auca, 3
Augustine of Hippo, 149
Austria, 212–13, 235, 245, 282–84, 376, 413
Austria and Hungary, Kingdom of, 282; see also: Austria, Hungary
authority, 9–10, 47
authority, spiritual, 129, 161–64
Ay, Pharaoh, 147n29, 148, 179n41
Ayar Auca, 3
Aziru (son of Abdashirta), 184–89
Aztecs, 15

B
Baber, Mughal Emperor, 125
Babylon, 129, 131, 152
Badoglio, Pietro, 342n90
Baikal, Lake, 59, 73, 85
Balfour Declaration, 306
Baljun, Lake, 81
Baltic Sea, 282
Baltic States (Lithuania, Latvia, and Estonia), 331
Bamyan, Afghanistan, 101
Bardèche, Maurice, 251n60, 357, 375, 387n25
Batu (son of Juchi), 108–10, 114–17
Beck, Ludwig (Chief of the German General Staff), 284–85

Beck, Józef (Polish Foreign Minister), 320, 323
Bektor (half-brother of Genghis Khan), 68, 77
Belgium, 324
Belgorod, 337
Belgutei (half-brother of Genghis Khan), 68, 72
Bengal, 252n63, 264–65, 300, 305, 336, 365, 392
Bengal Relief Association, 305
Berlin, 128, 131n5, 176, 315–20, 323, 331, 345, 349–54, 404
Bernard, Claude, 30, 32; see also: vivisection; Voronoff, Serge
Besant, Annie, 301–302
Bessarabia, 331
Bhagavad Gita, epigraph page, 19, 44, 46, 53–54, 101, 122–25, 199–200, 208, 239, 242, 256, 261, 275, 305, 332, 351, 363, 387, 410, 420n4
Bhen, Amala (Margaret Spiegel), 303–305
Bible, 6, 305, 365, 429
Biridiya of Megiddo, 184
Bismarck, Otto von, 211
Black Dragon Society (Kokuryūkai), 308–309n44; see also: Kenosha, Toyama Mitsuru
Blond, Georges, 346n95, 377, 380, 383, 385, 387, 393, 394, 409
blood, blood purity, 131–33, 155–56, 200–208, 212, 215, 228, 234, 237–39, 241–42, 245–47, 251, 260, 262–67, 269–76, 278, 289–90, 295, 297, 299–300, 304, 306, 308, 313, 317n53, 326, 328–30, 343–45, 350, 355, 365–69, 374, 378, 380–81, 385–87, 389–92, 396, 398, 400, 402, 411–13, 423, 430, 433, 435, 436; see also: race
Blood and Soil, 278, 308
Blue-Wolf, 69–72; see also: Borjigin
Blume, Heinrich, 413n50
Bock, Fedor von, 327
Boehm-Tettelbach, Hans, 284–85
Bombay, 297–98, 303, 397
Bonhoeffer, Dietrich, 284, 325
Boers, 275; see also: South Africa
Borguchi, 70
Borjigin, 69, 70, 74
Bormann, Martin, 349
Bortei the Fair (first wife of Genghis Khan), 65–66, 71–74, 78, 82, 106
Bose, Subhas Chandra, 307
Bosphorus, 332
Brahma, 418–21
Brahmo-Samaj, 301
Braun, Eva, 349, 405, 409
Braunau on the Inn, 212, 214–15, 217
Brauchitsch, Walther von, (German Commander in Chief), 326
British General Staff, 273
Buddha, The, 122, 157, 225, 229, 255, 299, 263, 420
Buddhism, 6, 43, 49, 82, 86, 93, 101, 118, 179n42, 180n43, 188, 191, 198, 201, 204–07, 245, 300, 304, 305, 363
Budge, Sir E. A. Wallis, 139, 145, 152, 156, 159, 181–83
Bullitt, William C., 318
Bunker (Hitler's), 346–54, 411
Burckhardt, Carl, 285
Burma, 111, 192, 336, 342
Byblos, 184, 186–87

C

Canaris, Wilhelm, 284–85
Carnot, Marie François Sadi, 314–15n51

Casablanca Conference, 339
Caserio, Sante Geronimo, 314n51
Caspian Sea, 74, 98, 336
caste system, 8, 10, 19, 218, 199, 199n7, 200, 203, 206, 218, 246n55, 251, 299–300, 304, 345, 363; see also: blood, India, race
Cathay, see China
Catholic church, 249, 272, 309, 357, 369, 371, 374, 380, 382, 383, 406, 408
Caucasus Mountains, 98, 104, 120, 332, 336–37
Celts, 155, 215
Central Europe, 281n17
Chagatai (son of Genghis Khan), 97–99, 101, 110, 118, 123
Chaitanya, 299
Chamberlain, Neville, 279, 285–87, 311–15, 319
Chancellory of the Reich, 354; see also: bunker
Chandogya Upanishad, 142
Ch'ang Ch'un, 105
change, principle of, 55, 100, 419–20; see also: Time
Charlemagne, 50, 272, 435n16
Charleville, 326
Charuk, 134
China, 72, 78, 79, 83, 87, 89, 91–94, 97, 105, 108–10, 112, 115, 117, 119, 120, 125, 129; see also: Kin, Yuan
Chinese, 4, 22, 79, 86, 89, 91, 92, 105, 108, 110, 117–18, 160, 307, 308
chosen race (Aryans), 260, 431
Christ (Jesus), 50–52, 149, 157, 204, 212, 225, 254–55, 364, 366, 407, 417, 430
Christian churches, 13, 204, 206, 252–53, 279, 310, 313, 364, 383, 385, 435n16
Christianity, 6, 32, 49–50, 72n8, 82, 93, 117, 138, 142, 151, 175, 197–98, 201, 206, 211, 215, 252, 253, 255, 265, 279, 284, 296, 300, 306, 334, 361, 363, 364, 365, 368, 369, 381, 382, 384, 385, 398, 399, 407, 432
Christianity, Nestorian, 49n2, 72n8, 82, 93
Christianity, original vs. historical, 255
Christians, 7, 13, 15, 20, 32, 50–51, 64, 86, 93, 126, 138, 142, 144, 157, 192, 206, 211, 215, 245, 249, 252–55, 265, 279, 284, 294, 296, 300, 306, 336, 341, 361–69, 371, 381–85, 398–99, 417, 425, 428
Chu (Tai-Tsong), 110
church (generic), 49, 49n1, 51, 251
Churchill, Winston, 274, 277–78, 283, 285, 288, 298, 309, 312, 329–39, 354, 357, 409, 424
Chvalkovský, František, 319
civilisation, 3–22, 52, 86, 100, 131, 160, 203, 215, 219, 223, 231, 278, 283–84, 315, 362, 365, 370, 373, 424
colonialism, 212, 275, 291, 308, 375, 399
collective responsibility, 343–44
commandments, 142, 147, 149, 239, 387, 412
Communism, 250, 253, 265, 275, 330, 357–61, 371–72, 382
communities, mystical, 204
concentration camps, 30n2, 33, 34, 175, 224n16, 259n70, 348, 376, 388, 393, 394, 398
Constantine, Emperor, 368
Cooper, Duff, 274
Crete, 129, 131
Cripps, Stafford, 333
Crowe, Eyre, 274, 276, 309
cruelty, to animals, 7, 18–19, 19n4, 30, 30n2, 387, 426; to

humans, 23, 34, 64, 78, 197, 224, 381, 426; and cowardice, 23
Csaba's Army, 417
Cuzco, 3n1
Cybele, 368

D

Dai Sechen, 65, 71
Damien, François, 15
Dance of Death, 96
Dance of Time, 96
Danube River, 109, 111, 115, 213, 215
Danzig, 282, 285, 320–21
Dardanelles, 332
Dark Age, 19, 25, 157, 160, 170–71, 180–83, 190–94, 195–208, 212, 215, 217–23, 227–35, 239–44, 247–48, 252–61, 265–67, 270–73, 276, 286, 293–96, 300–302, 310–15, 334, 338, 342, 344, 347, 351, 355, 361–73, 376, 380–88, 393, 398–413, 422–29, 434; see also: Age of Gloom, *Kali Yuga*
Dark Ages (Europe), 13
Dark Forces, 31, 36, 53, 126, 225, 244, 253, 257, 261, 265, 274, 275, 281, 300, 309, 310, 313, 317, 319, 323, 324, 327, 334, 335, 340, 349, 359, 370, 374, 402, 406, 407, 408, 412
Darré, Richard Walther, 380
death, Egyptian concept of, 143, 146, 156, 159, 179, 205; mystery of, 129, 368; see also: Death-forces; Powers, Dark, divine, Unseen, or invisible
Death-forces, 25–26, 35, 37, 247, 252–56, 276, 339, 347, 367, 427
Death-powers, 240, 247, 257
Deir-el-Bahri, 182
democracy, 10, 15, 20, 46, 175, 275, 292, 294, 315, 327, 334, 337, 339, 357, 360, 361, 399, 400
Denmark, 323–24, 417
Der Stürmer, 314, 401; see also: Streicher, Julius
Destiny, 54, 62, 66, 72, 132, 179, 214, 236, 386
destiny (small "d"), 3, 4, 8, 37, 43, 59, 60, 61, 65, 87, 89, 93, 94, 130, 164, 197, 221, 226, 228, 237, 243, 249, 353, 354
Detached Action, 305, 409, 410; see also: Detached Violence, Speculation vs. Action
Detached Violence, 102, 257, 261, 301, 302, 314, 359, 396, 421; see also: Detached Action; non-violence; violence
Deutsches Bund, 218
d'Harcourt, Count Robert, 388
Dibellius, F. K. Otto, 325
divine warrior, see warrior, apocalyptic, divine, eternal
Dodd, William, 317
Dostoyevsky, Fyodor, 51–52, 407; *The Brothers Karamazov*, 51–52; see also: Grand Inquisitor
Dravidians, 129, 201, 299
Dresden, 339
Dunkirk, 326–29
Dushratta, King of Mitanni, 131, 133, 135, 152
Dvapara Yuga, 227, 424

E

East Prussia, 282, 320
Eden, Garden of, 20, 263, 362, 422–23; see also: paradise, earthly
Eden, Anthony, 274
Edward the Eighth, King of England, 277, 279
Egypt, 3, 4, 44, 47, 109, 129–34,

135–41, 152–56, 161–94, 202, 256–57
Egyptian Empire, 129, 131, 136, 139, 156, 159, 162, 166, 168–70, 172–73, 183–89
Einstein, Albert, 295
Eisenhower, Dwight, 196n2, 339, 344, 371, 375
Elbruz, Mount, 336
electricity, 141, 143, 154
élite, 10, 16–17, 26–28, 31–36, 84, 144, 212, 233, 245, 247, 250, 266, 276, 313, 344, 373–80, 386–87, 402, 410
Elphinston College, Bombay, 303
Emperor cult (Japan), 126
Energy, cosmic, 53, 140–45, 152, 153, 154, 162, 167, 169, 310; divine, 157; life, 130; and matter, 141–43, 154; psychic, 308
England, the English, 15, 33, 46, 175, 228, 239, 254, 263, 266–67, 271–91, 298–99, 307–34, 338–40, 348, 402, 408–09, 428; see also: Great Britain
English Alliance, 271, 279, 309
equal treatment, 283
equality, equalitarianism, 7–12, 20, 40, 196, 211, 250–53, 265, 269, 270, 301, 306, 364, 369; see also: inequality
Essence, 141–48, 153, 167, 179, timeless, 419–20; see also: Brahma, Eternity, the one, *Tat*
Etana of Erech, 3
Eternal or Everlasting Blue Sky, 61, 69, 73, 74, 76, 81, 87, 90–92, 95, 106, 114, 122
Eternal Return, 20
Eternity, 146, 179, 200, 418, 421; see also: Essence, Brahma, The One, *Tat*
eternity, 42, 45, 102, 170, 354

ethics, 5, 11, 148–49, 269, 384, 388; see also: morality
ethnic (*völkisch*) attitude to life, 308
ethnic communities, 318
Europe, Europeans, 13–18, 26–28, 30, 50, 72, 75, 86, 97, 104, 108–11, 115, 120, 125, 126, 143, 158, 198n2, 201, 203, 206, 211–12, 214, 217, 243, 251, 253, 265, 269, 272, 278, 280, 281, 287, 288–99, 300, 303, 306, 308, 310, 315, 318, 327, 329, 331, 334–36, 339, 344–45, 348, 350, 351, 354, 355, 357, 358, 361, 369, 371, 374, 375, 383, 384, 394, 398, 409, 412, 417, 429; see also National Socialist Europe
Europe, tropical, see India
Ezra, David, 298n36

F
Fascism, 280, 282, 309, 325, 336, 342
Fegelein, Hermann, 405
Finland, 332
First World War, ix, 234–35, 245, 257, 271, 281–82, 289, 295, 342
Five Thousand of Verden, 435
Forces of Light (and Life), 24, 25, 35, 154, 219, 229, 240, 247, 302, 306, 308, 387, 411, 419, 433, 435
Fox, Ralph, 78n16, 87, 96, 104, 125
France, 15, 17, 228, 272, 281, 283, 287–88, 292n29, 317–26, 342, 375, 377, 424
Francis the First, King of France, 272
Frederic Barbarossa, Emperor of Germany, 417
Freemasonry, 211, 253, 270, 300–304, 309–17, 325, 330, 371

freedom, 7, 10, 11, 16, 54, 72, 94, 219, 239, 241, 289, 294–96, 339, 353, 382, 401, 424
freedom and bread, 219, 257
Frenssen, Gustav, 412
French *résistance*, 17, 374n10
French Revolution, 211, 259, 307, 369, 399
Freienberg (Linz), 352, 354

G

Galen, Clemens August Graft von, Archbishop of Münster, 325
Gandhi, Mohandas, 18, 45–46, 190, 290, 291, 302–304, 325
Gem-Aton (Nubia), 169
Genghis Khan, v, 40, 42, 53, 62–8, 78, 84–86, 87–106, 108–126, 134, 255, 419
Genyosha, 309n44; see also: Toyama Mitsuru
German Reich, 211, 224, 242, 258–61, 269–72, 279–86, 292, 297, 302, 307, 313, 315, 319–24, 333, 345, 347, 350, 358, 382, 388, 402, 404, 409, 411–13, 434 ; see also: National Socialist Germany; Third Reich
Germanic people of Northern Europe, 201, 205, 218
Germany, National Socialist, 19n4, 30, 293, 310, 317–18, 327, 329–34, 339–54, 357–71, 383, 397; see also: German Reich; Third Reich
Goa, 13, 50, 206
Gobi Desert, 78, 85
God, impersonal, 39, 42, 64, 76, 95, 100, 130, 141–45, 148, 153, 154, 157–58, 162–68, 172, 153, 172, 177, 189, 202–203, 207, 213, 229, 247, 249, 256, 266, 296, 301, 302, 324, 368, 380, 383–85, 386, 391, 429; see also: Aton, Godhead, Immanence, *Tat*
God, personal (Jewish, Christian, Muslim), 64, 138–44, 149, 203, 295, 362, 365, 368, 383–85; see also: Allah, Jehovah
Goddess, 42
gods, 4, 9, 13, 23, 26, 40, 50, 73, 104, 129–30, 132–133, 135–137, 139, 141–42, 145, 152–153 155, 158–68, 175, 180, 189, 195, 212, 215, 218, 262, 265, 295, 310, 347, 350, 355, 359, 373, 418, 429; see also: Aryan gods, polytheism, Sun-gods
Gods on earth, 4, 347, 359, 377, 392, 399–400, 435
Godhead, 133, 138, 140, 143, 144, 153, 158, 162, 178, 179, 218, 226, 230, 368, 391, 433; see also: Unknown
god-like men, dedication page, 20, 25, 40, 41, 65, 88, 108, 161, 173, 234, 260, 400, 422
Goebbels, Joseph, 30n3, 225, 233, 314, 329, 349–50, 396, 405, 411
Goebbels, Magda, 350, 405
Goebbels Children, 350
Golden Age, 4, 5, 20–36, 43–48, 53, 131, 146, 149–51, 156–58, 160–73, 183–94, 195–98, 202–208, 215, 221–29, 243, 247, 259–60, 265, 323–28, 347, 351, 355, 358, 362, 365, 370, 386, 408, 419–23, 433–36; see also: Age of Truth, *SatyaYuga*
Gomparst, Miss, 305
Göring, Hermann, 329, 401–404, 411
Goths, 218, 290 see also: Theodoric the Great
Govinda, Lama (Ernst Lothar Hoffmann), 305

goyim, 244, 248
Grand Inquisitor, 51, 396, 407; see also: Dostoyevsky
Grand Mufti of Jerusalem, 307
Great Britain, 19, 285, 287, 298, 319, 323, 327, 336, 397; see also: England
Great Wall of Cathay, 72, 78, 83, 85, 89–91, 93
Greeks, 4, 132, 139, 160, 295, 310, 366–67, 430
Greim, Ritter von, 350
Grimm, Hans, 226, 250, 265, 267, 273, 292–93, 295, 311–14, 328, 360–61 409, 434
Guénon, René, 250n59
Gujarat, 303
Gustloff, Wilhelm, 314

H

Habiru, 184, 185, 187–88, 203; see also: Hebrews
Hácha, Emil, 319
Halder, Franz, 284–85
Halifax, Lord (E. F. L. Wood), 324
Hall, H. R., 143, 146, 150
happiness, 11, 24, 39, 76, 168, 174, 196–97, 211, 221–22, 264, 426–27
Harshavardhana, 19
Hattusa, 129
Heat-and-Light, 141, 154–55, 157, 162, 167; see also: lightning
Heat-and-Light-within-the-Disk, 44, 140–41, 145, 147, 150, 153–55, 157, 162, 178, 202, 203
Hebrews, 184, 188; see also: Jews, Semites
Heliopolis, 132, 138–40, 144, 151, 158, 162, 165, 177, 183; see also: Anu
Heliopolitan Tradition, 140–41, 152, 177

Heidelberg, 218
Hess, Rudolf, epigraph page, 328–30, 401
hierarchy, natural, 26, 39, 150, 199, 204, 249, 296, 344; racial, 199, 249, 396, 430; sacred, 19, 23, 269, 306
Hierl, Konstantin, 228, 258–59
Himmler, Heinrich, *Reichsführer S.S.*, 341, 347, 388, 393–95, 397–402, 405–408, 411
Hindus, 4, 8, 10, 12, 19, 47, 48, 201, 300–311, 418, 425
History, Cyclic View of, 3–21, 53, 59, 194, 198, 219, 226
Hitler, Adolf, dedication page, 30, 52, 54, 67n5, 74n10, 122, 134, 214n3, 216, 217, 219–21, 223, 225–32, 233–35, 238–41, 244–45, 247–52, 254–63, 266–67, 269–360, 372–77, 381–84, 388, 392–96, 400–14, 421–22, 428, 432–35; as *the* Man against Time, 134, 214, 219, 220, 223, 229, 233, 239, 241, 247, 250, 255, 267, 270, 275, 280, 290, 324, 334, 335, 338, 341, 345–46, 351, 355, 358, 377, 395, 406, 408–409, 411; as the One-before-the-last Man against Time, 267, 324, 402–403, 409, 411, 422, 433–44; as *Welt-führer* (World-Leader), 343, 345, 409, 432–33; *Mein Kampf*, 214n3, 220, 221n4, 226, 228–29, 230n26, 231n32, 232–33, 234n39, 235n40, 236, 238n44, 240n47, 241–42, 249, 251n62, 252–53, 254n65, 260, 265n77, 271, 308, 328n72, 396, 412, 413n49; more Sun than Lightning, 348, 355, 406, 409; his "Political Testament," 345–46, 351, 354, 394n31; "Reichstag speech" (4 May

1941), 324n69; *Tischgespräche* (Table Talk), 344n91, 348n98, 388, 413n51; survival rumours, 350–51, 433
Hitler, Alois, 212
Hitler, Clara, 212–13
Hitler Faith, 230, 247, 259, 358, 374, 377, 381, 383, 407, 413–14; see also: Hitlerism, National Socialism
Hitler-Stalin Pact, see Russo-German Pact
Hitlerism, 306n40, 372, 373, 377, 392, 395; see also: Hitler Faith; National Socialism
Hittites, 129, 151, 153, 184
Hoang-Ho River, 91
Hoelun (mother of Genghis Khan), 59–62, 65, 68, 69–70, 72–73, 92
Holger Danske, 417
Holland, 324, 342, 375
Homer, 212, 262
"Horst Wessel Song," 412
Horuakhuti, 139
Hottentots, 290
Hulagu, 109–10, 117–18
Hsi-Hsia, 89, 93, 106
Huitzilopochtli, 15
humaneness, 7, 12–15
Hungary, 109, 116, 120, 282, 417; see also: Austria and Hungary, Kingdom of
Hymns to the Sun, 136, 138, 143–46, 152–53, 157, 181, 194
Hyksos, 202

I
Icarus, 3
Ikatama, the "man of Kadesh," 184
Immanence, Divine, 64, 138, 141–42, 150, 157, 385, 421, 429
Inca Empire, 179
India, 10, 46, 102, 122, 125, 129, 131, 134, 155, 160, 172, 175, 190, 203, 218, 239, 255, 275, 281, 290–92, 296–308, 325, 336, 348, 363, 385, 406, 418, 420
Indo-China, 308, 336
Indo-European, 143, 158, 201, 276
Indus Valley civilization (Mohenjo-Daro), 201–202
Inequality, Ordained, 249, 302, 385; see also: Equality
Infinity, 146, 154–55
Ingoda River, 62
Inn River, 212–15
Ise, Divine Wind of, 126
Islam, 6, 14, 49n2, 53n3, 96, 117–18, 122, 134, 142, 201, 206, 306–07, 363, 365, 398, 406, 409, 417n2
isms, 5–6, 20, 39
Israel, 293–94, 295, 428
Italy, 192, 218, 280, 309–10, 317, 342

J
Jamuga Sechen, 74–78, 81–83
Jainism, 190, 198, 204–208, 363, 389
Japan, Japanese, 4, 26, 49, 126, 179–80, 201, 280, 308–10, 317, 322, 330, 332, 336, 340, 342, 376, 392, 399
Java, 201
Jehovah, 142, 295; see also: Yahweh
Jelal-ed-Din, 102, 104–05
Jews, 20, 142, 211, 224, 234, 237, 244–47, 251n61, 265, 270, 280, 289–95, 296–302, 303–15, 321–22, 325, 338, 341, 343, 348, 362, 365, 367–71, 374, 376–77, 381, 385, 396–97, 400–401, 408, 417, 427–32; international, 211, 246–47, 248, 250, 267, 270, 280, 289,

296, 300, 354; see also: Hebrews, Jewish World Community, "Protocols of the Elders of Zion," Semites
Jezreel, Plain of, Palestine, 184
John of Carpini, 120
St. John of Patmos, 417
joy, 76, 80, 135, 146–47, 156, 165, 173, 193, 262, 351, 379, 419–20
Juchi (eldest prince of the Golden Family), 74, 96–98, 106, 108, 114, 116–17

K

Ka, 142, 145, 148; see also: Essence
Kabbalah, 365, 367
Kaidu Khan, 108–19, 125
Kaiser William the Second, 211
Kali Yuga, 19, 25, 47, 160, 273n3, 418, 424; see also: Age of Gloom, Dark Age
Kalki, 6, 20, 48, 53–55, 270, 311, 400, 406, 414, 417–18, 421–22, 427, 430–36; see also: One-Who-Comes-Back, Vishnu
Kara-Khoto, 106
Karakorum, 106, 108–109, 115, 117, 120
Karma Yoga, 122, 380, 410
Karnak, 135, 161, 165, 201n11
Kasar the Bowman, 68, 75, 81
Kassites, 152
Kelets (spirits of the Everlasting Blue Sky), 69
Kennedy, Joseph, 318, 321
Kerait Turks, 72, 79, 80–82
Kharkov, 337
Khepera, see Tem
Khorasan, 98, 100
Khudiram, 306n40
Khwarazmian Empire, 87, 93–103
Khwarizm Shah, 86, 94–5, 98, 102

Kin Dynasty (China), 87, 89, 91–93, 108
kindness, 7, 18–19, 30, 102, 381–88
Kingdom of the Sun on earth, 201
Kiyat (clan of Genghis Khan), 75
Kizil Kum Desert, 97
Kleist-Schmenzin, Ewald von, 285
Knossos, 4
Kogon, Eugen, 259n70, 312
Kordt, Erich, 284, 287n26
Korea, 92
Krebs, Hans, 218
Krebs, Hans, 282n18, 349, 404
Krishna, 44, 46, 101, 122, 208, 225, 255, 257, 261 (the Blessed One), 301–302, 348, 420n4; see also: Vishnu
Kronos, 4
Kshatriyas, 44–46, 125, 190–91, 200, 205, 208, 251, 299, 410, 420, 433
Kubilai Khan, 75, 109–10, 115–19, 126
Kubizek, August, 220–38, 352, 353n100
Kuchluk (Naiman chieftain), 93
Kulan (fifth wife of Genghis Khan), 83
Kuriltai, 84–86, 90, 109, 115–17
Kursk, 337
Kuyuk Khan, 108–11, 115–20

L

Labaya (or Lapaya), 184
labour, 7, 12, 174, 175, 196, 200, 234, 239, 248, 259, 262, 398
labour, intellectual, 43, 262
Lamb, Harold, 78n16, 95–96, 99, 113, 121, 123
Lange, Friedrich, 218
laws, cosmic, 4, 21, 31, 87, 136, 224, 256, 328, 385, 172; human, 19, 46, 84, 111–12,

114, 124, 147–48, 191, 207, 295; of Life, 6, 24, 122, 148, 252, 344, 355, 358, 362, 430; natural, 36, 142, 147, 290; Nuremberg, 218, 234, 262, 294–95; of Time, 136, 180, 217, 270, 358, 408, 432, 435; Unchanging, 24, 87, 122, 180, 435
Laws of Manu, 200
Leader, The, 87, 114, 120–23, 207, 244, 355, 409
League of Nations, 283, 285
Lebensraum, 218
Leibstandarte, 325
Leonding, 220
Libyan, 173, 338
Lichtvater, der Allwaltende (ancient Germanic god of Light), 158
Life, 5, 6, 19, 22–25, 35–39, 42, 100, 121–26, 130, 145–46, 148, 155, 158, 167–73, 182, 192, 199–203, 208, 215, 219, 229, 233, 239, 245, 247–48, 252–53, 257, 261, 265, 276, 290, 302, 306, 308, 311, 344, 346, 351, 355, 358, 362, 364, 372, 377, 380, 386, 387, 392, 407, 411, 418–19, 429–30, 432–35; see also: Forces of Light and Life, Light
Light, 24–25, 35, 130, 131, 136, 152, 154–56, 158, 169, 193, 203, 208, 218, 229, 239, 247, 253, 302, 308, 311, 346, 372, 378, 407, 411, 421, 432; see also: Forces of Light and Life, Life
Lightning, 53, 64, 88, 95, 141, 254, 329, 348, 355, 358, 395, 400–401, 406, 408–409, 420, 433; see also: Heat-and-Light
Lightning-man, 88, 254; see also: Man in Time
Linz, 220, 221, 223, 230, 238

Lipski, Józef, 320
literacy, general, 7–10
Living in Truth, 131, 147–51, 162, 191
London Anglo-German Fellowship, 277
love, 28, 30, 39, 52, 102, 136, 142, 144–45, 147–49, 191–92, 201–208, 212, 215, 225, 228, 244, 296, 300, 359–63, 369, 373–74, 386–91, 399, 412, 417, 429–30
Lugh Langhana (Lugh the Longhanded, Celtic god of Light), 155, 158
Lukasiewicz, Juliusz, 318n57

M

Mahakala, 41–42, 64, 100, 420
Mahavira (Founder of the Jain religion), 190
Mahdi, 417, 428
Maketaton, Princess (daughter of Akhnaton), 178n37
Malmédy case, 375, 412n48
Man-Centered and Equalitarian, 175, 250–53, 265, 269–70, 364, 369
Manchuria, 92
Manco Cápac, 3
Mangu (son of Tuli), 108–10, 115–19
Marx, Karl, 249, 253, 332, 359
Marxism, 175, 237, 245, 248–54, 265–66, 291, 296, 306, 321–22, 327, 333–37, 382, 398–99
matter, see energy and matter
Mattiuza, King of Mitanni, 152
Mayrhofer, Mr. (one of Hitler's schoolteachers), 220
men above Time, 35, 41–42, 43–55, 101–102, 105, 122, 131, 137, 146–47, 149–50, 154, 157–58, 161, 163, 166, 170, 171, 173, 175, 180, 182–83, 190, 192, 194, 198–207, 221, 225, 239, 253–56, 279, 296,

299–301, 363–64, 369–70, 389, 400, 407, 418–20; see also: Sun Men
men against Time, 31, 36, 43–45, 46–55, 68, 100–104, 122, 126, 134, 157–58, 160, 171, 180, 190–94, 198–208, 214–25, 229–39, 241, 243, 247, 248, 250, 254–63, 267, 270, 275, 280, 287, 290, 293, 299, 301–302, 310, 311, 321, 323–24, 329, 334, 335, 338, 341, 344–47, 348–60, 363, 364, 370–73, 374, 377, 379, 383, 386, 388, 389, 394–400, 401–403, 406, 408–14, 417–22, 425–27, 431–36
Men in Time, 38, 39–55, 76, 77, 88, 100, 101–104, 119, 122, 125, 157, 171, 192, 206, 247–249, 254–55, 266, 309, 317, 324, 338, 370, 396, 398, 409, 419–20, 426–27; see also: Forces in Time, Lightning Men
Menkheperura, see Thutmose the Fourth
Merkit tribe, 59–61, 72, 74, 77, 78, 81, 83
Mexico, 50
Milki-Ili, 184
Min, 132
Miracles, 87, 142
miscegenation, 123–24
Mitanni, 130–33, 135, 152–58, 202, 203
Mitchell, Sir Philip Chalmers, 273
Mithra, 132, 152, 368
Mohammed, 52–53, 122, 225, 255, 348, 364; see also: Islam; Mohammedans, Moslems
Mohammedans, 142, 144, 306, 417, 428; see also: Moslems
Molotov, Vyacheslav, 322, 331–32

Mongolia, 60, 65, 76, 104–105, 112, 115
Mongols, 60, 73–83, 87–107, 108–23, 124, 125, 335, 398
monotheism, 144, 166
morality, 33, 121, 137, 147, 148, 151, 159, 193, 197, 219, 221, 233, 252, 261, 364, 384; see also: Living in Truth
Moslems, 86, 93, 94, 142, 144, 307; see also: Mohammedans
Mosley, Sir Oswald, 277
Movement, the, 231, 234, 239–40, 245, 248, 252, 254, 263, 289, 310, 395, 406, 408–409; see also: NSDAP; Party, the
Mukherji, Asit Krishna (Savitri Devi's husband), 305, 308n42
Mukutin (son of Chagatai), 101
Munich, 238, 287
Munich Agreement, 286–87, 311, 319
Mutemwiya, 132
Mussolini, Benito, 18, 309, 323, 342; see also: Fascism

N

Napoleon, 104, 254–55
Naiman (tribe), 81-2, 93
National Socialism, v, 28, 208, 217, 220, 223, 225, 230, 233–34, 238, 244, 258–65, 269, 272, 274–75, 279, 284, 291, 295, 303, 307, 309–18, 322, 325, 327, 332, 333, 335, 345, 351, 354–55, 353, 357–58 360, 371, 373–74, 377, 383, 392, 394, 398, 400–401, 406, 408, 426
National Socialist doctrine, 215, 226, 330, 380, 396, 403, 405
National Socialist Europe, 334, 345, 351, 354
National Socialist Germany, 30, 293, 310, 317–18, 327–34, 339–44, 350, 354, 357–61, 371, 383, 397

National Socialist Idea, 217–18, 347
National Socialists, 194n73, 217, 244, 247, 308, 339, 371–72, 393, 412
nationalisms, false, 432; true, 248
nature, 11, 39–41, 100, 121, 142, 146–48, 212, 218, 226, 230, 235, 242, 250, 252–53, 264, 266, 272, 291, 345, 361–62, 368, 384, 386, 390–91, 423, 425, 429; laws of, 142, 147, 195, 235; living, 17, 23, 25, 30, 35, 362; see also: Living Nature
Nefer-kheperu-Ra, Ua-en-Ra, 138, 153, 179; see also: Akhnaton
negroes, 129, 165n7, 173, 181, 290, 295, 307, 425
Nenu (the primeval watery mass), 142
Neter (*the* God behind all gods), 142; see also: God, Impersonal
The New Mercury, 305, 306
New Order, 21, 26, 36, 54, 269, 286, 341, 397
Nile River, 166–71, 201
Nietzsche, Friedrich, 30, 215, 235, 262, 386–87, 412, 435
non-violence, 22–25, 34, 43–46, 190–92, 199, 204–208, 290, 299, 302, 305; see also: pacifism
Nordic race, 215, 245–46, 266, 275, 298, 313, 326, 328, 330, 344, 350, 381, 386, 390
Normandy, 338, 344, 346
North Sakhalin, 332
Norway, 323, 324, 343, 413
NSDAP (National Socialist German Workers Party), 217, 314, 372; see also Party, the; see also: Movement, the

Nubians, 129, 173
Nuremberg Laws, 218, 234, 262, 294–95
Nuremberg Trial, 33n5, 323, 330, 343
Nut-Amon (the City of Amon), 135

O

Ogodai Khan (son of Genghis Khan), 92n9, 108–11, 115–23
Olhonod clan, 59, 65, 71
Olaf Tryggvason, 50
One, The, 145, 151, 155, 199, 202, 418
One-Who-Comes-Back, The, 6, 219, 241–42, 267, 334, 351, 355, 400, 409, 417, 421, 433, 434; see also: Kalki, Vishnu
Onon River, 59–62, 65–73, 84, 86, 91, 107
order, cosmic, 18, 23, 31, 169, 224, 256, 328, 385, 433; divine, 8, 160, 181, 235; natural, 199, 264
ordu, 60–61, 66–67, 70, 75, 77, 79, 106

P

pacifism, pacifists, 22, 34–36, 188, 194, 197, 260, 310, 430; see also: Detached Violence; non-violence
Palestine, 136, 169, 183–92, 203, 246, 294, 306, 348, 428
Pan-Aryan Movement, 266, 306, 327, 345, 355, 407, 413
Papuans, 290
paradise, earthly, 146, 156, 157, 161, 168, 170–72, 180–83, 190–94, 196, 199, 223, 233, 256, 417; see also: perfection, earthly; Eden, Garden of
Paris, 15, 313, 317–19, 325
patience, 63, 64, 70, 71, 83, 84, 89, 91, 95, 103, 108, 110–11,

124, 223, 389
Party, The, 217, 218, 241, 249–50, 291, 380, 405; see also: Movement, The; N.S.D.A.P.
Pasteur, Louis, 19, 32
Paul of Tarsus, vi., 204, 310, 364, 368–69, 430n13, 432
Pavlograd, 337
peace, 23, 35, 81, 88, 103, 111–12, 113, 134–36, 147, 180, 188, 190–94, 201–202, 211, 234, 241, 256, 269–70, 278, 281, 286–88, 298–99, 307, 312–13, 323–30, 350, 369–70, 403, 418–25
peace, 35–36, 81, 82, 84, 88, 93, 103, 111–13, 134, 136, 147, 159, 180, 188–94, 201–203, 211–12, 223, 234, 241, 256, 257, 269–70, 278, 281, 286–88, 298–301, 312, 313, 323–24, 326, 328–30, 369–70, 403, 418, 420, 421, 425, 430, 431
Pearl Harbor, 336, 340
Pegolotti, Francesco Balducci, 111–12
Pendlebury, J. D. S., 145, 173n21, 174n23
perfection, earthly, 227–31, 247, 436; see also: paradise, earthly; Eden, Garden of
Persia, 110–11, 117–18, 123, 125, 251, 366, 368, 417n2
Persian Gulf, 94, 111, 340
Peru, 50, 206
Petrie, Sir Flinders, 132–34, 143, 151, 159, 177
Pharaonic state, 161, 165–66
Philo of Alexandria, 367
Pilate, Pontius, 255
Plato, 419
Pirow, Oswald, 311–15
Poland, 112, 282, 288, 293, 319–23, 417
polytheism, 144, 166; see also: Gods

Potocki, Count Jerzy, 317–18
Potsdam Conference, 330, 339 357, 371
powers, dark or sinister, 243, 247, 309, 311, 324, 367, 369, 427 (see also: Dark Forces; Death-powers); Heavenly or Everlasting, 96, 215, 247, 324; Invisible or Unseen, 248, 275, 367
Prakriti, 145
Prester John, see Togrul Khan
progress, 3–33, 211, 219, 226; technical, 425–27, 434
propaganda, iv, 8, 14, 22, 28, 89, 245, 278–79, 292, 302, 306, 309, 311–12, 324, 339, 330, 338–39, 393–95, 398, 401, 424; anti-Nazi, 279, 292, 306, 309, 330, 338, 398; Jewish, 292, 302, 311–12, 393, 401
"Protocols of the Elders of Zion," 428–29
Purusha, 145, 221n5
Pyramid Texts, 140
pyramids, 3, 162

Q
Quetzalcoatl, 417

R
Ra, 4, 138–39, 151, 161–68, 177, 195, 201, 203
Ra-Horakhti-Aton, 162
Ra-Horakhti of the Two Horizons, 132, 138–39, 151, 152, 176, 182
Rabinovich, Rabbi Emanuel, 429, 431
race, 7, 11, 18–31, 39, 44–46, 85, 100, 104, 125–26, 130–31, 133, 143, 150, 155, 158, 173, 188, 195, 199–208, 211, 218, 221, 226, 228–30, 233–34, 239, 241–43, 245–52, 257, 260, 262, 265, 275–76, 295–310, 330–33,

344–45, 350–51, 355, 360–65, 373, 377, 384–92, 397, 405, 413–14, 422–33; see also: *Altyn Uruk* (the Golden Family), Blood, Chosen Race
Raczyński, Edward Bernard (Polish Ambassador in London), 320
Rama, 255
Ramose, tomb of, 163
Rath, Ernst von, 313
Reading, Lord (Rufus Isaacs), 298n36
Red Army, 325, 335–39, 350
Reichstag, 258, 292, 324, 354, 434
Reitsch, Hanna, 346n94, 350
Religion of the Disk, 131, 143, 148–51, 156, 159–65, 179–88, 199, 201
responsibility, collective, 343–44
Rhineland, 283
Rhythm, of Life, 436; of Time, 217, 420
Ribaddi, King of Gebal (Byblos), 184–93
Ribbentrop, Joachim von, 271, 275–80, 285–88, 317–24, 331–47, 403
Rome, 66, 159, 273, 309, 366, 368
Romans, 4, 368
Roosevelt, Franklin Delano, 317, 321, 330, 338, 394, 409
Rosenberg, Alfred, 380, 387, 412
Rosicrucian Order, 301
Rostov, 337
Rudel, Hans-Ulrich, 346
Runciman, Walter, 286
Rundstedt, Gerd von, 326
Russia, 98, 104, 108–109, 117, 120, 123, 125, 263, 266, 282, 317, 321–24, 329–49, 353–55, 357–60, 371, 382, 385, 394, 397, 404, 408–409, 412
Russia, Soviet, 317, 322, 329–32, 339, 341, 357, 360, 394
Russian Revolution, 259

Russo-German Pact, 322; see also: Hitler-Stalin Pact

S

S.S., men, 376, 378, 380; Outlook on Life, 374–97, 407–13; S.S. state, 259, 312; see also: Waffen S.S.
Saarland, 283–84
Sabarmati, 303
sadhana, 12
Sagas, Germanic, 227–32
Salzburger Turm, 212, 213, 214, 215
Sartak (Batu's eldest son), 117
Satan, 51, 311
Satya Yuga, 4n2, 160; see also: Age of Truth, Golden Age
Savita, 153
Savitri (Savita's Energy), 152–53, 155, 158
Savitri Devi, 17n3; husband, Dr. Asit Krishna Mukherji, 308n42; works: *And Time Rolls On: The Savitri Devi Interviews*, 306n40, 413n50; *A Son of God*, 133n12; *Defiance: The Prison Memoirs of Savitri Devi*, 306n40; *Gold in the Furnace*, 35n7, 306n40; "Hitlerism and the Hindu World," 306n40; *Impeachment of Man*, 18n; *Pilgrimage*, 345n93, 413n50
Saxons, 272
Schirach, Baldur von, 307
Schliemann, Heinrich, 8
science, 20, 31, 33, 142, 151, 211, 219, 264, 427, 434
scientific spirit, 133, 141–44, 151, 156, 158, 159
"Scourge of Allah" (Genghis Khan), 99
Seat of Truth, 54, 170, 192, 194, 198; see also: Akhetaton
Second German Reich, 211

selfishness, 22, 38–42, 49, 50, 54, 121, 196, 235, 312, 363, 408, 423
Second World War, 17, 28, 224–25, 251–57, 262–67, 275–76, 281, 288, 297, 302, 311–15, 321–23, 330, 338, 343, 345, 354, 358, 361, 373, 375, 434
Semites, 129, 173, 203, 245–46; see also: Hebrews; Jews
Sequenen-Ra, Pharaoh, 202
seriousness, deadly, 222–23
Sevagram, 303
Shantiniketan, 303, 305
Shigi-Kutuku, 102–103
Shinto, 126, 308, 309
Shiva, 55, 418–21
Shu-which-is-in-the-Disk, 138, 139–40, 151–52
Shubbiluliuma, King of the Hittites, 152, 184
Sicily, 338
Silver Age, 160, 195, 400; see also: *Treta Yuga*
Simovitch, Dusan, 331
Simyra, 186–87
Singapore, 336
"Sixteen Points," 323
Sixth Army, German, 337
Siyurkuktiti (wife of Tuli), 82, 116
Skorzeny, Otto, 342
slaughter, kosher, 30n2, 295
slavery, 15, 125, 197, 353
Smuts, Jan, 311
Solar Disk, 138, 139, 141, 165; see also: Atem, Sun-Disk
Sommer, Martin, 224n16
soul, individual or personal, 43, 164, 166, 198–204, 368
South Africa, 265, 275, 311
South-East Asia, 336, 342
Spandau Prison, 329, 412; see also: Hess, Rudolf
Spain, 17, 376
Spanish Civil War, 17

Speer, Albert, 404–405
Spiegel, Margaret (a.k.a. Amala Bhen), 303–305
speculation, vs. action, 130, 161, 200, 208, 248, 300, 429
Stalin, Josef, 322, 330–31, 337–38, 346, 357, 409, 419
Stalingrad, 337–38, 346
state, above Time, 180, 198, 207, 255; against Time, 180,198, 243, 258, 259, 260, 287, 310, 321, 334, 341, 347, 350, 354, 359, 360, 371, 388, 409, 414; in Time, 206, 409; theocratic, 161, 164, 201; see also: Kingdom of the Sun on earth, theocracy
state cult, 159
Streicher, Julius, 396, 401
Subodai, 75, 97–98, 103, 108–11, 115, 120–22, 124
Sumeria, 3, 131, 160
Sumerians, 3–4, 201
sun, 53, 130–34, 135–36, 138–57, 168–69, 172, 174, 177–79, 183, 185, 220, 245, 254, 276, 329, 348, 336, 355, 358, 365, 395, 400–401, 406, 407, 409, 433; see also: Solar Disk, Atem
Sun-Disk, 133, 140, 143, 145, 152, 157, 161–62, 178, 199, 202; see also: Solar Disk
Sun-Gods, 132, 139, 140, 158, 165; see also: Aryan Gods, gods
Sun men, 254; see also: men above Time
Surya, 132, 152, 154–55, 158
swastika, 220n2, 269, 276, 306, 308, 325, 350, 387, 400, 407–408
swastika Flag, 224, 255, 336
Syr Daria (river), 96–97

T

Tagi, 184

Tagore, Rabindranath, 299
Taijiut (chieftains), 66–71, 77–8
Tai-Tsong (Chu), 110
Tamerlane, 125
Tandava Dance, 420; see also: Shiva
Tangut, 89, 106
Tat, 142; see also: God, Impersonal; Immanence
Tatars, 79–82
Targutai-Kiriltuk, 70, 78
Tayan Khan, 82, 93
technology, 3–4, 7, 196, 382, 425–27, 434
Tefnut (Moisture), 140
Teheran Conference, 339, 357
Tell-el-Amarna, 131n5, 135n1, 145n26, 147, 162–69, 185, 188–89
Tem, 139–41
Temple of the Sun (Cuzco), 3n1
Temujin, see Genghis Khan
terror, 237, 253, 254, 265, 308n44, 345, 396, 406; Mongol, 78, 80, 91–92, 96, 99–100
Thebes, 129, 132, 133, 134, 135, 153, 155, 161–66, 170, 202
theocracy, 161, 163–66, 170, 176, 202–203, 207, 355, 364; see also: State, Theocratic
Theodoric the Great, 218, 290; see also: Goths
Theosophical Society, 301–302
Theosophists, 245, 304
Third Reich, 224, 259–60, 287n26, 294, 299,306, 308, 312–14, 317, 324, 331, 339, 350, 354, 388, 393, 396, 403, 408; see also: German Reich; National Socialist Germany
thunder, 141
Thutmose III, 186
ThutmoseIV, 129–31, 202
Tilak, Bal Gangadar (Lokomanya), 301
Time, All-devouring, 64, 100, 247; Endless, 96, 161, 420n4; Merciless, 64; see also: *Mahakala*, Men above Time, Men against Time, Men in Time, Time-Cycles
Time-Cycles, 18, 20, 22–24, 26, 43, 47, 53, 55, 131, 158, 160, 167, 171, 180, 190, 194–96, 201–202, 202–203, 214, 219, 224, 227, 229, 230, 234, 235, 240, 243, 247, 250, 256–57, 262–63, 267, 276, 341, 347, 351, 358, 360, 362, 400–401, 417–22, 427–33, 435, 436
Timur Khan, 118
Tirpitz, Admiral, 273
Tiso, Jozef, 319
Tiy, Queen of Egypt, 132–33, 135
Todoyan-Girte, 70, 78
Togrul Khan, 72, 74–75, 77–80
Tōjō Hideki, 126
Toktoa (Merkit chief), 83
Tokugawa Dynasty, 399
toleration, 7, 12–15, 29, 33–34, 112, 159–60, 183, 303
torture, 13–19, 27–34, 78, 102, 339, 348, 374, 388, 399, 405, 411, 412n48, 423, 435
Tōyama Mitsuru, 126, 308n44
Tower of London, 329, 401
Tradition, ix, 23, 48, 129, 137, 140, 160, 172, 176, 195, 219, 232, 243, 267, 299–306, 363, 400, 417–18, 422, 431, 433
Treta Yuga, 160, 400n33; see also: Silver Age
Trojan War, 134
Troy, 9
Truth, 20, 36, 52, 122, 131, 134, 137, 149, 155, 229–30, 261, 392; Cosmic, 204, 240, 258, 261, 266–67, 354, 359, 366, 400, 412, 421; Eternal, 13, 25, 29, 44, 51, 124, 215, 226, 267, 290, 313, 354, 370, 435;

Timeless, 9, 52–53, 157, 198; see also: Age of Truth, Living in Truth, Seat of Truth
Tuat (Egyptian afterworld), 156
Tuau (mother of Tiy), 132–33
Tuka, Vojtech, 319
Tuli (son of Genghis Khan), 82, 98, 108–109, 116–17
Tumans, 93, 96–97, 108
Tunip, 186, 193
Turks, 272, 295
"Twenty-Five Points," 249, 289

U

United Nations, 28, 325, 337, 342n90, 374
United States of America, 281, 287, 317–18, 330, 333, 338, 340, 371, 397, 409; actions in World War II, 315–21, 330, 338–42, 371, 375, 389
Unknown, 130; see also: Godhead
Untermeyer, Samuel, 293–94, 297, 304, 314, 394
Ur-ma, 140
Utley, Freda, 375

V

vaccination, 19
Vaishnavas, 252n63, 300, 304, 365
Van Roden, Edward L., 375, 412n48
Vansittart, Robert, 274, 276, 279, 283, 285, 298, 309
Varuna, 152
Vatican, 279
Vedas, 141, 201, 304
Vedic Gods, 152, 218
vegetarian question, 30n3; see also: animals; slaughter, kosher; vivisection
Versailles Treaty, 217, 219, 243, 281–82, 298, 318–20, 323, 331

Vienna, 109, 230–31, 238, 331
violence, 22–30, 33–36, 42–46, 49–50, 54, 134, 137, 149–50, 156–57, 159, 166, 180, 183, 190–94, 197–99, 202, 204, 207–208, 224–25, 255–57, 261, 288–302, 305, 314, 364, 375–76, 382, 387, 398, 419, 421; see also: Detached Violence
Vishnu, 6, 46, 55, 414–17, 418–21, 429, 433
vivisection, 19, 208, 261, 384, 388
Vladivostok, 340, 342
void, 154–55, 355
Volga River, 336
Voronoff, Serge, 32, 32n4
Voss, Hans-Erich, Admiral, 349

W

Waffen S.S., 376–83, 393, 407, 410
Wagner, Richard, 227, 231–32, 352
Wailing Wall, 401
Wang Khan, 79–82
war, 14–17, 24–27, 31–35, 52, 76; 83–85, 89–95, 103, 111, 129, 137, 164–65, 180, 183–92, 196, 200, 223–24, 236, 241; Holy War, 248, 293, 297–98; modern war, 379, 410
war criminals, 31, 223, 375, 382
war crimes, 197, 357, 375–76, 381–82
Warner, Sir G., 285
Warrior, apocalyptic, divine, eternal, 239, 432
warriors, 16, 17, 44, 74, 77, 80, 104, 120, 125, 200, 212, 215, 261, 272, 307, 380–81, 410, 433; Aryan, 410, 433; Muslim, 398
Weimar Republic, 292, 318
Weizsäcker, Ernst Ulrich von, 284–86
Wenck, Walther, 349

Wiesbaden, 128, 176n30
Wilhelm II, Kaiser, 211, 237
William of Ruysbroek, 117
wisdom, 28, 95, 122, 386; above Time, 173; against Time, 201, 310, 358, 359, 363, 374, 436; Ancient, 214, 221, 226, 228; aristocratic, 426; Aryan, 201, 215, 242, 261, 306, 332, 351; Chinese, 117, 118; Christ's, 407; Cosmic or Divine, ix, 219, 242, 248, 250, 317, 377; Egyptian, 140; Golden Age, 183, 192; life-centred, 269, 370; National Socialist, 355; Nature, 195, 215, 218, 391; other-worldly, 188; solar, 201, 203; perennial, 208; timeless (above Time), 47, 200, 363; traditional, 243; Vedic, 201
workmen, 172, 174–75, 181, 234, 240–41, 348
World-Jewry, 248, 250, 317, 331–41, 347, 428; see also: International Jewry
World War I, see First World War
World War II, see Second World War

Y

Yahweh, 429, 430; see also: Jehovah
Yakka Mongols, 60, 62, 66, 106
Yalta Conference, 330, 339, 357, 371
Yao Chow, 117
Yapa-addu, 186
Yasa, 80, 84, 111–16, 119–25
Yellow Sea, 108
Yesugei, 60–62, 63–77, 81, 86, 89, 94, 97
yoga, yogis, 53, 200, 420; *Karma Yoga*, 122, 380, 410
Yuaa, 132
Yugoslavia, 331
Yuan Dynasty (China), 92, 110, 118–19

Z

Zimrida of Sidon, 186
Zionist Movement, 251, 428

ABOUT THE AUTHORESS

SAVITRI DEVI (1905–1982) is one of the most original and influential National Socialist thinkers of the post-World War II era. Born Maximine Julia Portaz in Lyons, France on 30 September 1905, she was of English, Greek, and Italian ancestry and described her nationality as "Indo-European." She earned Master's degrees in philosophy and chemistry and a Ph.D. in philosophy from the University of Lyons.

A self-described "nationalist of every nation" and an Indo-European pagan revivalist, Savitri Devi embraced National Socialism in 1929 while in Palestine. In 1935, she travelled to India to experience in Hinduism the last living Indo-European pagan religion. Settling eventually in Calcutta, she worked for the Hindu nationalist movement, married a Bengali Brahmin, the pro-Axis publisher Asit Krishna Mukherji, and spied for the Japanese during World War II.

After World War II, Savitri Devi embarked upon an itinerant, ascetic life. Her two chief activities were tireless witness on behalf of National Socialism and caring for homeless and abused animals.

Savitri Devi influenced such leading figures of post-war National Socialism as George Lincoln Rockwell, Colin Jordan, William Pierce, and Miguel Serrano. In 1962, she took part in the Cotswolds camp, where the World Union of National Socialists (WUNS) was formed.

Her books include *A Warning to the Hindus* (1939), *L'Etang aux lotus (The Lotus Pond)* (1940), *A Son of God: The Life and Philosophy of Akhnaton, King of Egypt* (1946), later republished as *Son of the Sun* (1956), *Akhnaton: A Play* (1948), *Gold in the Furnace: Experiences in Post-War Germany* (1952), *Defiance: The Prison Memoirs of Savitri Devi* (1958), *Pilgrimage* (1958), *Impeachment of Man* (1959), *Long-Whiskers and the Two-Legged Goddess* (1965), *Souvenirs et réflexions d'une Aryenne (Memories and Reflections of an Aryan Woman)* (1976), *And Time Rolls On: The Savitri Devi Interviews* (2005), and *Forever and Ever: Devotional Poems* (2012).

Savitri Devi died in England on 22 October 1982.

www.ingramcontent.com/pod-product-compliance
Lightning Source LLC
Chambersburg PA
CBHW021825220426
43663CB00005B/136